BUILDING THE CONSTITUTION

This revisionary perspective on South Africa's celebrated Constitutional Court draws on historical and empirical sources alongside conventional legal analysis to show how support from the African National Congress government and other political actors has underpinned the Court's landmark cases. Standard accounts see the Court as overseer of a negotiated constitutional compromise and as the looked-to guardian of that constitution against the rising threat of the ANC. In reality, South African successes have been built on broader and more admirable constitutional politics to a degree no previous account has described or acknowledged. The Court has responded to this context with a substantially consistent but widely misunderstood pattern of deference and intervention. Although a work in progress, this institutional self-understanding represents a powerful effort by an emerging court, as one constitutionally serious actor among others, to build a constitution.

JAMES FOWKES is a former clerk of the South African Constitutional Court and studied law at the University of the Witwatersrand, Johannesburg, and Yale Law School. He is currently a senior researcher at the Institute for International and Comparative Law in Africa, University of Pretoria, South Africa.

CAMBRIDGE STUDIES IN CONSTITUTIONAL LAW

The aim of this series is to produce leading monographs in constitutional law. All areas of constitutional law and public law fall within the ambit of the series, including human rights and civil liberties law, administrative law, as well as constitutional theory and the history of constitutional law. A wide variety of scholarly approaches is encouraged, with the governing criterion being simply that the work is of interest to an international audience. Thus, works concerned with only one jurisdiction will be included in the series as appropriate, while, at the same time, the series will include works which are explicitly comparative or theoretical - or both. The series editors likewise welcome proposals that work at the intersection of constitutional and international law, or that seek to bridge the gaps between civil law systems, the US, and the common law jurisdictions of the Commonwealth.

Books in the Series:

Building the Constitution: The Practice of Constitutional Interpretation in Post-Apartheid South Africa James Fowkes

Dimensions of Dignity: The Theory and Practice of Modern Constitutional Law Jacob Weinrib

Reason of State: Law, Prerogative, Empire Thomas Poole

Bills of Rights in the Common Law Robert Leckey

The Guardian of the Constitution: Hans Kelsen and Carl Schmitt on the Limits of Constitutional Law, Translated by Lars Vinx, with an introduction and notes by Lars Vinx

Parliamentary Bills of Rights: The Experiences of New Zealand and the United Kingdom Janet L. Hiebert and James B. Kelly

Lawyering for the Rule of Law: Government Lawyers and the Rise of Judicial Power in Israel Yoav Dotan

Balancing Constitutional Rights: The Origins and Meanings of Postwar Legal Discourse Jacco Bomhoff

Judges on Trial: The Independence and Accountability of the English Judiciary Shimon Shetreet and Sophie Turenne

Proportionality and Constitutional Culture Moshe Cohen-Eliya and Iddo Porat

The Politics of Principle: The First South African Constitutional Court, 1995–2005 Theunis Roux

The New Commonwealth Model of Constitutionalism: Theory and Practice Stephen Gardbaum

Searching for the State in British Legal Thought: Competing Conceptions of the Public Sphere Janet McLean

Judging Social Rights Jeff King

Proportionality: Constitutional Rights and their Limitations Aharon Barak

Parliamentary Sovereignty: Contemporary Debates Jeffrey Goldsworthy

BUILDING THE CONSTITUTION

The Practice of Constitutional Interpretation in Post-Apartheid South Africa

JAMES FOWKES

Institute for International and Comparative Law in Africa, University of Pretoria, South Africa

CAMBRIDGE
UNIVERSITY PRESS

CAMBRIDGE
UNIVERSITY PRESS

University Printing House, Cambridge CB2 8BS, United Kingdom

Cambridge University Press is part of the University of Cambridge.

It furthers the University's mission by disseminating knowledge in the pursuit of education, learning and research at the highest international levels of excellence.

www.cambridge.org
Information on this title: www.cambridge.org/9781107124097

First published 2016

A catalogue record for this publication is available from the British Library

Library of Congress Cataloging-in-Publication Data
Names: Fowkes, James, 1984-
Title: Building the constitution : the practice of constitutional interpretation in post-apartheid South Africa / James Fowkes.
Description: Cambridge [UK] : Cambridge University Press, 2016. | Series: Cambridge studies in constitutional law
Identifiers: LCCN 2016026762 | ISBN 9781107124097 (Hardback)
Subjects: LCSH: Constitutional courts–South Africa. | South Africa. Constitutional Court. | Constitutional law–South Africa. | BISAC: LAW / Constitutional.
Classification: LCC KTL2620 .F69 2016 | DDC 342.68–dc23 LC record available at https://lccn.loc.gov/2016026762

ISBN 978-1-107-12409-7 Hardback

For Michaela

CONTENTS

ACKNOWLEDGEMENTS

Books, it seems, are like rolls of sticky tape: their owners often find themselves surprisingly attached to them, but until finished they are mostly an exercise in trying to find the end. And once finished, it takes a special kind of forensically archeaological mind to have much interest in going back to identify the precise point where they began. This book may have begun in Marius Pieterse's course on Human Rights at Wits Law School in 2006, or while writing for Thaddeus Metz in the Wits philosophy department the following year, or during my time as a law clerk to Justice Johann van der Westhuizen at South Africa's Constitutional Court the year after that, or indeeed after my arrival at Yale Law School a year later still. I'm not sure: I am, however, deeply grateful to all four.

It was, at least, at YLS that it took shape, and this book is owed above all to that institution and its generosity, of academic spirit and other things. It may be increasingly customary to be indebted to US law schools, but my debts are of the nicest kind. I owe them to the graduate programs office, to its mother, Maria Dino, its deans Toni Davis and her successor Gordon Silverstein, and to Steph D'Ambrose and Caroline Curtis; to Dean Robert Post; and to Yale's extraordinary librarians, not least for permitting me to check out portions of their South African collections sufficiently large to require returning by incredulous taxi. I owe them to teachers at YLS, including Akhil Amar, the late Robert Burt, Daniel Bonilla, Dieter Grimm, Frank Iacobucci, John Langbein, Jerry Mashaw, Nick Parrillo, Susan Rose-Ackerman, and Jim Silk, who although not directly involved in this book offered encouragement and afforded me, in various ways, the invaluable opportunity to watch them at work. I owe them to Ian Shapiro of Yale's Political Science department, who served on my doctoral committee and offered generous support and incisive criticism, and to my friends and colleagues in the Yale graduate community who had the misfortune to have parts of this book and, worse still, parts since deleted from this book, bounced off them, occasionally with their consent. And I owe them to Bruce Ackerman, whose scholarly interest in the breadth and richness of constitutional real life first made me want to go to Yale, who I was to discover possessed kindness to match as supervisor to the thesis on which this book is based, and who taught me too to disagree, although it is possible that there at least he was casting for type.

Parts of my time at Yale were supported by the Fulbright program and by South Africa's Skye Foundation; my thanks to Mareka Chabedi, Neville Passmore, and to the private benefactors and US tax-payers who fund these scholarships for their extraordinary beneficence. Parts of this book were written, post-Yale, during time at the Max Planck Institute for Comparative Public Law and International Law in Heidelberg, Germany, and the Institute for International and Comparative Law in Africa at the University of Pretoria, South Africa. I am grateful to the directors of the former, Anne Peters and Arnim von Bogdandy who extended my invitation, and of the latter, Erika de Wet and Christof Heyns, and to the people of both institutions. This book has also benefitted enormously from other scholars and observers, inside South Africa and out, who have offered me help and support on this and other projects along the way, including David Bilchitz, Michael Bishop, Steve Ellmann, Heinz Klug, Gilbert Marcus, Alistair Price, Ngwako Raboshakga, Theunis Roux, who graciously shared with me an earlier manuscript of his *Politics of Principle*, Wojciech Sadurski, Kristen Stilt, Mia Swart, Alexei Trochev, Dave Watson, Emma Webber, Stu Woolman and two annoymous reviewers for Cambridge University Press. I am also grateful to Finola O'Sullivan and the staff at Cambridge University Press, and to the editors of this series, David Dyzenhaus, who first showed an interest in this project, and Adam Tomkins.

Book acknowledgements are necessary because vital scaffolding is otherwise invisible in the finished construction; for the unfinished project that is this book's author, the scaffolding remains in place, notwithstanding the dust and occasional unannounced buckets of cement. An array of teachers, co-clerks, colleagues, conference attendees and friends, over an array of beverages, have been kind enough to tell me when they thought I was doing something right, when I was definitely doing something wrong, and when I might be missing out on something interesting and useful, a tangle of conversations that adds up, I think, to an education. Some timbers have been especially durable: Mieke Krynauw, conversations with whom represent another candidate for this book's beginning; Abby and Simon Marcus, curators of cities;

David and Rachel Fowkes, purveyors of banter and bánh mì, whom I assure that any dreadful puns in the book are accidental; and the rest of my impressively expanding family, support structure from the beginning. None has been around longer than my parents: no-one did more to provision this particular journey of a thousand miles, and while it may be that such journeys begin with a single step, someone was holding both my doubtless chubby hands when I took it. And no-one spent more time living with this book than Michaela Hailbronner, there from beginning to end, who first wrote down its title in the snow on the bonnet of a blue Honda Civic, owner unknown, at the start of a New Haven winter on Bradley Street. Writing books side by side in shared rooms on three continents may not be the most efficient dating strategy for picking a partner for life, but it is one I would highly recommend. To her, now my wife and mother to a small Edward very effectively distracting me from these acknowledgements, this book is dedicated.

TABLE OF SOUTH AFRICAN CASES

A

B

C

D

E

F

G

H

I

J

K

L

M

N

O

P

R

S

T

U

V

1

Introduction

Since the demise of apartheid, South African constitutionalism has been celebrated around the globe. The 1996 Constitution has been described as 'the most admirable constitution in the history of the world', and the process of drafting it and its 1993 interim predecessor has been held up as the fullest realization of the ideas and methods of post–Cold War constitution-making.[1] The Constitutional Court has quickly assumed a place among the world's highest profile judicial bodies; a South African amongst global constitution-watchers can often bask in reflected glory.[2] This constitutional success is an extraordinary result in a country where many in the 1980s did not think ordinary constitutionalism would even be possible.

But many scholars, particularly within South Africa, paint a picture in bleaker shades. The Constitutional Court's judgments often come in for sharp criticism, particularly because alongside its globally celebrated judgments the Court has, apparently inconsistently, handed down some deferent and seemingly stilted ones. The justices are attacked for not doing enough to develop South African law and respond to the manifest injustices of South African society. The concern extends beyond the Court. Threats to the Constitution from the dominant African National Congress (ANC) are regularly identified. Sujit Choudhry has argued that, given the ANC's continued electoral power, South Africa should now be treated as a dominant party democracy that will suffer 'the colonization of independent institutions meant to check the exercise of political power by a dominant party'. For Choudhry, the question is not whether this will

[1] C. R. Sunstein, *Designing Democracy: What Constitutions Do* (Oxford University Press, 2001), p. 261; A. Arato, 'Post-Sovereign Constitution-Making in Hungary: After Success, Partial Failure, and Now What?' (2010) 26 *South African Journal of Human Rights* 19, 21; A. Arato, *Constitution Making under Occupation: The Politics of Imposed Revolution in Iraq* (Columbia University Press, 2009), ch. 2.

[2] T. Roux, *Politics of Principle: The First South African Constitutional Court, 1995–2005* (Cambridge University Press, 2013), ch. 1.

spread to the judiciary; 'the only question is when'.[3] Veteran commentators have reached the point of lumping South Africa with Russia as a 'disenchanted democracy'.[4] Zapiro, South Africa's legendary and increasingly cynical political cartoonist, has drawn the Constitution with letters cut away from the title so that it reads simply 'The Con of the Republic of South Africa'.[5]

No serious observer can deny the concerns (although she also cannot deny that collapse has apparently been imminent in South Africa for some decades now). But this book is not an exercise in fortune-telling. Whatever might happen in the future, it is an attempt to look back and understand what has happened to date, to explain which forces and mechanisms have mattered, and to try and understand why some see so much going wrong while others see so much to celebrate and to envy. The discrepancy in views can be particularly sharp and puzzling when applied to this book's focus, the South African Constitutional Court. Somehow, the Court is seen as being on both sides of this dichotomy, with the very same judges apparently contextual, progressive guardians of social justice at one moment and closed-minded, heartless formalists the next. It is fair enough to charge a court with inconsistency, but the combined effect of the compliments and charges directed at the same group of judges can sometimes approach the point of implying judicial schizophrenia.

I believe that these uncertainties reflect more than just the truisms that no Court gets every decision right and that some level of reasonable professional disagreement about judgments is inevitable. I believe they speak of deep and basic disagreements about how we should understand the legal project in which the Court has been engaged. In the 2008 words of South Africa's constitutional law treatise, 'in the past nearly decade and a half of constitutional democracy in South Africa, no discernible theories of constitutional interpretation have emerged'.[6] The phrasing is suggestive of the problem: it is not merely a lack of acceptable accounts, but the lack of any plausible candidate at all. We are struggling even to take conceptual hold of the interpretative activity

3 S. Choudhry, '"He had a mandate": The South African Constitutional Court and the African National Congress in a Dominant Party Democracy' (2009) 2 *Constitutional Court Review* 1, 3.

4 B. Keller, 'How to Lose a Country Gracefully', *New York Times Magazine*, 6 March 2011.

5 *Mail & Guardian*, 6 August 2010.

6 L. du Plessis, 'Interpretation' in S. Woolman and M. Bishop (eds.), *Constitutional Law of South Africa* (2 edn., Cape Town: Juta & Co., OS 06–08, 2008), pp. 32–2.

that has been happening. My claim in this book is that the existing ways of understanding interpretation under the South African Constitution are inadequate to its actual operation. The reason why 'no discernible theories of constitutional interpretation have emerged', I argue, is because many scholarly accounts of constitutionalism in South Africa, focused on how it *should* work, have paid too little attention to how it *does* work.

As a result, I claim, some key mistakes are made. Scholarship is too court-centric, and gives far too little credit to the role that has been played by the ANC in government. There is a pervasive tendency to praise the ANC up to the point where the 1996 Constitution came into force, and thereafter to consign it to the role of threat. There is no point in being starry-eyed about the party. This book will not add much to the plentiful existing criticism of the ANC, but it by no means denies that many legitimate concerns that can be raised about the ANC, from specific policy areas like education to infamous scandals like the arms deal to general problems like corruption and mismanagement, nor that these concerns have been growing of late. But these points are already notorious, and this book is concerned with correcting an imbalance by focusing on the parts of the picture that are neglected. The ANC's contribution to the success of South African constitutionalism has been immense, and that contribution did not end when the drafting of the constitutional text did. It is inaccurate and unfair not to acknowledge this, whether we are thinking of giving due credit to the past or deciding more instrumentally how to think about the ANC going forward: we have more than one reason to want people living in South Africa, ANC members and not, to be aware of the prouder strains of the organization's recent history. And if we are trying to understand constitutional law or the Constitutional Court, the failure to acknowledge this contribution is also misleading. If we depart from the premise that the Court has mostly operated in a politically hostile environment, we will cast the Court as a somewhat precarious guardian at the gates, helped only by some resilient civil society actors – a story that we are primed for in any case by familiar understandings of impact litigation campaigns and the position of courts in emerging democracies. We will miss the way in which the Court's great cases have really been broader, public, political stories, and we will miss the extent to which the Court has had the luxury of being part of a significantly common exercise in building a new state and society. We will see the Court's great decisions as more unilaterally bold than they are, and so will find its decisions *not* to be unilaterally bold in other situations more puzzling than is actually the case. We will find it harder to take seriously the possibility that a decision by the Court to defer to another branch might not always be dictated by political fear or institutional caution or old-fashioned restrained legal habit, and that a decision to defer might really be a decision that the Court does not *need* to intervene because the other branches are also doing important constitutional work, and might be doing it better than the Court could. We will see how existing understandings of South African constitutional activity have problems with each of these ideas, and how each sheds important light on the Constitutional Court's approach to its cases. The Court has indeed played its hand well, and this book will argue that the Court is often better than its critics recognize. But the Court has also often held good cards, and we should not forget that in this metaphor the ANC has often been the dealer.

The result of this move to take more seriously the facts surrounding the Court and its cases is what I will call the *constitution-building account*, an account of the work that the Constitutional Court has been performing since its creation in 1995. This focus on the highest court has its ironies coming from someone ostensibly opposing court centrism. I adopt it partly because it is also the focus of most of the standard constitutional understandings with which a useful engagement has to start, but it also serves a broader goal. In the context of a broader enquiry into the surrounding facts, the focus on the Court forces us to engage with all the other institutions and actors its interpretative activity involves. Constitution-building compels us to stop seeing the Court as the place where all constitutional meaning begins and where all constitutional bucks stop, and to start seeing it as one institution among others. Constitution-building works best when it is a joint activity, and the successes of the South African system reflect that the Court's work has often been supported, in various ways, by the efforts of other actors and institutions.

The constitution-building account, however, aims to be an interpretative account – that is, a legal, constitutional account of the Court's work that can be used to explain and defend its activity in legal, constitutional terms, rather than merely the analyzed factual description one might get from a political scientist. It adopts a conscious strategy of trying to take the reality seriously as legal activity by seeking to articulate and test the constitutional arguments on which it rests. As such, it needs to explain how this social and political activity can fit into a book about legal activity, and how arguments that draw on these data can properly be treated as legal, constitutional arguments. This book is not a work of legal theory, but I will aim to say enough here to render plausible the claim that the constitution-building account is defensible as a legal account as well as a descriptively adequate one, and that it can therefore reply to other legal accounts on their own terms. Since the problem of how to relate legal activity to social and political activity arises in any legal system, my arguments in this regard borrow from abroad, and in particular on work from the United States. This may merit brief comment. Some perceive US constitutionalism as too old-fashioned, idiosyncratic, conservative and/or focused on negative rights to be useful to South Africans or other newer members of the global constitutional club. It is true that US doctrine is more often distinguished than followed by South African courts. But in drawing on US theory, I follow in the footsteps of leading scholars of South African constitutional law,[7] and I would add that there is much the long rich history of the US experience can teach us about how constitutionalism actually works.[8] It is mere chauvinism to rule all this out by stipulation.

But my focus in this book is on the South African case, and my analysis will be comparative only in the sense of looking outside in order to better understand within.[9] With five election cycles and two decades of post-apartheid government behind us, it is time to start taking stock. It is time to ask whether South African constitutionalism, poster child of the

[7] See e.g. J. Dugard, *Human Rights and the South African Legal Order* (Princeton University Press, 1978), p. 49: ('[s]pecial attention will be paid to the experience of the United States because South Africa and the United States share a common legal heritage as well as common social problems stemming from the diverse racial composition of their societies'), as well as the work of scholars such as Dennis Davis, Karl Klare, Heinz Klug, Theunis Roux and Stu Woolman discussed in this book.

[8] Thus although much US work of this sort will find little place in the footnotes of a book on South Africa, my approach has been informed in various ways by scholars including Akhil Reed Amar, Phillip Bobbitt, William Eskridge, John Ferejohn, Barry Friedman, Michael Klarman, John Langbein, Thomas McCraw, Jerry Mashaw, Nicholas Parrillo, Robert Post, Jed Rubenfeld, Reva Siegel, Keith Whittington and Gordon Wood, in addition to the US scholarship (and scholarship on South Africa by US scholars) that will find more specific acknowledgement in later pages.

[9] On this sort of comparative approach, see e.g. M. Tushnet, 'The Possibilities of Comparative Constitutional Law' (1998–1999) 108 *Yale Law Journal* 1225, 1269–84; P. W. Kahn, 'Comparative Constitutionalism in a New Key' (2002–2003) 101 *Michigan Law Review* 2677; R. Hirschl, 'On the Blurred Methodological Matrix of Comparative Constitutional Law' in S. Choudhry (ed.), *The Migration of Constitutional Ideas* (Cambridge University Press, 2007), pp. 41–43.

progressive and the transformative, whose birth was heralded around the world, has the resources to understand itself.[10]

A Beginning: *Makwanyane* Stories

S v. *Makwanyane*, the Constitutional Court's first significant decision which invalidated the death penalty, is the crown jewel of South African constitutionalism.[11] But if *Makwanyane* is an emblem, of what exactly is it emblematic? After more than twenty years, several hundred more Constitutional Court decisions, and a great deal of scholarship, local and international, we still do not have a good answer, and in this we will be able to start seeing the limitations of the ways in which South African constitutionalism is currently understood.

For many, *Makwanyane* is the model of a bold, value-driven approach to judging, and of a South African human rights jurisprudence that protects the interests of even unpopular minorities (murderers) against the position of the majority, without fear or favour. But if *Makwanyane* is to be understood in this way, as a decision that set the pattern for subsequent rights cases, it is striking that examples of its heirs are so hard to find. Although the many friends of this understanding of adjudication have kept a vigilant look-out, the truth of the matter is that the best example of this model today is still *Makwanyane*. Even the LGBTI equality decisions, the most likely candidates to be its successors, lack *Makwanyane*'s expansiveness.[12] So it is no surprise that those who saw *Makwanyane* as a promise of how the new court would be, or a symbol of how it should be, are often inclined to view this subsequent dearth as a betrayal, an abdication, a weakening of nerve, a failure to follow through.

Also interesting about this first view of *Makwanyane* is that it treats as *emblematic* of South African constitutionalism a decision that may be the Court's single most *un*popular finding among South Africans. It is not always attacked in name, or even as a court decision, but consistent majorities before and since have supported the death penalty. The 2005 decision in *Mohamed*, relying on *Makwanyane* to hold that South Africa should not have deported a criminal accused to the United States

[10] For this way of phrasing the enquiry, see B. Ackerman *We the People: Foundations* (Harvard University Press, 1991), ch. 1; J. Rubenfeld, 'Reading the Constitution as Spoken' (1995) 104 *Yale Law Journal* 1119.

[11] *S* v. *Makwanyane* 1995 (3) SA 391 (CC).

[12] I discuss these cases in Chapter 6.

without obtaining a guarantee that the death penalty would not be imposed, attracted undiminished public criticism.[13] A ban on the death penalty in the face of popular support for it is of course not unique to South Africa, but this first story does not spend enough time asking whether such an unpopular example represents a good model for a new constitution and court, nor why its unpopularity with a majority has not produced decisive backlash against *Makwanyane* and the stand the Court took in it. The role of the political party elected by that majority is conspicuous by its absence.

A second, more political *Makwanyane* story can be written. Its title might be 'Chronicle of a Death Penalty Invalidation Foretold'. The ANC had long supported the abolition of the death penalty by the time the Court decided the case in 1995. Black defendants had historically been strongly disproportionate recipients of the death penalty.[14] When the ANC and the ruling National Party (NP) moved towards negotiations in the late 1980s, a moratorium on the death penalty was one of the important concessions the government made. As the negotiations proceeded, the ANC wanted to abolish the death penalty, but reached deadlock with the NP, which wished to retain it. To get past the deadlock, they agreed on a right to life provision that was textually neutral on the issue, with the explicit intention that this arrangement would leave the issue to be decided by the Constitutional Court.[15]

Thus when the Court sat to consider the issue in 1995, its members could be as sure as judges in a counter-majoritarian case probably ever get to be that the ruling party intended them to decide the issue and would back up an anti-death penalty decision.[16] And the ANC

[13] *Mohamed* v. *President of the Republic of South Africa* 2001 (3) SA 893 (CC); see e.g. M. du Plessis, 'Between Apology and Utopia – The Constitutional Court and Public Opinion' (2002) 18 *South African Journal on Human Rights* 1, 5–7; R. N. Daniels and J. Brickhill, 'The Counter-Majoritarian Difficulty and the South African Constitutional Court' (2006–2007) 25 *Pennsylvania State International Law Review* 371, 381.

[14] See famously B. van Niekerk, '. . . Hanged by the Neck Until You Are Dead: Some Thoughts on the Application of the Death Penalty in South Africa' (1969) 86 *South African Law Journal* 457.

[15] For the background, see e.g. H. Klug, *Constituting Democracy: Law, Globalism and South Africa's Political Reconstruction* (Cambridge University Press, 2000), pp. 146–48); R. Spitz with M. Chaskalson, *The Politics of Transition: A Hidden History of South Africa's Negotiated Settlement* (Witwatersrand University Press, 2000), pp. 330–32; Roux, *Politics of Principle*, pp. 238–39.

[16] I use 'counter-majoritarian' here and in the rest of this chapter to refer to the court acting contrary to the view of a majority of members of the public, as opposed to the view of the majority party elected by that public. I owe to Or Bassok the knowledge that Alexander

has since repeatedly done so. Days after the decision (and just before local government elections) the NP demanded in Parliament that the issue of the death penalty should be put to a referendum, asking Parliament to '[a]llow South Africans to instruct the judiciary to let justice be seen to be done'.[17] Minister of Justice Dullah Omar and future Deputy Minister of Justice and then-ANC MP Johnny de Lange responded by praising *Makwanyane*, from which Omar quoted at length and which De Lange predicted 'shall go down in history as one of the great judgments that has been handed down'.[18] Joined by speakers from the Inkatha Freedom Party (IFP), Democratic Party (DP) and Pan Africanist Congress (PAC), they castigated the opportunism of the NP's populist pre-election appeal in light of the negotiated transition and the importance of respecting the new constitutional nature of the state and the Court's authority, while reminding the NP that other things could be put to referendum too. In Omar's words:

> The proposal that a referendum should take place calls into question the very basis of the constitutional state and the notion of the core values of the Constitution, which should be beyond the reach of temporary majorities and the role of the Constitutional Court ... The key to the whole negotiated settlement in South Africa is the move away from parliamentary sovereignty to constitutional supremacy. The constitutional state depends on the establishment and nurturing of an independent, impartial constitutional court. Every single party which is committed to the notion of a constitutional state needs, therefore, to ensure that nothing is done to undermine the new constitutionalism. This includes building respect for the Constitutional Court and helping to establish its independence ... The complex arrangement contained in the Constitution to place core values beyond the reach of a temporary majority will be at risk if the NP's proposal for a referendum is accepted. Not only does it undermine the Constitutional Court; it opportunistically invokes the principle of majoritarianism at the expense of constitutionalism, in respect of only one issue, the one in which it believes that the majority is baying for blood. However, it ignores others which are also controversial. Why should we not submit other issues of major concern to referendum, such as the future of languages in our country, the national anthem, the flag, the need for radical land redistribution, the unpopular property clause in Chapter 3,

Bickel used the term to refer to the latter situation, in the days before opinion polls became ubiquitous.

17 *Hansard*, 19 June 1995, Col. 2843 (GC Oosthuizen, NP).

18 *Ibid.*, Cols. 2850–52 (Minister of Justice [AM Omar]); Col. 2829 (JH de Lange, ANC).

> as well as the far-reaching amnesty provisions? Why should public opinion in these matters not also be tested by referenda? [Interjections].[19]

The referendum was not called. The ANC's position, of course, suited its preferences on the substance of the issue (although several senior ANC members also thought the issue of the death penalty should be put to a referendum).[20] But the terms in which Omar stated that position are notable nonetheless, and the ANC government has continued to hold this line. Although constitutional scholarship pays no attention, in the years since *Makwanyane* Parliament has heard many submissions from the public and in private member's bills seeking the reinstatement of the death penalty, and the ANC has consistently rejected them and upheld *Makwanyane*. A representative example comes from a 2008 parliamentary committee considering public comments. On a submission from a Mr. NK Govind, the minutes record: 'The first issue raised related to the re-instatement of the death penalty. The legal advisor recommended that the Makwanyane argument applied and therefore the amendment not be applied. Mr Gaum (ANC) agreed.' There the matter ended.[21] The most recent in a long chain of such small episodes, a November 2014 reply to a presidential question, continues to hold the *Makwanyane* line nearly twenty years on.[22]

This political detail offers an explanation for *Makwanyane*'s expansiveness – it will be rare indeed that judges can be as certain of a

[19] *Ibid.*, Cols. 2847–49 (Minister of Justice [AM Omar]); see also *Ibid.*, Cols. 2829–30 (JH De Lange, ANC); Cols. 2832–33 (MB Skosana, IFP); Cols. 2836–38 (AJ Leon, DP); Col. 2841 (RK Sizani, PAC). President Mandela took the same line at the time in a televised address: see A. M. Dodek, 'A Tale to Two Maps: The Limits of Universalism in Comparative Judicial Review' (2009) 47 *Osgoode Hall Law Journal* 287, 310.

[20] H. Klug, 'Participation in the Design' in P. Andrews and S. Ellmann (eds.), *Post-Apartheid Constitutions: Perspectives on South Africa's Basic Law* (Ohio University Press, 2001), p. 149.

[21] National Assembly, Constitutional Review Committee, 15 August 2008, record available at https://pmg.org.za/committee-meeting/9505.

[22] National Assembly, Internal Question Paper No. 2823, Question 940 for written reply from Mr. AM Shaik Emam (NFP), 21 November 2014, available at https://pmg.org.za/question_reply/497/. For other examples, selected from among many, see e.g. Private Members' Legislative Proposals and Special Petitions Portfolio Committee, Minutes, 9 September 1998, available at https://pmg.org.za/committee-meeting/6314/; Constitutional Review Committee, Minutes, 25 March 1999, available at https://pmg.org.za/committee-meeting/6684/; Joint Constitutional Review Committee, Minutes, 29 August 2003, available at https://pmg.org.za/committee-meeting/2779/; Joint Constitutional Review Committee, Minutes, 2 February 2004, available at https://pmg.org.za/committee-meeting/3411/.

ruling party's counter-majoritarian stance or its willingness to accept a counter-majoritarian outcome – and its durability. This second *Makwanyane* story, accordingly, illustrates the critical importance of taking social and political facts seriously. But the second story's most worrying deficiency is the account it offers us of *Makwanyane* as an interpretative act, or rather, the account it fails to offer. If the fearless rights-defender story seems to spend too much of its time inside the legal materials, the political story seems strangely removed from the judicial reasoning itself. The result matters, but there is a strong whiff of the legal realist idea that the Court's reasons were tacked on to a result preordained. Explaining *Makwanyane* as a product of the political circumstances seems to come at the cost of rendering rather vestigial or peripheral *Makwanyane* as the duly interpreted legal implications of a value-driven constitutional text.

The further effort to take the reality *interpretatively* seriously will respond to this concern, and I will be offering my own *Makwanyane* story based on that approach in a moment. But my prior concern is with the simple fact of these two stories and the divide between them. For my claim is that this pattern of a politically disinterested or naïve interpretative story running along in parallel with an interpretively barren political science story, neither of them completely satisfactory, is a general feature, and defect, of post-1994 understandings of South African constitutionalism. A key reason why a workable account of South African constitutional interpretation has not yet emerged is because accounts are only of one sort or the other, having the strengths and weaknesses of their type. If an account's *Makwanyane* story is court-centric and tends towards applauding bold, proudly value-vindicating counter-majoritarianism, it struggles to explain a post-*Makwanyane* world in which the Constitutional Court has almost always played a more cautious and subtle game, and in which much of what happens cannot be explained without considerable reference to actors outside of the Court. But if an account's *Makwanyane* story embraces the politics and the reality, it struggles to offer an account that can reasonably be considered interpretive, based on and resulting from fidelity to the legal materials.

Why does this divide matter? It is easy to imagine a possible world where it would *not* matter. After all, we are used to the idea that there is a gap between reality and the law: we are supposed to put the facts next to the rules and, to the extent that the facts do not match the rules, judge the facts as illegal, as unconstitutional, or at least as less constitutional. On this view, if post-*Makwanyane* constitutional practice has not lived up to *Makwanyane*'s promise, then that constitutional practice is failing to that extent to live up to what the Constitution demands. This is simple enough, and as we will see, many scholarly accounts understand the situation in just this way. The second *Makwanyane* story, on this view, states the facts that stand to be judged as constitutionally acceptable or defective, measured according to the legal standard of the first story. The political moment may explain the historical significance of the result, but this background is not seen as relevant to the legal question of whether the decision is correct or incorrect, satisfying or unsatisfying.

However, that is not the only possible world. Suppose the second, political *Makwayane* story is not only purporting to tell us what happened – the facts – but that it was the only way that so bold a decision *could* have happened – the political reality. Suppose it wants to tell us a causal story about how the system actually works and how the result actually came about, such that if we want another *Makwanyane*, its implication is that we will need the same causal factors, the same conducive political circumstances, or something else that can do the same work. In this world, those who view post-*Makwanyane* constitutional practice as (to some degree) a disappointment or a failure to follow through will find the relationship between law and reality more complicated. The gap between subsequent reality and the bold legal view of the first *Makwanyane* story is still present. But in this world, the causal account of the second *Makwanyane* account tells us of the extraordinary work needed to close that gap. It also suggests that whether the gap gets closed is not necessarily up to the Constitutional Court. If *Makwanyane* is to a significant extent a product of its political context, especially the stance of the ANC leadership, then we should expect that the work of closing the gap will be heavily a matter of such political factors in other cases too. In this world, if post-*Makwanyane* South Africa has failed to deliver on that decision's promise, the failure looks more like a failure of the polity, or a result of the limits of what was practically possible in that polity, than it does a failure of the Court's interpretations (with a legitimate debate still to be had about how much judicial activity alone can affect a polity and change what is possible within it). This account has a growing resonance as the glory days of the transition recede and less edifying ordinary politics resumes.[23]

[23] The distinction between 'normal politics' and times of 'higher law-making' or constitutional moments is Bruce Ackerman's, see Ackerman, *Foundations*, especially chs. 9 and 10; B. Ackerman, *The Future of Liberal Revolution* (Yale University Press, 1992), pp. 14–15.

Now consider a third and final possible world. In this world, the political *Makwanyane* story is not just telling us how things happened, or how they had to happen. It is pointing to how constitutionalism works – how things function, in a manner that is constitutionally appealing or at least acceptable. In this world, the gap between the first, bold *Makwanyane* story and reality is complicated still further. If the tale told by the first *Makwanyane* story is not only not happening, but the reality of what *is* happening is a functioning constitutional system, we should be willing to ask why we are hanging on to the first *Makwanyane* story. We will not necessarily want to say that it is wrong. It is a reasonable theoretical position of eminently respectable academic parents, and its place in the ongoing competition of ideal constitutional visions is fair enough. But we should question seriously whether we should proceed any longer with it as our blueprint to what constitutional adjudication is supposed to be. It might be a good blueprint or it might be a bad one, but it is not, apparently, an accurate blueprint of the functioning constitutional society before us. Whatever its virtues, then, it is likely to be a poorer guide to understanding the system, critiquing its actors, and thinking about reforms than an account that more accurately grasps what is going on.

My claim in this book is that post-apartheid constitutionalism in South Africa has existed much more in this third possible world than in either of the other two. The failure of post-*Makwanyane* South African constitutionalism to live up to the first *Makwanyane* story in fact reflects the inadequacies of the first *Makwanyane* story and the view of constitutionalism that it represents. It needs retelling. To the extent that post-*Makwanyane* constitutionalism *does* lie in the first two possible worlds, my claim is that it lies much more in the second than the first. Its features are shaped to a much greater extent by the limits of practical possibility and the nature of South African political activity than by interpretative choices made by the justices, the dominant target of most scholarly attention and criticism. The constitution-building account, situating constitutional activity in a broader institutional and political context, is intended to respond to this imbalance. Its conscious bid to offer an interpretative, constitutional account, in turn, will aim to show why this story can be a satisfactorily legal replacement for the first *Makwanyane* story.

If the second *Makwanyane* story were simply about naked political calculation, then this effort might well be doomed at the outset. We might be able to dress up the story in legal clothing, but it would not be an interpretative story worthy of the name. What is crucial to the argument about *Makwanyane*, and to this book's broader argument, is that the political story is much richer than this. As a result, it is possible to do what the second *Makwanyane* story does not: to see how the public, political story is part of, partly constitutive of, the legal reasons. In their different ways, the various judgments in *Makwanyane* seek to position the abolition of the death penalty as the necessary implication of the national decision to be a post-apartheid society. The abolition is powerfully understood as representing a desire to break out of the status of human rights pariah, to 'feel fulfilled that humanity has taken us back into its bosom', to 'never, never and never again . . . suffer the indignity of being the skunk of the world', as President Mandela had put it in his inauguration speech the previous year, in words written by Thabo Mbeki.[24] The full extent of what is included in the idea of rejoining the global human rights community is, of course, anyone's guess, but the death penalty is an unusually prominent symbol of what that community rejects, and it is the abolition of the death penalty as a symbolic, not-pariah, not-apartheid thing that *Makwanyane* is most deeply about. That *Makwanyane* is so celebrated by the international human rights community as a symbol is unsurprising, because the decision was in a real sense perfectly designed to be a symbol of all that was celebrated by that community, to mark South Africa's return to it.[25]

This presentation entirely suited the strategic interests of the Court, allowing it to represent itself as a fresh institution, not subject to the baggage of having been an apartheid-era body complicit in oppression, as the rest of the court system was.[26] But less often noted is how much it would have suited the ANC leadership, too. The ANC, too, wished to mark South Africa's return to the global community, as something

[24] As Mark Gevisser writes: 'These were Mandela's finest words since his speech from the dock at the Rivonia Trial in 1964. They were written by Thabo Mbeki. Seldom has Mbeki written as beautifully for himself as he has for others – and particularly for Mandela.' M. Gevisser, *Thabo Mbeki: The Dream Deferred* (Johannesburg: Jonathan Ball Publishers, 2007), p. 656.

[25] See Klug, *Constituting Democracy*, pp. 145–48; and see also Roux, *Politics of Principle*, p. 46, referring to Klug's general analysis and noting, in relation to issues including the death penalty, 'the non-accidental convergence of the political morality informing the post-Apartheid Constitutions and the political views circulating in the comparative law community'.

[26] H. Klug, *The Constitution of South Africa: A Contextual Analysis* (Oxford: Hart, 2010), pp. 238–40; see also D. Dyzenhaus, *Judging the Judges, Judging Ourselves* (Oxford: Hart, 1996).

achieved under the party's guidance and due to its commitment to human rights for all. The *Makwanyane* symbol had strategic value to the ANC just as it did to the Court, and it similarly spoke to something deep about the commitments of the organization.

What the second *Makwanyane* story gets wrong, therefore, is that it sees that the abolition *result* was favoured by the ANC and foreshadowed by the political history of the issue, but does not take the link between the politics and the decision any further. The result is its awkwardness as an interpretative story: if the Court was just following the politics, then the reasons it gave are relegated to secondary status. What the second story misses is that the link between the politics and the decision is much more extensive and happens at the level of the legal reasoning. I will refer to this kind of public backing or political support for an idea as its *public status*, something distinct from whether the idea can be located in the constitutional text (though public status and textual status are of course often linked). This public status, I argue, is something the constitution-building court can legitimately consider in its interpretative activity. That claim may raise concerns, but let us set those aside for a moment in order to see how taking such considerations into account can help us understand what the first *Makwanyane* story misses, which is how all the interpretative considerations lined up in the decision. The circumstances of the case were such that the *Makwanyane* court was operating in the context of powerful ANC preferences, but that strong pull was in very much the direction in which the Court wanted to go. The political leadership wanted the Court to exercise this counter-majoritarian power, wanted a bold human rights decision that abolished the death penalty and made manifest the constitutional achievement. And so the constitution-building pieces fell into place. In context, the Court could boldly assert its own, still-uncertain institutional authority and that of the Constitution, fulfilling the duty to advance and entrench the new constitutional arrangements. It could give strong voice to textual imperatives to give effect to the values of 'dignity, equality and freedom', and could show how this purposive obligation could give effect to the neutral provision that 'everyone has the right to life.' Indeed, such was the Court's sense of freedom that it could enthusiastically issue ten concurrences, each beginning the exploration of the new text, a number it has never subsequently got even close to approaching since. This sense of freedom stems from the fact that the Court could do all of this without in the least upsetting the ANC – as we have seen, the true position was completely the opposite. As a result, the Court could strongly and publicly emphasize the most critical premise of constitutionalism by asserting the Constitution as supreme over majoritarian politics, while actually strongly respecting the interests of the majority party.

That is not quite to say that every constitution-building imperative pointed to boldness in *Makwanyane*. The Court's decision does come with some potential legitimacy costs, since many South Africans would be upset by the Court's claim that South Africa had committed itself against the death penalty – as manifest in the regular bids to overturn the decision Parliament has received ever since. *Makwanyane* also sees the Court, unusually, stepping in to decide a deeply contested and potentially empirically complex question, rather than leave it to the legislature. That the Court elected to do this is a product of the unusual political situation. Given that the Court's institutional imperatives lay so strongly in presenting itself as a fresh institution, and given that its longer-term authority was so strongly bound up in the idea of being an institution not controlled by majoritarian politics, the legitimacy coin came down on the side of decision and abolition. But obvious differences of opinion among the judges about whether and how public opinion was relevant to their decision foreshadow the harder questions which later cases, arising in less conducive circumstances, would pose for the Court.[27] If *Makwanyane* is an emblem, what it signifies here is a question, not an answer, and we will see that it is an enduring question for a Court charged with enforcing a strongly aspirational constitution that applies to contested issues as much as settled commitments.

That some controversy existed can be detected in some notable features of the main judgment, written by then–Constitutional Court President Chaskalson, to which others have drawn attention. The judgment makes what remains a rare foray into the drafting history in order to find that the negotiating parties intended the Court to settle the question of the death penalty's constitutionality, providing an extraordinary kind of justification for the Court's decision to do so. The judgment also relies quite heavily on the absence of evidence that the death penalty would deter criminals or otherwise lower crime rates. Some see this as an area of weakness in *Makwanyane*'s abolitionist dam, because it represents a respect in which the decision does less than rule that the

[27] See H. Klug, 'Striking Down Death' (1996) 12 *South African Journal on Human Rights* 61; M. Zlotnick, 'The Death Penalty and Public Opinion' (1996) 12 *South African Journal on Human Rights* 70; Daniels and Brickhill, 'The Counter-Majoritarian Difficulty', pp. 380–81; Klug, *Constitution of South Africa*, pp. 76–78.

death penalty is inconsistent with South African constitutional values in any circumstances.[28] That concern is probably overdrawn, especially in light of the status the judgment has come to assume: *Makwanyane* would take some overruling, even if the death penalty really could be shown to reduce crime rates. But the observation is nevertheless important because it points to how, at least for Justice Chaskalson, the institutional considerations and the extent of public opposition remained reasons to craft the decision with some care, and some circumspection. *Makwanyane* is not the epitome of counter-majoritarian boldness, because the conditions, while unusually favourably, were not entirely conducive.

We are now in a position to see what the first *Makwanyane* story misses. It takes *Makwanyane* to stand for certain principles, such as dignity, and certain ideas, such as a commitment to a progressive vision of the global human rights consensus and a counter-majoritarian boldness in defending those ideas and those principles. Since the Court has not always followed through on these things in later cases, the first story cries inconsistency. But that conclusion only follows if we assume, as the first story does, that we should abstract the Court's findings from their context, and take the Court to be setting a precedent for how it will act in all future cases regardless of context. That assumption has its roots in a vision of the Court as an institution of moral principle, detached from politics and elevated above public opinion. This is, as I said above, a familiar and time-honoured picture, but it is not a picture of what the South African Constitutional Court is. Instead, there is an important sense in which *Makwanyane* is not an exercise in abstract moral reasoning. Theunis Roux has aptly noted the way in which, for all its many references to foreign law, the main judgment in *Makwanyane* makes little effort to articulate an understanding of the value-laden terms it works with, on the way to asking whether the death penalty complies with those understandings.[29] What this reflects, above all, is that the

[28] See e.g. J. van der Walt, *Law and Sacrifice: Towards a Post-Apartheid Theory of Law* (New York: Routledge, 2005), pp. 104–08.

[29] Roux, *Politics of Principle*, pp. 242–48. Roux understands this approach in strategic terms: the Court did not need to articulate abstract moral content to assert the supremacy of the Constitution, and such maximalism might have been politically risky, so the main judgment avoided it. He concludes: 'what is really going on in *Makwanyane*, then, is not a failed exercise in moral philosophy, but a largely successful exercise in judicial politics.' (*Ibid.*, p. 246). It is this sort of bifurcation *between* principle and politics that I resist in understanding *Makwanyane*, and this is a broader point of difference between the accounts. I do not see the ANC's stance as merely providing political cover for the

Court is not engaging in abstract constitutional reasoning and then considering a concrete issue in light of the result. Instead, it is receiving into constitutional law something of pre-existing public status – and that something is not a set of abstract principles of dignity and the right to life. If this conception of the Court's activity can be defended as a legally satisfying account of the Court's constitutional role, the assumption of the first story will stand exposed. We will not need to separate the Court's interpretative work from its political context, and we will recognize that constitution-building activity will usually have to play out in contexts less conducive to judicial expansionism than *Makwanyane*'s.

Makwanyane's importance, therefore, lies in the symbolic work it did as the first decision to establish the key ideas of constitutionalism in South Africa. Its significance as a matter of legal doctrine is only the more limited idea that these abstract ideas and principles will inform the Court's future assessment of its constitutional duty in future contexts, where other relevant factors might be different, the context might be less hospitable, and the case for judicial action less appealing. I submit that regular constitution-watchers will agree that this is a much more accurate description of what *Makwanyane*'s provenance has actually been: its ideas may be found, more or less diluted, in many of the Court's subsequent decisions – just seldom if ever as boldly as in the extraordinary circumstances of the original decision. The dominant theme has become *Makwanyane*'s secondary idea, mostly coming out in the concurrences, that the Court is not overruling the majority but instead expressing the nation's deeper will, represented by the Constitution. This classic constitutional line (and, sometimes, fiction) makes far more sense to the real life of a Court in ordinary times than the candid dismissal of public opinion, which only the extraordinary circumstances of *Makwanyane* could embolden the Court to employ.[30]

There is an epilogue to the *Makwanyane* story, which offers some support for my reading of what the case was really about and my more muted view of the picture of constitutional adjudication it represents.

legal work the judges wanted to do but which was difficult to sell to the South African public (and *Makwanyane*, notwithstanding its attempts to do so, has not done much to convince the public. See *Ibid.*, pp. 4, 246–48, 260). Activity in the political sphere was a key source of the content the Court expressed, and so has a deeper legal relevance.

30 See also Klug, *Constitution of South Africa*, pp. 76–78 (noting the bluntness of the *Makwanyane* main judgment's dismissal of the public opinion point); A. Cockrell, 'The South African Bill of Rights and the Duck/Rabbit' (1997) 60 *Modern Law Review* 513, 529–30, 532–34.

What seems to have been generally ignored at the time of the decision is what I will later call a question of *infrastructure* – how exactly was the order going to get implemented? What was to happen to the death row prisoners, sentenced to a now-unconstitutional sentence? The ironic epilogue to South Africa's constitutional emblem is that it would be over a decade before this question received an answer, while the prisoners languished in legal limbo, ignored by the authorities. The beneficiaries of the Court's first rights case would have to become the subject of the Court's first ever structural interdict before their status under the new constitutional dispensation would be finally resolved.[31]

Makwanyane's epilogue offers some support for the idea that the case was about symbolic commitments, not prisoners: once the constitutional trumpet was duly sounded, everyone stopped paying attention to Messers Makwanyane and Mchunu. That, admittedly, is not unusual for a constitutional case in a highest court, where the issue frequently transcends the facts that brought it there. But the real significance of the epilogue is as a salutary early reminder of the realities of constitution-building. Bold, progressive findings are not necessarily enough to affect concrete interests, even those as familiar and comparatively simple and close to the judiciary as the administration of prisoners. The limits under which the Court operates are not necessarily those posed by the much-discussed over-powerful party of liberation, but are often the basic limits of administrative and oversight mechanisms and other mundane problems of ordinary governance, and simple uncertainty. Thus this point is not much of a criticism of the Court, which would after all have had no reason at the time to issue a more intrusive remedy, given that the ANC government was, of course, supporting the court's order. But the third, retold *Makwanyane* story, with its epilogue, gives us a much better sense of the real nature of constitutional adjudication in South Africa after 1994. It illustrates why it is that, for all the importance of the bold principles of the first *Makwanyane* story, we need a more complete account of the realities of constitutional adjudication. It shows why it is crucial to remedy the limitations of the second *Makwanyane* story's view of political context so that we can use this to understand our interpretative practice better. Only then can we achieve an adequate view of what

[31] *Sibiya* v. *Director of Public Prosecutions, Johannesburg* 2005 (5) SA 315 (CC); *Sibiya* v. *Director of Public Prosecutions, Johannesburg* 2006 (2) BCLR 293 (CC). See also M. Bishop, 'Remedies' in Woolman and Bishop (eds.), *Constitutional Law*, 9-185–9-186.

this first great case really is: an admirable decision whose content was significantly formed by the political movements of South African society, whose proud counter-majoritarianism was and continues to be underwritten by the ANC; a decision whose boldness was already tempered by an awareness of the harder questions of legitimacy and deference to come, whose authors were without contradiction both sincere and astute, both politically aware and legally engaged, whose order turned out to be hampered by practical limits, failures of lower-level government, and problems of access to justice; its best admired around the world, its problems frustratingly ordinary – as *this* decision, *Makwanyane* is a true emblem of post-1994 South African constitutionalism.

Beyond *Makwanyane*

The pattern of the first two *Makwanyane* stories, I claimed, reflected general features of South African constitutional understandings, and it is in this light that we can see the wider significance of the retold *Makwanyane* story. As a rough but still substantially accurate generalization, we can think about two ways of writing about South African constitutional law, one associated with the first *Makwanyane* story and one associated with the second. Let us begin with accounts associated with the second. They can be called non-interpretivist or realist. The basic first question of this sort of account is: what do constitutional actors actually do in this system? To this question, accounts of this sort might give merely descriptive answers: politicians pressure courts in these sorts of cases, the courts resist or give in under these sorts of conditions. They might also go further and evaluate the data. They might try to show, for example, that a court's moves were strategically wise in that they helped the court avoid a destructive backlash or allowed it to build up its authority gradually in the face of a powerful party. Accounts of this sort are realist, in other words, because they aim to capture and analyze the behaviour that is really going on. What makes them non-interpretativist is that they have no resources to tell us whether what a constitutional actor did was constitutionally correct or at least constitutionally valid or permissible. At most, they can tell us whether what was done was strategically wise or foolish, good or bad for stability, and so on. They are legal accounts only in the sense of being accounts about legal things.

A small but notable school of writing on South African constitutionalism offers accounts of this sort. For example, an important paper by

Iain Currie describes the Constitutional Court as practicing 'judicious avoidance', using the sorts of minimalist tactics described by Cass Sunstein. Currie presents his argument as an attempt 'to describe and defend' this minimalism, following Sunstein's defences of minimalism as democracy-promoting, mistake-minimizing, agreement-facilitating, and so on.[32] But while Currie seems comfortable with the legitimacy of the behaviour he has described, he does not offer a constitutional argument for it in the sense of showing why the practice he describes is constitutionally permitted or required by a plausible reading of the constitutional text, as opposed to just being a good idea.[33] The most important work in this school is by Theunis Roux. He has argued that, in certain cases, the Court has 'compromised on principle' in order to avoid taking legally principled stands that would have risked serious political reprisal from the powerful ANC. Initially, Roux presented this as an accurate description defensible on simple pragmatic grounds, and therefore fell squarely in the realist camp.[34] His recent book offers a more general and more nuanced picture, in which some cases are still explained as blunt compromises on principle but in which this is part of a broader 'adjudicative strategy' which aims to explain what he views as 'remarkable about the Court's achievement', which is 'not just that it handed down some very fine decisions, or that it managed to stay out of political trouble, but that it did each of these things without compromising its ability to do the other.' On this picture, the Court's achievement is to have stayed legal enough to preserve its reputation as an adjudicator according to law and respond to 'the relatively strong pressure exerted by South African legal-professional culture to decide cases in a principled way', while being strategic enough to respond 'to the need to avoid a debilitating attack on

[32] I. Currie, 'Judicious Avoidance' (1999) 15 *South African Journal on Human Rights* 138, referring to C. R. Sunstein, *One Case at a Time: Judicial Minimalism on the Supreme Court* (Harvard University Press, 1999); the quoted text appears at p. 165. Note that Sunstein's views have evolved since: see especially C. R. Sunstein, 'Problems with Minimalism' (2005–2006) 58 *Stanford Law Review* 1889.

[33] Roederer, in his criticism of the Currie/Sunstein argument, repeatedly points to the lack of underlying normative justification for its features, most notably its understanding of democracy and the judicial role in it, although since Roederer is content to engage with Currie/Sunstein on their own terms he does not treat this as a particular failure to articulate a constitutional argument. See C. J. Roederer, 'Judicious Engagement: Theory, Attitude and Community' (1999) 15 *South African Law Journal* 486, 495, 504, 505–10.

[34] T. Roux, 'Principle and Pragmatism on the Constitutional Court of South Africa' (2009) 7 *International Journal of Constitutional Law* 106. On the characterization as straightforward pragmatism, see also Roux, *Politics of Principle*, p. 69 n. 201.

its independence'.[35] The result, then, is a set of decisions 'not absolutely determined by law' in which the Court gets away with a few genuine compromises on principle that are too infrequent to damage its reputation for principled decision-making, combined with a larger set of decisions in which the Court selects interpretations that are not the best reading of the text as a matter of pure legal principle but are at least legally plausible and are strategically more prudent.[36] The result is therefore still realist: Roux will repeatedly accept that the Court has articulated doctrines that are not the best legal interpretations of the Constitution, and only rarely thinks that the cases he examines are fully justifiable as a matter of constitutional principle.[37] Like the second *Makwanyane* story, his account can explain a great deal, but it is not able (because it does not set out) to rebut legally the standard interpretative criticisms of the Court, which indeed it often accepts are correct in strictly legal terms.

This matters when one compares the realists to the other school, classically interpretivist and associated with the first *Makwanyane* story. In contrast to realists, who look first to the world, the basic question of these accounts is: What do the legal sources mean? Accounts of the interpretivist sort try to tell us whether an interpretation was a good or a bad reading of the constitution and other legal materials, or whether an action was permitted according to such a reading. This is the core of traditional lawyerly business, so it will come as no surprise that most scholarly work on constitutional law in South Africa falls into this category (examples to follow). This school offers legal accounts not only in the sense of being about legal things, but also in the sense of working in legal terms.

The fact that these two schools operate in different terms means they constantly talk past each other. Realists argue that intepretivists are asking for what they cannot plausibly have, while interpretivists quite fairly respond that their legal arguments stand unrebutted and that if the Court does not follow them then this is illegitimate. Thus, for example, David Bilchitz, among many others, has devoted considerable attention to arguing that the Court's socio-economic rights interpretations are textually incoherent and do not do enough to make the protections of these vital interests real for impoverished

35 Roux, *Politics of Principle*, pp. 3, 8.
36 I return to his arguments about particular cases in later chapters.
37 See the discussion of same-sex marriage judgment in Chapter 6.

South Africans.[38] Roux explicitly accepts Bilchitz's arguments as legal criticisms of the Court's approach, but will dismiss the ultimate relevance of this: 'As soon as one accepts, however, that the [Court's] strategy in these [socio-economic] cases has been to devise a review standard that allowed it greater flexibility to manage its relationship with the political branches, much of the force of this criticism falls away.'[39] Each side appreciates the other's arguments but does not see them as an adequate response to their own. A similar problem dogs the debate between Currie's minimalism and the more expansive approaches of its opponents. He and opponents can at least engage on whether Sunstein's minimalism is an accurate way to describe what the court is doing or whether the virtues associated with minimalism outweigh its vices.[40] But for opponents such as Alfred Cockrell and Stu Woolman, the key objection to minimalism is instead that it is constitutionally inappropriate or incorrect.[41] The Constitution, they think,

[38] D. Bilchitz, *Poverty and Fundamental Rights: The Justification and Enforcement of Socio-economic Rights* (Oxford University Press, 2007); S. Liebenberg, *Adjudicating Socio-economic Rights under a Transformative Constitution* (Cape Town: Juta & Co., 2010).

[39] Roux, 'Principle and Pragmatism', 136; his later work accepts Bilchitz's legal arguments while explaining the strategic reasons the Court had for not following them: Roux, *Principle and Pragmatism*, pp. 263–64, 286–88, 291–92. I return to both arguments in the discussion of socio-economic rights cases in Chapters 8 and 9.

[40] See e.g. T. Roux, 'Transformative Constitutionalism and the Best Interpretation of the South African Constitution: Distinction Without a Difference?' (2009) 20 *Stellenbosch Law Review* 258, 284; S. Woolman, 'The Amazing Vanishing Bill of Rights' (2007) 124 *South African Law Journal* 762, 764–65 and n. 4. Woolman also makes the standard anti-minimalist argument, common in scholarship on South Africa, that a court must give guidance to other actors: *Ibid.*, pp. 785–87, 789–92.

[41] Woolman's claim, *Ibid.*, is built around a substantive constitutional argument about what is required by the various pieces of the constitutional mechanism that (are supposed to) govern its application. He sees the Court's minimalism as a failure to engage properly with this mechanism. Cockrell's criticism of 'shallow' thinly theorized adjudication styles – A. Cockrell, 'Rainbow Jurisprudence' (1996) 12 *South African Journal on Human Rights* 1 – is also bound up in a constitutional claim. He sees what was in his case the interim Constitution as importing into a previously formalist legal system a bill of rights and several constitutional provisions incorporating open-ended value terms (*Ibid.*, e.g. at 10). He considers this constitutional change to require that, instead of relying on 'shallow' reasoning, the Court must articulate a 'deep' vision of political morality according to which it will resolve the clash of incommensurables (he follows Isaiah Berlin – see esp. *Ibid.*, 37–38) that adjudicating such value terms will inevitably produce. Cockrell's article preceded Currie's. While Currie criticizes Cockrell's approach as 'impractical and inappropriate' in a nation with fractured ideas of the justification for law and judges still occupying a new and precarious court, he does not challenge Cockrell's argument on *constitutional* grounds (Currie, 'Judicious Avoidance', 144–46).

demands more than minimalism, and while Currie thinks more expansive action could be a mistake, he does not have an argument that the Constitution does *not* demand more (or, more strongly, that it really demands less). Unless we have an argument of this sort, this debate is as insoluble as the first one.

The suspicion may arise that the interpretativist ambitions of the constitution-building account are just a matter of taking prudential positions and dressing them up in legal clothing. After all, it is not too difficult to see how one might phrase Currie's argument, or Sunstein's, or Roux's, in terms of a constitutional argument about, say, the Court's duty to promote a constitutional good like democracy, or to defend the integrity of a constitutional structure, namely itself.[42] One might further suspect that merely redescribing the arguments like this does not take us any further towards resolving them. These are fair concerns. However, my claim in this book is that the real practice of South African constitutional law is not only different to what traditional accounts take it to be but often better than they acknowledge, and that if we take it legally seriously it will often yield richly satisfying legal answers. In this respect, my approach bears a family resemblance to Stu Woolman's recent book on South African constitutionalism. Woolman claims that some current 'understandings of freedom in the context of the self and the social' are 'errant' and that 'the way we think about the self is incorrect', but also that if we adjust our thinking and our ways of operating, including in the context of constitutional law, we may well find this reality appealing and be satisfied as lawyers by the sorts of answers to which it leads us.[43] I (like Roux) am more concerned with understanding what has happened in South Africa than offering my own theory of how to proceed, and this book is accordingly less theoretically ambitious than Woolman's and engages a smaller slice of reality, but it has a similar relationship to that reality. It will not always be the case that what actually happens is legally defensible or appealing, and it is important to insist on this if we are to retain the idea that law is not just what happens and so preserve law's autonomy. But even the less appealing parts of real practice will help us understand the Court's actions, something that will become important in contexts as awkward as

42 Roux has noted this possibility, which I return to in the next chapter.

43 S. Woolman, *The Selfless Constitution: Experimentalism and Flourishing as Foundations of South Africa's Basic Law* (Cape Town: Juta & Co., 2013); the quoted text appears at pp. 14–15.

Makwanyane's was congenial. And where the reality is more attractive, this approach will allow us to appreciate that some decisions seen as bad are in fact appealing exercises in constitution-building logic. The Court's approach will emerge at least as something legally intelligible and internally consistent, and, as I hope to show, something often more defensible and appealing than any existing account on either side of the current realist/interpretivist debate takes it to be.

Between us and this oh-so-neat finessing of the debates of South African constitutionalism stands the need to extend the lines of the third *Makwanyane* story to the broader record of the Constitutional Court's activity. Although my principle focus will be on cases and their broader social and political context, the enquiry will necessitate examining South African constitutionalism from a number of different angles and drawing on work from several disciplines. I begin in Chapter 2 by addressing the threshold resistance, should the reader feel it, to the idea of bringing social and political considerations in legal interpretation properly so called. I will offer reasons to think this is not a decisive objection to the constitution-building account, and that instead interpretative activity that takes account of social and political considerations might be not just legitimate but constitutionally better than interpretative activity that confines itself to more traditionally legal sources. Chapter 3 begins to confront real practice, defending the universally criticized decision on the right to vote in *New National Party* v. *Government of South Africa* and explaining how the constitution-building account can bring out the deep consistency in the Court's jurisprudence on voting rights. It will show the Court playing a particular institutional role, and Chapter 4 will seek to explain why the issue of the Court's role has been misunderstood, but also strangely neglected, by current understandings of South African constitutionalism. It will interrogate influential accounts based on the constitutional negotiations and the nature of South Africa's constitutional project, and discuss their limitations. Chapter 5, in turn, will move on to flesh out the constitution-building account as a constitutional argument in response. Chapters 6 and 7 apply this account to the Court's famous LGBTI equality judgments and its decisions, famous and infamous, on democracy. Chapters 8 and 9 will move into still more contested territory, considering the socio-economic rights cases and several decisions on equality and religious rights that represent some of the Court's most criticized judgments. The constitution-building account will allow us to see how the Court's socio-economic rights decisions are widely misunderstood, and are in fact much more defensible than they are usually thought to be once we understand their logic. It will also allow us at least to understand the vilified equality decisions, and to see why the real reason that they should be criticized is that there were better ways to approach the cases within the terms of the Court's own constitution-building logic than those the Court adopted. Understanding and developing these approaches is, I conclude, of the utmost importance to both bodies of law (which are far more similar than balkanized scholarship reflects) and to the future work of the constitution-building court.

A consequence of my approach is that the discussion of cases must often be broadly contextual and therefore sometimes detailed. For this reason, it is necessary not only to rely a little on the reader's forbearance but also to be selective, even in the context of a Court whose entire jurisprudence comprises only a few hundred decisions to date. This book therefore seeks to examine key members of the South African constitutional canon, testing its claims against the cases that would be seen as the Court's best and worst decisions by the professional community surrounding it.[44] In order to further combat sample bias, the chapters often engage comprehensively with the Court's decisions in the particular areas in which these canonical or anti-canonical cases fall. This approach aims to strengthen the claim that the constitution-building account really is descriptively adequate to the Court's practice in contexts good, bad and ordinary, rather than merely to the features of some hand-picked examples. It also aims to show the extent of the Court's consistency within and across its case law. I claim this is far greater than the divides between celebrated cases and failures, or principled cases and political compromises, would suggest, and it offers support to this book's claim that the Court's work regularly repays lawyerly efforts to take it legally seriously.

[44] On canons, see J. M. Balkin and S. Levinson, 'The Canons of Constitutional Law' (1997–1998) 111 *Harvard Law Review* 963; J. M. Balkin and S. Levinson (eds.), *Legal Canons* (New York University Press, 2000); B. Ackerman, *We the People: The Civil Rights Revolution* (Harvard University Press, 2014), pp. 7, 32–36; and see also J. Fowkes, 'Right After All: Reconsidering *New National Party* in the South African Canon' (2015) 31 *South African Journal on Human Rights* 151.

2

Taking Reality (Legally) Seriously

If it is old news that law and adjudication are political, under the surface it remains controversial exactly what this means and how far it goes. My concern in this chapter is with the claims that judicial activity that takes into account political and social considerations might be better judicial activity, in constitutional terms, as a result; that this includes interpretative activity, properly so called; and that there are therefore potentially rich rewards to taking the reality of South African practice more legally seriously in the ways illustrated by the *Makwanyane* stories. This idea implicates many theoretical questions, but for purposes of this book what matters is only to overcome the threshold objection that this is not a tenable way to think about law and that lawyers should not pursue it as a matter of theoretical principle. (Those who feel no resistance to this approach and are interested only in the concrete particulars of the Court's cases may therefore wish to skip to the next chapter.) Given this limited aim, I will be far from theoretically comprehensive here, and will confine myself to critiquing some assumptions and currents in thought about South African constitutionalism, working in terms of a small number of accounts picked for their illustrative value and familiarity in South African debates.

There remains in the South African context a good deal of (largely unspoken) traditionalism about such matters, and a result, a good deal of suspicion at the idea of strategy and politics affecting interpretation. Recognition that in a large vague sense it is all political does not alter this professional reaction. In the face of this, scholars have sought to bring South African law more firmly face to face with its politics. Theunis Roux, as we saw, draws on political science work on courts to show how they may need to act strategically, and argues that the South African Court indeed does act strategically in a variety of ways and that it is simply unrealistic not to take this into account. Karl Klare and Dennis Davis draw (inter alia) on Critical Legal Studies to argue that lawyers and judges should candidly confront how their use of traditional doctrines and approaches represents adherence to a certain political view which is not always in step with South Africa's radically changed society, and that this confrontation should affect their legal activity in various ways.[1] Stu Woolman draws on experimental constitutionalism to argue that interpretation should be both a shared activity and one based on trial-and-error and thus on a close and ongoing relationship with social and political activity.[2] Such arguments are (intentionally) startling to the traditional view, and join a significant body of work that sees a need to jolt South African law out of its traditional restrained professional habits.[3] The gap between the very vaguely political traditional view of law, and these stridently politically conscious challengers, can make it seem hard to reconcile politics and interpretation in a way acceptable to the South African legal community.

This appearance can be misleading. As we will see in more detail in Chapter 5, one reason things can appear this way is due to a tendency to think of the relationship between law and politics in terms of the bluntest cases: for example, a 'compromise on principle' where the Court deliberately chooses strategy as opposed to legal principle, an idea that has been a focus of recent important political science work on how young and fragile courts can survive in the sometimes hostile conditions of emerging systems.[4] This picture is indeed hard to reconcile with interpretation, more or less by definition. But that is only the bluntest of a range of possibilities, and so not necessarily a reliable guide to the general relationship between politics and interpretation. This is particularly brought out by the fact that many of the existing South African proposals that would have judges take account of social and political information look less blunt. As we will see, much of this work is either aimed at things other than interpretation, such as remedies and jurisdiction, or wishes the Court to listen to more people and more actively solicit more

1 See esp. Roux, *Politics of Principle*; K. E. Klare, 'Legal Culture and Transformative Constitutionalism' (1998) 14 *South African Journal on Human Rights* 146; D. M. Davis and K. Klare, 'Transformative Constitutionalism and the Common and Customary Law' (2010) 26 *South African Journal on Human Rights* 403.

2 Woolman, *Selfless Constitution*; see esp. chs. 4 and 5.

3 See further the discussions of these accounts in Chapters 4 and 5.

4 Notable examples include T. Ginsburg, *Judicial Review in New Democracies: Constitutional Courts in Asian Cases* (Cambridge University Press, 2003); T. Ginsburg and T. Moustafa (eds.), *Rule by Law: The Politics of Courts in Authoritarian Regimes* (Cambridge University Press, 2008); A. Trochev, *Judging Russia: Constitutional Court in Russian Politics, 1990–2006* (Cambridge University Press, 2008); see also the discussion in Roux, *Politics of Principle*, pp. 17–32, drawing inter alia on this work.

information before it interprets, or concerns details of the way in which the Court presents its reasoning. The influence of social and political considerations in these things looks less bluntly inconsistent with the idea of interpretation according to law, and I doubt their proponents think them inconsistent with that idea, though they would certainly understand themselves to be challenging traditional views of law and judging to some extent. Davis and Klare will certainly think that more political conscious judging and lawyering can be constitutionally better judging and lawyering, inter alia because it yields better interpretative activity, and Woolman will say the same about reasoning based on experimentalism and shared interpretation. I will be making arguments in a similar spirit.[5]

From the perspective of the argument of this book, the reason this matters is that it is these less blunt relations between judging and politics, which are less obviously inconsistent with idea of interpretation, that I see as having been more important in the South African context since 1994 simply as a matter of contingent fact. The suggestion implicit in the third *Makwanyane* story is that South Africa has been a more conducive space for adjudication than could well have been the case. As a result, reality has tended not to confront the South African Court with the stronger versions of the tensions between the commitments of interpretation according to law and the imperatives that social and political considerations can entail. Put another way, the more one sees the Court as a lonely actor, in a hostile political environment, matched with an ineffective and/or recalcitrant government, the more one will focus on the Court and the strategies it will have to employ in order to survive and uphold the Constitution in the face of these obstacles. The more one thinks the Court has had to do by itself, the more one it will seem vital to resist a legal tradition in which courts were secondary to Parliament and to explore creative alternatives to this view. This book, by contrast, emphasizes more than any previous study the quality of South Africa's constitutional politics since 1994 and the degree to which the ANC and the Court, among other actors, have been working on a common project. I do not therefore rebut the more dramatic arguments so much as see less need for them (although since the basis for this view is about how well those

[5] Klare, 'Transformative Constitutionalism'; D. Davis, *Democracy and Deliberation: Transformation and the South African Legal Order* (Cape Town: Juta & Co., 1999); Woolman, *Selfless Constitution*.

arguments fit the South African context, this might change as and when that context does). On this view, preferring an account in which judicial activity including interpretative activity is importantly supported by political activity is simply more realistic, while at the same time also being satisfying to classical interpretivist views *and* adequate to the position of the court operating in a particular political context and charged with participating in a particular political project. That these things can be reconciled reflects, not theoretical sleight of hand, but that key South African actors in the years since 1994 have regularly done the work of reconciling them.

A final preliminary point. I do not claim that the justices of the Constitutional Court (or other actors) have necessarily consciously operated on the basis of the constitution-building account or always had its elements clearly in mind. I only argue that it fits what they have done: as with Dworkin's chain novel, a judge can participate in a constitution-building exercise without necessarily having a comprehensive sense of the larger enterprise or where it will end up. My claim is only that, as political and socially aware but also legal actors, the justices have sought to build a legally credible court and jurisprudence, but have also sensed and responded to the sometimes non-traditional imperatives of their position, and would (I hope) recognize in the constitution-building account the sort of work that has fallen to them to do and the context in which they have had to do it. One reason this point matters is that much existing critical work, as we have begun to see, understands itself to be opposing various traditional legal ideas and assumptions. While I do not think the justices of the Constitutional Court have been prisoners of their legal culture, it is certainly true that the legal culture in which they were situated when the new Constitution was handed to them to enforce has had an important influence on how they have responded – as one would expect, especially given that observers, including those in the other branches of government, would equally be expected to assess the Court in terms of the ideas of legitimacy traditional in that legal culture.[6] ('The Court is being political, it should stick to being legal.') To the extent that one can show that more institutional creativity would have been valuable in these

[6] For a project understanding the development of another constitutional system in this kind of way, see M. Hailbronner, *Tradition and Transformation: The Rise of German Constitutionalism* (Oxford University Press, 2015). I discuss existing debates on legal culture and legitimacy in Chapter 5.

circumstances, this can be (and commonly is) a basis for criticism, and one I will make in certain respects in later chapters. But to the extent that the context has been more conducive than is recognized, the Court has had the luxury of more time to evolve its responses and more room to be persuaded by various plausible reasons for caution than would have been true under, for example, conditions of sharper political conflict or greater state failures. Critics who seek a sharp break with aspects of the legal culture often look for signs that the Court recognizes the need for that sharp break, and as we will see this can lead to criticism that is not so much directed at what the Court did in response to certain facts as the failure of that response to evince those signs. That sort of criticism can overread cases and underestimate the costs of sharp breaks with prevailing legal culture, but it can also overestimate the extent to which this has been necessary – not in principle or as matter of how much South Africa and thus by extension South African law needs to change, but in response to the actual situations before the Court. The Court, I claim, often gets where it needs to by the time it (really) needs to. That this evolution has sometimes been quite slow – whether this is attributed to reactionary professional habit, a lack of creativity, political caution, fear of mistakes, indifference to the urgency of social justice claims and the plight of the poor, or something else – has indeed sometimes been a problem. But it has also often reflected the relative luxury of the position from which the Court has acted, a thing not be taken for granted in the future but also not to be taken lightly in the past.

The Work of the Constitution-Building Court

The traditional account of the separation of powers leads us to think reflexively of the judiciary's task as being 'to interpret the law'. The constitution-building account asks us to look at interpretation in a slightly different way: it is more useful to think of the Constitutional Court as the bearer of a duty to make the constitution work.

By 'make the constitution work' I mean several things, some of them obvious. First, any court bears this duty in the sense that adjudicating cases is part of what makes any constitutional system work. Second, we understand that courts of constitutional jurisdiction bear a responsibility to decide who decides: they are not merely focused on being their part in the machine, but have some responsibilities for the machine as a whole. This duty takes on a particular character in a system where the constitutional machine, or part of it, is *new*.[7] The power to decide who decides, with respect to a new system or mechanism, is often a matter of deciding how the machine should work in the first place. There is a sense in these cases in which the court takes on not merely an umpiring role but also a design responsibility. Of course, any case in any system can confront a court with novel questions about how the constitutional system should function, so the distinctive feature of newer systems is only the extent of this responsibility. Third – and this duty, too, arises in any system, but to a greater degree in newer ones – making the constitution work entails making the present form of society in which the court operates into the society described by the constitution. This is a question of implementation, of making effective. It extends to all aspects of the court's work: it is not confined to the narrow idea of ensuring that the situation of the particular applicant before the court changes in the way implied by the text, but encompasses the full reach of the duty to make the real world work as the constitution envisions.

Of course, implementing the Constitution is not the court's duty alone. Other actors have responsibilities to make the constitution work too, and both they and the court must make sense of how their responsibilities relate to one another's. The claim is only that the court is among the actors with responsibilities for how things are to get implemented and how constitutional change is to be brought about.

Some parts of these claims are entirely uncontroversial; to some, perhaps, they will all seem so. Nevertheless, their implications are large. A court charged with making a constitution work, in all these senses, is a court that is charged with bringing about certain results in the world. This concern with results does not imply that the court is unprincipled (nor does it necessarily imply consequentialism, that only consequences matter, at least in any simple way).[8] The court has to make the principle-laden decisions about which results must be brought about and in which ways this may constitutionally be done. It is just that such a court also has to be concerned with what will actually realize principles in the world, including decisions about what blend of institutional activity will best achieve this. And this is why the work of such a court – its constitution-building work – can involve social and political awareness and practical

[7] I discuss the idea of newness in detail in Chapter 5 and apply it thereafter; I describe mechanisms or principles as new to the extent that they are not entrenched in institutional functioning or associated with settled public understandings.

[8] See the further discussion of this point in Chapter 5.

judgment and strategy alongside more conventionally legal considerations about the text and its purposes.

If we substitute this broader constitution-building duty to make the constitution work for the more traditional idea of the court as the institution with the duty to interpret the law, it is also helpful to think of interpretation a little differently. When we think of interpretation, we might well have an image of the judge at her desk, books and papers spread out, law reports on the shelf, or we might just think of the judgment and its legal reasoning. To understand constitution-building, however, a different image will be more useful. When we think of interpretation, we should think of the moment when the judge has to announce that interpretation. As it happens, the real image of the South African Constitutional Court will serve well here. The Court announces its judgment to a chamber that is sometimes packed with plaintiffs or supporters, but is often empty, save for the journalists up in the press box. The judges are making a claim out into space, talking to the audiences to whose imagined scrutiny they are releasing their judgment.[9] It is no doubt true that few South Africans pay attention to Constitutional Court judgments, and that most decisions attract little close scrutiny outside the government, the profession and the academy. But the moment I want to grasp is not when someone sits down to read the judgment. It is when the judge is contemplating releasing it, contemplating the claim, exposed to potential examination and attack by all and any, that *this* is what we, South Africa, have committed ourselves to, and so *this* is what constitutional and judicial authority require should be made to happen in this society.

We should not miss presumption of this claim, although it should be familiar enough. There is the presumption implied by courts asserting authority they have little ability to enforce. There is also the presumption of telling other people what they believe, particularly if one is a Constitutional Court justice and the other people are not afforded a right of electoral response and, if they are government officials, are expected to be careful and formally respectful in their disagreements. Both kinds of presumption will be well known after decades of scholarship on the counter-majoritarian dilemma, but they have their own special twists in South Africa. The 1996 Constitution is an aspirational and visionary

[9] My use of the word 'audience' reflects that I have benefitted here from L. Baum, *Judges and their Audiences: A Perspective on Judicial Behavior* (Princeton University Press, 2006). See also A. Sachs, *The Strange Alchemy of Life and Law* (Oxford University Press, 2011), ch. 6.

document whose implications are often more progressive than public opinion. It resulted from negotiations, and even if the extent and impact of the negotiated compromises is often exaggerated,[10] in this context that matters less than the fact that many South Africans think of the text that way. As Theunis Roux has pointed out, for example, it is not actually true that the Constitution requires that land reform be nearly as slow and expensively compensated as it has been, but many people involved in the process think the negotiated pact is the reason that it is.[11] It is relevant here that the Constitution was not put to a referendum. While constitutionalism cannot be considered a 'Western' idea in a world where it is everywhere, the 1996 text makes little overt attempt to be 'African'. And finally, constitutional supremacy and the extensive associated powers of judicial review are inherently somewhat uncertain in a state that went straight from the strong parliamentary supremacy of a whites-only electoral system to the strong supremacy of an expansive Constitution, with everyone having to come to terms with the change, including the very powerful national liberation movement that drove it. All in all, the feeling of presumption inherent in judges claiming that South Africans have bound themselves to the 1996 text, and to everything that one might be able to read in it, can at times loom very large indeed.

To properly understand the tasks of constitution-building, we must understand not only that the judges are under a duty to make the Constitution work, but that they must fulfil this duty in this context, in which their judgments are public announcements exposed to being seen as presumptuous in all these ways. It is in this society, into which they are announcing the judgment, that the judges must produce that effect, an effort which will almost always also depend on other actors. I suggest it is readily apparent why a range of social and political considerations beyond the traditional legal materials will often seem highly relevant to a judge in this position, whether they concern obstacles the court must overcome or support that it can enlist.

Realism, Law and Karl Llewellyn

At least one familiar response to suggestions like these is that once we go down this road there is no going back. If it is true that judges take account of political and social factors when they interpret, this should

[10] See the discussion of this issue in Chapter 4.
[11] Roux, *Politics of Principle*, pp. 311–12.

end our interest in interpretation. We should accept that judging is just another exercise in power, pursuing the entrenched and possibly subconscious preferences of the elites, and is not about drawing meaning from texts, assuming that idea even make sense. The only sensible response is to give up on interpretation and become something else: a social scientist, a judicial psychologist, a journalist, a protestor, a trasher. This avoids the difficulties by giving up on the whole exercise of interpretation. If we are not to accept this conclusion, we must try a more moderate strategy – as some notable accounts have done.

A widely adopted approach uses a separation strategy. It recognizes the reality of judicial strategy and social and political awareness but seeks to keep this separate from interpretation. Ronald Dworkin, for example, included a little sentence in *Law's Empire* in which he said that a judge 'must sometimes adjust what he believes to be right as a matter of principle, and therefore as a matter of law', for strategic ends: 'to gain the votes of other justices and to make their joint decision sufficiently acceptable to the community'.[12] He earlier refers to the same activity while trying to put it on one side so he can focus on interpretation, properly so called:

> . . . nor do I discuss the practical politics of adjudication, the compromises that judges must sometimes accept, stating the law in a somewhat different way than they think most accurate in order to attract the votes of other judges, for instance. I am concerned with the issue of law, not with the reasons judges may have for tempering their statements of what it is.[13]

This tries to preserve the traditional idea of interpretation, while recognizing the reality of 'the practical politics of adjudication', by placing them in separate spheres: generalized beyond Dworkin's stray remarks, this approach recognizes that judges do respond to politics and social facts, but effectively argues that when we detect this happening, we should take the resulting interpretation somewhat less seriously. It is not what the judges *really* think the law *really* is, or what they really think the best reading of the law is, but a pragmatic reaction to the micro-politics of a particular situation. Roux makes a similar point in his nice description of the 'sense in which the Chaskalson Court's opinions were intended as diplomatic missives of some sort',[14] and indeed he employs a

[12] R. Dworkin, *Law's Empire* (Harvard University Press, 1986), pp. 380–81.

[13] Dworkin, *Law's Empire*, p. 12. See also his intriguing brief discussion of *Brown* v. *Board of Education*, 347 U.S. 483 (1954), *Ibid.*, pp. 389–92.

[14] Roux, *Politics of Principle*, p. 130; see also pp. 383–86 and Roux's discussion of this feature of Dworkin's argument, *Ibid.*, p. 69.

similar separation strategy in the division between cases where the Court for strategic reasons retreats from interpretation or offers a legally plausible interpretation that it knows is nevertheless not the best one, and cases where it interprets properly according to legal principles. On such views, the influence of social and political factors might be inevitable or necessary, but it is still an embarrassment to interpretation. Realists might be more willing than classical interpretivists to acknowledge the 'practical politics' of judging, but both see this as being in tension with best legal practice, as we saw in Chapter 1.

Against this, as noted, I seek to raise the possibility that a court might be a better interpreter if it takes social and political considerations into account, and not merely, say, a safer one. How might we accommodate this possibility? The traditional law/politics divide asks us to preserve the autonomy of law by keeping non-legal things out of the sphere of legal activity.[15] In this, we see the roots of the separation strategy. It asks us to define a set of non-legal things and exclude them from the sphere of interpretation, and that exclusion usually includes political calculation. But that is not the only way we might proceed. We could also permit judges to take social and political considerations into account whenever that is compatible with the traditionally legal considerations and commitments. We would exclude such considerations not by definition at the outset, but only after weighing them up against the set of traditionally legal materials and commitments. We therefore permit the possibility that we might reach a better – constitutionally, legally better – answer by taking these considerations into account then if we do not, instead of excluding that possibility in principle. And we therefore leave space for the possibility raised by the third *Makwanyane* story, which is that we might find that a reality in which social and political considerations play a role in interpretation fits more satisfactorily with our legal ideas and commitments and so should lead us to reject or reconsider more traditional legal accounts accordingly. Whether we gain anything by doing

[15] I stay agnostic in this book on precisely what is considered 'non-legal', including in relation to debates about whether particular considerations should be considered as legal, or as non-legal but permissibly considered in legal decision-making, or as something else. See e.g. J. Raz, *Between Authority and Interpretation: On the Theory of Law and Practical Reason* (Oxford University Press, 2009), ch. 14; see also the discussion of Raz and this issue in Roux, *Politics of Principle*, pp. 49–58. Here, I need only the claim that considerations of non-traditionally legal types can properly count in legal interpretation in some way; it does not matter for present purposes precisely what way that is or exactly which considerations' legitimacy is in dispute, on which views will differ.

so, of course, depends on the reality being more attractive – constitutionally, legally more attractive – than the existing understandings. The strategy would be a waste of time in the world of the first *Makwanyane* story, where the reality of practice cannot be reconciled with legal ideas and arguments and where the legal ideas and arguments are better than the reality of practice, and where it would be naïve at best and disingenuous at worst to pretend otherwise.

The idea of testing the judicial consideration of social and political factors against our legal ideas and commitments is not in itself outlandish. The traditional image of the common law judge, for instance, is of a socially aware actor who adjusts the law in response to social trends (albeit only slowly and incrementally). Common law legal systems have long accepted this approach and asserted its superiority against continental lawyers who are more suspicious of this and aim for judicial behaviour to be determined by written law.[16] Or consider attitudinalism, which tells us that judges' personal backgrounds and social positions influence their judgments. Classically, in the hands of the more sceptical legal realists, this is supposed to dampen our enthusiasm for the idea of interpretation according to law. It is supposed to imply that we should see this influence as, at best, an inevitable result of the fact that judges are human beings, and at worst a reason to think that we should not take legal interpretation too seriously. But if we were to ask members of the South African legal community, we are likely to encounter a different reaction to this idea, and that reaction finds a ready basis in the constitutional text. That text sees South Africans as 'united in diversity', celebrates difference in a variety of ways, and states that the 'need for the judiciary to reflect broadly the racial and gender composition of South Africa must be considered when judicial officers are appointed'.[17] It is common to read all this to mean that the judges' personal backgrounds *should* influence their own thinking and each others' (especially given the Court's deliberative, consultative judgment-writing process), and that the resulting judgments will be the better for it. That implies that interpretative activity should or at least properly can reflect the influence of these factors.[18] If so, attitudinalism is at least to this extent to be accepted – and not merely accepted as something inevitable and

[16] See e.g. M. R. Damaška, *The Faces of Justice and State Authority: A Comparative Approach to the Legal Process* (Yale University Press, 1986).

[17] 1996 Constitution, Preamble, ss 16, 17, 30, 31, 174(2).

[18] See e.g. Sachs, *Strange Alchemy*, pp. 142–45.

unavoidable, but as something whose influence represents a *better, more constitutionally satisfying* understanding of the judicial role and interpretation than the classical rejection of attitudinalism does. This shows the utility of being willing to ask whether the reality of practice, though it may not fit with traditional views, might nevertheless be constitutionally superior to them.

This point is also particularly well illustrated by the work of Karl Llewellyn, chief amongst the legal realists and one who did not see his realist insights as a reason to be sceptical about the idea of legal activity in general. Sometimes, Llewellyn is simply a realist, talking about legal things but not in legal terms.[19] But sometimes, he takes the crucial further step of treating the reality that he observes as *legally* appealing. At the beginning of *The Common Law Tradition* he notes that for all the complaints about how appellate judging does not conform to the black letter law, 'the work of our appellate courts all over the country is reckonable . . . far beyond what any sane man has any business expecting of a machinery devoted to settling disputes self-selected for their toughness'.[20] The social scientist in Llewellyn is admiring, but so is the lawyer – this was, after all, a man who made his students sing songs of his own composing in honour of the common law tradition.[21] And he is making this lawyerly judgment despite believing, in good legal realist fashion, that a lot of what was going on in courts could not be explained on the basis of doctrine and traditional ideas of law and judging. Llewellyn, in other words, is looking at the real-life system and finding that for all its failures to match the traditional doctrine it is still legally attractive, and he takes it seriously as such. He thought that the US contract law of his day did not follow the rules set out in the textbooks, and understandably saw that as a reason to take those textbooks less seriously. But he did not think it was a reason to take contract law less seriously, because he thought the contract cases did run on rules, just different ones that

19 See e.g. his essays 'A Realistic Jurisprudence – The Next Step', 'Legal Tradition and Social Science Method' and 'Law and the Social Sciences – Especially Sociology', all in K. N. Llewellyn, *Jurisprudence: Realism in Theory and Practice* (Chicago University Press, 1962)

20 K. N. Llewellyn, *The Common Law Tradition: Deciding Appeals* (Boston: Little, Brown & Co., 1960), p. 12.

21 As related by former pupil M. A. Glendon, *A Nation Under Lawyers: How the Crisis in the Legal Profession Is Transforming American Society* (Harvard University Press, 1996), pp. 177–78.

had more to do with fact-patterns.[22] The result is not to show that the traditional approaches in the textbooks were necessarily bad theories of contract law in principle, but that we should lose interest in them because the existing practice is legally satisfying (as well as being more socially responsive) and so we adjust our accounts to it rather than the other way round. Llewellyn's work is a founding illustration of the rewards of taking reality legally seriously.

Strategy, Legal Legitimacy and Alexander Bickel

The chief question, then, is not whether our ideas of law and judging are compatible with the consideration of social and political factors, but how far this can acceptably be taken before we think we face a hard choice between politics and law, between strategy and interpretation. Alexander Bickel's work offers a good way to see why and how we might be able to take this approach further than we often think possible.

Bickel's account in *The Least Dangerous Branch* illustrates how lawyers who wish to take strategy seriously end up juggling three apparently incompatible propositions: first, the realist insight that strategy is something that judges sometimes do that sometimes looks useful for advancing legal ends; second, that judges can legally only do non-strategic things; and third, that presumably judges are only supposed to do legal things. Bickel wishes to take the first idea seriously. But he also wishes to adhere to strong, classical notions of what legitimate interpretation requires. He therefore again ends up pursuing another kind of separation strategy: in his case, separating the preliminary decision about whether to hear a case from the decision on the merits. Expediency is appropriate at the preliminary phase, where a judge can refuse to hear a case simply because she thinks it best that the court not decide it now. But if the judge decides to hear the case, then expediency is inappropriate, and the judge must decide the merits in a principled fashion, come what may, without any strategic calculation colouring the decision on the merits. The result, famously, is a certain awkwardness, because Bickel likes what politically informed strategy can do for legal ends, but cannot bring himself to accept it fully as a legal means. He is firmly committed to principled

[22] K. N. Llewellyn, 'The Crafts of Law Re-valued' in Llewellyn, *Jurisprudence*; K. N. Llewellyn, *The Case Law System in America* (P. Gewirtz, ed., M. Ansaldi, tr., Chicago University Press, 1989); W. Twining, *Karl Llewellyn and the Realist Movement* (London: Weidenfeld & Nicolson, 1973), pp. 128–52.

adjudication. His solution is therefore to let judges be unprincipled (his word) at the pre-merits stage. This sense of awkwardness is what drives Gerald Gunther's impeccable line that Bickel's account offers '100% commitment to principle, 20% of the time'.[23] Given that on Roux's account the Court compromises on principle or otherwise strategically sacrifices the best legal interpretation where necessary, something similar would be true of Roux's Court.[24]

This sort of reputation can make us think of Bickel's approach as beyond legal redemption, as can the impression that he uses doctrines like standing and jurisdiction as pretexts for purely strategic exercises in legal avoidance. As a result, while we can easily enough imagine redescribing Bickel's account in legal terms, we probably do not think the result would be credible. For example, we could argue that there is a constitutional reason for courts to protect their own institutional integrity by not becoming too politicized, and so we could argue that Bickel's court is 100% committed to a constitutional principle that effectively calls for it to decide on the merits, without considering politics, 20% of the time. But this ploy may look too glib for its own good, and legal observers are unlikely to think it promising.[25]

Consider, however, how this impression might change if we add in some details. For example, underlying Bickel's account is a principled argument about democratic legitimacy. If the judge actually decides the merits, that for Bickel means that the judge is taking over a decision from the democratic process. Accordingly, it is only justifiable for the judge to take over a decision if that can be justified in a democracy, and for Bickel, that means that the decision must be based on a 'principled process of enunciating and applying certain enduring values of our society' in an 'even-handed' fashion.[26] If that condition is not met, then the judge is not better placed to decide the question than the democratic process is, so it is not justifiable for the unelected judge to take over the decision. Bickel doesn't treat this as a legal argument – he presents it as a piece of political philosophy[27] – but we can readily see how it might be cashed out as a

[23] G. Gunther, 'The Subtle Vices of the "Passive Virtues" – A Comment on Principle and Expediency in Judicial Review' (1964) 64 *Columbia Law Review* 1, 3.

[24] See also J. Fowkes, 'The People, the Court, and Langa Constitutionalism' (2015) *Acta Juridica* 75, 82–83.

[25] See Roux's discussion of legitimacy conditions in relation to his account in Roux, *Politics of Principle*, pp. 58–66, 99–100.

[26] A. Bickel, *The Least Dangerous Branch*, 2 (Yale University Press, 1986), p. 58.

[27] *Ibid.*, chs. 1 and 2.

constitutional principle of democracy affecting, among other things, legal arguments about jurisdiction. Or, to take another example, it is important that while Bickel argues that judges should use doctrines like standing and ripeness and mootness and other rules of jurisdiction as grounds for avoiding cases, he doesn't think these are legally empty things stuck on afterwards to justify a strategic decision. He thinks, for example, that the test for ripeness and the jurisdictional 'case or controversy' test are good ways of identifying the cases that are still the subject of an ongoing debate in political arenas and that therefore cannot be resolved by 'enduring principles'. He also thinks that a court should take these legal doctrines seriously in order to stay within the bounds of judicial legitimacy.[28] It is not necessary to decide whether we would ultimately accept these legal arguments to see how although something is not being called legal in traditional terms it might nevertheless start to look legal, and how one might start to look at Bickel's picture as Karl Llewellyn looked at the reality of US contract law or appellate practice – and thus how we might start to more credibly understand the Bickellian court as displaying 100% fidelity to a respectably legal principle about when judges should articulate interpretations in a constitutional democracy.

This sort of re-imagining can show us how one can build legal arguments for judges to take account of political and social considerations and respond strategically to them, if we do not exclude this possibility at the outset by definition. That we can build them, of course, does not mean we have to accept them. Whether we accept the argument just made, for example, would no doubt depend on whether we think the democratic institutions to which Bickel wants courts to defer on unsettled matters offer adequate rights protection, which will be a crucial issue in later chapters. This is just a matter of the ongoing testing of arguments against our legal commitments. In the same way, we might have difficulty accepting the idea of compromises on principle as legal, but in Roux's nuanced statement of the argument we will find less blunt versions that are more appealing possibilities for legal argument, and then keeping strategic arguments separate from legal ones may seem less important.[29]

[28] This part of Bickel's argument, discussed mainly in *The Least Dangerous Branch*, ch. 3, should be read with his later work, esp. A. M. Bickel, *The Supreme Court and the Idea of Progress* (New York: Harper & Row, 1970), pp. 58–59, 107–08, 173–76.

[29] Roux's argument on socio-economic rights, for example, sees the Court picking, on strategic grounds, a plausible legal interpretation that is nevertheless not the best legal interpretation, a less starkly strategic as opposed to legal decision than a true compromise on principle, and one closer to my own account – see Chapter 8.

There is one more lesson to draw from Bickel's example. It is generally the legal legitimacy of Bickel's account that is attacked, but it may be that its realist credentials are a weaker point. Bickel's theory can only account for strategic behaviour at the pre-merits phase. This is not unlike limiting a poker player to a single up or down decision to go all in or decline to play the hand: as a matter of realism, it is incomplete, since strategic calculations based on social and political facts happen, and are thought valuable, more generally than that. Indeed, Bickel himself argued that judges should adopt democracy-forcing interpretations that decline to resolve insufficiently resolved issues and thus pass them back to the legislature or to the political process, which potentially affects the merits phase.[30] His firm adherence to a traditional legitimacy criterion therefore produces a less realistic and attractive account – and yet might be unnecessary, given that today we would have little difficulty with the idea that such dialogic strategies constituted legal activity properly so called, and given the possibilities for legally redescribing his whole account that we have already seen. We can see, in short, how the apparently impeccable abstract legitimacy condition that precludes courts from considering political and strategic factors at the merits stage might actually be a red herring, and an approach that simply took the reality of judicial strategy legally seriously might be able to produce a more appealing yet still legitimate account. Whether this can be done with Bickel's account in the US context need not detain us here; what matters is to see the argumentative strategy and where it can lead.

Dworkin, Ackerman and the Relevance of Political Activity to Interpretation

Bickel's account brings the consideration of social and political factors to bear on decisions not to advance a judicial interpretation (of which his democracy-forcing interpretations are a species). This type of decision is

[30] See his discussion of the doctrines of delegation, vagueness and desuetude, and of 'colloquies' between the judiciary and other branches in Bickel, *Least Dangerous Branch*, pp. 200–07; and see also Bickel, *Supreme Court*, p. 91: 'Virtually all important decisions of the Supreme Court are the beginnings of conversations between the Court and the people and their representatives.' Thus Bickel is rightly recognized as a founding father of dialogue theory – see e.g. K. Roach, 'Sharpening the Dialogue Debate: The Next Decade of Scholarship' (2007) 45 *Osgoode Hall Law Journal* 169, 177–80. I have also benefitted from the discussion of this aspect of Bickel's work in P. Bobbitt, *Constitutional Interpretation* (Oxford and Cambridge [Mass.]: Blackwell, 1991).

important to the constitution-building account, as we will see, but I am equally interested in their relevance to *which* interpretation to advance. Ronald Dworkin's account is instructive here. Dworkin's work has had a considerable impact on South African scholarship both directly and via his chief early importer, Etienne Mureinik, whose idea of a 'culture of justification' has Dworkinian roots.[31] Dworkin's account can help us to understand the interpretative significance of social and political considerations, not least because it and the way it has been used in South Africa can also tend to obscure these points and direct interpretative attention to more abstract matters.

One of the most powerful features of Dworkin's account in *Law's Empire* is a realist insight. The reason why we should accept that moral principles play a role in judging, and that judges respond to less certain areas of the law by drawing on these principles, is that this is actually what happens. When Dworkin produces his famous examples of snail darters and decisions to allow claims for pure mental shock, he is arguing that the real world reveals a behaviour that we should recognize in our account of the law, because it is more satisfying, including more legally satisfying, than other accounts. Whether his particular argument is right need not detain us here; the interesting question for present purposes is how far we should take this realist insight. Cutting rather jaggedly across its face in *Law's Empire* is the normative legitimacy condition Dworkin stipulates, which is that exercises of legal authority must be able to justify themselves to those who are subject to law's coercive authority. This, especially in Dworkin's later writings, becomes heavily an exercise in moral philosophy. In 2004 he placed himself to the abstract side of Rawls' account of judges as grounded in the political commitments of society, and criticized Rawls for this grounding. He increasingly engaged constitutionalism as a branch of moral philosophy rather than as a public or political activity, and his final work on law and philosophy reflects this view.[32]

[31] See the citations to Mureinik's own writing in note 35 below; see also D. Dyzenhaus, 'Law as Justification: Etienne Mureinik's Conception of Legal Culture' (1998) 14 *South African Journal on Human Rights* 11; E. A. Christodoulidis, '"End of History" Jurisprudence: Dworkin in South Africa' (2004) *Acta Juridica* 64, 68–72; D. Davis, 'Dworkin: A Viable Theory of Adjudication for the South African Constitutional Community?' (2004) *Acta Juridica* 96, 115.

[32] R. Dworkin, 'Keynote Address: Rawls and the Law' (2004) 72 *Fordham Law Review* 1387, 1397–99; R. Dworkin, *Justice for Hedgehogs* (Harvard University Press, 2011). For this characterization, see also D. Cornell and N. Friedman, 'The Significance of Dworkin's

In the midst of all this, one can almost forget that on Dworkin's account judges are not just doing abstract moral philosophy, but are supposed to be working from commitments they draw from society itself. Judges are supposed to seek, not the morally best interpretation of the law, but the best interpretation of the law in light of the morally best reading of society's commitments. This was why Dworkin thought his theory of interpretation broke down in apartheid South Africa: no interpretation of apartheid society's commitments could be reconciled with a defensible moral philosophy, and that meant no judging could satisfy his normative legitimacy condition of justifying law's use of coercive authority to those subject to it.[33] To be fair, Dworkin's dozen post-*Law's Empire* books invite the focus on moral philosophy, and so do his debates with positivists over the place of morality in law, but we should not forget that however much of this judges are meant to do, they are meant to start by looking at society's actual commitments. His legitimacy condition is a way of stipulating how judges are supposed to relate to social commitments in a manner consistent with (Dworkin's understanding of) law and its justification.

Two more specifically South African trends have emphasized the part of Dworkin that is about the role of abstract moral principles in interpretation and downplayed the link to social and political ideas. One is due to apartheid. The first South African borrowings of Dworkin were by pioneering legal critics of apartheid judging who sought to bring more moral resources legitimately into interpretation. This served their argument that South African law had moral resources judges could use to oppose or at least soften the effects of apartheid laws, meaning both that judges could still do useful work within the law and were not morally obliged to resign, on the one hand, and that they could not excuse their adherence to harsh apartheid laws on the grounds that they had no legal

Non-Positivist Jurisprudence for Law in the Post-Colony' (2010) 4 *Malawi Law Journal* 1 e.g. 3–4 (arguing that Dworkin has moved from an account of law as a social fact to one increasingly based on political morality)

33 See R. Dworkin, 'Keynote Address: The Practice of Integrity' (2004) *Acta Juridica* 16 (replying to Christodoulidis, '"End of History" Jurisprudence'): 'How does [the principle of integrity] relate to bad or evil legal systems, like the apartheid legal system? Such a legal system is one in which the process values that we are drawn to respect could be respected only at the cost of assigning principles to that legal system which are wholly disreputable principles. When that is the best we can do, then, my view, legality has nothing further to offer us. Then it is a time for revolution, it is a time for dramatic measures, because we have reached a point at which legality can no longer serve.' See also Dworkin, *Law's Empire*, pp. 101–04.

choice but to uphold their letter, on the other. The most famous early argument of this sort, by John Dugard in 1971, preceded Dworkin's work and offered a troubled 'legal realist-cum-natural law' theory to bring this morality in.[34] Later scholars, including Edwin Cameron and Mureinik, could draw on Dworkin's much more sophisticated devices to the same end.[35] But that, naturally, meant downplaying the actual commitments of apartheid society and playing up the abstract moral principles deduced from long-standing precedents – indeed, it meant straining further away from social commitments and towards abstract morality than Dworkin himself thought was theoretically tenable under the apartheid system, as we saw.

This type of thinking has persisted in the post-apartheid world because although there have been many positive changes in society's commitments, there has also been a new constitution. While we recognize the social and political roots of these positive changes – and celebrate the transition and the constitution-drafting accordingly – this makes it easier thereafter to treat the constitutional text as the embodiment of the social commitments from which judges are supposed to work. Thus, for example, one can argue that South African society has committed itself to various rights and values, like equality and dignity; that these are now in the text as guiding legal principles; and that what the judges charged with interpreting this text now owe us is accounts of these principles of

[34] J. Dugard, 'The Judicial Process, Positivism and Civil Liberty' (1971) 88 *South African Law Journal* 181; see also the work at this early stage by Tony Mathews and Barend van Niekerk cited by du F. du Bois, 'Preface: The Practice of Integrity' (2004) *Acta Juridica* i; for further discussion, see J. Fowkes, 'Apartheid Judging and Dugard's Question: Re-examining the Legend' (forthcoming).

[35] For Cameron's use, probably the first one in South African legal writing, see E. Cameron, 'Are Dworkin's "Principles" Really Rules?' (1979) 96 *South African Law Journal* 450; E. Cameron, 'Legal Chauvinism, Executive-Mindedness and Justice – L C Steyn's Impact on South African Law' (1982) 99 *South African Law Journal* 38, 59 n. 101, 74 n. 167. For Mureinik's explicit reliances on Dworkin, see esp. E. Mureinik, 'Dworkin and Apartheid' in H. Corder (ed.), *Essays on Law and Social Practice in South Africa* (Cape Town: Juta & Co., 1988); and also E. Mureinik, 'Fundamental Rights and Delegated Legislation' (1985) 1 *South African Journal on Human Rights* 111, 119–20; E. Mureinik, 'Administrative Law in South Africa' (1986) 103 *South African Law Journal* 615, 619–24; E. Mureinik, 'Security and Integrity' (1987) *Acta Juridica* 197; E. Mureinik, 'Emerging from Emergency: Human Rights in South Africa' (1994) 92 *Michigan Law Review* 1977, 1981 n. 18, 1984–88. See also Davis, 'Dworkin', 96–97 (referring also to the work of David Dyzenhaus drawing on Dworkin); Davis, *Democracy and Deliberation*, p. 30 n. 22 (recalling that Mureinik was 'almost solely responsible for introducing the work of Ronald Dworkin into local legal debate'); and the review of Dworkin's impact by Du Bois, 'Preface', xi–xv.

equality and dignity. That looks like a job for moral philosophy in a way that resonates especially with Dworkin's later work, and it is no coincidence that the most sophisticated recent Dworkinian work in South African constitutional law, by Drucilla Cornell and Nick Friedman, concludes that it is the later Dworkin of *Justice for Hedgehogs* that South Africans should follow.[36] Recalling the arguments of the apartheid era, this argument follows from the authors' sense that the actual social and political commitments of South Africans might not always square with the progressiveness of the text and with an account of law they consider morally justifiable. Once again, this encourages an emphasis on abstract moral principle, and a tendency to fall back on the argument that we saw in *Makwanyane* that judges are only upholding the principles South Africans have already committed themselves to – regardless of how implausible that claim is as a matter of political fact in particular cases and how presumptuously exposed judges may therefore feel when they contemplate having to announce this out to the people themselves. This is once again the world of the first *Makwanyane* story, in which the social and political context do not affect the legal expectation that judges should be as bold, principled and counter-majoritarian in every case alike.

This, conversely, can encourage us to think of social and political facts as *obstacles*, impediments to upholding and promoting progressive constitutional values that are therefore in tension with best-practice interpretative activity. Thus David Bilchitz has argued that, on its best interpretation, the South African Constitution protects animal rights. He recognizes, however, that South African society mostly does not yet accept this, and treats this adverse public opinion as a practical obstacle which judges should work around as much as possible.[37] This, of course, implies that judges are taking social and political considerations into account, though only in the same sort of way, separate to interpretation, as Dworkin's judges might temper their statements of the law to make their interpretations acceptable to the community. But recognition that the South African polity is rather less settled in its commitments than Dworkin's home in the incremental common law tradition can also point the way to less oppositional relationships between social and political

[36] Cornell and Friedman, 'Significance of Dworkin's Jurisprudence'.

[37] D. Bilchitz, 'Does Transformative Constitutionalism Require the Recognition of Animal Rights?' in S. Woolman and D. Bilchitz (eds.), *Is this Seat Taken? Conversations at the Bar, the Bench and the Academy about the South African Constitution* (University of Pretoria Law Press, 2012).

activity and interpretation. Davis argued early on that South African judges, faced with a society whose commitments are unsettled or fractured or plainly contrary to the Constitution, should do more to promote constitutional dialogue. He accordingly thought they would do better to follow Habermas than Dworkin, because it might be hard to come up with the unifying best readings of society's ideas entailed by Dworkin's legitimacy condition without being overly dictatorial.[38] Others have followed Davis in supporting dialogic approaches; I have already noted Woolman's experimentalist account.[39] What these approaches imply is that constitutional meaning is formed on an ongoing basis, rather than being enshrined in some way in a text. And in that case, judges have a firmer ongoing reason to consider social and political activity. We might understand this simply as a strategic response to the obstacle posed by public opinion, with dialogue being understood chiefly in terms of education, persuasion or at least trying to head off opposition. But there is something altogether richer at stake.

Thaddeus Metz has responded to Bilchitz's animal rights argument by relying on the *early* Dworkin and the importance of maintaining the links between a constitution and its political community.[40] This illustrates how the prudential reasons for engaging the public are only the negative, cautious side of a broader positive argument which sees constitutionalism, at its best, as a richly public activity and asks us not to act in ways that might damage or stunt its future growth. Social ideas and political activity need not only be an intolerant, hostile constraint on constitutional judging; they may also inform and underpin and enforce it. Judges charged with upholding the Constitution, therefore, are not only concerned with managing and responding to hostile or uncertain public opinion, but may ride its waves, receiving into constitutional law meaning formed by political activity.

Bruce Ackerman's work illustrates this richer point.[41] At ordinary times, in his view, judges are supposed to uphold the constitutional text

38 Davis, *Democracy and Deliberation*, esp., pp. 6–11, 23–48; Davis, 'Dworkin', 113–16 (although Davis' remarks make it clear his opposition to Dworkin is not confined to the specific South African context). See also Currie's early defence of minimalism on this basis: Currie, 'Judicious Avoidance', 144–46.

39 See further Chapter 5.

40 T. Metz, 'Animal Rights and the Interpretation of the South African constitution' in Woolman and Bilchitz, *Conversations*, pp. 211–14; Fowkes, 'Langa Constitutionalism', 80.

41 See esp. Ackerman, *Foundations*; B.A. Ackerman, *We the People: Transformations* (Harvard University Press, 1998); B. A. Ackerman, 'Holmes Lectures: The Living Constitution' (2007) 120 *Harvard Law Review* 1737.

against political threats in traditional fashion. But sometimes political mobilization behind a set of ideas is extraordinarily sustained: these are the times that change a country, as the Civil War and the New Deal and the Civil Rights era changed the United States.[42] This extraordinary mobilization may succeed in expressing its ideas as a formal constitutional amendment, and then there will be no legal difficulty in explaining why judges should adjust their interpretations to take them into account. But what if it does not result in a formal amendment? The traditional view will tell us that judges should not then change their interpretations – the legal materials have not changed – and should resist the political pressure to do so. But judges do in fact change their interpretations at these times. We could treat that as a purely strategic response to political pressure. But we could also seek to take this reality more legally seriously. Thus Ackerman argues that these extraordinary mobilizations represent expressions of popular sovereignty, which has serious legal status. If we believe that popular sovereignty is what underwrites the authority of a constitution, then what we care about ultimately is the popular sovereignty, and not whether the popular sovereignty happens to get expressed in a formal legal way (though we no doubt *prefer* it to be expressed that way for reasons of legal certainty). If so, then judges are not merely being strategic in taking these social and political events into account when they interpret, nor are they even merely doing something legally permissible: instead of being obliged to uphold the constitution against these ideas, they are positively obliged to take them into account and harmonize them with the other, earlier expressions of popular sovereignty already in the text. Once again, by taking reality legally seriously, though it may not fit traditional understandings, we might end up with an understanding that is not only more accurate but also more satisfying.

Other accounts have followed, offering expanded ways in which social and political activity affect legal activity, sometimes presented simply as a descriptions of what happens, but sometimes normatively asserted as accounts of how what happens is legally appealing or at least defensibly legitimate.[43] The degree to which these various US accounts might or

[42] He speaks of a change in 'constitutional regime': see e.g. Ackerman, *Foundations*, p. 59.

[43] See e.g. J. Rubenfeld, *Freedom and Time: A Theory of Constitutional Self-Government* (Yale University Press, 2001); R. Post, 'Foreword: Fashioning the Legal Constitution: Culture, Courts and the Law' (2003) 117 *Harvard Law Review* 4; J. Rubenfeld, *Revolution by Judiciary: The Structure of American Constitutional Law* (Harvard University Press, 2005); W. N. Eskridge, Jr. and J. Ferejohn, *A Republic of Statutes: The New American Constitution* (Yale University Press, 2010); J. M. Balkin, *Living Originalism*

might not fit the South African context is a question for another day. What matters here is to see the counterpoint this offers to the Dworkinian view, especially in the form in which that view tends to be deployed in the South African context. On that view, judges should be doing the principled work of articulating South Africa's commitments and then must diplomatically try and present the results to South African society as best they can. The public, once its authority has been invoked to pass the constitution, is rather passive on this view, confined thereafter to supporting the Court's activity by dutiful obedience, civil society support, or well-designed litigation campaigns. In reality, broader public activity, in and out of government, can be much more than this. It can be a *source* of efforts to reconcile principles and ideals with social and political realities, and so judges are not necessarily the only ones doing this work and the constitutional project does not necessarily depend on their bold moral leadership. If society is a source rather than merely a recipient of interpretative activity, judges will have a powerful reason to take ongoing account of social and political activity, not only for strategic reasons, but as something to substantively inform the interpretations they announce.[44]

Raising this issue prompts many other questions, but to understand the Constitutional Court's activity since its creation, what matters most of all is to raise it. If a court that is often seen as cautious and modest and convinced of the value of restraint has also reached bold results, this says a lot about the help it has had. That it has apparently also been inconsistent in its boldness and restraint may instead reflect variations in that help, variations to which understandings that approach interpretation as an exercise in applying abstract principle will be blind, but which are central to understanding how the constitution-building task in front of the Court shifts from case to case even if the abstract principles at stake

(Harvard University Press, 2011); Ackerman, *Civil Rights Revolution*. See also the constitutional experimentalist work important to Woolman's account – see Woolman, *Selfless Constitution*, esp. ch. 4 – and the historical institutionalist work important to Roux's' – see Roux, *Politics of Principle*, pp. 24–27; T. Roux, 'The South African Constitutional Court's Democratic Rights Jurisprudence' (2013) 5 *Constitutional Court Review* 33, 46–47. Scholarship which simply describes constitutional activity in these terms is vast; M. J. Klarman, *From Jim Crow to Civil Rights: The Supreme Court and the Struggle for Racial Equality* (Oxford University Press, 2004) is an extraordinarily rich exercise of this sort, but it is perhaps representative in taking it that social and political considerations are pervasively relevant to judicial interpretation while explicitly leaving aside the question of whether they *should* be: *Ibid.*, pp. 5, 449.

44 See further Fowkes, 'Langa Constitutionalism'.

are the same. Albie Sachs, reviewing Cass Sunstein's earlier, strong-form argument for judicial minimalism, accepted that the arguments for minimalism made good sense, but that they would make more sense at some times then at others. As Sachs put it, '[t]he question becomes not one of whether but of when: I would love to see a theory of when . . . '.[45] The constitution-building account is not a full theory of when. But I will hope to oblige the Justice at least in offering an account which takes this as the central question of the work the Court has been called to perform since 1995, and it is a question we can grapple with only if we begin with the reality and not the law.

[45] Albie Sachs, 'Book Review: Cass R. Sunstein, One Case at a Time: Minimalism on the Supreme Court and Ian Loveland, Racial Discrimination and the Right to Vote in South Africa 1855–1960' (2001) 51 *University of Toronto Law Journal* 87, 90.

3

Voting Rights, Politics and Trust

Having now given some reason to think there is theoretical room for the constitution-building account's approach, I now return to the purchase it can have on South African constitutional practice, including on cases far less celebrated than *Makwanyane*. *New National Party* v. *President of the Republic of South Africa* ('*NNP*') is among the most criticized decisions in the South African Constitutional Court's emerging body of case law.[1] Part of the reason for this, I will suggest, is that *NNP* is standardly misread. But coming to terms with the decision is much more than a matter of arguing over how to read its treacherous 24th paragraph. There is a deeper and far more interesting reason for its pariah status, which will require examining the case and its surroundings in some detail, but which will show us how the most prevalent ways in which South African constitutional law understands itself struggle to accommodate some of the imperatives that are most prevalent in South African constitutional practice. For *NNP* should not be a pariah. It is at least an eminently debatable and defensible decision, and in my view it is right.

The standard view that it is clearly wrong reflects, not the quality of the decision, but the degree to which it falls into blind spots in existing South African constitutional understandings. The *NNP* Court confronts a real, significant threat to rights and chooses to make no order. What is more, it does this in a voting rights dispute that appears to be a textbook case for strong judicial review. It also acts in a deferent manner that appears to recall the methods of the apartheid judiciary and its complicity in injustice,[2] and does so in a political context where it appears to be backing down in the face of the powerful ANC rather than standing its constitutional ground. It is because of these features that the decision is criticized as universally and as strongly as it is. We will come to see that,

[1] *New National Party* v. *Government of the Republic of South Africa* 1999 (3) SA 191 (CC) *(NNP)*. For the critical reaction, see notes 9–15 below.

[2] Dennis Davis has compared *NNP* to judging in the apartheid era; see note 15 below.

in the story in which *Makwanyane* is the hero, *NNP*, at least as it is usually read, is almost perfectly cast to be the villain.

Rereading *NNP*

NNP arose as the country was gearing up for its second post-apartheid election for national and provincial government. In 1998, Parliament passed a law requiring citizens to have new, barcoded identification documents in order to vote, and in order to register to vote.[3] Several million South Africans, at the time of the law's passage, were unable to meet this requirement, about half because they had various older documents without barcodes, and about half because they had no identification documents at all.[4] It was unclear that those with the incorrect documents would know to apply for new ones, and it was also unclear whether the Department of Home Affairs, often a troubled institution, would be able to issue all the new barcoded documents in time to those who did apply for them. The government had acknowledged the problem and had launched two public awareness campaigns and initiated a contingency plan to ensure the documents would be provided. There was no decisive evidence about how these initiatives were working – they were not obviously inadequate or failing in practice, but nor was it clear whether they would be enough to address the problem in time.[5]

The applicant was the party of apartheid, subtly rechristened as the *New* National Party. Presumably because of the uncertain evidence about the plan's implementation, the party chose to challenge the constitutionality of the underlying statutory provision imposing the documentary requirements. In another application decided at the same time ('*DP*'), the Democratic Party, another opposition party with mostly white supporters, brought a similar challenge.[6] On top of this, both parties also alleged that the ANC government was infringing the independence of the Electoral Commission. The majority chose to make no order of any kind,

[3] Electoral Act 73 of 1998. For a succinct summary of the relevant provisions, see *NNP*, paras. 108–10 (judgment of O'Regan J). Citizens were also able to register, and to vote, on the basis of special temporary documents, but since they had to apply for these too, this can be left to one side for purpose of this discussion.

[4] *Ibid.*, paras. 28–30 (Yacoob J.), 132–36 (O'Regan J.). The surveys on which these figures were based are considered later in this chapter.

[5] *Ibid.*, paras. 18, 37–46 (Yacoob J.), paras. 139–41 (O'Regan J.).

[6] *Democratic Party* v. *Government of the Republic of South Africa* 1999 (3) SA 254 (CC); see also *NNP*, para. 4.

while O'Regan J, in lone dissent, would have struck down the new ID requirement. Most of the important arguments raised by the two applications were dealt with in the *NNP* decision, and so I shall refer mainly to it.

The standard disparaging view of *NNP* understands it as a case that turns on the interpretation of voting rights. This view runs as follows. The *NNP* majority holds that voting rights challenges are to be interpreted according to a weak, deferential standard (although we will see that, significantly, there is some disagreement about precisely what that standard is), while the O'Regan J dissent uses a more rigorous reasonableness standard.[7] Her dissent is preferable as a matter of general principle because of the importance of voting rights and, following John Hart Ely, the importance of judicial protection of them.[8] Her dissent is also preferable on the particular facts because the government's decision posed a real threat to the voting rights of several million South Africans. For some adherents to the standard view, these facts have sinister overtones. Theunis Roux, for instance, has argued that 'underlying the case . . . was the fact that many of the people who were prevented from voting were members of South Africa's white minority' who were likely to vote for the opposition.[9] On that view of the case, the Ely argument for judicial review is of course particularly strong. For others, the facts suggest an unwise or callous policy rather than a nefarious one. For example, Patrick Lenta understands its effects as 'being that the Electoral Act would exclude approximately ten percent of the electorate, mostly rural blacks, from voting in the 1999 elections'.[10] Since many rural black voters could be expected to support the ANC, the two explanations are

[7] I survey the relevant scholarship in Fowkes, 'Right After All', 155 n. 15.

[8] J. H. Ely, *Democracy and Distrust: A Theory of Judicial Review* (Harvard University Press, 1980). For explicit reliance on Ely (whose theory probably underlies other thinking as well), see T. Roux, 'Democracy' in Woolman and Bishop (eds.), *Constitutional Law*, 10-56–10-57; P. Lenta, 'Judicial Restraint and Overreach' (2004) 20 *South African Journal on Human Rights* 544, 557– 58. I discuss Ely's account and its ambiguities in this context later in this chapter.

[9] Roux 'Principle and Pragmatism', 126. In his more recent book, Roux notes that the group without any documents mostly consisted of 'young Africans living in rural areas' but argues that the NNP challenge was focused on the other group holding older identification without barcodes, 'who were predominantly coloured, Indian or white voters' and repeats his view that the exclusion of likely minority party voters underlay the case: Roux, *Politics of Principle*, p. 342.

[10] P. Lenta, 'Looking Sideways: Constitutional Interpretation, Ethics and Theory' (2004) 15 *Stellenbosch Law Review* 3, 11 n. 54.

rather at odds, but either way the case for judicial review looks strong. It is easy to see why someone with this sort of view of the case would expect a firm response from the Court, and why she would strongly criticize the majority's failure to respond at all. Thus Iain Currie and Johan de Waal, in the standard text on the South African Bill of Rights, describe *NNP* as 'unfortunate' and state that the approach taken there 'cannot be accepted'.[11] Jason Brickhill and Ryan Babuich, writing the chapter on political rights in the country's constitutional law treatise, call the judgment 'far too deferential' and worry that 'it does not sufficiently protect the right to vote'.[12] Roux initially called the decision 'hard to fathom' and argued that on reading the O'Regan J dissent 'it is difficult to come to any conclusion other than that the majority failed to give a principled reading of the Constitution'.[13] He therefore classifies *NNP* as one of his cases in which the Court 'compromised on principle'.[14] Dennis Davis finds a 'similarity in approach between [the *NNP*] judgment and those in the rather darker days when the [judiciary's] trust of the executive constrained review activity' – by which he means judging during the apartheid era.[15]

To start seeing our way around this view, let us begin with the misreading it involves. As noted, the most common view is that *NNP* favours a weak, rationality standard for assessing voting rights violations. This offers a neat explanation for the outcome: an overly weak understanding of the right produces an overly weak response, while O'Regan J's more robust test leads her to take more robust action against the threat of disenfranchisement. However, it is simply false.[16] The *NNP* majority in fact does not employ a rationality test in relation to the voting right and instead uses one based on reasonableness. Yacoob J, writing for the majority, says that the s 19 voting right requires Parliament to ensure that eligible voters who take 'reasonable steps' (he uses the term in

[11] I. Currie and J. de Waal, *The Bill of Rights Handbook* (6th edn., Cape Town: Juta & Co., 2013), pp. 438–39.

[12] J. Brickhill and R. Babuich, 'Political Rights' in Woolman and Bishop (eds.), *Constitutional Law*, 45-19–45-20.

[13] Roux, 'Democracy', 10-56–10-57; Roux, 'Principle and Pragmatism', 125–28.

[14] Roux, 'Principle and Pragmatism', 125–28; Roux, *Politics of Principle*, p. 363. I should note that Roux may have revised his views in response to the arguments presented here; see Fowkes, 'Right After All', 155 n. 13.

[15] Davis, *Democracy and Deliberation*, p. 174.

[16] Some of *NNP*'s critics recognize that the true subject of Yacoob J's rationality analysis is not the voting right but the legality principle, then a nascent doctrine – see further Fowkes, 'Right After All', 156 n. 16.

relation to the voters' efforts, too) in pursuit of the right to vote are able to do so: 'Parliament is obliged to provide for the machinery, mechanism or process that is *reasonably* capable' of meeting this requirement, and '[a]ny scheme which is not sufficiently flexible to be *reasonably* capable of achieving [it] ... has the potential of infringing the right ... The appellant bears the onus of establishing that the machinery or process provided for is not *reasonably* capable of achieving that purpose' (my emphasis).[17] Yacoob J never once uses the words 'rational' or 'rationality' in his paragraphs about the voting right.

If it is simply not true that O'Regan J is the only one in *NNP* using a test based on reasonableness, what then explains the difference between her outcome and the majority's? Under the next heading, I will set out the considerations that really drive the majority judgment. But a much quicker way to see what separates the two judgments is to note what, in the midst of all the criticism of the majority, goes unnoticed: that O'Regan J's position in *NNP* is highly, even unprecedentedly, expansive. She engages in direct balancing – directly reconsidering the legislature's weighing up of cost and benefit, sometimes referred to as proportionality in the narrow sense – and does so not after finding that a right is being infringed but *in order to establish* that a right is being infringed. This is what her interpretation of the reasonableness test in the case amounts to: she asks whether the legislature's plan is acceptable given the right to vote, and she finds that the risks involved in the plan are not proportional to the rewards, and that the legislature accordingly did not fulfil its duties in terms of the right to vote when it decided to pass the legislation.[18] A number of scholars have argued that proportionality is implicit in the reasonableness test for rights interpretation created in *Grootboom*, but they also all agree that the Court has yet to actually apply the test in this way.[19] O'Regan J effectively concedes what her approach entails: '[g]iven the definition of the right I propose and have applied, the exercise under s 36 [the limitations clause, where proportionality is usually conducted]

[17] *NNP*, para. 23. [18] *Ibid.*, paras. 146–58.

[19] See e.g. S. Liebenberg, 'The Interpretation of Socio-Economic Rights' in Woolman and Bishop (eds.), *Constitutional Law*, 33-39 – 33-40; T. Roux, 'Legitimating Transformation: Political Resource Allocation in the South African Constitutional Court' (2003) 10 *Democratization* 92, 96–97; A. Price, 'The Content and Justification of Rationality Review (2010) 25 *SA Public Law/SA Publiekreg* 345, 356–59, 361 n. 71; G. Quinot and S. Liebenberg 'Narrowing the Band: Reasonableness Review in Administrative Justice and Socio-economic Rights Jurisprudence in South Africa' (2011) 22 *Stellenbosch Law Review* 639, 646–47, 650–51, 654–55, 659–61.

in this case is similar to the exercise carried out to determine whether the challenged provisions were reasonable [under s 19]' and so 'it is not necessary to undertake a full and separate limitations analysis'.[20]

That her approach is expansive does not, of course, make it wrong. Several scholars have also argued that she would have done better to treat the barcoded ID scheme immediately as a limitation of the right to vote – in which case her proportionality analysis could have been conducted at the limitations stage where everyone accepts it belongs, though it would still be an unusually expansive approach.[21] But the most striking thing here is not her position but the fact that, given how expansive it is, *NNP* should at least be seen as an eminently arguable case. We should surely not be particularly surprised to see O'Regan J's colleagues expressing caution. Yet everyone *is* surprised. *NNP*'s critics all quickly reach the conclusion that her approach is preferable to the majority's, usually without even noting how expansive it is.

What explains this? The critics' stance appears to be that O'Regan J is correct because she is acting to protect rights under threat. This is the key premise: when faced with a threat to rights, a judge must do whatever is necessary to protect and vindicate the right, at least within the bounds of reasonable legal creativity. Adopt this premise, and *NNP* is indeed a largely straightforward case and O'Regan J is indeed clearly right. Understanding why the majority might be right instead means understanding how and when this premise might be wrong, or at least disputable. But this can be heretically difficult in South Africa, for reasons that run deeper than voting rights. In fact, this premise represents *the* key dogma of existing understandings of South African constitutional law, and the idea of imposing limits on it is *the* key thing those understandings struggle to conceptualize.

We saw in the first *Makwanyane* story the importance attached to the bold judicial defence of rights. We will see in Chapter 4 that this arises in part from a sense that it was the failure of apartheid judges to act boldly to protect rights that led them to be complicit in apartheid's injustices.

[20] *NNP*, para. 160. See also S. Woolman and D. Brand, 'Limitations' in Woolman and Bishop (eds.) *Constitutional Law*, 34-27–34-28, discussed further in Fowkes, 'Right After All', 161 n. 32.

[21] For this suggestion, see Currie and De Waal, *Handbook*, pp. 439–40; Roux, *Politics of Principle*, pp. 345–46, 349; I. M. Rautenbach, 'Means-End Rationality in Constitutional Court Judgments' (2010) *Tydskrif vir die Suid-Afrikaanse Reg* 768, 776 and his earlier work there cited; for analysis and comparison to the approach in other voting rights cases, see Fowkes, 'Right After All', 163–64.

The importance attached to rights protection also follows from the general tendency of progressive lawyers to want to expand judicial rights protection rather than not. And it stems, too, from the tendency to see the ANC as a looming threat. If it is the Constitution alone that will keep South Africa on the right path, then the Constitutional Court must live up to its role as fearless guardian. The idea that judges might *not* do everything in their power to protect rights is therefore likely to be seen as suspicious on several levels, and this accounts for why it is so unquestioningly accepted that the *NNP* majority must be wrong.[22]

The Constitution-Building Court at Work: Structural Concerns in *NNP*

If *NNP* falls into a conceptual blind spot, what exactly is it that we are being prevented from seeing? We should start with the threat to voting rights. If the government's plan would exclude large numbers of voters, opposition or not, then judicial inaction would be hard to defend. But what were the facts?

The available evidence consisted of two reports by the Human Sciences Research Council (HSRC, a government research institution created by statute), and a survey.[23] The HSRC reports, compiled at the request of the Independent Electoral Commission, found that as of June 1998 only about 80 per cent of the voting population could meet the new barcoded ID requirement. The survey broke down voters without the proper documentation by likely party affiliation. The group with the highest proportion of valid documentation among its likely voters was the Inkatha Freedom Party (IFP), an ANC rival and its chief opposition in one of the only two potentially competitive provincial races, in KwaZulu-Natal. There was also none of the usual evidence that accompanies efforts to subvert elections: no signs, for example, that the government was or had been selectively targeting its awareness campaigns or its plan to provide the new documents to exclude opposition areas or voters. (Later evidence revealed that the province with the greatest Home Affairs delays was, by a considerable margin, the ANC stronghold of the Eastern Cape,

[22] See further Fowkes, 'Right After All', 163–68.

[23] *NNP*, para. 29; *DP*, para. 11; Human Sciences Research Council, *Opinion 1999: Voter Participation in the 1999 Elections* (Pretoria: Human Sciences Research Council Press, 1999). The survey was conducted by the Institute for Democracy in South Africa (IDASA), the SABC (the public broadcaster), and Markinor, a market research firm.

long a site of capacity problems. The white opposition strongholds of the Western Cape and, to a lesser extent, Gauteng had only a small percentage of the problems.)[24] It is true that while the survey ranked likely IFP voters first on the list of those with correct documentation (84%), likely ANC voters were a close second (82%) and likely NNP and DP voters were much lower on the list (71% and 65%, respectively).[25] It is easy to see why the two parties chose to litigate. What is much harder to see is what basis the Court had to conclude that dirty work was afoot.

It is worth adding that none of the members of the Court, including O'Regan J, expressed any concern about white voters or opposition voters. The concern was instead with the young, poor, rural, mostly non-white voters discussed by Lenta, presumably because this was the group least likely to learn about the new requirements or to be able to act to get hold of the new documents. This is a population that would have tended to vote ANC. Indeed, it was reported at the time (based on an unnamed internal source) that ANC election strategists had opposed the barcoded ID requirement for precisely this reason: that it might hurt the ANC at the polls.[26] The most plausible explanation for why the ANC leadership pursued the plan despite this concern is policy (over-) ambition. The stricter documentary requirements were partly aimed at enhancing voting security, especially given that, at the time, many people had more than one type of ID document as a consequence of apartheid policies.[27] But as O'Regan J noted in her dissent, their introduction was also part of a wider policy to modernize the administration of social grants and other government benefits. In fact, the barcoded IDs themselves were to be replaced by a system of identity cards (now the 'Smart ID Card' system, whose roll-out is only now under way). This evidence, too, supports the view that the ANC was not playing dirty electoral games.

[24] In an HSRC exit poll, 32% of those who had experienced delays at Home Affairs were from the Eastern Cape. The figures for Gauteng and the Western Cape were 5% and 8% respectively. M. O'Donovan, 'Election Day Exit Poll' in Y. Muthien (ed.), *Democracy South Africa: Evaluating the 1999 Election* (Pretoria: Human Sciences Research Council, 1999), p. 34.

[25] *DP*, para. 11.

[26] 'How Many People Will Be Able to Vote?' 13(1) *Focus* (1999), available at www.hsf.org.za/resource-centre/focus/issues-11-20/issue-13-first-quarter-1999/how-many-people-will-be-able-to-vote.

[27] See e.g. A. Wall, 'South Africa' in A. Evrensel (ed.), *Voter Registration in Africa: A Comparative Analysis* (Electoral Institute for the Sustainability of Democracy in Africa, 2010), p. 319 and further sources there cited.

Even so – and here the O'Regan J argument looks powerful – why shouldn't the Court play it safe? It did not need to make a finding that the ANC was trying to steal the election in order to worry, as she did, that an obstacle was being placed between millions of people and the exercise of their right to vote. The obstacle, moreover, was posed by a policy that made sense but did not seem critically necessary. The new documents provided greater security and efficiency (which had been serious concerns during the 1994 election, as we will see in detail later) and also served to replace a variety of apartheid-era documents that were a source of offense to many. However, as O'Regan J plausibly reasoned, these benefits do not seem worth the risk of potentially excluding 20 per cent of the voting population from an election.[28]

The *NNP* majority, however, did not view the case as a straight choice between adopting the O'Regan J approach and leaving millions under threat of disenfranchisement. One reason was that further options remained open. Yacoob J held that, if credible evidence *did* emerge that the government's plans were not working and the risk of disenfranchisement was actually being realized, the applicants could approach the Court on *that* basis and seek an urgent order.[29] That might be dismissed as an empty promise, except that the Court had issued just such an order only 12 days before. In *August* v. *Electoral Commission* ('*August*') the Court had ordered the Electoral Commission to make provision for prisoners to cast their votes in prison, in circumstances where such provision had simply not been made. Indeed, the simple fact that the very same judges at the very same time were willing to defend the voting rights of a minority as unpopular as prisoners is important evidence against views of the *NNP* Court as weak on voting rights – evidence that the standard critical accounts of the case do not confront.[30] If it is thought that too little time remained before the election for such a challenge to be effective, the evidence of the Court's behaviour in other cases similarly offers a rebuttal. Witness the fact that in the run-ups to

[28] *NNP*, paras. 146–58. [29] *Ibid.*, para. 46.

[30] Brickhill and Babuich, 'Political Rights', 45-21–45-22 note that *August* v. *Electoral Commission* 1999 (3) SA 1 (CC) used a reasonableness test but explain the discrepancy away because its statements were obiter – that is, because the result in the case was based on a requirement of the s 36 limitations clause and not the interpretation of s 19 and so its comments in that regard were not precedent-setting. This doctrinal technicality, however, hardly explains why the Court would use two different tests nor, as they note but do not explain, the fact that it has also used reasonableness-based tests in other cases concerning democracy (see Chapter 7).

the 1999 and subsequent elections, the Court has dealt with eight other election cases besides *NNP* and *DP*, and it has resolved almost all of them in a fraction of the 49 days that remained between the decisions in *NNP* and *DP* and the 1999 election date: in two cases, within 24 hours, and in five others, in less than two weeks. (The eighth case, which took two months to resolve and was concluded a week before the 2004 election, was a heavily court-managed process and so also stands as evidence that the Court will do what is necessary to resolve electoral cases in time.)[31] The *NNP* majority's promise to act later if necessary was not an empty one, and this option was an important reason not to act too hastily, on inconclusive and not very suspicious evidence.

Much more important to my broader argument, however, is the other reason the majority did not equate a decision to make no order with a decision to leave voting rights undefended. Simply put, it did not see the Court as the only protector of voting rights in the equation. Apart from the legislature and the Department of Home Affairs, both constitutionally obliged to uphold rights and both, for all the applicant could prove, ostensibly acting to do so, the Electoral Commission is the primary constitutional actor responsible for managing elections.[32] Yacoob J's judgment treats it as significant that, while the Commission had advised

[31] The relevant data: *NNP*: decision in 28 days, with 49 days to go. (Heard 15–16 March 1999, decided 13 April 1999, election 2 June 1999); *DP*: decision in 16 days, with 49 days to go (Heard 29 March 1999, decided 13 April 1999, election 2 June 1999). The other relevant cases: *August*: decision in 14 days, with 63 days to go (Heard 19 March 1999; decided 1 April 1999, election 2 June 1999); *Minister of Home Affairs* v. *National Institute for Crime Prevention and Re-Integration of Offenders (NICRO)* 2005 (3) SA 280 (CC): decision in 12 days, with 31 days to go (Heard 25 February 2004, decided 3 March 2004, election 14 April 2004); *African Christian Democratic Party* v. *Electoral Commission* 2006 (3) SA 305 (CC): decision in 1 day, with 4 days to go (Heard 23 February 2006, decided 24 February 2006, election 1 March 2006); *Richter* v. *Minister of Home Affairs* 2009 (3) SA 615 (CC) and *AParty* v. *Minister of Home Affairs* 2009 (3) SA 649 (CC): decision in 8 days, with 41 days to go. (Both heard 4 March 2009, both decided 12 March 2009, election 22 April 2009); *Electoral Commission of the Republic of South Africa* v. *Inkatha Freedom Party* 2011 (9) BCLR 943 (CC): decision in 4 days, with 8 days to go (Heard 6 May 2011, decided 10 May 2011, election 18 May 2011). To this list should also be added the decisions in *Premier, Western Cape* v. *President of the Republic of South Africa* 1999 (3) SA 657 (CC), heard on 26 May 1999 with 7 days until the election, where an order was made the same day but reasons where only furnished on 2 September 1999; and *Liberal Party* v. *The Election Commission* 2004 (8) BCLR 810 (CC), an irregular proceeding beginning with a letter to the Court on 10 March 2004 and resolved, substantially under court direction on the basis of written submissions, on 10 May 2004, with 8 days until the election.

[32] 1996 Constitution, s 190(1).

against requiring the new barcoded documents after the HSRC report it had commissioned revealed the number of voters who lacked them, it had not at the time of the *NNP* hearing made a finding that voters were going to be deprived of their right to vote by the policy and that the elections would be defective as a result. In other words, the Court (and the other government actors involved) could properly place some reliance on the Commission's stance in deciding whether it was necessary to step in and relax the documentation requirements to ensure fair elections.[33]

Thus in the majority's view, *NNP* actually presented a choice between three options. The Court could invalidate the statute based on its defective implementation. That was unacceptable: as all the judges agreed, the existing evidence about the policy's implementation was too inconclusive to ground that finding. It was this lack of evidence that compelled O'Regan J to take the second option: invalidating the statute not because it was being implemented defectively, but by directly second-guessing Parliament's decision to enact the statute given the uncertainty about whether it could be implemented in time and the resulting risk of excluding voters. The final option was to leave the vindication of voting rights, for the time being at least, in the hands of the other constitutional actors involved. The majority, therefore, saw *NNP* as a choice between O'Regan J's expansive judicial strategy, and giving other actors more time to do their constitutional jobs.

Why, in this position, might one favour the majority's option over O'Regan J's? The reasons that appear from the majority judgment all concern the sort of model of constitutional review that the new court was building. This helps us to see the profoundly institutional, structural concerns that drive the majority judgment.[34]

[33] *NNP*, para. 43: 'Parliament could derive comfort from the fact that the elections were to be facilitated, managed and controlled by the Commission which was independent and impartial, and had a continuing duty to satisfy itself that the elections would be free and fair. The Commission would be under a duty to report to Parliament if prospective voters were in fact unable to register or if it appeared they would be unable to vote because of the department's failure or inability to implement its assurances. No such report has been made.' See also the judgment of Langa DP at paras. 59–60; I discuss the Langa judgment later in this chapter.

[34] In taking this structural approach here and throughout the book, I have benefitted from the work of Charles Black; see esp. C. L. Black, Jnr., *Structure and Relationship in Constitutional Law* (Lousiana State University Press, 1969); C. L. Black, Jnr. *Impeachment: A Handbook* (Yale University Press, 1974); see also P. Bobbitt, *Constitutional Fate: Theory of the Constitution* (Oxford University Press, 1982), ch. 6; A. R. Amar, *America's*

One set of concerns arises from some technical doctrinal tangles about rationality and reasonableness tests, which are an important reason why *NNP* is so often misread but can be left to one side here.[35] More important is the way that standard understandings, focused on the strength of the Court's rights test, are not adequate to the larger institutional concerns that drive the *NNP* majority. It is intent on striking the proper structural balance between the jurisdiction of the Court and the authority of other institutions, which informs its concern with the precise thresholds of review, the sorts of burdens of proof required to trigger judicial intervention, and the issue of whether the subsequent implementation of a statute affects the constitutionality of the statute itself.[36] This concern with burden of proof has its counterpart in the *DP* judgment. The court of first instance had declined a request by the applicant to refer the case for the hearing of further evidence. On appeal, the applicant asked the Constitutional Court to rule this refusal had been wrong. The majority (O'Regan J dissented in *DP* as well, although she did not specifically address this question in *DP*) declined to do so.[37] Once again, this may look outrageous to the observer demanding a focus on rights-based substance. The majority in *NNP* and *DP* declined to act in large part because the available evidence was limited. So why should the Court not at least encourage the development of further evidence in future cases, in the hopes that future rights challenges would not arrive amidst similar factual uncertainty? For that matter – no-one raised this in the case – why did the Constitutional Court itself not seek further evidence more actively?

I will say more about this possibility in later chapters, but in *DP*, the majority gave several reasons for rejecting the argument that the court of first instance should have sought more evidence, and these apply equally well, in the context of the case, to the suggestion that the Court should have sought more evidence itself. Among them was that the Court saw what an expansive precedent it would set. Since the applicant was alleging that the implementation of the Electoral Act was defective,

Constitution: A Biography (New York: Random House, 2006). Black's work is not unknown to the Constitutional Court, and I am grateful to Kate O'Regan for pointing this out to me; see e.g. *Minister of Health* v. *New Clicks South Africa (Pty) Ltd* 2006 (2) SA 311 (CC), para. 581 n. 349.

35 I take up these doctrinal issues in detail in Fowkes, 'Right After All', 157–60.

36 *NNP*, paras. 43–45.

37 *DP*, paras. 14–17; O'Regan J's dissent in that case is one paragraph, referring only to her *NNP* dissent as its basis: *Ibid*., para. 21.

'to be of any value [the further evidence] would have had to traverse virtually every issue raised . . . including complex questions of causation and capacity relevant to the constitutionality of the electoral scheme'.[38] Furthermore, as the majority noted, there was nothing to suggest that even an enquiry of this scope would be decisive. One might learn everything there was to learn about the department's activities and it might very well show only that the problems might be addressed in time but also might not be – yet the precedent would be set that an applicant armed with some allegations but not much proof should be able to trigger a sweeping judicial investigation into all aspects of the statutory implementation work of a government department. That is not necessarily untenable, but it is very expansive and potentially very intrusive. It is also risky in an electoral context, and this is why the *DP* Court also mentioned the urgency of the matter and 'the need for a quick decision in the light of the pending elections'.[39] If the investigation had not yielded fairly definitive results quite quickly, it might serve only to place a cloud over the integrity of the election (a concern also crucial in the 2009 decision in *Richter*, discussed later in this chapter, which has provoked none of the criticism directed at *NNP* and *DP*).

To an observer who wants the Court to *act* in response to a threat to voting rights, all these concerns with burdens of proof and other quite technical matters can make it look as if the majority is focusing on fire department deployment regulations while Rome burns. This will provoke particular suspicion in a post-apartheid society familiar with the way in which apartheid judges engaged with technicalities while massive injustice happened around them (as Davis's comparison of *NNP* to apartheid-era judging reflects).[40] O'Regan J's strongly substantive approach will appear to be the only acceptable way to go. But the appearance is misleading. For one thing, once we recognize that the threat to voting rights in *NNP* was less serious and less immediate than it might appear at first glance, we can see why the Court could take account of considerations beyond the shortest term. If Rome is burning, worrying too much about broader policy issues is criminally negligent; if Rome is not burning, the negligence might lie in *not* worrying about them. For another, the majority's concerns might be technical, but it is not placing form

[38] *DP*, paras. 16–17. [39] *Ibid.*, para. 17.

[40] I discuss arguments from apartheid judging briefly in Chapter 4 and in more detail in Fowkes, 'Apartheid Judging'.

above substance. Such institutional considerations *serve* substance.[41] Most obviously, they aim to strike the proper relationship between the judiciary and the legislature, and to determine how quickly litigants can trigger judicial intervention in the work of other state organs. Arguments from apartheid notwithstanding, it simply is not obviously wrong to worry about these things when pondering the lines of a new constitutional machine, especially once we recognize the attenuated nature of the electoral threat, or to worry that the O'Regan approach might act too expansively in this area on too little evidence.[42] And with that said, it is worth noting that O'Regan J, too, is more institutionally minded than her supporters, her dissent's generally expansive attitude to judicial power notwithstanding. The most obvious reason why she did not just treat the barcoded ID scheme straight away as a limitation of the right to vote – thus neatly finessing the doctrinal controversy over using proportionality analysis at the stage of rights interpretation, as we saw – is that she wished to resist setting the precedent that any regulation of the right to vote is a limitation that must be justified immediately under the s 36 limitations clause. That approach, unanimously confirmed ten years later in *Richter*, reflects an institutional concern that electoral arrangements determined by other branches and particularly parliament should not be too quickly and easily challengeable in court.[43]

The majority's substantive concerns also extend outside the traditional tripartite conception of the separation of powers.[44] The institutional position of the Electoral Commission is crucial in *NNP* (and, as we will see, in the Court's voting rights jurisprudence more generally). Those who argue that *the Court* must do everything it can to defend rights may be guilty of operating with too simple a conception of the separation of powers, for the Commission cannot, constitutionally, be ignored. Of central importance here is the third judgment in *NNP*, which I have not

[41] I have in other work considered the tendency in South Africa and elsewhere to neglect, when applying he 'substance over form' slogan, the fact that form can often serve substance: see esp. J. Fowkes, 'Civil Procedure in Public Interest Litigation: Tradition, Collaboration and the Managerial Judge' (2012) 1 *Cambridge Journal of International and Comparative Law* 235, 235–36, 253; J. Fowkes, 'Constitutional Civil Procedure and the Limits of Party Autonomy in Private Cases: *Maphango* v. *Aengus Lifestyle Properties (Pty) Ltd*' (2013) 5 *Constitutional Court Review* 308.

[42] See also the discussion of John Hart Ely's account later in this chapter.

[43] *NNP*, paras. 15, 123; *Richter*, paras. 55–56.

[44] See e.g. B. A. Ackerman, 'The New Separation of Powers' (2000) 113 *Harvard Law Review* 633.

yet mentioned. Langa DP wrote for a unanimous court on the allegations that the government was interfering with the independence of the Commission. While the Langa judgment is a standard item in a South African separation of powers course, it tends to be kept separate from the other two judgments in the case. This is a mistake, for in fact it displays very similar structural concerns.

Allegations about threats to the Commission's independence will retrigger the suspicion that the ANC government was not respecting the integrity of elections, and it will cast doubt on the claim that the Court could rely on the Commission's views. However, the NNP failed to establish that any infringement of independence had occurred. The most telling indicator of the tenuousness of their allegations (in addition to the fact that O'Regan J, too, did not accept their argument on this issue) is that the NNP itself, recognizing the weakness of its argument, was driven to change tack in the Constitutional Court. It applied for permission to amend its papers in order to raise the rather less alarming point that even if the Commission's independence had not actually been infringed, the relationship between it and the government had not been structured in a manner in keeping with the Commission's constitutionally independent status. Witness also the fact that the Commission itself did not seek a finding that its independence was threatened.[45]

The NNP's allegation as amended was much closer to the truth of the matter than its original, and the judgment of Langa DP agreed with the substance of what it contended. The Court held that officials had treated the Commission, for budgetary and other purposes, as if it fell under the purview of the Department of Home Affairs. This was contrary to its constitutionally independent status, and the Court said so in unequivocal terms. But the Commission, whose chair at the time was Constitutional Court Justice Johann Kriegler (not, of course, sitting in *NNP* or *DP*), had firmly resisted this understanding of the Commission's status. As a result, no actual infringement of the Commission's independence had occurred. Similarly, the government had been slow to act on the appointment of staff, but the Chairperson had ultimately taken the necessary hiring steps himself. This again reflected insufficient commitment on the part of the government, but had not in fact impaired the Commission's functioning and its independence. There was therefore, the Court held, no basis to make the order originally sought by the NNP.[46]

[45] *NNP*, paras. 70–71, 106–07. [46] *Ibid.*, paras. 80–101.

Why, however, did the Court not make the amended order the NNP asked for – given that it essentially upheld the NNP's amended contentions? The reason is once again institutional. Like the Yacoob judgment, the Langa judgment is concerned to establish the proper relationships between constitutional institutions, and also about the precedent being set for the triggering of judicial interference in other bodies. It in fact rejected the NNP's application to amend its papers on the grounds that the party lacked standing to raise the issue of the Commission's independence. The judgment grounds this rejection on a view about how state institutions are supposed to relate to one another. Where there is disagreement, as there was in this case, institutions should seek to resolve it through good faith dialogue, making decisions as necessary about whether and when this dialogue is failing to the extent that it becomes necessary to approach the courts for a ruling.[47] On the facts, this is what had happened: the Commission had been quite capable of looking after its own interests, and had not itself felt it necessary to approach the courts, and so it did not need the NNP to do this on its behalf. The Yacoob judgment had declined to intervene where it had not been established that the government's efforts to vindicate voting rights had failed or were failing – where it had not been shown that the constitutional mechanism needed judicial fixing. (Where there *had* been a failure, in the omissions of *August*, the Court duly stepped in.) Similarly, the Langa judgment takes the position that the constitutional mechanism between the Department, the Commission and Parliament was not broken, and that outside actors like the NNP should not be granted standing to prompt judicial intervention in such circumstances.

The Langa judgment is thus also like Yacoob J's in that it chooses not to intervene even though it could have: it commented on the Commission's independence and what it implies, but made no order. If the

[47] *Ibid.*, paras. 97, 107. This is somewhat like the principle of co-operative governance set out in s 41 of the Constitution, but it is not entirely the same thing. The Commission is not a 'sphere of government' or an organ 'within' one – this being what the Langa judgement in *NNP* insists – and so s 41 does not apply to its relations. Furthermore, given the Commission's independent status the Court will likely exercise jurisdiction more quickly over a dispute, should the Commission chose to litigate, than it would over an intra-governmental dispute, though it has noted, without ruling definitively, 'that there may be good reasons for an organ of state not to litigate against the Commission except as a last resort'. See *Independent Electoral Commission* v. *Langeberg Municipality* 2001 (3) SA 925 (CC), paras. 27–31.

Commission's independence really had been under threat, the pressure on the Court to act may well have been insuperable. But as with the threat to voting rights, the danger to the Commission was not of this order of magnitude, so there was space to weigh other institutional considerations such as how easy it should be for political parties and other outside actors to involve themselves in intra-government separation of powers disputes. Issuing a declaratory order would have meant granting the NNP's application, accepting its standing to interfere, and thus once again setting a bad institutional precedent.

Democracy and Trust

This concern with institutional processes brings us to the argument of John Hart Ely. *NNP*'s critics rely on Ely and treat his argument as a key basis for preferring O'Regan J's judgment.[48] But Ely's account is actually distinctly equivocal authority here, in ways that are important to understanding the broader argument.

Ely defends processes. He responds to the counter-majoritarian difficulty by arguing that courts should police processes where there is a danger that the majority will be subverted or that groups will be excluded – but not otherwise. Ely's account is therefore highly ambiguous authority in a case where the key question is precisely whether or not democratic processes are broken, or breaking. *If* the government cannot be trusted or the election is threatened, it is strong authority for intervention, but if not, it is equally strong authority against it. His theory poses a question about when a court should *not* act as much as one about when it should, and *NNP*'s critics fail to take the second half of his question nearly as seriously as the Court did. Ely's account is also uncertain authority because it does not try to take account of the modern, multi-part separation of powers. He divides the constitutional world into democratic institutions and the judiciary, and so does not take account of other institutions insulated from democratic forces, such as the Electoral Commission. As a result, even if one thinks that the system in *NNP* was close enough to breaking that there is an Ely reason to override elected authorities, his argument doesn't necessarily offer a reason to choose

[48] Ely, *Democracy and Distrust.* Much reliance is implicit, given the degree to which Ely's argument for intervention has been absorbed into standard judicial review talk, but see note 8 for explicit reliance.

action by the Court over action by the Commission.[49] Finally, and perhaps most important of all, we usually think of Ely's argument in terms of courts policing *established* processes, and this does not fit a post-1994 South African reality where so much constitutional business is about establishing *new* processes.[50] (This is a key general point, which I will be returning to in detail later.) The *NNP* majority, as we have seen, is deeply concerned with the details of the constitutional system that it is building, and some of Justice O'Regan's concerns are also of this type. We saw her concerns about treating all regulation of elections as a limitation of the right to vote, and the primary concern of her judgment is not protection so much as insisting that the government and the Court should be doing everything possible to *promote* voter participation in a nascent democracy.[51] In both judgments, there is a concern about building that goes beyond mere protecting, but the tendency to focus on the famous part of Ely's argument about checking negative breaches by democratic institutions primes us to see the barcoded ID requirement simply as the government messing with a working electoral system, either suspiciously or just imprudently.

The reality was more or less the opposite. South Africa did not have a working electoral system in 1998. The 1994 elections, thrown together at speed, had been run with no registration process and no voters roll. All permanent residents had been allowed to vote along with citizens to avoid excluding those whose South African citizenship, as a result of the apartheid government's 'independent' homelands policy, might be in legal doubt or whose documents might not up to date. Very large numbers of temporary voters certificates had been issued to the same end, raising concerns about duplicate and underage voting. Ballots had to be shipped to central locations before they were counted. As a result of these and other concerns, irregularities had abounded in 1994, and if they did not ultimately become much of an issue it was only because the results were broadly acceptable to all the major interests and because the defects were overshadowed by the moment and the peace of that first

[49] Ely's US theory also fits the South African context imperfectly, because it entails a much more modest conception of the judicial role than the one that prevails in South African constitutional talk or the one that seems to underpin the O'Regan judgment. Ely, after all, thought courts should leave value judgments to the legislature. See *Ibid.*, e.g. p. 103.

[50] It is not clear that this is even an adequate way to understand his argument in the United States, since Ely saw the Warren Court's innovations as fuelled by an interventionist desire to promote a *new* openness of procedures. See *Ibid.*, e.g. p. 74.

[51] *NNP*, paras. 119–21, 156.

election. (Both Mandela and De Klerk successfully silenced calls within their parties to challenge aspects of the election results.)[52] The ANC government therefore faced the urgent need to build what was effectively a new electoral system that would be far more resistant to these potentially devastating weaknesses – which is why, notwithstanding the magnitude of its wider post-1994 tasks, it can be validly criticized for turning to electoral reform as late as 1998. The new, stricter documentary requirements were part of this effort.

In this context, it is far from obvious that the Court's task is only about restraining government, as both judgments reflect but as standard accounts seldom capture. This is not much of an obstacle to understanding the O'Regan J judgment, because her efforts to build by intervening are compatible with simple ideas of protecting the right to vote by intervening. But it is serious conceptual block to understanding the majority, which wants to build by *not* intervening. Yacoob J, and Langa DP for that matter, want to build the electoral system, and the constitutional system more broadly, by letting the other pieces of the mechanism do their jobs, and by avoiding setting precedents that would make for a bad constitutional mechanism going forward. It is hard for conceptions that understand the judicial role only in terms of protection, and rights only in terms of *judicial* protection, to grasp this. Such conceptions accept judicial non-intervention only when nothing important needs

[52] See e.g. A. Guelke, *South Africa in Transition: The Misunderstood Miracle* (London: Tauris, 1999), pp. 114–31; H. *The Afrikaners: Biography of a People* (2 edn, UK: Hurst, 2009), pp. 646–47; D. Welsh, *The Rise and Fall of Apartheid* (University of Virginia Press, 2010), pp. 535–38, 541–43, 556–60, 562–65; Klug, *Constitution of South Africa*, pp. 38–39; P. Harris, *Birth: The Conspiracy to Stop the '94 Election* (Cape Town: Umuzi, 2010). The scale of potential abuse was large: 'A total of 19.7 million votes were cast [in 1994] but alleged widespread irregularities led political parties to question the validity of about 1.5 million of them. After investigation and intense consultation with the political parties, the IEC announced election results accepted as "substantially free and fair" – R. Alence, 'South Africa After Apartheid: The First Decade' (2004) 15 *Journal of Democracy* 78, 83. The final count was also convenient, giving all three of the largest players (the ANC, the NP and the IFP) results they could accept. Mark Gevisser's side comment, for example, is not untypical: 'In what many believe was a peacemaking rig, the IFP conveniently won 51% of the province of KwaZulu-Natal and, with that, enough votes to qualify it for a Government of National Unity (GNU) with the ANC and the National Party': Gevisser, *Dream Deferred*, p. 626; see also e.g. T. D. Sisk, *Democratization in South Africa: The Elusive Social Contract* (Princeton University Press, 1995), pp. 296–98; W. Gumede, *Thabo Mbeki and the Battle for the Soul of the ANC* (updated ed., Cape Town: Zebra, 2007), p. 53. The extent to which 1999 elections improved on the record of 1994 in these respects is discussed later in this chapter.

protecting, while *NNP* is all about the possibility that non-intervention might also be appropriate where there *is* something important to protect but it might be better to leave some or all of that protection to others.

This is not just an obstacle for classical legal accounts: realists, too, tend to focus on distrust. *Their* blind spot is their tendency to parse the Court's concern for institutional relationships simply in terms of political caution. (I discuss the political details of *NNP* in a moment.) This focus on political survival might be explained by the tendency to cast the ANC as a threat or by current trends in political science work on emerging courts noted earlier. It is only if we think of the Court as a fragile institution facing a looming threat from the regime that it makes sense to think of its work as dominated by political survival – just as it is only if we think voting rights were under imminent threat in *NNP* that it makes sense to dismiss Yacoob J's technical concerns as sacrificing substance for form. If we relax the assumption that *the Court* was under immediate threat, we can start to see what existing accounts do not adequately grasp: that if one is building a constitutional system, expressions of faith and respect are important, and they do not necessarily represent supplication.

Observers of South African constitutional law are unanimous in praising Nelson Mandela for making a point as president of publicly accepting Constitutional Court judgments and praising the Court, particularly when it ruled against his government. This, it is accepted, was an act of generous and far-sighted statesmanship, very valuable in establishing the authority of the Court in its first years.[53] And so it was. What needs to be recognized is that the positions adopted in the Langa and Yacoob judgments in *NNP* exemplify the same spirit. Part of building institutions is letting them exercise their authority. If a court seeks to establish intra-government dialogue and problem-solving, then it cannot insert itself too quickly into intra-government disputes. If a court wants to build the authority of the Electoral Commission and establish its place in the constitutional mechanism, it should not be too quick to intervene on its behalf. If a court wants to establish a system in which government takes responsibility for giving effect to rights, then it cannot insert itself too quickly when the government is trying to do that. And if a court itself wants to establish a reasonable dialogue with the government, part of that means acknowledging the other speaker as an equal and letting it speak too. This is not an argument about encouraging responsibility as one

[53] See e.g. Klug, *Constituting Democracy*, p. 150; Roux, *Politics of Principle*, pp. 33–34, 163.

might teach a child by leaving it In Charge, while keeping an eye on it from the other room. Quite apart from being inappropriately patronizing, that idea misses the fact that everyone in the post-1994 equation was new and learning, including a new Court taking its first stabs at some crucial issues. Instead, the best way to understand the argument is in terms of social trust. When we talk of trust as social capital, we mean that people are willing to rely on one other. That kind of social capital is created when people place reliance on others and find their trust justified.[54] It is far from obvious that a new court, seeking to build a new constitutional system, would be wise to start distrustfully, if given the choice, lest its distrust be repaid in kind. And the point is that the ANC's stance, as exemplified by President Mandela's actions (but not confined to him, as we will see), gave the Court that choice. It was possible to start as actors jointly working to build a new and better system – an utterly defining, and widely neglected, feature of the post-1994 South African polity.

This idea represents the strongest objection to the better-safe-than-sorry argument that otherwise looks like a powerful reason to favour the O'Regan J approach. If judicial intervention did not come with particular costs, then it seems reasonable to play it safe and not take any risks with voting rights. Even if the fears had proven groundless, at least firm protection would have been established for voting rights in the future (an argument that will be still more attractive the more one thinks of the ANC as a looming threat). But the argument from trust suggests that judicial intervention is far from costless. What is lost is the building work that can be done by letting other institutions do their jobs and by expressing trust in them. This can be understood as Jeremy Waldron's famous argument about the effect of expanding judicial review on democracy, but rewritten for a new, emerging system. Waldron worries that the more courts take over decisions, the less democratic institutions will take responsibility and the more they will atrophy. His is an argument explicitly set in an established system.[55] In a new system, with new institutions (or old institutions persisting in so new a context that they might as well be new), the issue is not one of atrophy, but of failing to grow at all. This argument, like Waldron's original, is vulnerable if rights

[54] See e.g. F. Fukuyama, *Trust: The Social Virtues and the Creation of Prosperity* (New York: The Free Press, 1995).

[55] J. Waldron, 'The Core of the Case Against Judicial Review' (2006) 115 *Yale Law Journal* 1346, 1360–64. See also Roux, *Politics of Principle*, p. 334.

will not be protected unless courts act.[56] But, as with the Ely argument, that is precisely what was up for debate in *NNP*.

This account of *NNP* does not rebut the idea that the judges were making political calculations. Some of its elements, like the trust-building argument, positively imply that the Court was thinking about the ANC's stance. It is also certainly true that one can tell a political story about *NNP*, the equivalent of the second *Makwanyane* story. The DP and the NNP had objected to the ANC's identification document policy soon after it was announced. Initially, in January 1999, President Mandela appeared to suggest that some compromise could be negotiated. Within days, this offer was withdrawn, possibly at the instigation of Mandela's anointed heir, Thabo Mbeki. Litigation by the DP and the NNP then proceeded.[57] In the meantime, the Commission was fighting several protracted battles with the government over staffing and funding arrangements, as we have seen. In February, the Commission's Chairperson, Constitutional Court Justice Johann Kriegler, resigned in frustration, citing the pressures of his twin commitments as Chairperson and Justice.[58] So when the Court heard the case on 15–16 March, it was in the context of a drawn-out political fight between the litigants before it, and a lengthy institutional battle between the government and one of the justices' own colleagues. A decision against the ANC would see the party lose quite a lot of face. It would risk the appearance of the judges siding with the NNP's combative suspicion of the ANC. (The NNP had walked out of the Government of National Unity just eleven months earlier.)[59] And it risked the appearance of the Court rushing to the defence of their brother judge.

I am in no position to deny that the Justices were thinking along political lines like these, and short of some unusually candid and reliable judicial autobiographies, it is hard to imagine how one could rebut such

[56] For a critique of Waldron's argument in the South African context, referring to the general debate, see Bilchitz, *Poverty and Fundamental Rights*, ch. 3.

[57] According the Electoral Institute of South Africa's compilation of sources, Mandela phoned DP and NNP leaders on 17 January 1999 to offer a compromise deal; and then again on 20 January to say the offer had been dropped. Thereafter, Mbeki's office repeatedly denied that any compromise or settlement had been offered – see Electoral Institute of South Africa, *South Africa's Second Democratic Election 1999: An Annotated Bibliography* (EISA, 2001), p. 2.

[58] E.g. S. Daley, 'Head of South Africa's Election Commission Resigns Suddenly', *New York Times*, 27 January 1999.

[59] On the Government of National Unity, see note 27 in the next chapter.

suggestions. It might therefore seem that we have reached the usual post-legal realism stalemate, in which the influence of the political is unrebuttable and so the pretensions of the legal explanations are seen as unrebuttably in doubt. It is true that the level of engagement with longer-term technical questions is inconsistent with the bluntest political explanations that the Court was just seeking the fastest route to dismissing the case, but one could readily offer a more sophisticated account. If the Court was strategically seeking to shore up its longer-term legal authority, then we would expect it to operate in as legal as fashion as possible, even (or especially) if it were using the flexibility of legal doctrines to avoid certain outcomes in a politically charged context. Similarly, if the Court was trying to design a model of judicial review that the powerful ANC could accept, or one that would minimize the possibility of destructive clashes going forward, then we would expect its answer to take a carefully legal form, but it would still be a political strategy.[60]

This result, however, only represents a stalemate if we believe that the presence of political factors is embarrassing to an interpretative account. Following the argument of the previous chapter, I do not see this as an inevitable conclusion. Instead, this depends on whether the consideration of political arguments detracts from or is incompatible with the traditional legal arguments. If politics led the court away from the law, as critics of *NNP* suspect, then the political story would indeed detract from the traditionally legal one. But now that we have all the pieces, we might wonder if that was true in *NNP*. In the first *Makwanyane* story, the standard account of that case as a bold rights defence missed the extent to which that deeply legal activity aligned with, and was partly a product of, the ANC's stance and the political context of the case. In *NNP*, where the standard account of the case is precisely the opposite of a bold rights defence, precisely the opposite point is missed: even the most sophisticated version of the standard political story misses the extent to which the action that aligned with the ANC's stance and the political imperatives of the case also represents deeply legal activity, an exercise in structural argumentation of a sort that would be familiar to constitutional lawyers all over the world. What we see is what we saw in the third *Makwanyane* story: the constitution-building pieces once again fall into place. Adjudicating a contest between parties in an electoral context may well have required circumspection, but these imperatives meshed with

[60] Roux's account of *NNP* is a good illustration: see *Politics of Principle*, 350.

the more general constitutional goal of building a workable system of constitutional review. That meant setting the bar for rights challenges and for opposition party challenges at a height the applicants did not manage to clear. It also meshed with the duty to give effect to the separation of powers, and with a judgment call that the system would be best built, in this sort of situation, by letting its parts do their jobs. The general result in *NNP* was of course not unwelcome to the ANC. But what the ANC would accept was also constitutionally acceptable, and an NNP loss, on the case it brought, is not a constitutionally unwelcome precedent.

Crucially, we should not think of this alignment merely as a fortuitous coincidence. If *NNP* just happened to be a case in which the threat to voting rights was not, after all, as serious as some feared, then this chapter would offer a mostly factual correction to existing realist accounts, and it would leave open the possibility that a deferent court just got lucky. But this way of thinking reflects the same disconnect between the political forces in the case and the constitutional reasons being offered in the judgment that we saw in the second *Makwanyane* story, and the same failure to take politics legally seriously. It was not coincidence that *Makwanyane* aligned with the ANC's position; this reflected the constitutional merits of that position. Similarly, in *NNP*, there is a deeper relationship between the nature of the political activity on offer and the Court's legal response. If Parliament and the Department of Home Affairs had not been making credible efforts to make the new policy work, or if that policy really had been a cheating move, or if the ANC really had been trying to compromise the Electoral Commission's independence, the various imperatives could not have been aligned. If the Commission had not vigorously asserted its own status, the Court would have been faced with the need to be heavier-handed in the Commission's defence and again the imperatives would have been harder to align. If the Commission had not made the HSRC poll happen in order to bring to everyone's attention the number of people who lacked the new IDs, the Court might have had to confront the issue much closer to the election with much less time for a contingency plan to be worked out by government, and it might then have had little choice but to step in and invalidate the restriction on documents. As with *Makwanyane*, this is not to take credit away from the Court, but merely to acknowledge that it is operating in a context in which others are doing constitutional work too. Indeed, it is *also* not a coincidence that the most troublesome feature of the case – what to do given that the limitations of the evidence made it hard to know whether intervention was yet required or not – represent the areas where the least work had been done by others.[61] The government had not been particularly forthcoming with information, the opposition parties had not been particularly successful in developing it, and, as we will see, other public bodies were only just starting to develop electoral data. (The 1999 elections would see South Africa's very first exit poll, for example.)[62]

None of this is proof that the Court might not have acted more politically, as opposed to legally, if these imperatives had been in greater tension. None of it, therefore, is proof that the straight realist accounts might not fit the Court in other cases. But it does show why these accounts are perfectly plausible blueprints that just turn out not to fit the constitutional activity we see in front of us in *NNP* – and later chapters will repeat this pattern. As long as law and politics are kept mentally separate, their alignment will be treated as a fortunate but coincidental matter. That will prevent us from giving the ANC and other actors proper constitutional credit for their activity in the political sphere, and it will prevent us from seeing that the successes of post-1994 constitutionalism in South Africa depend on far more than the Court's strategic ability to get away with articulating as much law as it politically can.

Epilogue to *NNP*

One way to bolster the legal credibility of my claims is to show that the Court's approach is consistent across a broader set of cases. I will conclude this chapter with arguments of that sort. Before that, I examine what actually happened after *NNP*, to test the naïveté or otherwise of the judgment calls made by the Justices and of my claims about trust and other consequences.

The DP and NNP never did take up the Court's invitation to bring another challenge to the policy when more information had come to light. This may have to do with the nature of that information. *NNP* was decided on 13 April 1999. On 12 May, the HSRC, whose initial report had formed the basis of the judgment, released an update. It found that whereas in July 1998 about 80% of potential voters had the required documentation (the figure used in *NNP*), as of March 1999 that figure

61 I return to this important issue in Chapter 9.

62 Y. Muthien, 'Introduction' in Muthien (ed.), *Democracy South Africa*, p. 8.

had increased to 93%. Given that a further 2% of voters had temporary certificates that would allow them to vote, by March 'about 95% of South Africans of voting age [were] in possession of the document required for voting in the elections'. The HRSC's project manager on the issue, Johan Olivier, stated: 'From [these] results it is clear that the IEC and the Department of Home Affairs have been successful in raising awareness about the need to have a bar-coded ID in order to participate in the upcoming elections.' He added that 'the Department of Home Affairs was able to issue significant numbers of [the barcoded] documents since the release of the HSRC's July 1998 study'. In numerical terms, the Department had issued somewhere between 3.4 and 4 million new ID documents between July 1998 and March 1999, when the final registration weekend was held.[63] Olivier would conclude after the election that 'possession or not of a bar-coded ID was not a significant factor' in whether people registered for the election.[64] The HSRC also noted that those who still lacked barcoded documents in March 1999 – about 1,3 million people – were 'mainly people who also did not register to vote in the upcoming elections'.[65] In other words, the barcoded ID requirement does not seem to have prevented many people from registering, and it does not seem that many of those who tried to vote were prevented from doing so because they could not get the required documents.

This does not mean there was no effect. There is some evidence that the barcoded ID requirement had some impact on voter participation. But on balance it seems to have been modest indeed.[66] With one telling

[63] See HSRC Press Release, 'Democracy SA: Update on Bar-Coded IDs', 12 May 1999, www.hsrc.ac.za/Media_Release-96.phtml; see also M. Khosa and Y. G. Muthien, 'Election Management in South Africa: An Evaluation of the 1999 Election' in International IDEA Conference–Towards Sustainable Democratic Institutions in Southern Africa, http://archive.idea.int/ideas_work/22_s_africa/elections_3_south_africa.htm, 65: 'The significant improvement in the possession of bar-coded IDs by March 1999 demonstrated the success of ID drive.'

[64] Johan Olivier, 'The Independent Electoral Commission (IEC): The Quest for Free and Fair Elections' in Muthien (ed.), *Democracy South Africa*, p. 28.

[65] HSRC, 'Democracy SA'.

[66] There is some evidence of last minute problems: it emerged in the HSRC's focus groups that some political parties apparently delivered documents to polling stations themselves in an effort to speed up delivery, suggesting a certain last-minute quality – see M. Khosa, 'Voting in Action: Focus Group and Workshop Findings' in Muthien (ed.), *Democracy South Africa*, pp. 74–75 – and the Violence Monitoring Project in KwaZulu-Natal observed that some voters had not collected their new documents from Home Affairs in time – R. Humphries, 'Assessing the 1999 Election Machinery: Views of Political Parties and Other Stakeholders' in Muthien (ed.), *Democracy South Africa*, pp. 58–59.

exception, discussed later in this chapter, the Election Commission's post-election report does not feel it necessary even to mention the barcoded documents, and they do not feature among the HSRC's nine policy lessons drawn from the election.[67] In HSRC post-election interviews with party leaders, only two parties, the DP and the UDM, complained that the requirement had impacted their results (although the DP had increased its share of the vote five-fold over 1994). No other party, with the notable inclusion of the NNP, raised the issue.[68] Ninety-six per cent of voters interviewed as part of the exit poll thought the elections free and fair. Among those who did not, the fear that other citizens had been excluded from voting was indeed one of the three main reasons given.[69] But the poll did not ask respondents to specify the reason for the exclusion – and it seems reasonable to speculate that the main concern here was not the ID requirement, which little of the other evidence points to, but instead that people were prevented from voting at a particular voting station because they were not on the voters roll for that district, which other assessments *do* identify as a problem. We would expect this to be a problem if we recall that there was no registration or voters roll in the 1994 elections and so most of the electorate had never dealt with these things before.[70] The post-election studies look consistent with the HSRC's assessment: the barcoded ID requirement did not exclude many people from voting.

Supporters of the O'Regan judgment may object that this is nothing to celebrate. Even if only 3 per cent, or 1 per cent, of the electorate was excluded or discouraged by the barcoded requirement – and the available evidence does not allow us to rule out exclusion on that sort of scale – that is unacceptable and her approach was still better. But if these are the true figures, then the overall balancing exercise looks rather different. Recall that Parliament was responding to a very real need to introduce

[67] IEC 1999; Muthien and Khosa, 'Election Management in South Africa', pp. 94–95.

[68] Humphries, 'Assessing the 1999 Election Machinery', pp. 53, 58–59.

[69] The other two were the concern that one party would dominate the election and voter intimidation.

[70] Fieldworkers attributed people being turned away to non-registration or their not appearing on the voters' roll for a particular station, and did not specifically mention ID books as a source of problems: S. Rule, 'Eyes on the Ground: Fieldworker Observations' in Muthien (ed.), *Democracy in South Africa*, pp. 48–49, 51. The Commonwealth observers noted that many voters were sent by officials to other polling stations to vote, which implies a problem of going to the wrong station rather than being ineligible to vote at all: Commonwealth Observer Group, *The National and Provincial Elections in South Africa 2 June 1999* (Commonwealth Secretariat, 1999), pp 34–36.

safer documentary standards to combat the fraud experienced in the 1994 election. That was important to protect everyone's right to vote, and in 1999, despite some reservations, the parties 'acknowledged that the new process limited the extent of the electoral fraud [experienced] in the founding election'.[71] That is a significant achievement in itself. Recall also that Parliament was also seeking a more efficient system, avoiding the delays inherent in a system in which officials would have to work with a number of different types of documents and to enter all information manually.[72] It is very important, in this regard, that the HSRC post-election evaluation suggested that '[l]ong queues were perhaps the single most important problem encountered by the electorate'.[73] They were the most common problem reported in the exit poll and in the focus groups, and delays and official inefficiencies, taken together, were the most common problems reported by field workers.[74] The HSRC expressed the concern that these delays caused disenchantment and led voters to leave queues without voting. (It would be reasonable to wonder at this point if the introduction of the new barcode-based system itself caused these delays, but the evidence does not bear this out.)[75] And so the question arises: if significant problems of delay arose during the election under the simplified barcode system, which avoided the need for manual entry and also avoided the need for officials to work with a range of different identity documents, how much worse might the delays have been if the barcoded system had not been introduced? Enough to make

[71] Humphries, 'Assessing the 1999 Election Machinery', p. 57.

[72] Yacoob J noted the problems of multiple document types: *NNP*, para. 16.

[73] Khosa, 'Voting in Action', p. 70.

[74] O'Donovan, "Election Day Exit Poll', pp. 34, 38; Rule, 'Eyes on the Ground', p. 49 (7% of fieldworkers mentioning delays, and 5% official inefficiencies. 11% reported shortages of voting materials, and 11% also reported delays due to the arrival of ineligible voters).

[75] The Commonwealth Observer team noted that 'in some instances where [the barcode system] was in use [it] did not enhance the efficiency of the station': Commonwealth Observer Group, 35; see also T. Lodge, D. Kadima and D. Pottie, 'South Africa' in T. Lodge, D. Kadima and D. Pottie (eds.) *Compendium of Elections in Southern Africa* (Electoral Institute of South Africa, 2002), p. 311. However, the inevitable teething troubles seem to have been mostly experienced, and dealt with, during the first voter registration weekend. It is also notable that most delays on that weekend occurred when the barcoded system broke down and officials had to enter data manually – IEC Report 1999, 30–33; Wall, 'South Africa', p. 320 – suggesting that whatever the problems with the barcoded system, manual entry would have been slower still. By the 2004 election, the objections had disappeared and the new system had become widely accepted – *Ibid.*, pp. 305, 308–09, 347–48.

one or three, or more, voters out of every hundred leave the line in frustration or decide not to join it at all after seeing the queues?

We are, of course, here in the realm of counterfactuals, and so there are no definite answers, but three points at least can be made with confidence. First, this epilogue supports my conclusion that it was not naïve for the Court to operate from a premise of trust in relation to other organs of government, absence credible evidence of a rights violation. Certainly, there were policy problems. But apart from the fact that the Department did succeed in issuing millions of barcoded IDs in time, it is also notable in this regard that, following the Commission's resistance to the funding procedure proposed by the Department and the Court's confirmation that this resistance was well-founded, the government altered its relationship with the Commission accordingly and shelved its earlier proposals.[76] The 'ANC-in-government', concludes Susan Booysen, 'by all explicit measures has conducted itself in an exemplary way in resourcing and only minimally interfering with the work of the successive election management bodies.'[77] Precise evaluations of the government's performance will differ. Perhaps it ultimately did a fair job in the circumstances; perhaps it pushed ahead too quickly with a nice-to-have policy without adequate information about its implications and was too cavalier about the real risks of disenfranchisement; perhaps it was too proud or stubborn in responding to criticism (although also, perhaps, that criticism was too quickly distrustful or partisan). But whatever one's judgment, the record contains sincere effort and significant success, and demands nuanced assessment. It is too simple to treat the party merely as a threat or a problem against which the Court must guard.

The second conclusion is about balancing and judicial intervention. All the evidence in the epilogue of course emerged after the *NNP* decision and so is of limited relevance in critiquing the judgments themselves. Given what was before the Court at the time, the majority and minority are both making defensible judgment calls about the consequences of non-intervention; this (and not differing interpretations of the right to vote) is what lies at the heart of their split. But the later evidence does illustrate why it might be thought controversial for courts to use proportionality analysis to directly reconsider legislative judgments in situations where judges have little to go on. Given that the subsequent evidence of

[76] Lodge et al., 'South Africa', 299; the issue has not arisen since.

[77] S. Booysen, *The African National Congress and the Regeneration of Political Power* (Wits University Press, 2014), p. 222.

voter exclusion due to the barcoded documents is modest and certainly did not place a question mark over the election, given that the efficiency gains of the new system may have been at least as important in preventing disenfranchisement by targeting the delay problems that seem to have been the largest concern for voters, and given the gains in security and efficiency which have become entrenched in subsequent elections, the conclusion is that South Africa, under Parliament's policy, got a credible second election that was not marred by the kind of fraud and other irregularities which had to be swallowed in 1994, and has since enjoyed a stable, reliable, trusted electoral system. If the Court had followed O'Regan J and ordered that multiple forms of identification be accepted again in the 1999 election, several of these gains might have been impaired – and if the sacrifice of the more efficient single-document barcode system had significantly increased delays, it might have excluded more voters than it brought in. Parliament may well have got the balancing exercise right after all.

Furthermore, consider what one would think in hindsight, as a member of the *NNP* majority, watching the 1999 elections. If they had turned out to be a catastrophe, O'Regan J's approach may not have been left nearly as much to one side as it subsequently has been. As it happened, the judges, and the nation, could watch the election happen freely and fairly without a disaster at Home Affairs or electoral fraud or the mass exclusion of voters, and take a very different moral to heart. This is how trust grows, and how a constitutional mechanism of many parts is built.

Finally, there are significant similarities between *NNP*'s epilogue and *Makwanyane*'s. If one were worried about voting rights in South Africa in 1999, the real challenges were mostly not the things raised in the court cases and were instead of the more mundane variety: queues, voter education, staff and capacity problems.[78] The Commission constructed a system for decentralized vote-counting based in the municipalities – and that required establishing the first internet network allowing all municipalities in South Africa to communicate with each other,

[78] Staff training was brief and sometimes haphazard. There were recruitment problems: IEC 1999 Election Report, p. 26. Owing to IEC funding shortages, it seems that voter education efforts were concentrated in urban areas, were often only available in English, and neglected key populations: Khosa, 'Voting in Action', pp. 64–66. Muthien and Khosa, 'Election Management in South Africa', p. 94, place voter education at the top of their list of policy guidelines for the future.

including placing computers in some offices that had never had them before and dealing with the fact that some municipal offices did not have electricity.[79] Because of staff shortages, the HSRC noted that 'many of the officials on duty at the voting stations on election day were too exhausted to count votes', and 'many fell asleep' while doing so.[80] Much of the business of giving effect to voting rights was much more prosaic, and much less about what went on in the courtroom, than standard understandings usually reflect.

In fact, the *NNP* epilogue has further echoes of *Makwanyane's*, because perhaps the most notable group neglected in the run-up to the 1999 election was prisoners. In *August*, which I return to under the next heading, the Court had held that the government's failure to make provision for prisoners to vote was unconstitutional. This is standardly held up as a bold rights defence, like *Makwanyane*, but once again there were hidden implementation problems. Prisoners were the one and only group the Electoral Commission's post-election report suggested were significantly impacted by the barcoded ID requirement. Prisoners presumably found it harder to obtain the new documents, especially in light of the uncertainty about whether they would be able to vote at all, and special efforts were not made to assist them. Together with other difficulties – the Electoral Commission managed to provide the voter education ordered in *August* to only 19 151 prisoners out of a total prison population of 146 000,[81] and many prisoners had been out of prison during the registration periods and so were not entitled to register in terms of the *August* order in any case – the result was that only 15 per cent of the prison population (21 998 of 146 000 prisoners) ultimately registered to vote in the 1999 elections.[82] There is some irony in the fact that for all the attention paid in *NNP* to barcoded IDs in general *without* proof that the government was failing to implement its policies, it was in the one area where the government *had* been shown to be neglecting its responsibilities, in *August*, that the issue actually became a serious problem. As in *Makwanyane*, it is quite hard to blame the Court for this outcome. It stems in the first place from the government's initial omission to make arrangements for prisoners, in the second place from the Commission's limited time and resources to give effect to *August* once

[79] IEC 1999 Election Report, p. 26.

[80] Muthien and Khosa, 'Election Management in South Africa', pp. 94–95. Staffing and training problems feature prominently in the HSRC's recommendations.

[81] IEC 1999 Election Report, p. 44.

[82] *Ibid.*, p. 36.

the omission was successfully challenged – something the Commission was candid about at the hearing[83] – and in the third place from the fact that civil society mobilization on behalf of prisoners was limited and so implementation of the *August* order was not pressed or supported as much as it might have been. The Court's remedy was also quite bold for the time: indeed, with narrative convenience, *August* (and its 2004 successor on prisoner voting rights, *NICRO*, discussed later) represent some of the most expansive relief the Court ordered until the more detailed supervisory process undertaken in 2005 in *Sibiya*, the follow-up case to *Makwanyane*.[84]

Consistency: *NNP* and the Rest of the Court's Voting Rights Jurisprudence

NNP's epilogue is one sort of evidence. Another way to support the claims made in this chapter is by demonstrating the Court's consistency across a wider range of cases. To this end, I compare *NNP* and *DP* to the rest of the Court's voting rights decisions, and also to another politically charged litigation between the main opposition party and the ANC, *Executive Council, Western Cape* v. *Government of the Republic of South Africa*, which is often analyzed as a counterpoint to *Makwanyane*.[85]

On the standard narrative, the Court's voting rights jurisprudence as a whole displays quite serious inconsistencies. In *August*, the Court vindicated the right of prisoners to vote, protecting the rights of an unpopular minority. Five years later in *NICRO*, it again upheld prisoners' voting rights in the face of a second, more focused attempt by the government to disenfranchise a narrowed class of prisoners. These decisions appear to be squarely in line with the first, bold rights-protecting *Makwanyane* story. They are praised or, more usually and more tellingly, simply treated as what should be happening. They stand in sharp contrast, on the standard view, to the deferent decisions in *NNP* and *DP*, and this contrast reinforces the view that the Court was playing politics in the latter pair of cases. (They are also contrasted with another restrained

83 *August*, para. 7.

84 The Court in *August* required the Commission 'to furnish an affidavit setting out the manner in which the order will be complied with' within two weeks of the judgment: *Ibid.*, para. 40. On the other cases and the Court's use of supervisory remedies see Bishop, 'Remedies', 9-185–9-186.

85 *Executive Council, Western Cape* v. *Government of the Republic of South Africa* 1995 (4) SA 877 (CC).

decision implicating voting rights, *UDM (2)*, which is criticized just as strongly as *NNP* and which I discuss in Chapter 7.)

This neat picture, however, is rather disrupted by two more recent decisions, because within those cases the Court vindicated one rights claim, apparently like *August* and *NICRO*, but rejected two others, apparently like *NNP* and *DP*. In *Richter* v. *Minister of Home Affairs* and *AParty* v. *Minister of Home Affairs*, the Court ruled that the government had to make reasonable arrangements for any citizen out of the country on election day to vote in national elections if they so wished, but it rejected the further claims that citizens overseas had the right to vote in *provincial* elections or the right to *register* to vote overseas. These three things – voting in national elections, voting in provincial elections, registering to vote – appear to be of very similar importance to the enjoyment of the right, yet the unanimous Court protected only one of them. If the first four voting rights decisions are understood as inconsistent, *Richter* and *AParty* must seem positively schizophrenic. But in fact they are an important warning against seeing a decision not to intervene necessarily as a political retreat. The distinctions within *Richter* and *AParty* are the same as the lines between *August* and *NICRO* on the one hand, and *NNP* and *DP* on the other.

The most important common theme in understanding *Richter* and *AParty* concerns the Electoral Commission. Indeed, the single best predictor of the outcome of all six cases is the Commission's stance. In *August*, the Commission did not indicate that making arrangements for prisoners would threaten the integrity of the elections and though it raised the formidable logistical hurdles involved it also undertook to do everything in its power to give effect to the order.[86] It abided the Court's decision in *NICRO*, and the Court's order in that case to reopen the voters' roll for prisoners was made on the back of the Commission's statement that this would be practically possible.[87] In *NNP* and *DP*, as we have seen, the Commission had not concluded that the elections would be compromised if the barcoded ID requirement were retained. But the point is most visible in *Richter* and *AParty*, where it is the key to understanding the Court's decision to accept one challenge and reject the other two. The crucial difference between national and provincial elections is that citizens *inside* South Africa, but outside their province of residence on voting day, could vote in the national election but not in the

[86] *August*, paras. 7, 40. [87] *NICRO*, paras. 49, 68, 76, 78.

provincial ones. Two million people had been in this position in the 2004 elections. If special provision were made for people overseas to vote in their provincial election, then it would presumably have to be made for all these people too, but the Commission claimed it was not possible to do this with the election fast approaching.[88] Giving overseas voters the right to vote in *national* elections, of course, did not pose the same inequality problem, since those inside South Africa but outside their own province enjoyed that right already. There was a similar sort of difference between voting and registration for people overseas. Giving people who were already registered the opportunity to vote overseas did not disrupt the election timetable. Giving people who were not already registered an opportunity to register overseas meant reopening the voters roll. Ordinarily, the roll closes when the President announces the date for the elections, and that point had already been reached. The Commission's stance was that accommodating the applicants' claims would threaten the electoral timetable.[89] The Court's position thus closely tracks the attitude of the Commission.[90] The partnership between the two institutions contemplated in *NNP*, and the deference shown by the Court to the Commission's judgment in that case, is strongly in evidence here as well. It is also important to see the work being done by the Commission in structuring the litigation. A good argument can be made that *Richter* and *AParty* were handled rather more smoothly than *NNP* because the Commission took a stronger lead role in resolving the latter two cases. It actively urged the consolidation of the cases in the Constitutional Court, and welcomed the inclusion of the political parties who applied to join the litigation at that stage.[91] Their participation might otherwise have been thought to raise the political stakes, and make the cases even more of an *Opposition Parties & Disgruntled Expats* v. *ANC*, but the result was something closer to the idealised collaborative model of litigation. The role of the Commission in producing this result, as an independent body focused on electoral realities, should not be underestimated – and this illustrates the wisdom of the institution-building effort made in *NNP* to empower the Commission and bolster its status as a responsible, independent body,

[88] *Richter*, paras. 14, 85–91; see also paras. 75, 80–83. [89] *AParty*, paras. 21–24, 56, 69.

[90] Note that the Court's deference to the Commission's views on the integrity of elections does not necessarily extend to issues less at the core of the Commission's role: see Fowkes, 'Right After All', p. 167 and n. 50.

[91] *Richter*, paras. 6–14.

separate to the Court. And in view of my earlier claims, I might be forgiven for suggesting that the greater electoral confidence and institutional trust that had been built up in South Africa since 1999 also contributed to the more collaborative resolution of *Richter* and *AParty*, and that this too demonstrates the wisdom of *NNP* – since things might have been very different if the 1999 elections had been conducted under a distrustful cloud of judicial intervention.

This institutional concern for the Commission also explains the pattern of a further set of cases where the Court has considered appeals against procedural decisions by the Commission. In *Liberal Party* v. *Electoral Commission*, in 2004, the Court upheld the Commission's decision to exclude a party which had sought to file its election papers 21 minutes after the deadline. But in 2006, *ACDP* v. *Electoral Commission* appeared to reverse course and adopt a substance-over-form approach to the requirements for paying deposits for the elections, ruling that a party which had paid a lump sum sufficient to cover its deposits, but had not paid specifically identified money for the deposit for a specific race, had met the requirement. It is, however, a mistake to read these cases as pursuing inconsistent approaches. The Court's line is simple, and strongly recalls the concerns of *NNP*. It will not override rules in order to permit someone to participate who would otherwise be excluded, because strict application of the rules usually preserves electoral integrity and so better serves the rights to vote of all citizens. Thus the Court will rule in favour of inclusion when this does not threaten the integrity of the elections – as in *ACDP*, where the Commission had taken this position in the Court – and where no purpose is served by insisting on strict compliance, as in *ANC* v. *Chief Electoral Officer*, where a candidate had been excluded essentially because of an (acknowledged) misconception by an Electoral Commission official, albeit one the candidate could have pre-emptively avoided.[92] But otherwise the Court will be strongly rule-bound, as it was in the *Liberal Party* decision. As the Court explained in the fourth and most recent decision in this set, 2012's *Electoral Commission* v. *IFP*, the Commission should not be held to have discretion to make ad hoc condonations of breaches of electoral rules, lest this create unfairness or the appearance of it. Sometimes, democratic rights and values are best advanced 'by the Commission's rigorous adherence to the provisions of the [Electoral] Act'.[93] Indeed, the

[92] *ACDP*, paras. 2, 17–18, 33; *African National Congress* v. *Chief Electoral Officer of the Independent Electoral Commission* 2010 (5) SA 487 (CC), paras. 13–14.

applicant in *IFP* had made precisely the mistake of reading *ACDP* simply as favouring a substance-over-form approach, ignoring the institutional considerations. The Court made a point of correcting this misinterpretation, which bears a family resemblance to the standard misinterpretation of the majority decision in *NNP*.[94]

The Commission is central, but the institutional concerns in the voting rights cases extend beyond it. Concerns for the structure of judicial review are also pervasive. Though *August* is celebrated as a defence of voting rights, it actually turned on the basic general point that rights can only be limited by a law of general application and not by mere omission. The basis for *NICRO*, too, was a standard point of limitations analysis, namely that government bears what the Court has called 'an onus of a special type' to provide justificatory evidence during limitations analysis.[95] The precise ground for rejecting the registration issue in *AParty* was jurisdictional: that it was not in the interests of justice to permit the applicants to come directly to the Court and compel the decision of important issues with little time to investigate and without the benefit of prior ventilation of the issues in other courts.[96] Institutional concerns loom largest here as they did in *NNP*. The Court's view of the right to vote matters, of course, but in none of these cases is it the decisive issue.

Something similar is true of *Richter*, which merits particular mention here because it has attracted no outcry even though it seems as if it should be the target of a number of the criticisms levelled at *NNP*. The *Richter* Court was stuck between two equality problems. Some citizens overseas, and all citizens inside South Africa but outside their province of residence on voting day, were not permitted to vote in provincial elections, but the electoral scheme made special provision for some groups, including government officials who were overseas at the time of the elections to do so.[97] Thus if the Court rejected the claim, the applicants, as citizens overseas, would be treated unequally in relation to groups such as government officials overseas; if it accepted it, then citizens inside South Africa but outside their home provinces would be treated unequally in relation to the applicants. (Recall that the Electoral

93 *Inkatha Freedom Party*, paras. 55, 52. See also *Richter*, para. 83.

94 *IFP*, paras. 23, 37.

95 *NICRO*, para. 34, citing *Moise* v. *Greater Germiston Transitional Local Council* 2001 (4) SA 491 (CC), para. 19.

96 *AParty*, paras. 71, 79.

97 Electoral Act 33 of 1998, ss 24A and 33, read with Election Regulations, GN R12 *Government Gazette* 25894 (7 January 2004), Regs. 9(4) and 12(4).

Commission had indicated that, at the stage at which the case was brought, extending the right to vote in provincial elections to *all* citizens outside their province of residence would 'create very real logistical difficulties'.)[98] *Richter* acknowledged the equality difficulty but decided to make no order on the point – not even a legal finding, lest this prejudge consideration of the matter by another court after the election. *Richter* thus reached a similar result to *AParty* for similar reasons: the issue was complex, the evidence was limited, and the applicants were the authors of their own misfortune because they had waited until very late in the day to challenge legislation in force for years.[99]

However, *Richter*'s facts were a little different. It is debatable whether the right to vote is being limited if one excludes would-be voters who had made no effort to return to South Africa to register nor, until the last moment, to challenge their inability to register to vote overseas (*AParty*). But it does seem at lot clearer that rights are being limited if one permits some people outside their province of residence on voting day to vote in provincial elections but not others, on a basis everyone accepted was at least questionable – counsel for both the Minister and the Commission were openly concerned about the equality issue.[100] Inaction in *Richter* thus looks more constitutionally suspect than inaction in *AParty* – and also looks even further from the bold rights-protecting model than *NNP* is said to be. *Richter*, after all, had rather blunter implications for rights, since inaction in *NNP* left the matter in the hands of other institutions (with the option of further Court action), while inaction in *Richter* meant a final decision that people overseas could not vote in the 2009 provincial elections unless they fell into the existing law's exceptions. The constitutional basis for *Richter* is also trickier, as a result. The Court seems to accept that there is an equality problem, and so its decision not to make any finding to that effect seems to fly in the face of the peremptory obligation in s 172(1)(a) of the Constitution that a court encountering unconstitutional law or conduct 'must' make a declaration of invalidity accordingly.[101] *Richter* bears an important similarity in this regard to the decision in the Langa judgment in *NNP*, which finds a constitutional problem with the government's understanding of the Commission's status but nevertheless does not make a declaratory order. Scholars have not objected to either of these sorts of practical, institutional calculations

[98] *Richter*, para. 90. [99] *Ibid.*, para. 91. [100] *Ibid.*, para. 91.

[101] I discuss the Court's flexible approach even towards s 172(1)(a), the textual *in*flexibility of which makes it unusual in the 1996 Constitution, in Chapter 5.

to decline to take matters out of the hands of other actors– so why do they object to it in the rather milder form of Yacoob J's majority judgment in *NNP*?

It is worth adding, in light of the multi-institutional story told about *NNP*, that the Court found itself in a more difficult position in *Richter* because other constitutional actors had done less work. Parliament's engagement with the issue was obviously patchily inadequate, so unlike *NNP* there was no credible statutory scheme to defer to. As in *August* or *NICRO*, the status quo reflected selective exclusion inadequately justified, but in *Richter* civil society actors had not raised the issue timeously, and so unlike the prisoner cases there was no remedy available that would be practicable in time. This is why the Court ended up awkwardly declining relief while also not being able to declare the status quo to be constitutionally valid. The constitution-building imperatives of the case that reached it were much harder to align.

A final common theme is that while political stories can be told about at least some of these cases, there are good grounds to take the Court's actions interpretatively seriously. That the cases are sometimes decided on technical grounds, rather than the details of the right to vote, may imply avoidance. But as I noted in discussing Bickel, even he does not actually think that the technical devices he advocates using in this way are empty labels. The importance of establishing the requirements of limitations analysis in *August* and *NICRO* is evident. *Richter*'s refusal of a claim on the basis of jurisdiction might also look like a dodge, but the decision spends fully sixty-seven paragraphs on the direct access issue. Some avoidance strategy. The fact that all the cases show similar concerns – and that there are no grounds for thinking that the Court is weakening its understanding of the voting right at the times when it does not act – also cuts against at least the blunter versions of arguments that the Court is being principled in some of these cases and strategic in others. *Richter* is especially hard to understand as deference to the ANC, not only because the Court makes findings both for and against the government, but also because *Richter* was written by none other than O'Regan J. I say this not to suggest that O'Regan J is being caught out in some sort of inconsistency in having a penned a judgment that is similar in several ways to the majority's in *NNP*. It is perfectly consistent for her to believe that she was doing what best promoted voting rights and sound elections both times, just as it was consistent of her to follow the rest of the *NNP* Court on the Commission's independence but not on the issue of liberalizing ID requirements. But the fact that the unanimous O'Regan

Richter judgment shares features with the *NNP* judgment should make *NNP*'s critics take those features more seriously, and accept that such institutional calculations are not necessarily unprincipled strategy.

Another *NNP* v. *ANC*

The final piece of evidence for this chapter concerns another politicized dispute between the parties in *NNP* – and another matter resolved under pressure of an electoral timetable – but in a different legal terrain.[102] *Executive Council* was a standard sort of intra-governmental power dispute: national and provincial leaders disagreed about the validity of presidential actions at the local government level. The issue crystallized into a dispute over whether the authority under which the President had purported to act had been duly delegated by Parliament or not.[103] But the political context was not so standard. *Executive Council*, handed down just after *Makwanyane*, was one of the Court's very first decisions. The National Party (it had not yet added the cosmetic 'New' to its name at that point) controlled the Western Cape province after the 1994 elections, and so the case pitted the NP against the ANC national government at a time when the two parties were still negotiating the 1996 Constitution. It concerned transitional government arrangements that the two parties had been negotiating for the previous two years, which would underpin the first post-1994 local government elections whose proclaimed date was fast approaching. The dispute had grown bitter, and the stakes, at that juncture, were obvious and large.[104] The Court was called upon to adjudicate the matter.

Much can be said about the decision; what I seek to note here is that it is generally acknowledged among scholars that the Court in this case actively sought to give something to both sides. It found in favour of the NP provincial government on the due delegation question, but it offered several olive branches to the ANC, including a careful

[102] *Executive Council*; see paras. 1, 14–17 on its speedy resolution so as not to disrupt pending local government elections, and see also J. Sarkin, 'The Political Role of the South African Constitutional Court' (1997) 114 *South African Law Journal* 134, 140.

[103] For details, see J. Klaaren, 'Case Reports: Executive Council, Western Cape Legislature, and Others v President of the Republic of South Africa and Others CCT/27/95, 1995 (4) SA 877 (CC); 1995 (10) BCLR 1289 (CC)' (1996) 12 *South African Journal on Human Rights* 158.

[104] *Executive Council*, paras. 3, 11–17; Klug, *Constituting Democracy*, pp. 148–50.

acknowledgement of the importance of the national government's constitutional role in provincial and local affairs, and a deferent remedy which gave Parliament time to correct the constitutional defects of its process.[105] It is also fair to say that this is generally accepted as appropriate: it is action in line with a long-standing argument from political science that courts have a power-balancing role in resolving disputes between parts of government. Heinz Klug's well-known analysis of the case is a representative example. Klug sees the Court in *Executive Council* as engaged in 'a judicious style of intervention reminiscent of *Marbury* v. *Madison*', generally upholding national powers while finding against the national government on the particular facts.[106] He notes that the case 'may be viewed as an example of the Court mediating a conflict between different levels of government', but considers its greater significance to lie in 'the Court's exercise of its role as final arbiter in a conflict over the Constitution's allocation of power to decide highly politicized questions'.[107] Klug does not go out of his way to make these points in particularly legal, rather than merely realist, terms, but that is because he does not have to. Whether one resorts to the separation of powers or federalism or some other legal basis, he knows that most lawyers will accept that a court can do this sort of work in this sort of context and that it can take these sorts of considerations into account when it does.

If so, why is it thought legally controversial if this sort of work is also part of what the Court is doing in a case like *NNP*? Klug's analysis is of special interest in relation to this question because he sets up a comparison between *Executive Council* and *Makwanyane*. He notes the 'clear' differences and 'marked contrast' in the tone of the two decisions.[108] *Executive Council* 'involved the allocation of powers between levels of government under an Act negotiated by all parties as part of the transition to democracy'. *Makwanyane* 'involved the interpretation of fundamental rights and the striking down of law and practice that was closely associated with the violations and inequalities of the apartheid era'. 'The salience of this difference', he concludes, 'lies in the distinction between a court's role in the adjudication of rights and in the allocation of powers.'[109] The same distinction, it is evident, is

[105] *Executive Council*, paras. 102–115, 124; see also Sarkin, 'The Political Role', 140–41, describing the decision, significantly for this reason, as 'a well-crafted compromise which ultimately favours the national government'.

[106] Klug, *Constituting Democracy*, p. 150. [107] *Ibid.*, p. 154. [108] *Ibid.*, pp. 153, 148.

understood be salient in a case like *NNP* as well: the Court should not be strategic in a rights case, as opposed to a power-balancing case about federalism and governmental powers.

Given that this argument would probably be received without demur in much talk about South African constitutionalism, it is important that Klug's point is immediately called into question by his own analysis. He thinks that deciding power allocation cases raises the risk that the branches of government will 'ignore or publicly disregard the Court's decision', so caution and strategy is appropriate.[110] But that, of course, is a risk that arises in rights cases too, where the government is usually involved as well and dissent or defiance is obviously also a possibility. Klug also offers the argument that *Makwanyane* was overturning an apartheid-era practice that had been 'laden with racial disparity' and 'a tool used against those who fought against apartheid,' whereas *Executive Council* was about overturning the enactment of a newly-elected parliament flushed with the legitimacy of South Africa's first multi-racial electoral mandate, and a product of the multi-party negotiated transition.[111] As my *Makwanyane* stories will have made clear, I think this sort of consideration is important. But on this logic, the Court needs to be strategically cautious whenever it is tackling policies of a powerful, legitimate legislature, rights case or no rights case (as is evident in the plausibility of realist narratives like Roux's). Similarly, on this logic, it will have much more freedom to act when overturning apartheid polices – again, rights case or no rights case.

These objections are hardly confined to Klug's analysis.[112] They go to the heart of the realist/interpretivist debate. The interpretivist argument here depends on accepting (or expecting) that the Court will consider these sorts of political or strategic factors in non-rights cases, while insisting that it ignore or override them in rights cases. This is why *NNP*, understood as a case demanding *Makwanyane's* boldness in *Executive Council*'s politically trickier context, is viewed as an abdication.

[109] *Ibid.*, pp. 152–53. [110] *Ibid.*, p. 153. [111] *Ibid.*, p. 148.

[112] Instructive examples are to be found even among the more candid engagements with political and structural questions, which tend to cash the point out in terms of federal power disputes, including *Executive Council*, and not rights enforcement: Sarkin, 'The Political Role'; J. Klaaren, 'Structures of Government in the 1996 South African Constitution: Putting Democracy Back into Human Rights' (1997) 13 *South African Journal on Human Rights* 3. Klaaren proposes a structural approach that resonates with the themes of this book; see esp. *Ibid.*, 19–20 and note 34 in this chapter.

A very great deal, then, depends on the argument for why rights cases are different. It is hardly fanciful to think that this argument can be made out – indeed, it probably represents the canonical theoretical position – and the constitution-building account is not an outright rejection of it. But at the end of this chapter, we should be able to see how the argument that rights imply courts renouncing strategy might be qualified without this necessarily amounting to a stark betrayal of rights.

For one thing, we have seen the error of treating any of the voting rights cases as being above all about the content of the voting right. Questions of institutional structures and relationships were key – and that meant a good chunk of the legal considerations in these rights cases looked quite a lot like the considerations in cases like *Executive Council* that the standard view files separately as power-brokering cases. (And conversely, given that *Executive Council* itself is motivated in part by the need to ascertain the legal framework underpinning imminent elections, it itself can readily be understood as a mix of power-brokering case with voting rights implications). For another, we have seen that it is misleading to think of law and politics as always pulling a court in different directions. They can, of course, but whether they actually do depends on which way politics pulls. If a state has contested but sincere constitutional politics, the relationship between law and politics is far more nuanced, and that means that the relationship between rights and other constitutional imperatives is potentially far more nuanced too.

This points us to the theoretical space in which the general constitution-building account can be constructed. But I close this chapter with a non-theoretical question, which is simply this: is an analysis like Klug's, whatever its normative advantages and problems, descriptively adequate? Whatever its theoretical merits, does it *fit*? For we can now see that this kind of analysis rests, to a significant extent, on caricatures of South African constitutional practice. It treats *Makwanyane* as bold counter-majoritarianism, whereas we saw in fact that it was more complex than this: it was a strong rights defence, to be sure, but it was only counter-majoritarian in the sense of going against the views of the majority of South Africans, and was in fact closely aligned with the wishes of the majority party leadership. It treats *NNP* as unprincipled politicking, whereas we have spent considerable time seeing that the case was much more plausible, on traditional legal grounds, than its critics accept and that a great deal of very interpretative construction work was going on in the judgments. And it treats *Executive Council* as astute diplomacy, whereas in fact a great deal of legal work was also being done.

Seven judgments were filed in the case, and there was extensive disagreement about theories of due delegation and other issues – whereas one would suspect that the Chaskalson Court, known for its preference for unanimity, would have produced one judgment if political concerns were paramount. The Court's stance *was* carefully diplomatic, and it *is* once again very plausible to speculate that it was thinking about the ANC and its reaction to the decision, but its work is nevertheless deeply interpretative and is taken seriously as such.[113] No scholar takes *Executive Council*'s due delegation arguments as somehow less interpretatively serious because of the politics of the case. *Makwanyane*, *Executive Council* and *NNP* are much more similar than is currently recognized.

These caricatures are also caricatures of the ANC: as a bystander whose significance peters out after the constitutional negotiations in *Makwanyane*, as a heavy-handed and possibly unscrupulous ogre in *NNP* against whom only the Court an stand, and in *Executive Council*, as the powerful actor whom the Court can find against but must offer judicious olive branches, without adequate recognition that the astute and careful constitutional politics of the Court in that case was matched by the astute and careful politics of the ANC government. It was after the adverse finding in *Executive Council* that President Mandela made the first of his carefully public acceptances of the Court's decision. Scholars *do* recognize this, as we saw, but the President rather than the ANC gets the credit. I hardly begrudge Mandela the praise, but it is a mistake to analyze a party man separately from a party with a long tradition of treating its leaders as subordinate to itself, especially since respect for the courts continued to be a feature of the ANC government after Mandela left it.

We should not miss the inconsistency between the standard view of *Executive Council*, where the astute strategy apparently lay in finding for the NP while mollifying the ANC, and the view of *NNP*, where political pressure apparently led the Court to find for the ANC and resist being seen as the defender of the party of apartheid. Each story sounds plausible enough on its own, but if the Court could find for the NP against the ANC in 1995, we cannot easily accept that it was forced to find for the ANC against the NNP in 1999 – especially given Mandela's pointed acceptance of the finding against his government in *Executive Council*. Witness the fact that in the same nine month period that the Court

[113] See e.g. M. Bishop and N. Raboshakga, 'National Legislative Authority' in Woolman and Bishop (eds.), *Constitutional Law*, 17-45–17-51.

decided *NNP* and *DP*, it decided at least four other disputes about governmental powers that pitted the opposition-controlled Western Cape against the ANC, finding mostly for the ANC national government in one case, wholly for the Western Cape government in a second, and partly for and against each in the other two.[114] And witness also the fact that another of Mandela's famous affirmations of judicial authority arose in the *SARFU* case, in which a judge (an apartheid-era appointee) summoned the President, with few courtesies, to submit to cross-examination. President Mandela quietly complied – and the Court was dealing with the appeals in this matter in the months on either side of *NNP*, with Mandela still President.[115] Even pending my attempt to show that the ANC in general should not be caricatured as a threat, it is hard to accept, in this context, that the justices could have believed that a finding against the ANC in *NNP* would have brought vengeance upon their heads or were operating on that assumption. It is especially hard to accept this when we do not even *need* to try and explain the decision away as a blunt exercise in politics, because, properly understood, it is very far from a blunt failure to be principled.

114 See *Premier, Western Cape*, handed down 29 March 1999, finding for the national government on all but one issue of a dispute over the national regulation of provincial administration; *Premier of the Western Cape* v. *Electoral Commission* 1999 (11) BCLR 1209 (CC), handed down 2 September 1999, finding in favour of the Western Cape on an issue of the number of seats in the provincial legislature, on the basis of a finding made against the objections of the ANC and the national government during the Certification of the Western Cape Constitution (see *Premier*, para. 10; *Certification of the Constitution of the Western Cape* 1997 (12) BCLR 1653 (CC), para. 51); *Executive Council of the Province of the Western Cape* v. *Minister for Provincial Affairs and Constitutional Development; Executive Council of KwaZulu-Natal* v. *President of the Republic of South Africa* 2000 (1) SA 661 (CC), handed down 15 October 1999, finding against the national government on some of the challenges to the new legislation on local government structures and their establishment raised by the Western Cape (and KwaZulu-Natal); and *Ex Parte President of the Republic of South Africa: In re Constitutionality of the Liquor Bill* 2000 (1) SA 732 (CC), handed down 11 November 1999, upholding, in a case initiated by a presidential referral but which saw the Western Cape government opposing the national Department of Trade and Industry, some of the arguments of each side.

115 President Mandela gave evidence in the High Court on 19 and 20 March 1998. The Constitutional Court handed down its first judgment in the matter on 2 December 1998, a few months before it became seized of the *NNP* matter, and held its second hearing on the case on 7 and 10–13 May 1999, a month after handing down the *NNP* judgment. See *President of the Republic of South Africa* v. *South African Rugby Football Union* 1999 (2) SA 14 (CC); *President of the Republic of South Africa* v. *South African Rugby Football Union* 2000 (1) SA 1 (CC).

It is often said that *Makwanyane* and *Executive Council* were a fortunate pair of early decisions for the Court: the first allowing it to trumpet its guardianship of rights, the second allowing itself to establish its credibility as a body that would stand up to the ANC when necessary. This is usually understood as an argument that the legal nature of the cases turned out to be such that the Court could, without bending the law, reach strategically or politically valuable results. But then *August* and *NICRO*, too, are fortunate cases, allowing the Court to assert important structural points about rights review without having to take a final position on the controversial question of prisoners' voting rights. *AParty* and *Richter* also look like fortunate cases (aside from the technical difficulties in *Richter* surrounding s 172(1)(a)). They permitted the Court to vindicate some inconsistent limitations of rights while the strategic weakness of the litigation meant that the Court did not have to consider the more sweeping and problematic relief sought. And, as retold, *NNP* and *DP* might look fortunate too, since the deficiency of evidence allowed the Court to avoid having to decide just how much policy discretion the voting right affords the state.

A lucky court indeed. And yet if it was fortunate to be able to make findings aligned with the ANC position in *Makwanyane* and against it in *Executive Council*; and for the ANC in *NNP* and *DP* and against it in *NICRO*; and fortunate to be able to make findings on the direct merits in *Makwanyane, Executive Council, ACDP, IFP, Liberal Party* and part of *Richter* and *Aparty* and also fortunate to be able to avoid making findings on the direct merits in *August, NICRO, NNP, DP* and the rest of *Richter* and *AParty*, we will see that this is not fortune but careful work; not luck, but a constitutional system being built, across the kinds of cases that arise in practice, by actors with serious commitments to that project. Producing a general account of this sort of activity as legal activity is the task of the next two chapters. But it does not look so hard to call this the work of the law. Indeed, lawyers, and South Africans, might be proud to call it so.

4

The Role of the Court: Standard Conceptions

In 1952, the new German Federal Constitutional Court issued a memorandum called the Statusdenkschrift.[1] It was in part an assertion of independence. But it was also an attempt by the Court to articulate the nature of its own authority, and as such it is an attempt to answer an interesting kind of question. Everyone knows what a court is and does, basically. But if a new court is created to do the new things implied by a new text (whatever those might be), then while everyone knows what a court is, no-one quite knows what this new institution is.

Thus to the German judges in the new institution called a court, for example, its position as ultimate constitutional interpreter meant that it had to enjoy status equal to that of the other highest organs of government, a matter not clear from the text of the Basic Law, and had to have control of its own budget and administration instead of these matters being controlled by the Ministry of Justice. But for present purposes, the particular answer they gave is less interesting than the question itself. It is a similar question to the one confronted in *Marbury* v. *Madison*. In a context in which it had not been settled whether judicial review under a system of constitutional supremacy implied a judicial power to invalidate unconstitutional law and conduct, the US Supreme Court had to answer an institutional question about its own authority, as an inference from what the text said.[2] It similar to the question that László Sólyom found himself confronting as first Chief Justice of the Hungarian Constitutional Court – so much so that Sólyom found his most important source of answers by looking

[1] I was referred to the Statusdenkschrift by L. Sólyom, 'The Role of Constitutional Courts in the Transition to Democracy, with special reference to Hungary' in S. A. Arjomand (ed.), *Constitutionalism and Political Reconstruction* (Leiden: Brill, 2007), p. 289 n. 11. For further discussion in English see M. Hailbronner, *Tradition and Transformation*, pp. 101–02, 192; J. Collings, *Karlsruhe Republic: A History of the German Constitutional Court* (Oxford University Press, 2015), pp. 50–56.

[2] *Marbury* v. *Madison* 5 U.S. 137 (1803).

back to the German Court's Statusdenkschrift itself.[3] The examples could be multiplied, but the point is clear: once we get beyond the fact that the South African Constitutional Court is a court, the same kind of question about its institutional role lies before us, and we have seen in the last chapter how important ideas and expectations about this role can be. In the next chapter, I will be fleshing out how the constitution-building account can be inferred from the constitutional text and from the work that text implies needs doing. But first it is important to work through some existing ideas that strongly influence the way observers think of the Court, to see why the question of just what the Court is and what role it plays is still in need of a more adequate answer.[4]

The Intentions of the Drafters

The 1996 Constitution, like all constitutions, is an incomplete contract: it is an agreement that does not deal with all the contingencies that might arise because of the various costs of reaching agreement on all of them.[5] This is a standard idea in constitutional scholarship, but it might in fact tell us rather less about the role of the South African Constitutional Court than is sometimes thought. There is a common assumption that the

[3] Sólyom, 'The Role of Constitutional Courts', pp. 288–90; on German influences in the Hungarian case more generally see G. Brunner, 'Structure and Proceedings of the Hungarian Constitutional Judiciary' in L. Sólyom and G. Brunner (eds.), *Constitutional Judiciary in a New Democracy: The Hungarian Constitutional Court* (University of Michigan Press, 2000), pp. 93–94.

[4] I discuss several of the arguments in this chapter in more detail in J. Fowkes, 'More Power than Pact: The Over-Emphasis on the Negotiated Origins of South Africa's Constitution' (forthcoming); I do not cite it repeatedly in what follows.

[5] For a survey of incomplete contracting as a concept in economic analysis, see e.g. J. Tirole, 'Incomplete Contracts: Where Do We Stand?' (1999) 67 *Econometrica* 741: 'For lack of a better definition, we will say that a contract is incomplete if it does not exhaust the contracting possibilities envisioned in the complete contracting literature.' (*Ibid.*, 753–54). Alec Stone Sweet, following P. Milgrom and J. Roberts, *Economics, Organization and Management* (Englewood Cliffs, NJ: Prentice Hall, 1992), pp. 127–33, offers a less technically precise but for present purposes more useful definition: 'Generally, contracts can be said to be "incomplete" to the extent that there exists meaningful uncertainty as to the precise nature of the commitments made': A. Stone-Sweet, 'Constitutional Courts and Parliamentary Democracy' (2002) 25 *West European Politics* 77, 90. On various forms of deciding not to decide, see e.g. C. R. Sunstein *Legal Reasoning and Political Conflict* (Oxford University Press, 1996), esp. pp. 35–48; Sunstein, *Designing Democracy*, esp. pp. 49–66; R. Dixon and T. Ginsburg, 'Deciding Not to Decide: Deferral in Constitutional Design' (2011) 9 *International Journal of Constitutional Law* 636.

open-endedness of the constitutional text reflects an intention on the part of the negotiating parties that the Court should fill in what they did not, or what they for contracting reasons could not. Put another way, incomplete contracts often include agreements about how future disputes over constitutional meaning are to be resolved. The common assumption is that the South African incomplete contract includes an expectation that these future disputes are to be resolved by the Court. For example, Richard Spitz states (in relation to the interim Constitution) that the Bill of Rights 'was littered with fudges requiring judicial intervention'.[6] The first four words of the quote are no doubt true, but what about the last three?

It is worth noting that even if the last three words *were* true, that would still tell us rather little about the live questions surrounding the Court's role. It would not, for example, tell us very much about how readily or expansively the Court should fill in content, or how much deference it should give to the views of others in doing so. But the assumption itself is also much weaker than is sometimes thought. It is traditionally given credence by the two examples that are commonly cited in this context: *Makwanyane* and the certification process. In *Makwanyane*, the parties could not agree on the death penalty, so they left the issue open with the intention that the Court would settle the issue. The certification process saw the parties use the Court to solve the contracting problem of how the NP government could bind the constitution-drafting of a future elected and therefore surely ANC-dominated body sufficiently that the NP would feel secure enough to agree to the elections being held in the first place. They drew up basic principles in advance, and agreed that the Court would rule on whether the final text complied with them.

I have already argued that *Makwanyane* is a rather more modest exercise of judicial power than it is often made out to be, and the same is true of the two Certification judgments: the power inherent in the *idea* of a court ruling on whether a constitutional text complies with fundamental principles is an extraordinary one, but the actual exercise of that power by the Constitutional Court in 1996 was quite modest.[7] But that issue aside, the key point is that neither is a very representative example. Both are examples of incomplete contracting only as regards the

[6] Spitz, *Politics of Transition.*

[7] *Certification of the Constitution of the Republic of South Africa, 1996* 1996 (4) SA 744 (CC); Klug, *Constitution of South Africa*, p. 245, referring to the judgment as 'a very limited and circumscribed ruling'.

substance of the issue – the constitutionality of the death penalty, the compliance of the 1996 text with the negotiated Constitutional Principles. Neither is an example of incomplete contracting as regards the institutional issue of the judicial role. It was clear that the negotiating parties wanted the Court to resolve the question of the death penalty, and the whole point of the certification process was that the Court would ultimately be the decision-maker. In relation to *these* examples, the act of leaving open was definitely accompanied by a corresponding expectation of judicial filling in. But we can also see why both examples might be unusual in this respect.

Most of the time, when a constitution leaves something undecided, it leaves it more undecided than this. Drafters do not think about all the issues that are being left open, and they do not consciously decide who will settle all the issues they are aware of leaving open. Furthermore, even to the extent that drafters *do* accept a role for the court as a dispute-resolver, political scientists recognize that there will nonetheless be a perennial contest over how much judicial activity the parties will subsequently accept.[8] Ask an ANC negotiator about the vagueness of the right to life provision in relation to the death penalty, and she would no doubt have responded that the Court would resolve the uncertainty. But ask her about the open-endedness of, say, the provision on single-medium schools (another hotly contested issue, discussed later in this chapter), and she would likely respond that the ANC in government would make the decisions about most of what that provision left open. No doubt, if offered hypothetical scenarios about constitutional challenges that people might bring against future education policies, she would accept that there would be *a* role for the Court here. But she would not have accepted that the mere fact that a question was left open, the fact that it was one of 'fudges' to which Spitz refers, meant the Court would settle it. The *Makwanyane* judgment's reference to the drafting history to establish

[8] The approach in Alec Stone-Sweet, *Governing With Judges: Constitutional Politics in Europe* (Oxford University Press, 2000) offers a typical example. While Stone-Sweet argues that by including rights in their recent constitutional texts, political parties in European countries 'transferred their own entirely unresolved problems' about the meaning of rights and their relation to one another 'to judges' and that this 'transfer constitutes a massive, virtually open-ended delegation of policy-making authority' (*Ibid.*, 58), he also notes the ongoing political contestation over the extent and exercise of this delegation, which he, following Martin Shapiro, calls the triadic model (two contracting parties and a third dispute-resolving entity) – *Ibid.*, e.g. pp. 14–19, 22–25; M. Shapiro, *Courts: A Comparative and Political Analysis* (University of Chicago Press, 1981), ch. 1.

the negotiating parties' intention that the Court should settle the death penalty question remains rare, and the rarity reflects not only a suspicion of originalism, but also the rarity of this kind of clear intention.

There are only straw men who argue that the negotiating parties settled the role of the Court in precise detail. The point of the argument here is not to rebut that obviously implausible claim, but to start seeing just how open the question of the Court's role was left. It is, after all, quite an odd thing to claim that the Constitution leaves a good deal open and undecided, and then to claim – indeed, to *deduce* from this – that the role of the Court is comparatively clear. In fact, the exact role of the Court was left at least as undecided as everything else, and perhaps even more so.

Institutional Thinking during the Transition – the ANC

To see the extent of the uncertainty, it is necessary to look beyond the two examples of the death penalty and certification and examine the views of the negotiating parties in relation to the Court more broadly. The full story of the origins of South Africa's post-apartheid constitutionalism is a rich and complicated one that has yet to be told in full, and I do not take up that task here: the concerns of the present argument are narrower and it is suffices to draw out some important themes.

For its part, the ANC initially had little incentive to engage with the details of the Court's role. As an extra-parliamentary opposition movement, it was the substantive commitments that mattered.[9] At the UN in 1963, Oliver Tambo resisted discussion of the future shape of a post-apartheid state as a distraction from the primary goal of ensuring that apartheid became post. It was enough, he said, that all the major black South African leaders had committed themselves to non-racial equality, and that the Freedom Charter contemplated that 'South Africa belongs to all who live in it'.[10] A contemporaneous ANC discussion document for the UN meeting presciently observed that the NP government would ignore any more detailed proposals, 'an attitude [it] will maintain until it finds itself unable to practice the policy of Apartheid'.[11] Even when the

9 Sisk, *Democratization*, p. 149; Klug, *Constituting Democracy*, pp. 74–76.

10 African National Congress, 'United Nations Must Take Action to Destroy Apartheid' Statement at the meeting of the Special Political Committee of the General Assembly, New York, 29 October 1963, available at www.anc.org.za/show.php?id=4202.

11 African National Congress, 'Comments and Observations on Proposals for a United Nations Security Council Resolution on Apartheid', New York, 1 November 1963,

situation began to change, it remained desirable for party unity to avoid discussion of issues on which, as we will see, there were many disagreements. Rival proposals from the apartheid government made it important to take public positions on the substance of rights (discussed later), but not to take much of a position on the Court's role.[12] It was enough, for some time, simply to commit to an independent court to enforce rights. Everyone knows what a court is.

The results can be seen in the major policy documents of the period. The ANC's 1989 Constitutional Guidelines were entirely silent on the question of judicial review or a constitutional court, stating only that the Bill of Rights 'shall guarantee the fundamental human rights' and 'shall provide mechanisms for their enforcement'.[13] On 21 August 1989, under ANC lobbying, the Organization of African Unity (OAU) issued the Harare Declaration – the last great contribution of Oliver Tambo[14] – which set out plans for a transition and contemplated the creation of 'a new constitutional order' of non-racialism and equal rights 'protected under an entrenched Bill of Rights' with 'an independent and non-racial judiciary', but offered no further detail.[15] The joint ANC/NP Declaration of Intent of 21 December 1991 that launched the first CODESA talks included – only – the statements that 'the Constitution will be the supreme law and that it will be guarded over by an independent, non-racial and impartial judiciary' and that 'all shall enjoy universally accepted human rights, freedoms and civil liberties including freedom of religion, speech and assembly protected

available at www.anc.org.za/show.php?id=4265. Given the similarity in themes to his statement of 29 October, it is possible that Tambo was an author of this document.

12 See also Klug, *Constituting Democracy*, pp. 71–74, 80–85 noting that on both the ANC and NP sides, proposals for rights preceded recognition of judicial review to enforce them.

13 African National Congress, Constitutional Guidelines for a Democratic South Africa, 1989, available at www.anc.org.za/show.php?id=294.

14 L. Callinicos, *Oliver Tambo: Beyond the Engeli Mountains* (Claremont: New Africa Books, 2004), pp. 602–10; H. Macmillan, *The Lusaka Years: The ANC in Exile, 1963–1994* (Auckland Park: Jacana Media, 2013), p. 244.

15 Organization of African Unity, *Declaration of the Organization of African Unity (OAU) Ad Hoc Committee on Southern Africa on the Question of South Africa*, Harare, Zimbabwe, 21 August 1989, clause 16. The relevant portions are reproduced in H. Ebrahim, *Soul of the Nation: Constitution-Making in South Africa* (Oxford University Press, 1999), pp. 529–31. The anti-apartheid movement explicitly adopted the Harare Declaration a few months later: see *Anti-Apartheid Movement, Resolution by the Conference for a Democratic Future on Negotiations and the Constituent Assembly*, 8 December 1989, also reproduced in Ebrahim, *Soul of the Nation*, pp. 456–57.

by an entrenched and justiciable Bill of Rights and a legal system that guarantees equality before the law'.[16]

These documents concealed a good deal of internal ANC disagreement about the role of the Court and the judiciary. There were sharp disputes within the party, for example, over the judicial role in relation to socio-economic rights, discussed in Chapters 8 and 9, or as an agent of change in the private sphere, discussed later in this chapter. But even as the negotiating process moved towards substantive constitution-drafting, the ANC came under little pressure from the other negotiating parties to take more definite stances on the details of the Court's role (a striking point that I take up under the next heading). For its part, the ANC itself had little incentive to press the issue. In addition to avoiding internal controversy, it was of course the party that could expect to control government power in the future, and so questions left open were questions it would usually expect to be in a position to resolve for itself. This, we should note, has particular implications for the issue of the Court as an instrument of social change. As we will come to see in more detail, it is this issue that raises most of the difficult and novel questions about precisely what sort of institution the Court is. But the ANC, as the most important proponent of that change, was of course thinking primarily of pursuing that change via the branches of government that it would control directly. Provided the Court's design would not obstruct that enterprise, the ANC had little reason to try and lock in details.

Thus the focus of the ANC's attention during the negotiations was on the substance of rights as potential fetters on its future choices (discussed later) rather than on institutional details, and the two principal exceptions to this both follow from its concern about future constraints on its operations in government. One was to insist on the creation of a new Constitutional Court, rather than bestowing ultimate authority over the new text on the existing highest court, the Appellate Division, with its bench of apartheid government appointees.[17] That required little interrogation of the Court's role as such. The other was in the context of the application of the Constitution to private law and conduct. The ANC was here responding to proposals that posed a clear threat to its interests. Those who sought to protect the privileged position of the white minority had a reason to try and insulate a private sphere from state action. The South African Law Commission's 1991 proposal for a Bill of Rights, for

[16] The Declaration is reproduced in *Ibid.*, pp. 529–31.

[17] See e.g. Klug, *The Constitution of South Africa*, pp. 230–32.

example, limited the application of rights to legislative and executive acts. It thus precluded rights from being applied to strike down rules of common or customary law that might be discriminatory or serve to protect existing privileges. It also precluded rights from being used more actively to reform these areas of law. Elements within the ANC supported the horizontal application of rights in response.[18] That they settled only for indirect horizontal application of rights in the 1993 interim Constitution was partly due to the micro-politics, but also because the ANC preferred to leave controversial issues to the elected Constitutional Assembly where possible.[19] That body would provide for both direct and indirect horizontal application of rights to private persons.[20]

And even here, at the peak of the ANC's engagement with the more uncertain details of the new Court's role, the result raised more institutional questions than answers. Ensuring that the ANC's change agenda was not stopped at the border of some public/private divide produced a constitution with pervasive application to private conduct. But it did not necessarily produce clear intentions about what this meant for the Court's role. Was it just a prophylactic, an attempt to prevent the text being used to insulate the private sphere of white privilege in the manner contemplated by documents like the Law Commission's proposal? Did it imply an intention that the Court would play a quasi-legislative role to transform the common law? If so, was this role to be mainly about the Court removing apartheid-era obstacles to change, or more positively about the Court itself articulating the nature of that change and pursuing it? The mere incorporation of horizontal application does not answer such questions, nor did the ANC have a clear position on them at the time.[21] The debates within the party over horizontal application reflected concerns, for example, that judges might use rights to interfere with the horizontal relationship between employer and employee and undermine hard-won labour protections.[22] In this area, as in others, our hypothetical ANC drafter may well have expected the ANC legislature to take the lead in transforming the legal system. She would have resisted the idea that pervasive application equalled pervasive judicial primacy. Some of Albie Sachs' early judgments as Justice can be revealing about themes from the

[18] South African Law Commission, Project 58: Group and Human Rights: Interim Report, August 1991, Art 1; Klug, *Constitution of South Africa*, pp. 62–65, 67–78; Klug, *Constituting Democracy*, pp. 86–92.

[19] Spitz, *Politics of Transition*, pp. 271–77.

[20] 1996 Constitution, ss 8, 39(2).

[21] See e.g. Spitz, *Politics of Transition*, pp. 269–70, 273.

[22] *Ibid.*, pp. 271, 359–60.

debates he had just left as a key actor in the ANC's constitutional thinking, and the concerns he expressed in his 1996 judgment in *Du Plessis* v. *De Klerk*, the Court's first engagement with horizontal application, are instructive here:

> Much of the discussion on [horizontal application in the other judgments in *Du Plessis*] seems, in my view, to conflate two issues that should really be kept separate. The one is the question of the scope of [the Bill of Rights], and the other the matter of how the framers intended the chapter to be put into operation. By running the two issues into one, an argument in favour of the broadest constitutional reach is unfortunately converted into a claim for the widest possible judicial remedy.[23]

Sachs J went on to frame the debate instead in terms of legislative versus judicial competence, and to express the primary importance of parliamentary action on many questions.[24] Phrased more broadly, what he is rebutting is the claim that because the ANC drafters made choices for an expansive text, they made choices for an expansive court. This is closely related to the assumption that the incomplete contract of the Constitution contemplated that the Court would fill in its gaps. Both claims are false, and the truth is more uncertain than often seems to be assumed.

Institutional Thinking during the Transition – the NP and Other Minority Groups

If the ANC's position is natural enough, standard political science accounts tell us that the other negotiating parties, as future minority actors, should have been much more interested in the institutional details of the Court. The insurance conception tells us that an independent judiciary is usually the most important guarantee a departing regime can have that negotiated protections will be respected and laws and rights upheld.[25] The traditional idea of the court as a counter-majoritarian protector of rights should hold special appeal for those not in the

[23] *Du Plessis* v. *De Klerk* 1996 (3) SA 850 (CC), para. 176. [24] *Ibid.*, para. 178.

[25] See e.g. Ginsburg, *Judicial Review in New Democracies*, esp. pp. 22–33; J. S. Finkel, *Judicial Reform as Political Insurance: Argentina, Peru, and Mexico in the 1990s* (University of Notre Dame Press, 2008), esp. pp. 13–14, 29–37; T. Ginsburg, 'The Politics of Courts in Democratization' in G. L. Heckman, R. Nelson and L. Cabatingan (eds.), *Global Perspectives on the Rule of Law* (Routledge, 2010), pp. 181–82, 184–85; see also Roux, *Politics of Principle*, esp. pp. 1 n. 5, 29–32.

majority. So why did minority groups not force more engagement with the Court's role?

One part of the answer is that opposition groups seeking checks on the future ANC government only needed a very traditional sort of court: an independent institution enforcing negative rights against the state. This the ANC had already agreed to before the negotiations proper were under way. The incentives reflected in accounts like the insurance conceptions thus mostly led minority parties to focus on the details of substantive rights, and with details of the independence of the Court and the appointment of its judges. While the NP came to concede that a new Constitutional Court would be created, for example, it did ultimately secure an agreement that four Justices would be selected from those already on the bench. Such debates were contentious, but had few implications for the details of the Court's role.[26]

A second reason for minority party neglect of this issue is less obvious but probably more important, and it is again something that court centrism can cause us to miss: several minority groups in South Africa, including the NP, were for a long time primarily focused on forms of insurance other than rights in courts.

Illustrative here is the fact that at one point in November 1993, entirely contrary to what the standard accounts of its incentives would lead us to expect, the NP conceded that the future executive would have complete control over Constitutional Court appointments. The ANC spent the next 24 hours trying to spot the trap before it could quite believe its luck. Back-tracking, driven by a DP-led media campaign and facilitated by some ANC compromises, followed, leading to a less executive-dominated approach that included the agreement just noted to appoint four justices from the ranks of the existing judiciary.[27] But the episode should alert us to the way that the NP was far from fixated on the Court as the future protector of white interests. Its initial concession stemmed from a (mistaken) belief that it would exercise significant power from *within* the

[26] Klug, *Constitution of South Africa*, pp. 231–34; Spitz, *The Politics of Transition*, pp. 201–09.

[27] Spitz refers to this as an example of 'NP hubris', with some leaders having 'almost willed themselves to believe they would continue to be central to the workings of government even after April 1994': Spitz, *Politics of Transition*, pp. 204. On this episode, see also Ebrahim, *Soul of the Nation*, pp. 169–70; T. Leon, 'Etienne Mureinik's Role in Securing and Constitutionalising the Independence of the Universities and Judicial Selection' (1998) 12 *South African Journal on Human Rights* 190, 194–96; Roux, *Politics of Principle*, pp. 166–68.

post-1994 Government of National Unity (GNU). Under the GNU arrangement, winning 20 seats (about 5% of the national vote) in the 1994 election entitled a party to representation in the cabinet and 80 seats (about 20%, a threshold the NP expected to and did reach) to appoint a deputy president.[28] This focus on the GNU is illustrative of a broader NP tendency to think about its future power in terms of structures other than courts.

This is less surprising than it may appear in hindsight. Rights talk and the expansive actions of modern constitutional courts were unfamiliar ideas to a party that had long emphasized parliamentary supremacy.[29] Apartheid had been a legislative agenda, and it had worked to secure white interests by social engineering, by dividing up land and people and power. NP reform proposals took this as their starting point, and the history is important not only to see why the party focused less on courts than we might expect today, but also to start rebutting the persistent idea that the NP 'won' the negotiations and imposed a minority-protecting constitution and court on an unwilling ANC (an argument I discuss in detail later in this chapter).

When PW Botha was elected Prime Minister in 1978, he 'was in a hurry to grasp the nettle of constitutional reform'.[30] But the overwhelming focus of these efforts, leading up to the 1983 Constitution, was on mechanisms to protect white interests by means of electoral mechanisms and the structuring of sovereignty, together with a more inclusive politics. Suggestions for a modern justiciable bill of rights were rejected, and so no major changes to judicial powers were made in the 1983 text. The Constitutional Committee of the President's Council did note at the time that 'the role of the judiciary, particularly in a plural society' was 'of fundamental importance' and suggested it should be considered in subsequent reports, but that was as far as it went.[31] The subsequent failure of the 1983 Constitution led the government to consider rights proposals more seriously, but it did not quell the enthusiasm of policy-makers for

[28] Interim Constitution, ss 84, 88; Spitz, *Politics of Transition*, pp. 87–102; Ebrahim, *Soul of the Nation*, pp. 96, 155–56, 166; Giliomee, *Afrikaners*, p. 643.

[29] A point initially suggested to me by Ian Shapiro.

[30] Giliomee, *Afrikaners*, p. 603.

[31] Parliament of the Republic of South Africa, *Second Report of the Constitutional Committee of the President's Council on the Adaptation of Constitutional Structures in South Africa* (1982), § 10.67, 11.22. Proposals up to the 1983 Constitution went no further than considering the slight expansion of the tiny set of issues specially entrenched in the constitutions of 1910 and 1961 to include the independence of the judiciary and some structural features of the government – *Ibid.*, §9.35–9.36, 9.40.

the idea of power-sharing. This manifested itself not only in the emergence of an interest in group rights, but also in continued proposals to preserve white power by federal or consociational structures.[32] Indeed, apparently similarly misled by expectations about the NP's future power within the GNU, the South African Law Commission seems to have reduced its emphasis on group rights because the commissioners assumed 'that the NP would retain a key role in a future democratic government' and so could protect these interests from within.[33]

The mix of these ideas may be seen in President De Klerk's famous speech in Parliament on 2 February 1990 announcing sweeping reforms. De Klerk was 'one of the most enthusiastic supporters' of the 1983 system of race-based parliamentary representatives and believed late into the 1980s that each racial group 'should have a community life of its own' and be 'able to take care of its own affairs by itself'.[34] In his speech, he accepted 'the principle of the recognition and protection of the fundamental individual rights which form the constitutional basis of most Western democracies', and that 'the most practical way of protecting rights' would be by vesting them 'in a declaration of rights justiciable by an independent judiciary'. This was a reversal of the government's earlier thinking. But he immediately added that the approaches based on structuring sovereignty remained important, that '[t]he formal recognition of individual rights does not mean that the problems of a heterogeneous society will simply disappear', and that a constitutional structure which did not supplement individual rights with systems to protect 'minorities and national entities' would be 'inappropriate and even harmful'.[35] The President's Council's report on structures of government released later the same year repeated many of the themes as the pre-1983 proposals and spent the bulk of its pages on them, though it did also consider a justiciable

32 Klug, *Constituting Democracy*, pp. 72–73.

33 Gilliomee, *Afrikaners*, pp. 623, 676; see also Klug, *Constituting Democracy*, pp. 84–85, noting the shift away from group rights; Saul Dubow, *Apartheid, 1948–1994* (Oxford University Press, 2014), p. 247, noting the ANC's surprise at the Commission's stance.

34 H. Gilliomee, *The Last Afrikaner Leaders: A Supreme Test of Power* (Cape Town, Tafelberg: 2012), pp. 284–91; the quoted text appears at p. 284, and the last two phrases are De Klerk's own, speaking in Parliament in 1986; F. W. De Klerk, *The Last Trek: A New Beginning: The Autobiography* (Johannesburg: Jonathan Ball, 1999), pp. 95, 107–08, 229–37.

35 President FW de Klerk, Speech at the Opening of Parliament, 2 February 1990, reproduced in Ebrahim, *Soul of the Nation*, pp. 70ff.

Bill of Rights and a constitutional court.[36] The NP's insistence on a very decentralized federal system was a key cause of the breakdown of the first constitutional talks in 1992 – the party treated power-sharing as non-negotiable up to that point – and after their breakdown, one of De Klerk's initiatives was to hold a conference on regionalism and federalism.[37] 'Constitutionally-entrenched power-sharing and federalism' were key elements of the party's 1994 election manifesto.[38] Rights in courts were just one possibility for the NP, and often were not its first choice nor something it wanted to rely on exclusively.

Nor was it alone in this. The DP, a smaller white party to the left of the NP, was quite unusual on the early 1990s political spectrum in rejecting consociational arrangements along ethnic or cultural lines, though it did favour federal arrangements on classical liberal grounds as a check on the power of central government.[39] By contrast, the IFP, which would place third in the 1994 elections after the ANC and NP, had supported quite similar consociational arrangements to the NP in the 1980s. By 1992 the party was virtually proposing secession for KwaZulu: it envisaged, for example, that a future South African government would have to ask the KwaZulu authorities for permission to levy taxes there.[40] When the IFP sought something in exchange for its participation in the 1994 elections, it was concessions on provincial authority that it asked for, not on rights or courts.[41] It persisted in this vein even as the drafting of the 1996 Constitution was nearing completion. When the Constitutional Court certified the KwaZulu-Natal provincial constitution in 1995, it rejected a number of elements of it for attempting to preclude national powers in a way inconsistent with the

36 Parliament of the Republic of South Africa, *Report of the Committee for Constitutional Affairs on Decision-making and Conflict Resolution Mechanisms and Techniques in Constitutional Systems* (PC 1/1990), dated 20 September 1990. On the Committee's terms of reference and relationship to the Law Commission's work, see § 1.1–1.4.

37 H. Klug, 'Constitutional Law' (1992) *Annual Survey* 693, 693–95; on De Klerk's treatment of power-sharing as non-negotiable before the 1992 referendum see C. Jung, E. Lust-Okar and I. Shapiro, 'Prospects for Democratic Settlements: South Africa as a Model for the Middle East and Northern Ireland?' (2005) 33 *Politics & Society* 277, 294.

38 T. Lodge, 'The South African General Election, April 1994: Results, Analysis and Implications' (1995) 94 *African Affairs* 471, 484.

39 Sisk, *Democratization*, pp. 141–43, 182–84.

40 See Klug, 'Constitutional Law' (1992), 700–01; H. Klug, 'Constitutional Law' (1993) *Annual Survey* 1, 2–3; Sisk, *Democratization*, pp. 144–49, 184–86.

41 Klug, *Constitution of South Africa*, pp. 30, 255–57; Spitz, *Politics of Transition*, pp. 246–50.

1993 interim Constitution.[42] Similar ideas can also be found among white Afrikaner groups to the right of the NP. This shared support for ethnic autonomy and consociational or federal arrangements manifested in the unlikely Concerned South Africans Group (COSAG) alliance between the IFP and several of these groups at this time.[43] While De Klerk increasingly saw the positions of these groups as hopelessly unrealistic, they saw his as giving in. In the April 1991 words of Ferdi Hartzenberg, a former leader of the Conservative Party (a breakaway faction to the NP's right, which was its chief rival for white power in these years), 'If you are controlled by a majority and your only protection is a bill of rights, then you are bloody stupid.' Accordingly, he insisted: 'We will not build our future on a bill of rights, we will build it on sovereignty.'[44]

The significance of all this does not lie in its ultimate impact on South African constitutionalism, although some traces of it can be found.[45] Its chief significance is to counter the persistent sense that the ANC wanted power and whites wanted rights and so the fact that South Africa today is a constitutionally constrained majoritarian democracy shows the two met each other halfway. The ANC did make compromises, although they were often on transitional matters: the certification process, provision for power-sharing at national and local level subject to sunset clauses, pension guarantees for white civil servants.[46] But a constitutional democracy was long the ANC's starting point, while the NP and most other minority groups started out seeking a very different sort of state and largely failed to get it. The ANC successfully resisted attempts to dilute its majoritarian power, a pattern we will see again when discussing particular substantive rights. This background illustrates how minority groups focused rather less on the court than theories like the insurance conception might suggest, because they were seeking insurance via other mechanisms. Judicial review is sometimes understood in terms of parties delegating

[42] *Certification of the Constitution of the Province of KwaZulu-Natal* 1996 (4) SA 1098 (CC), esp. paras. 8, 14–16, 27, 32–34. The IFP was too committed to the national project by this point to retreat, and secession did not re-emerge as a concern: Klug, *Constituting Democracy*, pp. 172–76.

[43] Spitz, *Politics of Transition*, pp. 212–50; Ebrahim, *Soul of the Nation*, pp. 141–42, 155, 163–64; Sisk, *Democratization*, pp. 229–30.

[44] Quoted by Sisk, *Democratization*, pp. 133–34.

[45] Klug, 'Constitutional Law' (1993), 23–24, 28.

[46] See e.g. Klug, *Constituting Democracy*, pp. 104–07, 119–23; Klug, *Constitution of South Africa*, pp. 23–24, 28–31, 50, 86–92.

to the court a bundle of political decision rights – and several groups preferred, in the first instance, to hang on to their political decision rights and seek to insulate them from the ANC's majority authority.

This also meant that when these groups *did* think about the Court, it was often as an arbiter in power-sharing arrangements. Since those arrangements mostly did not come to pass, this meant minority group thinking about the Court was often concerned with a different kind of institution to the one it would actually become. This was often true even in relation to proposals that, like De Klerk's 1990 speech, contemplated a mix of judicial and structural minority protections. A 1990 Report of the President's Council makes striking reference to the guidance a 'value-tied' model of constitutionalism could offer a constitutional court in its 'law-making function', offering (West) German constitutionalism as an exemplar. The references are, however, tantalizingly brief, and the report's internal inconsistencies on these issues make it clear how much remained to be thought through.[47] The report is also typical in spending most of its pages on what it saw as its internationally groundbreaking thinking about consociational arrangements, whereas entrenching rights in a justiciable bill of rights was just a matter of doing what everyone else was doing: everyone knows what a (rights-enforcing) court is. In a related vein, the South African Law Commission's major report on the Bill of Rights in 1994 includes, amidst chapters of valuable comparative engagement with the substantive detail of various rights, only a few isolated sentences on the sorts of judicial activity their enforcement would require, mostly pointing to the need for judging to be more contextual.[48]

The enquiry into the drafters' institutional thinking about the Court once again ends, therefore, in something of a non-result. That is important – it is important to see how uncertain and open-ended the thinking about the Court was, including among minority groups. But it also means that the search must move to another area often seen as significant. Even if one cannot sustain the assumption that the negotiating parties generally left open textual questions in the expectation that the Court would

[47] The Report treats the court at one point as 'a body outside politics' which should therefore not be used to arbitrate parliamentary disputes, but also seeks to use it to arbitrate disputes between different cultural communities in consociational structures and at another point concludes that a court with the functions it contemplates has a 'function [that] lies partly in the political arena'. President's Council, *Decision-making*, § 2.153, 2.162, 3.7, 3.41.

[48] South African Law Commission, *Project 58: Final Report on Group and Human Rights* (1994), § 5.112.

fill in the gaps, and even if one cannot argue that they had a comparatively completely theorized conception of the new institution they were creating, perhaps we could draw firmer conclusions about the Court from a thing they certainly *did* spent a lot of time on: the rights and other more substantive details that they wrote into the text. In other words, what can we deduce about the Court's role, whether foreseen or not, from the context of the broader negotiated transition?

The Court as an Actor in an Elite Pact

The bluntest conclusion drawn about the Court's role in this context sees the text as an elite compromise and the Court as a pact-keeping agent intended to secure white interests against black/ANC majoritarian power. Michael Mandel argued soon after the 1996 Constitution came into force that elements of it, such as the right to property, reflected efforts by white elites to use the new constitution to preserve their privileged position.[49] Ran Hirschl has made a similar claim, arguing that South Africa is a case of his hegemonic preservation thesis: departing white elites, facing the loss of political power, converted to constitutionalism and rights as a way of insulating their position from majoritarianism. He too thinks the NP 'won out conclusively on the property rights front', and he understands the Court to have become complicit in this elite, minority-protecting project.[50] More moderate, and more plausible, versions of this argument see a more balanced process of compromise. Tom Ginsburg and Rosalind Dixon have argued that the property and socio-economic rights in the Constitution should be understood as 'insurance swaps' – effectively, they are the results of mutual compromises, mostly between the ANC and the NP. This implies, they argue, that the Court should persist in the spirit of the compromise by seeking to give something to both sides in its decisions and should retain flexibility so as to be able to do this; they claim this is a pattern that the Court can indeed often be seen to follow in these areas.[51] But even these more careful arguments are like the others in being perfectly plausible

[49] M. Mandel, 'A Brief History of the New Constitutionalism, or "How We Changed Everything so that Everything Would Remain the Same"' (1998) 32 *Israel Law Review* 250, 277–81.

[50] R. Hirschl, *Towards Juristocracy: The Origins and Consequences of the New Constitutionalism* (Harvard University Press, 2007), p. 95.

[51] R. Dixon and T. Ginsburg, 'The South African Constitutional Court and Socio-Economic Rights as "Insurance Swaps"' (2011) 4 *Constitutional Court Review* 1.

theoretical accounts that, as it has turned out, are an imperfect fit for what has happened in South Africa. Because they have a stubborn hold on thinking about South African constitutionalism and thus about the Court's position and role, it is important to set the record straight.

NP thinkers did indeed hypocritically convert to rights, after long supporting unfettered parliamentary sovereignty, once it looked like they might lose political power. They would have liked to insulate their interests from majority power using rights and judicial review, although as we have seen they would have preferred more direct means. But they mostly did not succeed. The ANC was well aware of the threat posed by the NP's strategy and saw early on, in Thabo Mbeki's 1985 words, that 'We've got to win the battle of ideas.'[52] It was in this context that Pallo Jordan argued in a December 1985 report that the Freedom Charter was 'insufficient' as a blueprint and that the ANC needed to 'adopt a Bill of Rights, setting out in extenso the rights all South Africans will enjoy under an ANC-led government'. Jordan proposed the formation of a constitutional committee, and Oliver Tambo 'jumped at the idea'.[53] ANC policy-makers were also thinking about economic policy, taking pragmatic cognizance of the real economic world in which they would have to take power and the importance of foreign investment, especially as South Africa's economic woes deepened under sanctions and the budgetary consequences of shoring up apartheid. The ANC began meeting with representatives of South African business, including black business, in September 1985 (although after that first meeting, it would not have another formal meeting with South African big business until 1990). These visitors, expecting hardline communists, were surprised to find the ANC representatives referring to countries like social democratic Sweden, already by this point the ANC's major source of funding.[54] Far from economically unsophisticated guerillas, the visitors were meeting veterans of the ANC's longstanding global diplomacy efforts. Several white leaders recalled, in the words of one, how '[w]ith hindsight one realizes how infinitely more accomplished they were as politicians ... [w]e were novices and like

[52] Gevisser, *Dream Deferred*, p. 536; see also Klug, *Constituting Democracy*, p. 76.

[53] Gevisser, *Dream Deferred*, pp. 535–36; emphasis in original. See also Macmillan, *Lusaka Years*, pp. 206, 215–17; Dubow, *Apartheid*, p. 249; Callincolis, *Oliver Tambo*, pp. 576–77; Klug, *Constituting Democracy*, pp. 76–78; and K. Asmal et al. (eds.), *Legacy of Freedom: The ANC's Human Rights Tradition* (Johannesburg: Jonathan Ball, 2005).

[54] Gevisser, *Dream Deferred*, pp. 473, 480, 496–505, 535–38; Callincolis, *Oliver Tambo*, pp. 494, 500–01, 583; Macmillan, *Lusaka Years*, pp. 100, 170–71, 203, 217.

putty in their hands'.[55] Suggestions that white elites duped the ANC in some way are wide of the mark. Indeed, if anything matters were the other way around. Thabo Mbeki was a central actor in these debates, and his biographer titles this chapter of his life 'The Seducer'.

These positions, on both rights and economic policy, were sharply contested within the ANC, and the evolution of the party's views was protracted (and continues today). But both positions were firmly in the ascendancy by the early 1990s. In this light, we can see why the mere presence of rights or capitalist policies did not represent a 'victory' over the ANC by the NP or white business elites.[56] We can also see why it will be misleading to see the Court as a preserver of that victory. But what then *do* they represent? The precise answer differs in each case.

In the economic context, it is true that the interests of the ANC and white capital were in substantial alignment: the corporations prized stability, including financial stability, and increasingly saw the ANC as the way to get it as conditions under the NP deteriorated, while key ANC leaders were pragmatic and recognized that the economy needed to keep running. As a result of this alignment, big business got rather more of what it wanted out of the transition than the NP government did.[57] Hirschl recognizes this when he argues, substantially accurately in this economic context, that black and white elites came to support the same project by the early 1990s (although it is also true that by 1994, Mbeki's relationship with white business had deteriorated dramatically even as

[55] Gevisser, *Dream Deferred*, p. 497, quoting Frederick Van Zyl Slabbert, former leader of the white opposition Progressive Federal Party who resigned from Parliament at the beginning of 1986 to pursue the fight for democracy in what he said were more meaningful channels; see also Callincolis, *Oliver Tambo*, p. 596.

[56] See also Roux, *Politics of Principle*, p. 304.

[57] On ANC economic policy, I have drawn especially on J. Michie and V. Padayachee (eds.) *The Political Economy of South Africa's Transition: Policy Perspectives in the Late 1990s* (London: Dryden Press/Harcourt, 1997); A. Hirsch, *A Season of Hope: Economic Reform under Mandela and Mbeki* (University of KwaZulu Natal Press, 2005); J. Seekings and N. Nattrass, *Class, Race and Inequality in South Africa* (Yale University Press, 2005); S. D. Taylor, *Business and the State in Southern Africa: The Politics of Economic Reform* (Boulder: Lynne Rienner, 2007), pp. 1–45, 152–191; A. Handley, *Business and the State in Africa: Economic Policy-making in the Neo-liberal Era* (Cambridge University Press, 2008) pp. 62–100; P. Green *Choice, Not Fate: The Life and Times of Trevor Manuel* (Johannesburg: Penguin, 2008); Gevisser, *Dream Deferred*, esp. pp. 663–73, 690–94; and D. Fowkes, 'The Democratic Escape from the Populist Cycle – A Comparative Case Study of Five Highly Unequal Democracies', unpublished PhD Dissertation, School of Advanced International Studies, Johns Hopkins University, 2011.

he was implementing the economic policies seen to favour them).[58] This recognition, however, points to the deep problem with Hirschl's thesis. Whatever one thinks of the ANC's economic policies, and wherever one stands on the debate about the role of international actors in the shifts in the ANC's economic policies in the early 1990s,[59] they are not something forced upon the government by a constitutional compromise, and nor are they insulated from ordinary majoritarian politics by the Constitution. The ANC has defended them as its own policies over five election cycles to date, not as a constitutional obligation or negotiated promise it is bound to follow – an implausible position in any case, since it has controlled the seats to amend the Constitution most years since 1994. Closer observers who share Hirschl's ideological view of these policies place the blame for them squarely at the door of the ANC government.[60] Indeed, as we will see, the Constitution has considerable space for redistributive policies and the standard complaint from progressive constitutional lawyers is that the ANC is not doing enough to fulfil these aspects of the Constitution; it is never that the Constitution is holding the ANC back.[61] Whatever this is, then, it is not a case of the hegemonic preservation thesis.

The degree of the ANC's control over the issue is borne out if we turn to examine the property right itself in more detail. Agitated writing on the subject often does not consider the wording, but as it appears in the 1996 Constitution, the right offers a rather weak basis on which to defend entrenched property rights against redistribution. The text makes specific provision for land reform, expropriation in the national interest, and redistributive redress for apartheid practices, and further provides that 'no provision in this section may impede the state from taking legislative and other measures to achieve land, water and related reform, in order to

58 Hirschl, *Juristocracy*, pp. 46–47, 91–92, 95–97; Gevisser, *Dream Deferred*, pp. 646, 685–86.

59 Compare e.g. Gumede, *Thabo Mbeki*, pp. 84–85: 'Never before had a government-in-waiting been so seduced by the international community' and G. Bauer and S. D. Taylor, *Politics in Southern Africa: State and Society in Transition* (Boulder: Lynne Rienner, 2005), p. 269, arguing that the ANC's economic policies were 'homegrown' and not 'imposed' on South Africa by the international financial institutions.

60 See e.g. D. T. McKinley, *The ANC and the Liberation Struggle: A Critical Political Biography* (London: Pluto Press, 1997); P. Bond, *Elite Transition: From Apartheid to Neoliberalism in South Africa* (London: Pluto Press, 2000). Hirschl's analysis (e.g. *Juristocracy*, pp. 95–97) reflects awareness of the ANC's stance, but he does not address the inconsistencies between this and his hegemonic preservation thesis.

61 I discuss socio-economic rights further in Chapters 8 and 9.

redress the results of past racial discrimination', provided that any departure from the section meets the general limitations clause.[62] Quite apart from the ANC's potential amendment powers, as it stands this surely permits considerable redistribution. It should not therefore come as a surprise that just two property rights challenges have ever succeeded in the Constitutional Court, neither of them involving the protection of white entrenched property interests against redistributive policies.[63] The rate of failure of property right claims has been higher than for any other right.[64] But what really crowns the present argument is that we still do not *know* just how much redistribution this text permits. This is partly because the Court prefers to avoid deciding cases in terms of the property right when it can.[65] But it is mostly because the issue has yet to arise. The limits of redistribution under the right have mostly not been tested in the Court. And the most important reason for this is that the ANC has to date chosen not to pursue the sorts of more radical redistributive policies that might produce litigation and defensive invocations of the property right. Thus even though it is true that the ANC started from the position of resisting a property right, while the NP was among the actors strongly arguing for one, that initial pattern is a misleading basis on which to understand subsequent events. ANC economic policy was simultaneously evolving, and in line with this it has chosen in government to stay well within the constraints of the property right.[66]

62 1996 Constitution, s 25; for an overview, see A. J. *Constitutional Property Law* (3 edn., Cape Town: Juta & Co., 2011), ch. 2. The clause thus displays much more use of the carve-out approach than acknowledged by Dixon and Ginsburg, 'Insurance Swaps'; indeed, more than the Zambian clause they offer as an example of the approach – *Ibid.*, 4, 8.

63 *First National Bank of South Africa Ltd t/a Wesbank* v. *Commissioner for the South African Revenue Services; First National Bank of South Africa Ltd. t/a Wesbank* v. *Minister of Finance* 2002 (4) SA 768 (CC); *National Credit Regulator* v. *Opperman* 2013 (2) SA 1 (CC).

64 K. O'Regan, 'Helen Suzman Memorial Lecture: A Forum for Reason: Reflections on the Role and Work of the Constitutional Court' (2012) 28 *South African Journal on Human Rights* 116, 124.

65 Thus one of its most important (though still limited) defences of property rights was not decided in terms of the property right: *President of the Republic of South Africa* v. *Modderklip Boerdery (Pty) Ltd.* 2005 (5) SA 3 (CC).

66 This is a key objection to the argument in Dixon and Ginsburg, 'Socio-Economic Rights as Insurance Swaps'; they recognize the evolution in the ANC's views – see *Ibid.*, 6–7, 12–15, 20; Dixon and Ginsburg, 'Deciding Not to Decide', 647–48 – but not the implication that the ANC came to support *both* property rights and socio-economic interests and sought to strike the balance between these interests itself in policy. See also Roux, *Politics of Principle*, p. 304.

The nationalizations and land grabs feared by some whites have not been prevented by negotiated checks: the government has chosen not to try them in the first place.

Unless and until this changes, the only important sense in which the post-1994 trajectory of this issue continues the lines of the transition is that the original concerns, on both sides, are still powerfully present. Some still fear the onset of more radically redistributive economic policies; others still await them with impatience. This is why debates about the property right have often been about what its presence symbolizes, which is at least one reason why the detail of the wording is often not considered. This is also important to understand the Court: that the right is symbolically freighted with this battle, which the ANC's policies have postponed but have not been successful enough to defuse, has certainly affected its decisions in this area.[67] Having seen what the text permits, we can see why Roux is correct that the Constitution does not require the expensively compensated approach to land reform that prevails; instead, in line with the argument made here, it is a statutory scheme of the ANC government that provides for this. But that does not alter the fact that many people associate this kind of economic policy with the constitutional negotiations. The sense of compromise is perfectly real, and everyone including the Court is acutely conscious of it. But it is the ANC in government, and not the Constitution or the Court, which has struck this compromise between its goals and its perception of economic realities, and it is the ANC's power that maintains it.

This pattern on economic issues can also be seen in the other areas where the white minority sought protection from rights during the negotiations; the main difference is the extent to which the ANC has shared the goals in question. Apart from the death penalty, already discussed, the issues which were responsible for much of the protracted disagreement around rights during the negotiations were Afrikaans language and culture rights, particularly in the context of education; affirmative action, including in the civil service; and the extent of labour rights and management's powers to respond, including the right to lock-out. The final results on all of these issues favoured the position of the ANC.[68] Single-medium schools ended up being mentioned only as one among possible 'reasonable educational alternatives' to 'ensure effective access' to education. The position of Afrikaans-language schools, in other words,

[67] Fowkes, 'More Power than Pact'; see also Roux, *Politics of Principle*, ch. 8.

[68] Klug, *Constitution of South Africa*, p. 53.

was left subject to post-1994 government policy discretion.[69] Cultural and language rights were protected, but their exercise was made explicitly subject to the rest of the Bill of Rights – these are not group rights that may be used to limit the individual rights of others.[70] While sunset clauses did offer white civil servants and their pensions some protection from affirmative action policies, the equality clause explicitly provides for such measures to redress past discrimination.[71] The right to strike, favoured by the ANC, made it into the text, while the employer's right to lock-out, favoured by the NP, did not.[72] These results are not very surprising. The ANC increasingly held the cards by the time the final form of these rights was being determined. Elections had been held, and the ANC firmly controlled government power. It had also secured an arrangement in which a failure to agree in the Constitutional Assembly would lead to a majoritarian deadlock mechanism.[73] Omission or delay, therefore, would allow the ANC to dictate the outcome, and so others had to strike what deals they could while they could. Consistent with standard accounts of the incentives of a negotiating party confident of securing majority power, the final form of the text reflects the ANC's success in resisting constraints inconsistent with its own intentions once in government.

This point about the drafting, however, is perfectly consistent with the ANC later choosing, within the space afforded it by the text, to sometimes use its governing power in a way that was closer to white minority interests than the text strictly required. We saw this in economic policy and land reform; similarly, while the ANC resisted constitutional protection for the right to lock-out, that entitlement was nevertheless granted employers by statute.[74] Conversely, reflecting the same policy freedom, the ANC government has adopted positions that would have been less amenable to white minority negotiators on other issues. Single-medium

69 1996 Constitution, s 29(2); Ebrahim, *Soul of the Nation*, pp. 216–17; S. Woolman and B. Fleisch, *The Constitution in the Classroom: Law and Education in South Africa 1994–2008* (Pretoria University Law Press, 2009), pp. 45–46, 49–51, 60–67. Hirschl accepts that the NP lost on this issue: *Juristocracy*, p. 94.

70 1996 Constitution, ss 30, 31.

71 1996 Constitution, s 9(2). On these sunset clauses, see e.g. Klug, *Constituting Democracy*, pp. 104–05; Ebrahim, *Soul of the Nation*, pp. 116–17.

72 1996 Constitution, ss 23(2) and (3); Ebrahim, *Soul of the Nation*, pp. 216–18; on disputes during the drafting of the interim Constitution, which did offer protection for the right to lock-out, see Spitz, *Politics of Transition*, pp. 357–62.

73 For details of this mechanism, see Klug, *Constitution of South Africa*, pp. 70–71.

74 Labour Relations Act 66 of 1995, s 64(1).

Afrikaans schools have declined significantly (though teaching of the language remains widely entrenched), with the ANC's attention focused on broader problems in education.[75] Similarly, the government has pursued affirmative action policies and redistributive taxation arrangements in a wide array of contexts.

This policy freedom is highly significant for the present argument. Accounts that emphasize the Constitution as a negotiated compromise operate on the basis that majority parties will not pursue policies unpopular with their majority. The assumption in the South African case is therefore that policies suiting white or other minority interests must reflect the intrusion of counter-majoritarian mechanisms like entrenched constitutional provisions and negotiated concessions, and courts charged with policing them.[76] This assumption is false. Other incentives exist, and other counter-majoritarian mechanisms are possible, and both have been crucial in the South African case. The ANC was not motivated entirely by narrowly sectional motivations during the constitution-drafting. It was also partly aiming to draft an admirable new founding document for the country, in line with the party's long understanding of itself as morally better than the NP government.[77] The inclusion of protections against discrimination on the basis of sexual orientation (discussed in detail in Chapter 6) is a powerful example of this. This self-understanding of the ANC as the responsible leader of the country, not just the representative of its constituency, has continued to inform its policy choices in government.[78] Both factors mean that the party's positions do not always follow straightforwardly from what a majority of the country might prefer in an opinion poll. Second, what

[75] For a discussion also conveying the particular impression of the Afrikaner community, see Gilliomee, *Afrikaners*, pp. 658–65, 690–99. See also M. Smit, '"Collateral irony" and "insular construction" – justifying single-medium schools, equal access and quality education' (2011) 27 *South African Journal on Human Rights* 398, 421, noting a 61% decline in Afrikaans single-medium schools between 1994 and 2010 (although a majority had become dual or parallel medium, with English, rather than dropping Afrikaans entirely). For an update on the government's language policy, see S. Woolman and B. Fleisch, 'The Problem of the "Other" Language' (2013) 5 *Constitutional Court Review* 135.

[76] See Dixon and Ginsburg, 'Insurance Swaps', 6 (also noting that this is the starting assumption of insurance theory; see also sources cited in note 25); Hirschl, *Juristocracy*, pp. 41–42, treating insurance theory as 'quite insightful' in transitions, though this should be read in light of his broader hegemonic preservation thesis.

[77] See e.g. Gilliomee, *Afrikaners*, p. 668: 'Like all other leaders of the organization, Mbeki displayed a deep belief in the ANC's moral virtue'; this was also central to the ANC's international branding in exile: Gevisser, *Dream Deferred*, pp. 397, 412–13.

[78] See generally Booysen, *African National Congress*.

has maintained this gap between majority preference and majority government policy, where it exists, is the ANC's political slack.[79] Slack arises to the degree that voters do not punish elected representatives for decisions contrary to the voters' preferences, and since 1994 the ANC has enjoyed this to an extraordinary degree. The party enjoys considerable trust from voters, and exerts considerable effort to maintain it. Plentiful criticism from alliance partners and citizens is much less often accompanied by a loss of support come election time.[80] These two features explain why models based on standard majoritarian incentives, in negotiations or government, are imperfect guides to the South African case.

The central importance of ANC policy positions on these issues, rather than constitutional or court compromises, is further reflected in the way they have subsequently played out in the Constitutional Court. I work through the relevant cases elsewhere; here, it suffices to summarize the trends.[81] The first point, which we can now anticipate having seen the still-untested limits of the property right, is that there are a strikingly small number of decisions on most of these issues. Consider, for example, that it took 20 years for the Court to decide its first case on affirmative action in the workplace, and that it has yet to decide a case on this issue in the other classic context of higher education.[82] The issue may be contentious, but it has mostly played out elsewhere. The second trend – which goes some way to explaining why white minorities have not litigated more[83] – is that the Court usually hews close to the government's line. It upholds redistributive policies and substantive equality in

[79] Political slack is the freedom elected representatives can enjoy, essentially, to make choices without being scrutinized by their voters (because particular choices are secret, or because they are low-profile, or because voters are not monitoring them closely, and so on). See M. E. Levine and J. L. Forrence, 'Regulatory Capture, Public Interest and the Public Agenda: Towards a Synthesis' (1990) 6 *Journal of Law, Economics and Organization* 167. The concept of slack has its origins in economic literature – see A. O. Hirschman, *Exit, Voice, and Loyalty: Responses to Decline in Firms, Organizations, and States* (Harvard University Press, 1970), pp. 10–15 and sources there cited.

[80] See generally Booysen, *African National Congress*. Hirschl recognizes that the ANC's economic stance has been underwritten by its '[m]assive, almost unconditional public support' – *Juristocracy*, p. 96 – but again does not consider the implications for his hegemonic preservation thesis.

[81] Fowkes, 'More Power than Pact'.

[82] *South African Police Service* v. *Solidarity obo Barnard* 2014 (6) SA 123 (CC).

[83] This pattern has begun to shift in recent years, with several groups litigating regularly to assert white minority rights: see S. Budlender, G. Marcus and N. Ferreira, *Public Interest Litigation and Social Change in South Africa: Strategies, Tactics and Lessons* (New York: The Atlantic Philanthropies, 2014), pp. 13–21.

strong terms across these policy areas.[84] In line with what we saw in the property context, the most accurate generalization is not that the Court has been delegated the task of striking ongoing compromises between the interests of the negotiating parties that they, for contracting reasons, chose not to settle. It is that the ANC government strikes most of these compromises itself, and the Court in these cases is more often than not concerned with implementing the government's policies and statutes rather than with reconciling competing rights claims.

Third, insofar as the Court does substantively push against the government's line, it is frequently in a pro-poor, pro-redistributive, direction, albeit not as much as its critics would like. It is virtually never, on these issues, in the direction that white minority negotiators would have favoured. The most significant example is eviction, where (as we will see in Chapters 8 and 9) the Court has been relatively expansive. But its intervention in this area has not been to try and strike a position somewhere between the ANC government's stance and that of property owners. It has above all consisted of enforcing more protections for occupiers against eviction efforts by ANC-controlled authorities acting in favour of property rights and markets.[85] This reflects the degree to which arguments based on negotiated compromises have been superseded, including by the ANC's own economic policy stances.

And finally, insofar as the Court has invalidated redistributive policies or interventions aimed at promoting substantive equality, it has invariably been on procedural or other good governance grounds, accompanied by affirmation of the underlying substantive goals. This is not, in other words, a strategy of using technical or procedural pretexts to invalidate policies whose substance the Court's members oppose. The Justices and the government have usually been in broad agreement on the substance of issues – which is unsurprising if one considers that the ANC had much the greatest say in appointing judges and that those on the bench and in government have often shared historical political backgrounds or commitments.[86] What it reflects is that instead of being

[84] Fowkes, 'More Power than Pact'.

[85] This holds true for the Court's most important cases on eviction protections, which I discuss in Chapters 8 and 9; see further *Ibid.*

[86] Hirschl's work is important in emphasizing the way courts are seldom persistently out of step with the stances of political elites: see Hirschl, *Juristocracy*, pp. 147, 155, 171–72, 201–11; R. Hirschl, 'Reply: Constitutionalism, Judicial Review, and Progressive Change: A Rejoinder to McCain and Fleming' (2005) 84 *Texas Law Review* 471. For a discussion of some of the relevant literature, see J. Fowkes and M. Hailbronner, 'Courts as the

the centre of an ongoing mediation of transitional compromises on contentious issues from the early 1990s, much of the Court's diplomatic effort has been devoted to things whose constitutional inclusion was largely *un*controversial as between the negotiating parties: procedural fairness, the rule of law, the separation of powers. It has been an exercise in holding the ANC to its *own* commitments much more than to negotiated compromises, and it follows the standard pattern of a court holding an elected government to constitutional tenets much more than some South Africa-specific pattern following from the negotiated nature of the transition. The main tension the Court has had to navigate is the *intra*-ANC one between the party's identity as a dominant political organization seeking to concentrate in itself the power to rule, and as a party of national liberation with a commitment to rights, of a different order of moral magnitude to its apartheid predecessor, with the aim of building a globally credible state and delivering social goods to its people. The latter led the party to pass an expansive constitution symbolic of South Africa's return to the global community; the former has meant that the implications this expansive text has for expansive judicial authority have been a perennial source of tension.

The certification process is thus a doubly misleading example from which to extrapolate. It not only overemphasizes the degree to which those at the constitutional negotiations deferred to judicial power or anticipated doing so, but also simply overemphasizes the negotiations. Negotiated concessions do matter – those on federalism are probably the most important example, as noted – and the Court does often take a conciliatory stance when it engages with these controversial issues, as is reflected, for example, in its respectful statements on the value of the Afrikaans language and culture in judgments on single-medium

Nation's Conscience: Empirically Testing the Intuitions Behind Ethicalization' in S. Vöneky et al. (eds.), *Ethics and Law: The Ethicalization of Law/Ethik und Recht: Ethisierung des Rechts* (Heidelberg: Springer, 2013). On judicial biographies of the South African justices over the bulk of the period considered by this book, see Roux, *Politics of Principle*, esp. ch. 5. I do not consider in detail the nuances of the appointment story in recent years – see e.g. R. Calland, *The Zuma Years: South Africa's Changing Face of Power* (Cape Town, Zebra Press, 2013), ch. 11 – except to note that insofar as the government may be seeking to appoint more deferent judges, this reflects that the disagreement is often not so much about the substance of the issues as it is about the power of the government as opposed to the court to decide matters. This will be a regular theme in subsequent chapters.

schools.[87] But to a degree that might seem surprising, the key to understanding the Court's role in South Africa's post-apartheid constitutionalism does not lie in the celebrated negotiated process that produced South Africa's constitutions. It is only if we engage with the years before and after the transitional moments that received so much international attention, and thus consider political events other than those crystallized in the text, that we can appreciate the true context of the Court's work.

Post-Apartheid Judging and Transformative Constitutionalism

The final approach considered here is the attempt to deduce an account of the Court's role from the text and the broader idea of the constitutional project in which the Court is a participant. In South Africa, this exercise is associated, above all, with the concept of transformative constitutionalism. The concept stands for very important things and I am more sympathetic to this way of thinking than the others in this chapter (this book could be viewed as an account of transformative constitutionalism in practice). But, at least as the concept is used in South African constitutional talk, it can also mislead us in ways that we must guard against.[88]

At its simplest, transformative constitutionalism has clear conceptual edge. It points to the considerable textual evidence that the 1996 Constitution aims to be a blueprint for a new society and a powerful engine for change to realize that vision. It understands this vision in contrast to a more traditional kind of constitutionalism focused on negative rights and checking the state.[89] In turn, this implies that a transformative court is

[87] See *Ex Parte Gauteng Provincial Legislature: In re Dispute Concerning the Constitutionality of Certain Provisions of the Gauteng School Education Bill of 1995* 1996 (3) SA 165 (CC), esp. the judgments of Sachs J at paras. 47–49, 74, and Kriegler J, paras. 38–43, the latter being written symbolically in Afrikaans.

[88] I discuss the arguments in this section in more detail in J. Fowkes, 'Two Concepts of Transformative Constitutionalism' (forthcoming).

[89] This approach takes as its starting point the claim that '[t]he South African Constitution is *different* – it is a transformative constitution': Davis and Klare, 'Transformative Constitutionalism', 403, 404. It proceeds by understanding transformative constitutionalism in terms of what it is not or what it rejects. See e.g. Klare, 'Legal Culture and Transformative Constitutionalism' (distinguishing liberal and post-liberal constitutionalism); D. Davis, 'Transformation and the Democratic Case for Judicial Review: The South African Experience' 5 *Loyola University Chicago International Law Review* 45 (2007–2008) (distinguishing negative, preservative constitutionalism and transformative constitutionalism); S. Sibanda, 'Not Purpose-Made! Transformative Constitutionalism, Post-Independence Constitutionalism and the Struggle to Eradicate Poverty' (2011) 22

one that embraces its role as an agent of change, of legal reform and of the pursuit of social justice. A court that considers itself confined to more traditional tasks or acts with indifference or hostility to the project of social change will thus be failing in its constitutional duty. This is a powerful and important idea in post-apartheid South Africa. Its power, however, is confined to a particular target. It tells us that judges should pursue change as a legitimate and important part of their legal role, and so it is powerfully applicable to those who resist that idea. But it does not itself tell us much about how a judge who does *not* resist that idea should go about deciding *what* change to pursue, or how, or when. It is thus entirely convincing when deployed against judges and others who are declining for whatever reason to move beyond the old ideas of law and judging – and this, unfortunately, remains a perfectly real category of legal professionals in South Africa – but, at the same time, is almost entirely beside the point in relation to the judge who has already grasped the imperative to change and is grappling with the details. In that situation, the concept is useful, at most, as a goad or a heuristic.

In this respect, the way this simplest concept of transformative constitutionalism is deployed is similar to simple arguments from apartheid judging. Arguments about what post-apartheid judges and lawyers must do to avoid being complicit in injustice as apartheid-era judges and lawyers were are naturally powerful in post-1994 South Africa. What, then, did apartheid judges and lawyers do that their post-apartheid successors must avoid? The prevailing diagnosis is a persistent tendency to uphold or condone a whole gamut of injustices while paying them little attention, instead focusing throughout on technical legal reasoning about jurisdiction or the separation of powers or fine points of doctrine. This, in turn, is usually blamed on crude positivist or formalist approaches to law, excessive deference to parliament and 'executive-mindedness', and a tendency to abstract from moral concerns, human rights and social context.[90] By implication, then, *post*-apartheid judges should do the opposite and be bold opponents of injustice, driven by moral values and rights and social awareness. Like the simple concept of transformative constitutionalism, this is an important and powerful

Stellenbosch Law Review 482 (distinguishing orthodox or liberal democratic constitutionalism and transformative constitutionalism). This distinction is only a starting point for these authors' more sophisticated analysis, but the simplest usage is important in general constitutional talk: see further Fowkes, 'Transformative Constitutionalism'.

90 For discussion, see Fowkes, 'Apartheid Judging' and sources there cited.

counter to judges who cannot see any way to judge except the old ways, and who are dissuaded from being bold agents of change because they think it is incompatible with ideas of judging and law, or with professional habit. But, also like the simple concept of transformative constitutionalism, it can be entirely beside the point when confronting a different sort of judge who decides for different reasons that restraint is called for in a given case. This possibility arises especially because the spirit of criticism directed at apartheid judges – judges should do whatever they can within legal bounds to combat injustice – came from a society where the state was positively bent on an unjust agenda and where the judiciary was as a result often the only hope for justice, short of extra-legal activity. In *that* context, the sort of institutional calculations we saw in the previous chapter are often empty: any judicial resistance, whatever the concerns, will probably be better than no action at all. But in a post-apartheid society where the government pursues a much more just agenda (though of course not always, and not always successfully), that picture is much more complicated, and so too, therefore, is the argument for judges to do all they can.

One can naturally respond by trying to make these simple arguments less simple. Much valuable writing aims to spell out the concept of transformative constitutionalism in more detailed ways, or to critique it (although this has been done rather less in relation to arguments from apartheid judging). I engage with the results of this work throughout this book, which can itself be thought of as an exercise of that kind. But I have spoken about the simplest versions of these ideas because that is often how they are used in talk about South African constitutionalism. Even writing that offers more nuance tends much of the time to be cited as authority for these simpler conclusions and for the critical attitude it they implies we should adopt towards more restrained judicial activity. Transformative constitutionalism and post-apartheid judging, as ideas, spend most of their time being deployed against things that are seen as failing to transform. It is therefore easy for those who use these ideas to divide the judicial world into the part that is bold and creative and acts expansively in the interests of social justice, and that part that is not these things, and to label the one as transformative, properly post-apartheid constitutionalism and the other as its lamentable betrayal. It is also easy, for those who take a more generally sceptical view of the current record, to draw the same division between a bold constitutional idealist view of what judging could be, and the current practice. But the danger is that they also make it deceptively easy to lump together a judge who is technical and deferent and restrained in a particular case because she considers herself professionally unable or personally disinclined to do more, and the judge who is these things in a particular case because she thinks this is the best way, in that case, to further the cause of the new constitutional project. Thus I would argue that both the majority and the minority in *NNP* deserve to be acknowledged and debated as competing exercises in transformative constitutionalism. But because the majority does things superficially associated with the apartheid-era picture and not things associated with the simple concept of transformative constitutionalism, it gets excluded from the debate.

If we rule out restrained, deferent or technical decisions in this way, we risk entirely begging the question. We will purport by conceptual reflex to diagnose cases as failures to pursue change when they really stand or fall on the complex issue of whether the judge has picked the best *way* to pursue change – a question usually heavily about politics, economics, science, public administration or other technical, practical matters, which the concept of transformative constitutionalism, on its own, has no resources to answer. Put another way, we can rebut blunt failures with simple concepts – and that is important because blunt failures are sadly real – but we are in danger of making large mistakes if we are not careful to upgrade the sophistication of our concepts when dealing with more sophisticated judging.

It may seem obvious enough, even truistic, to argue that sometimes judging will involve flexibility and various degrees of boldness. Those who make sophisticated arguments about transformative constitutionalism certainly do not understand themselves to be making arguments that rule out the sorts of possibilities I have been talking about. Davis and Klare, for example, the most cited scholars in this area, accept that their exhortations about how judges under the 1996 Constitution are supposed actively to reform the common and customary law do not 'banish pre-transition values' from this development, that '[i]ndividualist values (autonomy, conscience, privacy, self-determination) endure in the new constitutional dispensation', and that '[t]ransformative methodology is attentive to the values of stability, predictability and administrability'.[91] The most nuanced understandings of transformative constitutionalism in the transition to a post-apartheid state understand the practice of law in this context as a balance of stability and change, activity and restraint.[92]

[91] Davis and Klare, 'Transformative Constitutionalism', 412.

[92] I discuss this scholarship in Fowkes, 'Transformative Constitutionalism'.

That this work on transformative and post-apartheid constitutionalism does not *mean* to rule out more restrained approaches is one obvious reason why it is problematic if these concepts get used lightly to do just that in constitutional talk.

But furthermore, while this sophisticated scholarship does not deny the arguments I have been making, it is nevertheless usually concerned to insist on the bolder approaches. There are several reasons for this. Scholars, not unreasonably seeing the insufficiency of change as the main problem, are inclined to focus on that. They are also perhaps disinclined to make arguments that might provide cover for those who are unwilling to change. Insisting that a transformative judge can be restrained no doubt facilitates restraint borne of other motivations as well, and dilutes sharp challenges to restraint designed to shake a legal culture that prizes it too highly.[93] But strategy is not, I believe, the whole story. When we want to move beyond the simplest ideas of transformative and post-apartheid judging, we naturally draw on prevailing understandings of rights and courts and justice and the South African political context. Scholarship that fleshes out these ideas therefore tends to draw on content with the general biases I discuss in this book. It is content that tends to be court centric and bullish about judicial action, and to be sceptical about the constitutional contributions of other government institutions or at least not to pay all that much attention to them. It lends itself to equating an imperative to change with an imperative for bold judicial-led change, and to equating expansive constitutionalism with expansive judicial action. If one fleshes out ideas of transformative constitutionalism and post-apartheid judging using this sort of content, then even nuanced versions of the argument will tend not to *emphasize* or *insist* that more restrained behaviours find a legitimate place in the transformative judge's toolbox, albeit that they do not deny that place either. Even nuanced arguments, then, will readily support conclusions that look quite a lot like the simplest ideas of transformative constitutionalism. More judicial work to produce more change will seem the overwhelming priority, and the recognition that restraint has a place too will be easy to push to one side, along with distinctions about the

[93] For concerns about such limits, including internally to the concept of transformative constitutionalism, see generally M. Pieterse, 'What Do We Mean When We Talk About Transformative Constitutionalism' (2005) 20 *SA Public Law/SA Publiekreg* 155; Sibanda, 'Not Purpose-Made!'; this concern is also central to the work of Davis and Klare cited previously.

different reasons judges may have for being restrained I have just been insisting on. By the same token – and here the dominant view generates its own momentum – this view of the powerful ideas of transformative constitutionalism and post-apartheid judging will reduce the space for arguments about trust, and for empirical evidence that trusting the ANC is not always naïve, which might serve to bring out other aspects of what these ideas can properly entail. This is what has happened to *NNP*, as we saw.

If the arguments of this book are correct, therefore, it will be important to exercise care when using concepts like 'transformative constitutionalism' and when encountering their use by others. That the concept has nuance might be obvious as a matter of principle, but this will need assertion against a dominant scholarly usage that may sideline nuance in its (praiseworthy) efforts to dislodge a hegemonic target of its own. If we do this, we may be too quick to prescribe bold, court-led options when they might not be the best way, in a particular case, to further the cause of transformative constitutionalism. We risk misunderstanding judges who are more alive to other options, and risk missing opportunities to assist them with the difficult decisions they are grappling with. We therefore risk being counter-productive. What lies at the heart of transformative constitutionalism is too important not to challenge those who fail to take it seriously. But it is also too important for us to risk blinding ourselves by mere conceptual looseness to things that are and have been crucial tools in the pursuit of constitutional change in South Africa.

Bridge-Building

In this chapter, I have discussed a number of different perspectives from which South African judicial activity in general and the Constitutional Court in particular are commonly viewed. We have seen that while they all have some explanatory power, this is often much less than is sometimes claimed or assumed, and the perspectives can easily mislead us if we are not careful to observe their limitations.

If we stop to think about it, it may seem rather odd to find that deep and prevalent ideas are sometimes rather irrelevant to the Court's practice. There is more than one cause: the degree of international attention paid to a few years in the mid-1990s has had a distorting effect on assessment of the transition, for example. But ultimately, in my view, this situation is due to the position I outlined in Chapter 1. These accounts and ideas are plausible and sometimes normatively appealing views of constitutional activity that just turn out, to varying degrees, to be imperfect fits for the South Africa case. That this has gone more unnoticed than one might expect also follows from the argument of Chapter 1: if I am using the wrong ideas, but believe that it is the world that is wrong, then the fact that the world does not fit the ideas will seem like a reason to insist on them all the more strongly, not a reason to reconsider them. If the Court – obviously – should articulate the content of rights, then institutional questions about what other actors might also be able to do are easily glossed over in favour of the substantive question of what that content should be. If the Court – obviously – should do everything it can to promote rights, then the question of what it could do is the focus, not what other institutions are doing do, or could do, or might be able to do better. The fact that questions about the Court's role in relation to other institutions have not forced themselves into the discussion more often reflects a deep court centrism, and often also a distrust of more directly political institutions.

Nowhere is this glossing over of institutional considerations more apparent, and more overlooked, than in South Africa's main constitutional metaphor.[94] Metaphors can be telling things, and the ubiquitous image of the constitution as a bridge is an image all about the past and the destination, about transformation and moving away from apartheid, a single glorious span that completely elides any notion of separate institutional roles. It is well known that the image was used in the text of the *interim* Constitution (though as an image in South African constitutionalism it actually pre-dates that text as well).[95] But what that interim span represented was the work of several years of negotiations,

[94] L. Pretorius, 'A response to Professors Michelman and Van der Walt' (1998) *Acta Juridica* 282, 283–86; A. J. van der Walt, 'Dancing with Codes – Protecting, Developing and Deconstructing Property Rights in a Constitutional State' (2001) 118 *South African Law Journal* 258; H. Botha, 'Metaphoric Reasoning and Transformative Constitutionalism' (Part 1) (2002) *Tydskrif vir die Suid-Afrikaanse Reg* 612; (Part 2) (2003) *Tydskrif vir die Suid-Afrikaanse Reg* 20; H. Botha, 'Freedom and Constraint in Constitutional Adjudication' (2004) 20 *South African Journal on Human Rights* 249; W. le Roux, 'Bridges, Clearings and Labyrinths: The Architectural Framing of Post-Apartheid Constitutionalism' (2004) 19 *SA Public Law/SA Publiekreg* 629.

[95] Interim Constitution, Postamble: 'This Constitution Provides a Historic Bridge . . . '; E. Mureinik, 'A Bridge to Where? Introducing the Interim Bill of Rights' (1994) 10 *South African Journal on Human Rights* 31. The bridge imagery pre-dates the 1993 text by at least ten years: see the evaluation of the 1983 Constitution by F. de Villiers (ed.), *Bridge or Barricade? The Constitution – A First Appraisal* (Johannesburg: Jonathan Ball, 1983), and in particular the contribution by L. Schlemmer, 'Bridges That Have to Be Built', *Ibid.*, p. 63: 'What are the minimum requirements for a transitional constitution? . . . First, a constitution must start to build bridges across the basic conflicts in our society.'

an exercise in institutional and political co-ordination by many actors of which the court was only one, and by no means the most important. Those may have been special times, but it is a mistake to assume that producing future change by constitutional means will be sharply different in these respects. If the interim Constitution, with its limited life and narrow purposes, was a bridge, then the 1996 text, intended to endure, may be better thought of as a guide to bridge-building, and each building exercise will entail the kinds of work by multiple actors that the first great crossing did, albeit of course not always to the same degree. Oversight of such constitutional activity will be heavily an exercise in institutional co-ordination. The image of the bridge does valuable work as a constant reminder of past wrongs and the fine goals ahead. But if we do not pay attention to the court's role as one institution among many we cannot be sure that we will be working towards that hopeful destination in the best possible way.

5

The Role of the Court: Constitution-Building

If the approaches of Chapter 4 are imperfect guides to the Court's institutional role, how can we improve? As previous chapters have noted, there already exists a substantial body of scholarship, often critical of the Court, that aims to rethink specific aspects of its role and ways of operating. Among the more important innovations this scholarship proposes are the increased use of the direct access procedure (making the Court less an appeal court and more a constitutional forum separate from the ordinary judicial hierarchy);[1] a creative, expansive approach to remedial jurisdiction (reflecting a concern with implementation going well beyond the usual adjudicative function);[2] and a maximalist approach to interpretation that favours deep, broad articulations (reflecting a desire for the court to be more legislative, in the name of offering greater guidance and protection, and sometimes also in the name of provoking more dialogue and debate)[3]

[1] J. Dugard, 'Courts and the Poor in South Africa: A Critique of Systemic Judicial Failures to Advance Transformative Justice' (2008) 24 *South African Journal on Human Rights* 214; J. Dugard, 'Judging the Judges: Towards an Appropriate Role for the Judiciary in South Africa's Transformation' (2007) 20 *Leiden Journal of International Law* 965; J. Dugard and T. Roux, 'The Record of the South African Constitutional Court in Providing an Institutional Voice to the Poor' in R. Gargarella, P. Domingo and T. Roux (eds.), *Courts and Social Transformation in New Democracies: An Institutional Voice for the Poor?* (Hampshire: Ashgate, 2006); J. Dugard, 'Court of First Instance? Towards a Pro-Poor Jurisdiction for the South African Constitutional Court' (2006) 22 *South African Journal on Human Rights* 261; L. Seafield, 'South Africa: The Interdependence of All Human Rights' in A. A. An-Na'im (ed.), *Human Rights under African Constitutions: Realizing the Promise for Ourselves* (University of Pennsylvania Press, 2003), pp. 322–23, 334–35.

[2] See generally Bishop 'Remedies'; I return to this theme in later chapters.

[3] Important contributions here include Klare, 'Legal Culture'; Davis, *Democracy and Deliberation*; Van der Walt, 'Dancing with Codes'; Botha, 'Metaphoric Reasoning'; Botha, 'Freedom and Constraint'; Van der Walt, *Law and Sacrifice*; Woolman, 'Amazing Vanishing Bill of Rights'; Davis and Klare, 'Transformative Constitutionalism'; David Bilchitz, 'Does Sandra Liebenberg's New Book Provide a Viable Approach to Adjudicating Socio-economic Rights?' (2011) 27 *South African Journal on Human Rights* 546; Woolman, *Selfless Constitution;* see further Chapter 9.

and/or favours more candidly political judgments (on the grounds that if judges are expected to more open about their political motivations they will be forced to confront them and their implication that judges create law, and this will be good both for transparency and because it will challenge a traditionalist legal culture's suspicion of this lawmaking role).[4]

These proposals all represent attempts to respond to the kind of question I identified in the previous chapter: yes, this is a court, but exactly what sort of institution should it be? They also all rest on practical judgments about what will best give effect to the Constitution in South African society, in line with what I said in Chapter 2 about the Court's task of making the constitution work. In simple terms, these proposals all depend on judgments, informed by social and political factors, about the effects that their adoption will have. Arguments about maximalism, for example, are often disagreements about effects: if the court speaks more, will this prompt debates or foreclose them, produce progressive change or mistakes and backlash?[5] Arguments for more candidly political judgments rest, inter alia, on claims that abandoning the traditional foundations of legal legitimacy in South African society will not have net deleterious effects on the Court's status.[6] And so on. A final thing that is true of all these proposals is that those who make them believe that judges should be engaging all these questions – implying that judges should be in the business of making judgments about the consequences of possible actions in light of social and political and practical factors. Presumably if judges should adopt the most pro-poor procedures or the most effective remedial responses, then they will have to be constantly making practical judgments about what fits the bill.

[4] Most notably Klare, 'Legal Culture' esp. 163–66; see also e.g. Pieterse, 'Transformative Constitutionalism'; Sibanda, 'Not Purpose-Made!'.

[5] In addition to the sources cited in note 3, see also the terms of the debate over minimalism between R. Dworkin, 'The Order of the Coif Lecture: In Praise of Theory' (1997) 29 *Arizona State Law Journal* 353 and C. R. Sunstein, 'The Order of the Coif Lecture: Response: From Theory to Practice' (1997) 29 *Arizona State Law Journal* 389; see also Sunstein, 'Problems with Minimalism'.

[6] In their debate over whether judges under a transformative constitution should be candidly political, both Roux and Klare recognize that this could be risky given that it clashes with established notions of judicial legitimacy in the South African system; the difference is only that Roux thinks this is a decisive objection against the idea: see Klare, 'Legal Culture', p. 166; Roux, 'Transformative Constitutionalism', 267–69, 281–82; Roux 'Democratic Rights Jurisprudence', 58–59. See also D. Davis, 'Transformation: The Constitutional Promise and the Reality' (2010) 26 *South African Journal on Human Rights* 85, 100 n. 60 (noting that a more detailed reply to Roux is forthcoming).

The body of scholarship that offers these proposals, therefore, represents just the sort of rethinking of the judicial role that I believe is necessary, and I am sympathetic to a number of its proposals and concerns.[7] If I have an objection to this work as a body, it is that its creativity is not always aimed at the real tasks that have lain before the Court. In this chapter, I refocus this sort of institutional imagination on the picture of the Court's activity that has been emerging so far in the book.

The Constitution-Building Account and Newness

Key to understanding the Court's work is the idea of *newness*.[8] We can imagine a hypothetical stable and settled constitutional system, one in which the constitution is old and familiar and where no major social changes have raised questions about what the old constitution means in a new kind of society; one in which everyone is mostly accustomed to complying with the constitution and keeping to its well-worn paths. In such a society, any operative part of the constitution will be associated with familiar understandings, settled expectations, an existing infrastructure with procedures and officials for its enforcement, and so on. For a constitutional court charged with enforcing a text in this context, the tasks of constitutional design and giving effect to that design represent largely completed work. When a judge resolves a case, she will need to give little or no thought to larger institutional questions or how to give effect to her order beyond getting the familiar functionary to put it in the proper file. The judicial role would consist almost entirely of the adjudicative function emphasized in traditional accounts of the separation of powers.

The more we move along the spectrum towards more unsettled, unstable constitutional systems, the less all this is true, and in such systems I describe the law as displaying characteristics of *newness*. Law that is new in this sense is law that is not accompanied by settled understandings, familiar expectations and institutional frameworks with established procedures and officials who are accustomed to them.

[7] See J. Fowkes, 'How to Open the Doors of the Court – Lessons on Access to Justice from Indian PIL' (2011) 27 *South African Journal on Human Rights* 434; Fowkes, 'Civil Procedure'; Fowkes, '*Maphango*'.

[8] See also J. Fowkes, 'Normal Rights, Just New: Understanding the Judicial Enforcement of Socio-economic Rights' (forthcoming).

This is a matter of degree. For example, even familiar laws with established infrastructures will display some characteristics of newness if the aspect of society to which they apply changes in some significant way – the classic situation in which the law evolves in response to changing social needs or views. In South Africa, where the Constitution self-consciously goes out ahead of society and leaves many of the implications of this to be worked out, constitutional law is often a great deal newer than this. And in a hypothetical maximally new system, a judge asked to enforce a piece of text would be unable to take for granted everything that the judge in the hypothetical maximally settled system can assume when she simply hands her judgment to the clerk. The responsibility of enforcement will necessarily implicate large questions of the constitutional design and how effect is to be given to it and by whom, and these questions would dominate any act of adjudication. To the degree that aspects of a particular legal system are new, its enforcement will tend to involve tasks beyond the traditional adjudicative function and the role of the Court charged with enforcing the text will require rethinking accordingly. Newness, finally, is a state that can shift over time. It denotes a contingent property of social understandings and structures and processes, and so any institution or person can do work to try and make an idea more established and less new. New legal protections can become settled and entrenched, and their judicial enforcement can become easier and more routine, but this is not inevitable. The work can go undone, or it can fail and the point can stay unstable and contested, or new social needs or forces can re-unsettle a point that was becoming less new.

The best way to understand constitution-building, in a legal system like South Africa's that has displayed considerable (though far from total) newness, is in terms of this notion of doing judicial work in a context where law is often significantly new but can be made less so. The degree to which ideas display newness will be crucial to how difficult a judicial task their enforcement represents. But at least as crucial will be the question of how much support the Court enjoys when it must confront newness. The presence of other actors, inside or outside government, whose efforts can assist the Court in its work can transform the calculus of judicial action, because the real difficulties often come when a court must confront newness *unilaterally*.

Considerations relevant to when the court must confront newness and not, and when it must confront newness unilaterally and not, will therefore be of crucial importance to the constitution-building judge, along with more traditionally legal considerations. Two factors will be of particular importance, the second of which is really a special form of the first: *infrastructure* and the *public status of ideas.*

Infrastructure

The constitution-building judge concerned with producing results must be deeply concerned with the presence and adequacy of mechanisms for producing constitutional change in the real world. I call these mechanisms *infrastructure.*[9]

Newness is deeply associated with infrastructural questions. The judge who can take for granted everything after reaching a verdict on the narrow legal issue is above all a judge who can take infrastructure for granted. Giving effect to a traditional protection like a fair trial right implies, in addition to interpreting what the guarantee means, a range of decisions about how to enforce the order and how to monitor its enforcement and how it affects the processes of arrest, incarceration, pre-trial and trial. But in a functioning legal system, all these questions already mostly have answers – there are networks of lawyers and registrars and prison officials and prosecutors doing tasks to which they are accustomed in institutions that already exist and are used to judicial oversight and direction. The fact that complicated effects-based decisions underpin all this activity can fade into the background in stable, successful systems, but comes rushing back into view as soon as we encounter any kind of systemic problem with a familiar institution. When we confront problems about how to respond to police abuses or incapacity in the prosecutor's office or corruption by court officials, we quickly realize how tough it can be to give proper effect to a constitution without this infrastructure in place, and also how tough the problem of bringing about that infrastructure can be when it cannot be taken for granted. The challenges only deepen when one is dealing with new kinds of rights for which a legal infrastructure may never have existed. Here, infrastructural considerations may implicate not only the adjudicative function, but also the Court's larger design responsibility.

[9] My account here owes a transparent debt to C. R. Epp, *The Rights Revolution: Lawyers, Activists, and Supreme Courts in Comparative Perspective* (University of Chicago Press, 1998), but my use of infrastructure extends well beyond social movements and so is broader.

The relevance of infrastructural considerations to the judge contemplating announcing an interpretation will be patent. But we may have difficulty seeing past the two most familiar ways in which this point is understood, which in fact by no means exhaust it. The bluntest implication of infrastructural problems is that a judge will have a reason to avoid issuing an order where it is unclear how it will get enforced. Conversely, the presence of infrastructural problems is also often understood as a reason for the Court itself to act expansively to make good the defect: it should still make the order, but invest much more effort in the remedial stage to ensure that the order is effective. These points stand, but it is the subtler implications of infrastructural factors in between these poles that I see as more important to understanding constitution-building and the South African Court's post-1994 practice.

A willing government or other institution that can be trusted to act allows a court to delegate infrastructural questions. The epilogues to *Makwanyane* and to prisoner voting after *August* and *NNP* illustrate the inevitable stakes and pitfalls of this sort of decision, and we will see more examples, but the general line in the voting cases was that the Court could also successfully place reliance on other institutions primarily responsible for certain tasks. The value of being able to rely on other institutions in this way is large. The more a court can do it, the more it can act without facing the invidious choice suggested by the bluntest implications of the infrastructural argument: the choice between trying to do more itself to compensate for the absence, thus stretching judicial capacity and ability, or risking issuing an order that will not be implemented, leaving the underlying problems unresolved and damaging the credibility of the text and the Court. The value of avoiding this predicament is such that the Court has a powerful reason to support other institutions and build trust. This we saw in operation in *NNP*, and it is one of the most important and neglected parts of the Court's work.

Where the official institutional infrastructure cannot, for one or other reason, be relied on to some degree, the presence of civil society groups can be vital because they can serve as temporary infrastructure. Given the tendency to view the ANC as a threat, it is no surprise that this particular aspect of the infrastructural argument is much more commonly acknowledged in the South African context.[10] The Treatment

[10] See esp. Budlender et al., *Public Interest Litigation*; this is also a standard feature of writing especially on LGBTI equality (discussed in Chapter 6) and on the TAC itself (discussed in Chapter 8).

Action Campaign (TAC) has already entered South African constitutional legend, and it played a well-known role in assisting with the monitoring and implementation of the Court's order in *TAC*, which I will discuss in Chapter 8. The general point illustrated by that case is that a reliable and effective civil society body is an actor to whom the Court can delegate infrastructure-related work if need be, and so its presence can transform the calculus of judicial action. But while this form of temporary infrastructure is popular and well known, two important points need to be added to it. One is that much of the way that we understand the work of civil society bodies (and much of the reason that their role is fashionable) comes from the context of impact litigation. Whether we are thinking about lawyers fighting for justice against the apartheid government, or civil society bodies around the world trying to produce change in status quos they deem unjust, we most commonly understand the work of these actors in a context where they are prodding change forward and where, absent their work, that change may well not happen at all. The most commonly discussed aspects of the work of the Treatment Action Campaign, which is in turn the most prominent South African example, are usually understood in these sorts of terms. This can encourage a view of the lawyer as combatant, with the state as the enemy and the Court as the potential guardian, if it can just be convinced to act. Sometimes, that is a perfectly good way to think, in South Africa as elsewhere. But as noted in the previous chapter, post-apartheid South Africa features a government with much more just intentions and much more electoral legitimacy than its predecessor, and in that context the paradigm of impact litigation is not always the most accurate one. Legal talk rightly remains a means to protest injustice and express anger, but just as a politics of protest is not enough for nation-building, so a scholarship of protest is not enough for constitution-building.[11]

This is especially true because even in situations where the government does present an obstacle to change for some reason, and the Court and civil society find themselves having to respond, temporary infrastructure is usually just that, and this is the second point. Effective social change usually requires the government. Wherever one stands on the debate about the effects of *Brown* v. *Board of Education*, it is beyond argument that a great deal of what the civil rights movement achieved and the changes that followed *Brown* and other cases were produced by non-

[11] See further Fowkes, 'Apartheid Judging'.

judicial government action.[12] The example of the Treatment Action Campaign, too, lends support to this point. Its leaders, who have a good claim to be the most successful strategists of social change in post-1994 South Africa to date, recognized the need to be able to work with government. They therefore co-operated with it where they could, and emphasized the need to keep open the possibility of future partnership even in the midst of the most antagonistic disagreements.[13] This sort of consideration has important implications for how the constitution-building court uses temporary infrastructure. Any use of temporary infrastructure is potentially a missed opportunity to build trust and permanent infrastructure, and while that will sometimes be an unavoidable if the government is not acting in a manner that merits trust, it is nevertheless a cost. As a result, while the constitution-building court will often have a reason to rely on temporary infrastructure, it will also often have a reason to try to do so in ways that are complementary of permanent structures, or that conduce to the continued ability and willingness of those structures to support the court going forward. That will be especially true where the impact litigation

[12] Klarman, *Jim Crow to Civil Rights*; Ackerman, *Civil Rights Revolution;* G. N. Rosenberg, *The Hollow Hope: Can Courts Bring about Social change?* (2nd edn., University of Chicago Press, 2008).

[13] The idea of co-operation with the government was a regular theme of former TAC Chairperson Zackie Achmat's speeches at the time. See e.g. Z. Achmat, 'The Treatment Action Campaign, HIV/AIDS and the Government' (2004) 54 *Transformation* 76; Z. Achmat, 'Law, Politics and Social Transformation' (2004) 32 *International Journal of Legal Information* 237. Long-standing member of the TAC executive Mark Heywood has described the TAC as having 'approached the state, government and private sector pragmatically' and 'engaged continuously with politicians and government during Mbeki's rule' – M. Heywood, 'Civil Society and Uncivil Government: The Treatment Action Campaign versus Thabo Mbeki, 1998–2008' in D. Glaser (ed.), *Mbeki and After: Reflections on the Legacy of Thabo Mbeki* (Wits University Press, 2010) pp. 154, 155; see also M. Heywood, 'Shaping, Making and Breaking the Law in the Campaign for a National HIV/AIDS Treatment Plan' in P. Jones and K. Stokke (eds.), *Democratizing Development: The Politics of Socio-Economic Rights in South Africa* (Leiden: Martinus Nijhoff, 2005). This feature of the TAC's approach is well documented in scholarship: see e.g. S. Friedman and S. Mottiar, 'A Rewarding Engagement? The Treatment Action Campaign and the Politics of HIV/AIDS' (2005) 33 *Politics & Society* 511; K. Endresen and A. Kotze, 'Living while Being Alive: Education and Learning in the Treatment Action Campaign' (2005) 24 *International Journal of Lifelong Education* 431, 437–38; R. Ballard, 'Social Movements in Post-Apartheid South Africa: An Introduction' in Jones and Stokke, *Democratizing Development*, pp. 78–79, 87; C. Campbell et al., 'Heeding the Push from Below: How Do Social Movements Persuade the Rich to Listen to the Poor?' (2010) 15 *Journal of Health Psychology* 962.

paradigm is misleading and the government is something more than just an obstacle.

It is perfectly possible to take an absolutist position, and argue that even these more fine-grained sorts of infrastructural calculations are inconsistent with the judicial role and should play no part in how judges interpret the law and decide cases. But there are reasons to question this absolutist position on constitutional grounds. After all, such considerations are standardly deemed relevant in remedial decisions, so why should interpretation itself be any different? *NNP* will help us understand this point. What we saw there was that many of the decisions at the interpretation stage were influenced by institutional considerations. Rulings about burdens of proof and thresholds for when a court will interfere in another institution or permit others to do so (recall the question of the standing of an opposition political party to enforce the Electoral Commission's independence, for example) are, in part, about the relationship between courts and other actors going forward. They are about realizing the Constitution in the world, and more specifically about realizing the parts of it that are about institutions and their functioning. This shows the tenuousness of separation strategies that try to draw a distinction between the interpretative stage and the remedial stage, in order to claim that strategic and practical judgments and social and political considerations are appropriate only at the latter stage.

The precise reason for attacking the distinction between the interpretative and remedial stages follows from the discussion of newness. In a system that does not display significant newness, where infrastructural questions have settled answers, the only thing riding on a novel question of interpretation is whether the text means what the applicant alleges it means in a particular case. The more a system displays newness, however, the more any interpretation is also a decision about institutional relationships, because for the court to decide to decide a question is for it to rule that another institution will not decide that question and must obey instead, and that this will be the pattern henceforth. For the court to decide to rule in circumstances in which another institution has not yet expressed its position, or to overrule another institution that has asserted it is competent to handle the issue, is for it to make a determination about its relationship to that institution going forward. (And for it to decide to defer to other institutions in circumstances like these is for it to make a similar kind of institutional decision.) The act of interpreting, therefore, is often bound up in calculations about how to relate to other institutions and give effect to the Constitution that look a lot like remedial calculations, which are affected in just the same way by considerations of newness and infrastructure.[14] It is only if infrastructural questions are settled and trust is strong that no remedy will be necessary beyond a declaration of what the law requires, and that it will not be necessary to be strategic and make political judgments.

I quite acknowledge what this implies: if one adopts the absolutist position that infrastructural considerations and related non-traditional considerations are not relevant to the interpretation stage, then one may indeed insist on the distinction between the interpretative and remedial phases. (Indeed, one will have just stipulated it.) We can see, however, why the constitution-building judge confronting the text and its implications might not find the distinction particularly meaningful.

The Public Status of Ideas

In one sense, all constitutional ideas are created equal. They are in the Constitution, and that fact is an important public reason that can be offered as justification for upholding the idea, and an important reason for a court to do so. But in another sense, we know they are not equal. Ideas, too, display degrees of newness. Some things that can be read into a constitution represent ideas that are already strongly entrenched in a given society. Some have more political backing or historical weight. Some remain stubborn sites of contest. Some are, if anything, negatively entrenched: the dominant public status of the idea is its rejection. LGBTI equality is the global example of the moment of an idea whose public status is moving from negative to positive in many places, to different degrees from issue to issue.

I shall refer to these properties as the *public status* of ideas. Infrastructure and the public status of ideas are, of course, closely related and often correlated: if ideas matter in society, this will often have an effect on government and civil society structures, and conversely the presence of government or civil society activity structures will affect the public status of the ideas involved. One can usefully think of public status as a species of infrastructure, because a set of familiar or politically supported ideas that can be invoked in favour of a ruling can greatly assist a court just as concrete infrastructure can. However, some special considerations apply

[14] See also the discussion of *Executive Council* and *Makwanyane* in Chapter 3.

to the question of public status and so it can be helpful to talk about this factor separately.

The most traditional view here, again, is that public status is irrelevant: the *constitutional* status of an idea is all that matters, and all parts of the constitution should be enforced the same regardless of socio-political factors. We saw this bold view in Chapter 2. But as I noted there, if we imagine ourselves as the judges, with the fresh, open-ended text in our hands, confronting the prospect of telling society what it has committed itself to, this stance might make us feel rather uncomfortably exposed. Part of this is the fear of being reckless. If one is granted a new and potentially fragile judicial authority, one will be sensitive to the need to safeguard it.[15] Roux's work responds to this important intuition. But the idea of weighing institutional self-preservation against the protection of rights is again only the bluntest version of the point, and again it is the subtler ones that are crucial to understanding the work of the Court. *NNP*, after all, does not show the Court failing to protect rights in order to build its own authority (which as noted would be hard to defend legally). It shows it selecting an approach that plausibly protects rights and *also* builds its own authority *and* that of other institutions all at the same time. In light of this example, insisting that judges observe the classical interpretivist distinction and keep the sphere of rights interpretation free from other considerations looks less imperative. In fact, it shows how that insistence may prevent a judge from considering optimal courses of activity that could promote multiple goals at once, and so hamper her ability to do the complex balancing work that, according to the constitution-building account, she confronts.

Whether this sort of optimal solution actually exists depends on the constitutional politics of a society. In the blunt case in which the constitution strongly points one way and political forces and public opinion strongly point another, there may be no good options for the constitution-building court. But the reality of a democratic society is often much more nuanced than this. For one thing, as noted, the ANC has taken some positions that are supportive of constitutional ideas, including positions that run contrary to public opinion which would therefore otherwise be problematic for an emerging court to defend. This is why the ANC's stance has been so crucial: it is sometimes what has

[15] See esp. the interviews Mark Kende conducted with Justices Ackermann, Goldstone, O'Regan and Sachs – M. S. Kende, *Constitutional Rights in Two Worlds: South Africa and the United States* (Cambridge University Press, 2009), pp. 10, 271–73.

permitted the Court to have its cake and eat it, to vindicate aspirational constitutional ideas while limiting its political and institutional risks. But even if political and legal imperatives do not align this neatly, there are many possibilities beyond the absolutist positions of ignoring politics or giving in to it. The position here parallels the argument about remedies in the discussion of infrastructure, and the separation strategy attempted there. Many scholars would prefer the court to make orders even in the absence of infrastructure, and then do the expansive, creative work to make sure these orders are meaningful. In similar vein, the classical view is that courts should make orders regardless of whether they are unpopular, startling, distasteful or alienating to the public, and then do more work outside the context of interpreting the constitution to try and soften the blow and the impact on the courts' image. For example, there are familiar proposals that courts should improve their media relations capabilities, and that judges should make more public speeches to try and acquaint the public with their role and educate the public about their rulings.[16]

If one adopts this position, then one may insist on the distinction between the relevance of public opinion to curial activity, and to extra-curial activity, just as one can insist on the distinction between the relevance of infrastructural defects to the interpretative phase and the remedial one. But as we saw in Chapter 2, at least some erosion of this absolute rule is often accepted, as when judges alter the way they write judgments with a conscious eye to its anticipated public reaction in the ways mentioned by Dworkin and Roux. If we are willing to accept at least this erosion of the distinction, we will be able to see how the judge contemplating announcing an interpretation will have reason to think about the public reception judicial pronouncements will receive and to make adjustments accordingly.

How far we are willing to go along with this argument probably depends above all on whether rights protection might be eroded as a result of judges adjusting their activities in response to social and political

[16] Du Plessis, 'Between Apology and Utopia'; Brickhill and Babuich, 'Political Rights'. Seafield, 'South Africa', reflects some of the nascent tension in such views. While supporting counter-majoritarian rulings such as *Makwanyane* (*Ibid.*, 320–22), and the need to establish respect for the rights-protecting court and educate the public (*Ibid.*, 329, 331–32, 336, 338), Seafield also argues for an interpretative concession to public relations: '[t]he increase in crime has resulted in a backlash against the constitution; people are now blaming the ills of society on the bill of rights and are calling for the reinstatement of capital punishment. A balancing act between the dictates of the constitution and being tough on crime is required' (*Ibid.*, 336).

considerations. One of the most common sorts of reason given for thinking that rights protection is not eroded is the claim that judicial deference to action in democratic institutions might produce more enduring change. Thus, for example, at times during the pursuit of same-sex marriage around the world it has been debatable whether or not the cause would be best furthered by firm judicial pronouncements going out ahead of public opinion and other institutions, an issue we will see in the South African case as well.[17] The public status of ideas before the court can also be important because constitutionalism is at its most effective as a public activity. Public support for a court is relevant to its institutional independence and security. The legitimacy of a constitution depends in some way on its remaining a document that members of the public can think of as 'ours'. A Court aiming to establish the Constitution's authority will have a reason to worry about stretching the constitutional writ too far out ahead of public opinion, which is what we saw Metz being concerned about in response to Bilchitz's animal rights proposals in Chapter 2. These considerations also matter because public opinion can in itself be an extraordinarily important piece of infrastructure for giving effect to ideas. A good deal of what the 1996 Constitution envisages entails changes to individual conduct. Full effect can be given to a range of rights and values only if private attitudes change. For example, at least in the more public spheres, racist speech is seen as unacceptable in South Africa and so is policed by individuals who react adversely to it, or is self-censored by people seeking to avoid that adverse reaction. This is a key way in which the constitutional ban on discrimination is enforced, and it is when this kind of enforcement mechanism is absent that racism, and other kinds of discrimination, can be the hardest to target by other, heavier-handed methods. As the late Chief Justice Langa put this point in a closely related context: 'Reconciliation and forgiveness are beyond the power of the law. We cannot legislate reconciliation and we cannot order forgiveness.'[18]

These considerations mean that courts will also have a reason to relate to the public in ways that serve to promote the relationship, just as they have a reason to approach other institutions with trust so as to build

[17] Compare e.g. Rosenberg, *Hollow Hope*, pp. 339–429 with e.g. W. N. Eskridge, Jnr., 'Backlash Politics: How Constitutional Litigation Has Advanced Marriage Equality in the United States' (2013) 93 *Boston University Law Review* 275; see further Chapter 6.

[18] Pius Langa, 'Transformative Constitutionalism' (2006) 17 *Stellenbosch Law Review* 351, 358; see also Fowkes, 'Langa Jurisprudence'.

infrastructure and promote the judicial ability to rely on it. We can expect that the public will be a less effective constitutional institution if they think of the Constitution or the Court's interpretations of it as foreign or distasteful, an elite exercise, or simply something with unwelcome consequences. Again, the bluntest implication, that the Court should not make unpopular rulings, is less interesting than the subtler implications about how the Court might try to shape its actions in light of this important concern. It will give the Court a reason to choose its moments to be bold, to select reasons and argumentative strategies with care, and to make full use of supportive government activity.

The final point is that if the public's stance on an issue matters, then it also matters how visible the public status of an idea is to the Court. The judge contemplating announcing to society that it is committed to something will want to know something about the reaction of the audiences out there, and this might be uncertain. Given the breadth and ambition of the 1996 Constitution, it is sometimes not especially clear how the public would react to a particular constitutional commitment. This state of uncertainty will generally give a court a reason to be cautious, just as (to borrow the climate scientists' metaphor) one will have a reason to go slowly if one is driving near a cliff in a fog. It will make support from the public's representatives of particular value. And it can make the role of social movements especially important. Charles Epp has famously argued that social movements can trigger rights revolutions by getting courts to act.[19] The most obvious hypothesis to explain this causal relationship is that social movements jolt judges out of their contented status quo, and effective social movements can also, of course, do work to alter social opinion on an issue and so bolster its public status. But I would also offer the hypothesis that social movements, by raising an issue and compelling others to react to it, might simply make the public stakes of an issue clearer to courts, so that they can approach the issue with more precise knowledge of how judicial intervention needs to be handled.

An Illustration: HIV/AIDS Discrimination

An example will be helpful here to illustrate how these types of considerations can impact on the work of the Court. *Hoffman* v. *South African Airways* ('*Hoffman*') shows the court confronting the newness of an issue

[19] Epp, *Rights Revolution*.

in a case that is more ordinary and typical than *Makwanyane*, and that also involves simpler and more familiar institutional calculations than *NNP*. The case arose because the airline in question refused to employ Mr Hoffman solely on the basis that he was HIV-positive. The judgment found for the applicant in strong terms and has been well received; I seek only to note to a few pertinent points.[20]

The case saw the Court doing quite a familiarly judicial thing – regulating discrimination in the workplace – but in relation to HIV/AIDS, a disease still (and especially at the time) working its way from being a subject of stigma and fear and a symbol of irresponsibility and 'deviant' sex to being a category for legal protection. The issue of its constitutional status therefore displayed some degree of newness (as is reflected in the fact that the decision is considered a groundbreaking one). *Hoffman* takes a strong stand on this contentious, sensitive social issue on behalf of a vulnerable minority group. Indeed, the Court's stand is stronger than was necessary to dispose of the case: the judges chose to skip over the first, rationality stage of the equality enquiry in order to make the stronger finding that the airline's actions constituted unfair discrimination.[21] (This is particularly important because HIV/AIDS is not included in the Constitution's list of presumptively unfair grounds of discrimination, so the finding represents an important extension of equality protection to those living with HIV.) The Court also strongly resists the idea that commercial interests or the prejudices of customers can be a basis for justifying discrimination against people living with HIV and AIDS.[22] This firmly upends some of the innocent-looking rocks under which prejudice can hide. An examination of pre-*Hoffman* High Court decisions on HIV and AIDS shows how some judges could also treat the disease with suspicion and distaste and could permit the exclusion and differential treatment of people living with it as a result.[23]

20 *Hoffman* v. *South African Airways* 2001 (1) SA 1 (CC). Criticism of the judgment is technical only: see e.g. I. M. Rautenbach, 'Die konstitusionele hof se riglyne vir die toepassing van die reg op gelykheid II (The Constitutional Court's guidelines for the limitation of the right to equality II)' (2001) *Tydskrif vir die Suid-Afrikaanse Reg* 329.

21 *Hoffman*, paras. 26–29. Under the equality test set out in *Harksen* v. *Lane NO* 1998 (1) SA 300 (CC), the first step is to ask whether a differentiation is rational, and only if it is to proceed to ask whether it constitutes discrimination.

22 See e.g. M. Christianson, 'People with Disabilities Inside (and Outside) the South African Workplace: The Current Status of the Constitutional and Statutory Promises' (2012) *Acta Juridica* 286, 290–91; E. Cameron, 'Legal and Human Rights Responses to the HIV/AIDS Epidemic' (2006) *Stellenbosch Law Review* 47, 70–79.

23 The case law is surveyed by Cameron, 'Legal and Human Rights Responses', 72–87.

Hoffman, then, seems to be everything supporters of the first *Makwanyane* story could want. And the *Hoffman* Court, again, does indeed deserve credit. But the decision's salutary stance is built on a lot of work by other actors, whose actions meant that the Court had to confront a less newness or confront it a lot less unilaterally than might otherwise have been true in relation to an issue of this kind. Government policy provides one key support for the judgment. By the time the Court decided *Hoffman* on 28 September 2000, the ANC government had instituted a number of important protections for HIV-positive persons, which the Court could refer to in a long footnote as authority for the proposition that HIV-positive persons 'enjoy special protection in our law'.[24] A glance at the list shows the particular relevance these existing instruments had to HIV/AIDS issues in the context of employment and the workplace. *Hoffman* could therefore situate itself squarely in line with a clearly expressed policy trend from the ANC government. These legal instruments, in turn, mostly had their roots in work done by the South African Law Reform Commission, especially after 1997, and their spirit is to be traced back still further to the work done by legal scholars in the early 1990s and positions adopted by key actors during the negotiations.[25] The NP government and the ANC formed the National AIDS Co-ordinating Committee of South Africa (NACOSA) in October 1992, and it produced some salutary policy proposals, with meetings proceeding even at times when the broader constitutional talks were suspended.[26] These proposals were generally stillborn, but '[the Committee's] legal ideas were a significant exception'.[27] At the request of the Department of Health in 1993, the Law Commission set to work, and its proposals over the next decade laid the groundwork for the government's responses to AIDS in the workplace, in education, in relation to testing

[24] *Hoffman*, para. 28 n. 25, referring to the national testing policy issued in terms of the National Policy for Health Act 116 of 1990; the National Education Policy Act 27 of 1996; the Employment Equity Act 55 of 1998 and the draft code of good practice issued in terms of it; the Medical Schemes Act 131 of 1998; and the Promotion of Equality and Prevention of Unfair Discrimination Act 4 of 2000.

[25] Cameron, 'Legal and Human Rights Responses', 51, 55–56.

[26] See e.g. H. Klug, 'Five Years On: How Relevant Is the Constitution to the New South Africa?' (2001–2002) 26 *Vermont Law Review* 803, 805; E. Wouters, H. C. J. van Rensburg and H. Meulemans, 'The National Strategic Plan of South Africa: What Are the Prospects of Success after the Repeated Failures of Previous AIDS Policy?' (2010) 25 *Health Policy and Planning* 171, 174.

[27] Cameron, 'Legal and Human Rights Responses', 56 and sources there cited.

and in the context of discrimination more generally.[28] At the same time, work was being done to alter the public status of the idea. Key individuals were advocating human rights-based approaches to the epidemic. Cameron, himself an obvious hero of this story as the first openly gay and HIV-positive person to hold high public office in South Africa, highlights the stance taken in 1992 by Ishmail Mohamed, a future Chief Justice, in support of a measured, ethical and rights-based response to the AIDS issue.[29] Activists from the anti-apartheid and LGBTI equality context like Simon Nkoli and Zackie Achmat, whom we will meet again in later chapters, were forerunners in being open about their HIV-positive status and fighting stigma.

The other key support of *Hoffman* is consensus on the scientific evidence. The Aids Law Project (ALP), admitted as an amicus, served to bring some of this evidence to the Court's attention, including a finding by experts that the Project had engineered as part of an earlier Labour Court case.[30] The *Hoffman* Court took a robust stance on the scientific evidence, overturning a number of findings of fact made by the court of first instance.[31] The most critical thing underpinning this stance was the consensus: even South African Airways's own expert did not contest the evidence, and so much of the case was not really in dispute by the time it reached the Court.[32] The Court did not in fact need to resolve any factual disputes between the parties, and it could firmly rely on scientific evidence in finding the applicant fit for flight service. This consensus is of considerable significance, because the newness of an issue can mean that pertinent details about it, which courts are not usually in a good position to resolve, are unsettled. If the Court had confronted a genuine dispute of fact about whether HIV-positive flight personnel could safely take the necessary vaccines, for example, it would have been much more difficult for it to order responsibly that airlines could not

[28] For a summary, see Cameron, 'Legal and Human Rights Responses', 55–72.

[29] Cameron, 'Legal and Human Rights Responses', 55.

[30] *Hoffman*, para. 3 and n. 3, para. 13 and n. 14, referring to the minutes of a meeting of medical experts in the context of a similar, unreported case involving SAA in the Labour Court, *A* v. *South African Airways (Pty) Ltd*, Case J1916/99, which ended in settlement. The minutes are part of the *Hoffman* case file available at www.constitutioncourt.org.za. See also S. Gumedze, 'HIV/AIDS and Human Rights: The Role of the African Commission on Human and People's Rights' (2004) 4 *African Human Rights Law Journal* 181, 186–87.

[31] See also N. Smit and S. Cornelius, 'South African Perspectives on HIV/AIDS in the Workplace' (2005) 36 *Cambrian Law Review* 73.

[32] *Hoffman*, paras. 16, 62.

refuse to employ HIV-positive people. These features of the case supported its boldness. Like *Makwanyane*, *Hoffman* is a minority-protecting decision that is nevertheless not counter-majoritarian in relation to the stance of the government. It is also a bold decision in a technical, policy-laden area that does not involve the court independently having to make any bold, technical, policy decisions.

The final observation to make about *Hoffman* is that, on the subsidiary issues that lacked the same foundations in existing policy, public work and scientific evidence, the Court's boldness was replaced by restraint. The Court declined to express a view on the issue of HIV testing as regulated by labour legislation, which had been raised for the first time in the Constitutional Court, on the grounds that Parliament had created the Labour Court as a specialist tribunal to deal with labour issues and it should deal with the regulation of testing in the first instance.[33] (The question did indeed require some working out in the Labour Court after *Hoffman*.)[34] The Court also avoided making further general pronouncements on discrimination and disabilities in the workplace, beyond the obvious symbolic import of its findings specifically on HIV and AIDS. The ALP, as amicus, had expressed significant reservations about treating HIV-positive people as 'disabled' for the purposes of the Employment Equity Act.[35] The Court's avoidance may reflect agreement on this point, but it is more likely that the Court simply felt it better not to speak on a complex issue given that other actors were engaging it. Thus in line with what we saw in *NNP*, the *Hoffman* Court is making careful institutional judgments about when and when not to assert its jurisdiction. This reflects a further luxury that a Court enjoys to the extent that it does not have to confront a new issue unilaterally. In *Hoffman*, the Court could be confident that government policy instruments were progressive, that there existed a labour court structure

[33] *Hoffman*, paras. 18–20.

[34] See esp. *PFG Building Glass (Pty) Ltd* v. *Chemical Engineering Pulp Paper Wood & Allied Workers Union* (2003) 24 *Industrial Law Journal* 974 (LC); *Irvin & Johnson Ltd* v. *Trawler & Line Fishing Union* (2003) 24 *Industrial Law Journal* 565 (LC); *Joy Mining Machinery, A division of Harnischfeger (SA) (Pty) Ltd* v. *National Union of Metalworkers of SA* (2002) 23 *Industrial Law Journal* 391 (LC). For summaries, see A. Leonard, 'To Test or Not to Test Employees for HIV' (2003) *Juta's Business Law* 140; Cameron, 'Legal and Human Rights Responses', 67–68.

[35] *Hoffman*, para. 40; F. Bhabha, 'Disability Equality Rights in South Africa: Concepts, Interpretation and the Transformation Imperative' (2009) 25 *South African Journal on Human Rights* 218, 232. On *Hoffman*'s symbolic importance in the general disability context, see Christianson, 'People with Disabilities', 290–91.

charged with giving effect to those instruments, and that civil society groups like the Aids Law Project were active in the area. This not only meant that it needed to give little thought to infrastructural questions in relation to the issues it did decide. It also meant that the Court had some room to tailor its intervention to the places where it was least risky. It could be quite confident that leaving issues undecided in this way would not come at the cost of their neglect, because they could be left to other institutions and actors who were apparently engaging with them productively.

The Text and Its Questions: Constitution-Building as a Constitutional Argument

So far in this chapter, I have simply been describing the Court's work. But in line with the arguments of Chapter 2 I also aim to take this work legally seriously, and in concluding this chapter I seek to show how the constitution-building work I have been discussing can be understood as an implication of the text, and how the tasks constitution-building involves can thus be seen to rest on a powerful constitutional argument. This argument is largely not a matter of explicit textualism, reflecting the fact that, as we saw in the previous chapter, the drafters did not always pay a good deal of attention to the details of the Court or its role. Instead, it is an argument about what the text leaves open and the work that it therefore implies needs to be done by an institution charged with its enforcement. That potentially applies to every constitutional institution, not just the Court, but it means that if and when it falls to the Court to enforce a particular aspect of the Constitution the Court impliedly has the constitutional duty to do that work, or at least is permitted to do it if that is what is required to ensure that the Constitution is enforced.

Because the argument can apply to other institutions as well, it falls short of being an argument that the Court in particular must do this work and this can make it easy to stick to old habits. It is often possible to respond to the openness of the text by falling back on a traditional conception of the judicial role: the text implies that certain things must be done, some of them by the judiciary and some of them by other actors, and the way to decide which is which is with reference to a traditional conception of what courts should so and should not do. This kind of thinking is the chief concern of arguments about the constraining effects South Africa's traditional legal culture can have on constitutional work. Such an approach reads the Constitution in light of a rather limited judicial tradition instead of using the Constitution to challenge that tradition and re-imagine the judicial role. Everyone knows what a court is, but an old court asked to perform new tasks will be a new court, and it is in this spirit that we should approach the text and the work it implies needs doing.

As a starting point, consider s 172(1)(a).[36] In this section, the judge will find quite definite guidance about her job: judges are obliged to declare invalid law or conduct that is inconsistent with the Constitution. That of course leaves the not unimportant question of whether something is inconsistent with the Constitution. But the section is nevertheless quite definite in the sense that it tells a court what question to ask and what to do when it has answered that question. By way of comparison, consider what the text says about the judicial task in the following subsection, s 172(1)(b).[37] Once unconstitutional law or conduct has been declared as such, the courts have the power to order any remedy that is just and equitable. Presumably, that requires some kind of action to bring an unconstitutional situation into line with the text, but it is left to the courts to make the causal judgment about what will best achieve this. Thus, in addition to the interpretative decision about whether there has been a departure from what the Constitution requires, this section implies that the Court must make a further, practical decision about how to bring the world in line with the Constitution. Something analogous can be said about ss 8(2) and 39(2), which oblige the courts to interpret, and if necessary to develop, the common law and customary law to give effect to the Bill of Rights and its values. That implies that courts should make judgments about what the rights and values mean and whether the existing law is consistent with this meaning, but also causal judgments about what to do to vindicate this meaning when some inconsistency is found. They must ask, for example, whether it is enough to announce a re-interpretation of an existing rule and rely on others to learn about the gloss, or whether the rule itself must be rewritten, and if so whether the court can do the re-writing or whether the legislature or someone else should do it instead. These arguments will be familiar enough, but I pause to underline the practical concern with producing

[36] 1996 Constitution, s 172(1)(a) reads: 'When deciding a constitutional matter within its powers, a court must declare that any law or conduct that is inconsistent with the Constitution is invalid to the extent of its inconsistency.'

[37] 1996 Constitution, s 172(1)(b) reads in relevant part: 'When deciding a constitutional matter within its power a court … may make any order that is just and equitable … '.

certain effects or results they display. Where s 172(1)(a) apparently requires a declaration of invalidity to be made regardless of its consequences for general constitutional ends, ss 172(1)(b), 8(2) and 39(2) instruct courts to bring about constitution-serving results: just and equitable vindication of its provisions, and effect to its values in other bodies of law.

In fact, s 172(1)(a) is unusual in seemingly removing this kind of judicial discretion. The section stipulates that it is never constitutionally good for unconstitutional conduct not to be declared as such, but this kind of purportedly absolute rule is rare in the 1996 Constitution. The strict rules on the Court's obligations in relation to certain mechanisms for abstract review during legislative processes are another example, but beyond that, instances are hard to find.[38] Generally, the text leaves space for judicial discretion to do what will best serve constitutional ends, and the Court has further reserved as much of this discretion for itself as possible, even in areas where the text is comparatively prescriptive about judicial obligations. For example, the Court has recognized the clear restrictions on judicial review of bills still passing through the legislative process, but otherwise has reserved its right to do what best serves the interests of justice in relation to legislation before it comes into force (while subjecting that power to intervene in the legislative process to very heavy fetters).[39] Constitutional Court confirmation of a lower court's invalidation of legislation or presidential conduct is required if the confirmation is to have any force or effect, but the Court has ruled that this only means that lower court rulings will not have force unless they are confirmed, not that the Court is obliged to hear confirmation cases.[40] Indeed, we saw the *Richter* Court reserve discretion for itself even in relation to s 172(1)(a), despite the apparently clear wording, deciding not to pronounce on a constitutional issue where this might affect the administration of an election.

All this may look like an argument for expansive judicial authority, and so may seem odd coming from an opponent of court centrism. But the question left open by the text, of how to produce results, cuts both

[38] 1996 Constitution, s 167(4)(b) and (c).

[39] See *Doctors for Life* and *United Democratic Movement* v. *President of the Republic of South Africa (No. 2)* 2003 (1) SA 495 (CC), discussed in Chapter 7, and see also *Glenister* v. *President of the Republic of South Africa* 2009 (1) SA 287 (CC).

[40] *President of the Ordinary Court Martial* v. *Freedom of Expression Institute* 1999 (4) SA 682 (CC), paras. 14–18; *Langeberg Municipality*, paras. 9–14; *Khosa* v. *Minister of Social Development* 2004 (6) SA 505 (CC), para. 32.

ways: it can leave room for court action, but it can also be answered in favour of other institutions. We saw the *NNP* majority defer to other bodies on the decisions about means to give effect to the right to vote, while also making its own decisions of this kind – about certain approaches to judicial review, the burden of proof, and the rules on judicial orders for the collection of additional evidence as means to the establishment of a sustainable model of judicial review. It was also making decisions about means to promote the end of the Electoral Commission's authority. And so on. Both the decisions on which it deferred to others and the ones that it made are similar kinds of practical judgments about what would best move the world towards what the text sets out.

Note, however, that *NNP* did not make these kinds of decisions in terms of the explicit empowering provisions in ss 8(2), 39(2) or s 172(1)(b), none of which are implicated by the decision. *Hoffman* also made several decisions of this sort that were not part of the order it made in terms of s 172(1)(b), including, most obviously, the decisions not to make an order in respect of certain issues. From where, then, does the duty or authority of courts to make these sorts of judgments arise? The most direct answer is the s 165(2) duty of the courts to apply the Constitution.[41] But that answer simply shifts the focus to the question of what applying the Constitution entails. Why precisely does the text at large prompt the need for the Court to make these sorts of judgments, or to find answers to them in the judgments of others? The answer lies in the text's undoubted purposivism, a familiar point but one whose full implications merit comment here.

Purposive Text and Results-Driven Constitutionalism

A purposive text contemplates change and the bringing about of results, and those things in turn imply consideration of the sorts of factors I have been discussing. Any action done in terms of the text is supposed to be done in furtherance of its values, and so an interpreting judge will have a general obligation to ask whether a particular judicial action actually serves to advance the text's values or not. The overall textual embodiment of this point is the sometimes-neglected s 1, setting out the

[41] 1996 Constitution, s 165(2) reads: 'The courts are independent and subject only to the Constitution and the law, which they must apply impartially and without fear, favour or prejudice.'

founding values of the Constitution.[42] The courts have not quite come to terms with its role, but I have argued elsewhere that the best way to make sense of s 1 is as a source of descriptive principles. They describe the most important values that the 1996 Constitution is supposed to further, and the effect of that description – when s 1 is read in conjunction with s 74(1), requiring a special super-majority to amend s 1 – is to super-entrench the parts of the text that give effect to those values.[43] Here, the significance of this argument lies in its implication that s 1 raises a constant question about whether an interpretation or action in terms of the text vindicates the constitutional description of the text in s 1. It imposes a duty to ensure that the description is vindicated whenever constitutional activity engages the values set out in s 1, and that in turn implies the need for practical judgments about the consequences of particular judicial choices. Several other sections of more specific application than s 1 also impose value-based obligations of this variety.[44]

This utilitarian-sounding account of purposivism may startle, as may my general concern in this chapter with results. But I am not proposing that all law-based social reform is about consequences, in the manner of a Jeremy Bentham, and I am not claiming that we can or should reduce constitutional law to a utility sum or a rational choice calculation in some reductionist version of law and economics. Nor, as the arguments of Chapter 2 made clear, am I arguing along with some of the legal realists that we should put away doctrine and just do social science. Instead, the claim is one exemplifying the best of movements like legal realism and

[42] 1996 Constitution, s 1 reads: 'The Republic of South Africa is one, sovereign, democratic state founded on the following values:

(a) Human dignity, the achievement of equality and the advancement of human rights and freedoms.
(b) Non-racialism and non-sexism.
(c) Supremacy of the constitution and the rule of law.
(d) Universal adult suffrage, a national common voters roll, regular elections and a multi-party system of government, to ensure accountability, responsiveness and openness.'

[43] James Fowkes, 'Founding Provisions' in Woolman and Bishop (eds.), *Constitutional Law.*

[44] The Bill of Rights has an internal value-based mechanism establishing the 'democratic values of human dignity, equality and freedom' as the ultimate goals of the Bill and therefore of activity in terms of it – see 1996 Constitution, s 7(1), 8(1), 36(1), 39(1) and (2). Overall statements of the values and goals associated with a particular institution are also common: see e.g. s 152(1) (local government), s 195(1) (public administration), s 198 (security services), as well as s 41(1) (general principles for intra-governmental relations). Many individual provisions use value terms.

law and economics, which is that the point and worth of many legal practices has a great deal to do with their effects and that these are accordingly worth trying to use to understand and reform legal activity. To worry about results is not to be unprincipled; to the contrary, it is to show the deepest concern that principles are actually realized.

The point is worth emphasizing, but it is not all that startling or novel. Ran Hirschl calls our attention to the important fact that most constitutional claims are really empirical ones, even though scholars do not always think of them that way. Evaluating a constitutional arrangement – such as how to balance ideas of judicial review and democracy – is often a question of 'the nature of its substantive outcome', a matter of whether it 'has produced or is likely to produce practical outcomes closest to the meaning of social justice'.[45] Hirschl makes his point about these largest-scale questions, but the same logic applies generally. We already accept this idea, for example, in relation to affirmative action. Although Hirschl is right to note that Dworkin does not generally rely on empirical evidence for his broader claims about judicial review, affirmative action may be the best example of an area where Dworkin does do this.[46] In *Sovereign Virtue*, he rests his defence of affirmative action on the consequences it produces and in particular on a large-scale empirical evaluation of 30 years of affirmative action policies in US universities that identified a range of positive effects.[47] His argument fits our intuitions: no-one would defend affirmative action if it didn't produce certain results, and the same is true of many other policies. South African constitutionalism must confront an array of practical questions in the context of trying, for example, to tackle poverty. This is a general

[45] Hirschl, *Towards Juristocracy*, p. 3, referring to M. A. Graber 'Review: Constitutional Politics and Constitutional Theory: A Misunderstood and Neglected Relationship' (2002) 27 *Law and Social Enquiry* 309.

[46] See also e.g. his comments on remedies, Dworkin, *Law's Empire*, pp. 390–91.

[47] R. Dworkin, *Sovereign Virtue: The Theory and Practice of Equality* (Harvard University Press, 2002), pp. 386–426. Dworkin divides his discussion into two parts: 'Does It Work?' and 'Is It Fair?'. The first part focuses on the empirical study, W. G. Bowen and D. Bok, *The Shape of the River: Long-Term Consequences of Considering Race in College and University Admissions* (Princeton University Press, 1998). But both parts rest on the consequences. Dworkin concludes by referring to what affirmative action does – 'it produces no balkanization, but helps to dissolve the balkanization now sadly in place' – and sees this as part of the (consequentialist) project of trying to 'achieve, if we really want it, a more perfect union.' (*Sovereign Virtue*, pp. 425–26). The study on which Hirschl relies for his claim about Dworkin's use of empirical evidence included *Sovereign Virtue* but examined only indexes: Graber, 'Constitutional Politics', 315 n. 9.

consequence of constitutionalism in modern welfare states, but as we saw at the beginning of this chapter it applies to many other aspects of the Court's activity. Justice Sachs' desired theory of when must be in large part a theory about what effects an intervention will or might have in a particular case.

Purposivism in the South African context is usually understood in terms of giving effects to rights and values. We are familiar with the idea that the constitutional text is aspirational in this regard, and that when it refers to rights that persons 'have' and the values on which the state 'is' based it is referring to a significant extent to states of affairs that still have to be brought about. But it is important to see that this applies equally to all parts of the Constitution. It is possible to imagine a constitution that is not institutionally new, meaning that the structures and arrangements it refers to are all already in functioning existence, but the 1996 Constitution is not in that position. It is institutionally aspirational as well. The stuttering beginnings of many of the newly created Chapter 9 institutions may offer the most obvious illustration of this.[48] But it is true of arrangements that are much more traditional, too: this is, after all, a state in which constitutional supremacy is new and in which its entrenchment across the full scope of potential judicial action is not a foregone conclusion. Thus, as we saw, *NNP* is not merely a case about giving effect to the voting right, but in truth also a case about how to do that *and* give effect to s 43 on legislative authority, s 190 on the Electoral Commission and the s 181(3) obligation to assist and protect it, and so on. Textually, the Court has to vindicate these provisions just as much as the right to vote, and they can produce the same effects-based questions in a context were these institutions and their institutional relationships were often still unsettled. That protecting rights might be very important does not alter the fact that the Court's responsibilities to enforce the text do not stop at the end of the Bill of Rights.

This argument can locate judicial discretion about practical effects in relation to any provision of the text, even one like s 172(1)(a) that apparently forecloses judicial discretion. Interpreted purposively, the section's injunction that judges encountering unconstitutional conduct must make a declaration accordingly is about a rule of law state policed

[48] See e.g. Klug, *Constitution of South Africa*, pp. 212–15; Parliament of the Republic of South Africa, *Report of the ad hoc Committee on the Review of Chapter 9 and Associated Institutions* (31 July 2007). On aspirational constitutionalism and newness, and why the latter concept does not collapse into the former, see Fowkes, 'Normal Rights, Just New'.

by courts. Insofar as that kind of state is not yet entrenched, and partly represents an aspiration, how is this purpose to be served? The standard position – which is an answer to this question whether it acknowledges it or not – is that courts should not consider this issue, but should fearlessly declare all unconstitutional conduct as such. That answers the question by leaving it up to political actors and their supporters to establish the rule of law state by respectfully accepting the Court's rulings. Conversely, a familiar political science position is that courts might wish to avoid making orders when there is a good chance that they will be ignored and the finality of judicial decisions will be called into question as a result, or, more actively, when they may provoke attacks on judicial authority, constitutional supremacy and the rule of law. In light of the discussion of other absolutist positions earlier in this chapter, however, we can again see that other answers might be possible. The standard legal position is willing to make some limited concessions that reflect a concern with effects, such as the suggestions about media relations, judicial public appearances and phrasing of judgments considered earlier. Here, the purposive arguments that can be linked even to s 172(1)(a) are most readily linked to the point about trust made in Chapter 3. I argued there that existing accounts tended to miss the general significance of trust when they applauded President Mandela's authority-building reaction to court rulings in *Executive Council* and *SARFU* but failed to note how the majority in *NNP* was doing the same thing in relation to other institutions.[49] If part of giving effect to the Constitution is establishing a system in which the Court makes the final decision about the constitutionality of presidential and other conduct, then building institutional relationships and trust such that the judicial authority to do this will be accepted and respected will be a legally relevant consideration in everything the court does. It means that in situations like *NNP* in which it is less than clear whether judicial intervention in other institutions is necessary to protect a right, there will always be a (non-decisive) reason to express trust and establish the judiciary's bona fides as an actor that exercises its powers responsibly and respectfully.

Just how far such arguments can be taken is, of course, the key question for the constitution-building court, and one that depends heavily on context. I suggested that the constitution-building pieces fell rather neatly into place in *NNP*. We can now see that what I meant by this was

[49] See Chapter 3.

that it was possible to find a plausible way to give effect to all the different pieces of relevant text at once. That will not always be so: sometimes judges will face harder choices, and there will thus be more contentious debates about whether the balance struck is compatible with our constitutional commitments such that we are willing to ratify it as an exercise in legal interpretation, as opposed to a constitutionally indefensible (though possibly prudent) piece of strategy. The point of the argument in this chapter is only to show that the types of decisions I have discussed are inescapably prompted by the text itself. It is perfectly open for traditionalists to resist some or all of these implications of the text, using arguments about what the judiciary should and should not do, and by insisting on absolutist distinctions like those I have noted. But we can now see that this is just one response to an open-ended text, and not obviously the best one. This is the result I sought in Chapter 1: the arguments of realists and classical interpretivists, of traditionalists and radicals, all stand alike as readings of the same text, and all stand alike to be compared as rival constitutional arguments.

6

LGBTI Equality

If adherents to the first *Makwanyane* story are asked to identify the cases in which the Court has lived up to that story's promise and engaged in the bold defence of rights, they are most likely to point to the series of LGBTI equality decisions that begins with the decriminalization of consensual sodomy in 1998.[1] These are globally celebrated decisions, and they are often seen as a *judicial* achievement. Even Hirschl, so suspicious of the Constitutional Court, gives it credit for these judgments.[2] They are also often celebrated as achievements of the sophisticated civil society bodies that brought several of the cases and masterminded the broader litigation strategy.[3] But like *Makwanyane* and *Hoffman*, these decisions are only judicial achievements as part of a broader, multi-actor story, and among those actors is the government: once again, the apparently bold, counter-majoritarian stance of the Court in these famous cases is underpinned by an ANC stance. Here, however, the story is more complex, because that stance has been more reluctant, and there is therefore much to learn about how the Court confronts newness in choppier political waters. Although parts of the story have been told before, it has not been brought into constitutional legal scholarship, and it is also a story that bears repeating.

The Emerging Public Status of LGBTI Equality in South Africa

In 1986, a delegation from the National Union of South African Students met with the ANC in exile. One of its questions was about gay equality. The party's response, as a NUSAS pamphlet recorded it,

1 The Court's decisions are cited later in this chapter; for explicit links to *Makwanyane*, see e.g. Currie, 'Judicious Avoidance', 160.

2 Hirschl, *Juristocracy*, p. 79.

3 See e.g. Budlender et al., *Public Interest Litigation*, pp. 25–34; M. F. Massoud, 'The Evolution of Gay Rights in South Africa' (2003) 15 *Peace Review* 301, 301, 305–06.

was 'that it had taken no policy on the issue of gay liberation' (sic) but it added that 'ANC policy grows as it confronts social questions that need to be addressed' and that '[a] democratic state should restructure and accommodate issues related to oppression'. The party's response also noted that freedom of association was protected in the Freedom Charter.[4] Underneath this no-policy policy, the ANC's characteristically broad tent contained a range of positions. It contained Simon Nkoli, anti-apartheid and gay rights activist, UDF and ANC member, founding member of the National Coalition for Gay and Lesbian Equality and an early force in the civil society response to HIV/AIDS, who caused considerable consternation among his fellow accused when he came out to them in detention while awaiting trial for treason in 1984.[5] The ANC's tent also contained many others who were more conservative on the issue. Some shared his prison cell. Fellow treason accused Mosiuoa Lekota, later Defence Minister and later still one of the ANC leaders to break away and found the Congress of the People (COPE) in 2008, recalls how his arguments with Nkoli changed his views on sexual orientation.[6] Others were in London. In August 1987 British journalist Peter Tatchell concluded an interview with ANC member Ruth Mompati by asking about the ANC's stance on homosexuality. Her initial reply was to repeat the ANC's no-policy stance, but when pressed, she expressed puzzlement about the need for gay and lesbian rights, suggested that it was a distraction from the anti-apartheid struggle,[7] and notoriously stated that lesbians and gays are 'not normal' and that 'I hope that in a liberated South Africa people

[4] 'NUSAS talks to the ANC: Report back on meeting between the National Union of South African Students and the African National Congress held from Sunday, 31 March to Tuesday, 2 April in Harare, Zimbabwe' (1986), available at www.disa.ukzn.ac.za/index.php?option=com_displaydc&recordID=pam19860400.026.022.000, 27–28.

[5] See inter alia the obituary by Z. Achmat, 'We Mourn Simon Tseko Nkoli' (4 June 1999) *Equality*, No. 4, 8–9, reproduced in N. Hoad, K. Martin and G. Reid (eds.), *Sex and Politics in South Africa* (Cape Town: Juta & Co., 2005), pp. 168–69; B. M. Munro, *South Africa and the Dream of Love to Come: Queer Sexuality and the Struggle for Freedom* (University of Minnesota Press, 2012), pp. 47–56; K. Davis, 'Hamba Kahle (Farewell) Simon Nkoli', *Green Left Weekly*, 20 January 1999, www.greenleft.org.au/1999/345/19684.

[6] P. M. Lekota, 'Address at Simon Nkoli's Memorial Service, St Mary's Cathedral, Johannesburg, December 1998', reproduced in Hoad et al. (eds.), *Sex and Politics*, pp. 150–53.

[7] See also H. Kleinbooi, 'Identity Crossfire: On Being a Black Gay Student Activist' in E. Cameron and M. Gevisser (eds.), *Defiant Desire: Gay and Lesbian Lives in South Africa* (New York: Routledge, 1995) e.g. p. 264: 'my black liberationist comrades told me, whenever I brought up the issue of gay rights, that I was "hijacking the struggle"'.

will live a *normal* life. I emphasize the word *normal* ... '.[8] (Years later, Dr Mompati would rather splendidly be invited to write the foreword to a collection of sources on the gay and lesbian rights movement. In it, she notes the steps taken by the ANC to oppose discrimination on the basis of sexual orientation, and concludes: 'times change and attitudes change ... Looking back, I like to think that the debate that was sparked by that interview had a positive outcome'.)[9]

At the time, Mompati's statements received a high-profile retraction. Two months after she made them, in November 1987, Tatchell received a telex that read in part:

> The ANC is indeed very firmly committed to removing all forms of discrimination and oppression in a liberated South Africa ... That commitment must surely extend to the protection of gay rights. I would like to believe that my colleagues... did not want to suggest in any way that a free South Africa would want to see gays discriminated against or subjected to any form of repression. As a movement, we are of the view that the sexual preferences of an individual are a private matter. We would not wish to compromise anybody's right to privacy both now and in future, and would therefore not wish to legislate or decree how people should conduct their private lives. We have, consequently, never been opposed to gay rights. That position remains unchanged.[10]

The telex is signed 'Yours in the common struggle, Thabo Mbeki'. ANC spokesperson Frene Ginwala, later Speaker of Parliament, also gave an exclusive interview to the publication in which Tatchell's piece had appeared, in which she stated that 'The raison d'etre of the ANC's existence is to fight discrimination, and deprivation of gays and lesbians cannot be excluded from that process.'[11]

The support is not completely full-throated, focused as it is on privacy and non-opposition, no doubt reflecting the discomforts about LGBTI sexuality inside and outside the ANC. Some of the motivation for the support was also doubtless strategic. The ANC did not want to lose the support of the international anti-apartheid

[8] P. Tatchell, 'ANC Dashes Hopes for Gay Rights in SA', *Capital Gay*, 18 September 1987, reproduced in Hoad et al. (eds.), *Sex and Politics*, p. 148.

[9] R. Mompati, 'Foreword' in Hoad et al. (eds.), *Sex and Politics*, p. 7.

[10] Telex from Thabo Mbeki to Peter Tatchell, dated 24 November 1987, reproduced in Hoad et al. (eds.), *Sex and Politics*, p. 149.

[11] *Capital Gay*, 4 December 1987, quoted by D. Fine and J. Nicol, 'The Lavender Lobby: Working for Lesbian and Gay Rights within the Liberation Movement' in Cameron and Gevisser (eds.), *Defiant Desire*, pp. 270–71.

movements, and English, Dutch and Scandinavian organizations had reacted strongly against the Mompati interview.[12] But it remains true that as the 1990s dawned, the ANC was moving towards an admirably principled stance on the issue. Following the 1987 expulsion of South Africa's national gay and lesbian association from the International Gay and Lesbian Alliance due to its weak stance on apartheid and racial issues, the new Organization of Lesbian and Gay Activists (OLGA) joined the UDF and began lobbying for LGBTI rights from inside the anti-apartheid movement.[13] In February 1990 Sachs had warned a visiting gay and lesbian lobby group that there was 'no guarantee' that a majority of the ANC would endorse constitutional protections.[14] But considerable debate at an ANC Women's League meeting in March 1990 in Lusaka, at which members of the ANC's National Executive Committee were present, yielded a resolution opposing discrimination on the basis of sexual orientation.[15] In 1991, the ANC included in its draft Bill of Rights, under the heading of 'Gender Rights', a provision that '[d]iscrimination on the grounds of gender, single parenthood, legitimacy of birth or sexual orientation shall be unlawful'.[16] In 1992, support for such a provision was included in the party's *Ready to Govern* policy

[12] See e.g. E. C. Christiansen, 'Ending the Apartheid of the Closet: Sexual Orientation in the South African Constitutional Process' (1999–2000) 32 *New York University Journal of International Law and Policy* 997, 1025.

[13] S. Croucher, 'South Africa's Democratization and the Politics of Gay Liberation' (2002) 28 *Journal of Southern African Studies* 315, 318–19; Christiansen, 'Ending the Apartheid of the Closet', 1023–25; L. Newstrom, 'The Horizon of Rights: Lessons from South Africa for the Post-Goodridge Analysis of Same-Sex Marriage' (2007) 40 *Cornell International Law Journal* 781, 786; P. de Vos, 'The "Inevitability" of Same Sex Marriage in South Africa's Post-Apartheid State' (2007) 23 *South African Journal on Human Rights* 432, 435–36.

[14] P. Tatchell, 'The Moment the ANC Embraced Gay Rights' in Hoad et al. (eds.), *Sex and Politics*, pp. 146–47. On Sachs as a supporter of gay and lesbian rights within the ANC, see e.g. Fine and Nicol, 'Lavender Lobby', p. 271; Christiansen, 'Ending the Apartheid of the Closet', 1053–54; Massoud, 'Evolution of Gay Rights', 302–03.

[15] Christiansen, 'Ending the Apartheid of the Closet', 1026–27, citing correspondence with Albie Sachs. Two years before, at a conference on social welfare funded by Sweden, Adelaide Tambo had raised the issues of 'wife and girlfriend battering' and 'issues like lesbianism and homosexuality'; see Macmillan, *The Lusaka Years*, p. 183. The vital role played by women within the ANC in supporting LGBTI rights, as part of a broader concern with gender, remains under-researched.

[16] Art 7(2); 'A Bill of Rights for a Democratic South Africa – Working Draft for Consultation' (1991) 3 *African Journal of International and Comparative Law* 608, 613.

statement, making the ANC the first mass movement in Africa, and one of the first in the world, to express support for LGBTI equality.[17]

While the ANC richly deserves this distinction, it should also be noted that it was not the only South African political actor taking this position. OLGA conducted a survey in 1991 among political parties, which produced open support for the explicit constitutional protection of gay and lesbian rights from the DP (although only from it; the ANC had only just been unbanned at that stage and was not included in the survey).[18] And often forgotten is the fact that in December 1992, the KwaZulu Legislative Assembly, controlled by the IFP, passed a resolution in favour of the constitutional protection of gay and lesbian rights.[19] It was the DP and the IFP who first proposed the inclusion of 'sexual orientation' as a listed ground in the main equality clause, as opposed to the ANC's initial proposal of inclusion under a separate 'Gender Rights' heading.[20] Other factors were also favourable. The interim Constitution drafting process was conducive to elite influence, and forces at this level supported the LGBTI equality trend.[21] Edwin Cameron personally lobbied Hugh Corder, a member of the Technical Committee drafting the interim Constitution's Bill of Rights, to include the sexual orientation clause

17 Fine and Nicol, 'Lavender Lobby', p. 269. Sadly, the ANC remains an outlier in this respect in Africa: see e.g. S. Maguire, 'The Human Rights of Sexual Minorities in Africa' (2004–2005) 35 *California Western International Law Journal* 1.

18 Christiansen, 'Ending the Apartheid of the Closet', 1029–30.

19 KwaZulu Legislative Assembly Resolution, 'The Constitution of the State of KwaZulu/Natal' (1 December 1992), clause 10(a), to which I am referred by E. Cameron, 'Sexual Orientation and the Constitution: A Test Case for Human Rights' (1993) 110 *South African Law Journal* 450, 468 n. 107.

20 See 'A Bill of Rights for a New South Africa – Preliminary Revised Text, February 1993', available at www.anc.org.za/show.php?id=231, Art 8(2) 'Gender Rights', Art 1 'Equality'. The 1991 draft has a similar split, though its equivalent of the equality clause is entitled 'General' – 1991 draft, Art 1.; E. Cameron, 'Sexual Orientation', 450, 468–70; Christiansen, 'Ending the Apartheid of the Closet', 1031.

21 S. Croucher, 'South Africa: Opportunities Seized in the Post-Apartheid Era' in M. Tremblay, D. Paternotte and C. Johnson (eds.), *The Gay and Lesbian Movement and the State: Comparative Insights into a Transformed Relationship* (Surrey: Ashgate, 2011), p. 159; Christiansen, 'Ending the Apartheid of the Closet', 1055–56; see also Munro, *Dream of Love to Come*, xxi, and De Vos, 'The "Inevitability"', 441–42, 446, noting that LGBTI rights were consciously pursued by discreet lobbying rather than grassroots political activity or other more confrontational political activity.

in the draft.[22] The Technical Committee, in turn, was strongly supportive of LGBTI rights.[23]

The pattern of civil society forces was also conducive, though public opinion itself was not. The National Coalition for Gay and Lesbian Equality was formed in 1994 to lobby for the 'sexual orientation' clause in the interim Constitution to be retained in the 1996 text, given doubtful levels of public support. But no populist backlash emerged. LGBTI rights around the world have often met with strong resistance from religious groups, but South Africa to a substantial degree did not follow this script. The fight against apartheid had made allies of LGBTI activists and some religious groups.[24] Anglican Archbishop Desmond Tutu, a figure of international stature whose church has generally been 'vocally pro-gay rights', would write a letter to the Constitutional Assembly urging the inclusion of the sexual orientation clause in the 1996 Constitution.[25] The more conservative white churches, on the other hand, were experiencing a crisis of their moral authority in the wake of their support of apartheid.[26] In 1998, Gerrit Grové, another member of the Technical

22 Spitz, *Politics of Transition*, pp. 306, 404, 406. Cameron himself does not mention this intervention in his memoir of AIDS, where he simply states that 'by an almost certain causal sequence, assisted by the stand of brave leaders like Simon Nkoli' the ANC's stance in the Mbeki telex and its negotiating positions was translated into the sexual orientation clause – E. Cameron, *Witness to AIDS* (Cape Town: Tafelberg, 2005), pp. 125–26 – but he did acknowledge the impact of his 'personal contacts and interventions' in a 1999 interview: see Croucher, 'South Africa's Democratization', 323. See also his positioning of LGBTI rights as 'the logical consequence of the liberation process' and its general values of dignity and equality, rather than 'some special dispensation, based on special pleading, for gays and lesbians in South Africa' in E. Cameron, 'Constitutional Protection of Sexual Orientation and African Conceptions of Humanity' (2001) 118 *South African Law Journal* 642, 647.

23 One commentator has gone so far as to suggest that the Committee 'very favourably interpreted' the existing international and comparative materials on gay and lesbian equality rights to show a trend in their favour to a degree that was 'less than fully honest': Christiansen, 'Ending the Apartheid of the Closet', 1034–36.

24 See e.g. R. Abel, *Politics by Other Means: Law in the Struggle Against Apartheid, 1980–1994* (London: Routledge, 1995), ch. 4.

25 Submission to Theme Committee Four, Constitutional Assembly, from Desmond Tutu, Anglican Archbishop of Cape Town, 2 June 1995, reproduced in Hoad et al. (eds.), *Sex and Politics*, p. 222; the quoted description is from Munro, *Dream of Love to Come*, p. xvii.

26 See the recent papers by P. Strauss, 'Church Polity in a Changing South Africa: A study of two Reformed churches' (2013) 39 *Studiae Historiae Ecclesiasticae* 129; and J. van der Merwe, 'The Dutch Reformed Church from Human Relations and the South African Scene in the Light of Scripture to Church and Society: The Struggle Goes On' (2013) 39 *Studiae Historiae Ecclesiasticae* 137; and the unpublished research on trends on sermons

Committee, recalled his amazement at the 'silence of the Afrikaner and other churches' and their 'tacit response to a clause that they might have been expected to oppose with vigour'.[27] This silence is an under-acknowledged part of the success story of LGBTI rights in South Africa. In this context, the NP grudgingly came to accept the clause, and the contrast with its greater defiance on the issue of the death penalty is telling. The result, combined with the high levels of mobilization among LGBTI groups, was that submissions to the Constitutional Assembly in favour of including protections for LGBTI rights far exceeded those opposing it (7032 responses to 564), despite majority opposition in opinion polls.[28] All this combined to produce a certain sense of inevitability.[29] Once included in the 1993 text, the clause became part of the rejection of apartheid and a manifestation of the responsibility to produce a better society for all. Private prejudices and discomfort ill fit the politics of the moment.[30] By the time the 1996 Constitution was passed,

and a 'syndrome of apathy' by J. Cilliers, 'Preaching between Assimilation and Separation: Perspectives on Church and State in South African Society', paper delivered at the Homilectics Seminar for Danish Pastors, Copenhagen, 19–20 June 2008, available at http://academic.sun.ac.za/theology/Profiles/Profile_documents/Johan_Cilliers_PREACHING_BETWEEN_ASSIMILATION_AND_SEPERATION.pdf (sic). These churches were not entirely detached from the negotiations, however: see T. R. Lave, 'A Nation at Prayer, a Nation in Hate: Apartheid in South Africa' (1994) 30 *Stanford Journal of International Law* 483, 523–24.

27 Spitz, *Politics of Transition*, pp. 306–07.

28 Massoud, 'Evolution of Gay Rights', 303–04; Christiansen, 'Ending the Apartheid of the Closet', 1040; Croucher, 'South Africa's Democratization', 323; De Vos, '"Inevitability" of Same Sex Marriage', 439–43; for the figures, see M. Palmberg, 'Emerging Visibility of Gays and Lesbians in Southern Africa: Contrasting Contexts' in B. D. Adam, J. W. Duyvendak and A. Krouwel (eds.), *The Global Emergence of Gay and Lesbian Politics* (Philadelphia: Temple University Press, 1999), p. 273.

29 Hugh Corder believes that once the sexual orientation clause was included in the draft equality clause, it was almost impossible to remove it – Spitz, *Politics of Transition*, p. 307. Spitz himself sees the clause as the best example of what he calls the general 'once-in-never-out' dynamic of the drafting process – *Ibid.*, pp. 307, 407. P. de Vos and J. Barnard, 'Same-sex Marriage, Civil Unions and Domestic Partnerships in South Africa: Critical Reflections on an Ongoing Saga' (2007) 124 *South African Law Journal* 795, 797–98 conclude that, given the history of activists like Simon Nkoli and the ANC's stance, 'it is no surprise' that South Africa came to include sexual orientation in its equality clause. Edwin Cameron, as we have seen, refers to an 'almost certain causal sequence' – Cameron, *Witness to AIDS*, p. 126.

30 See E. Cameron, 'Nepal's New Constitution and Fundamental Rights of Minorities – Lessons of the South African Experience', paper delivered at a civil society constitution drafting seminar, Kathmandu, Nepal, 8 January 2007, reproduced in (2007) 23 *South African Journal on Human Rights* 195, 200–01.

only the tiny African Christian Democratic Party (ACDP) opposed the text because of the sexual orientation clause.[31]

The Two *National Coalition* Decisions: Criminalization and Immigration Law

As with *Makwanyane*, recognizing this political context should already make us see the resulting LGBTI equality decisions as more than judicial achievements. What might in the abstract be thought an issue displaying substantial newness was in fact less new than it might have been, and we will see that subsequent government activity also offered support to the Court. We will also see a familiar constitution-building logic: the same type of institutional calculations that we saw in *NNP*, and the same decisions to settle some issues but not others that we saw in *Hoffman*.

In 1996, with its textual goals secured, the National Coalition turned its attention to a carefully designed litigation campaign, steering clear of the most contentious issues initially and prevailing on other would-be litigants to do so as well.[32] However, the first concrete manifestation of the new dispensation was not, as it is often taken to be, its successful 1998 challenge to the criminal prohibition of sodomy in *National Coalition for Gay and Lesbian Equality* v. *Minister of Justice* ('*National Coalition (1)*').[33] That honour instead goes to the Special Pensions Act 69 of 1996. The Act provided for pensions for those involved in the anti-apartheid struggle, and for their spouses and dependants, and the Act is explicit that 'spouse' includes same-sex partners. This inclusion followed lobbying by lesbian members of Umkhonto we Sizwe, the ANC's armed wing.[34] These women, and the Parliament that listened to them, have gone unremembered in legal scholarship.

31 Cameron, 'Sexual Orientation', 465–70; Croucher, 'South Africa's Democratization', 320–24; Christiansen, 'Ending the Apartheid of the Closet', 1029–31, 1038; De Vos, '"Inevitability" of Same Sex Marriage', 442.

32 Budlender et al., *Public Interest Litigation*, pp. 28–30; generally De Vos, '"Inevitability" of Same Sex Marriage'; see also Cameron, 'Sexual Orientation', 471.

33 *National Coalition for Gay and Lesbian Equality* v. *Minister of Justice* 1999 (1) SA 6 (CC).

34 Special Pensions Act 69 of 1996, s 31 definition of 'spouse' read with s 31(2)(a)(iii) definition of 'marriage relationship' as including 'a continuous cohabitation in a homosexual or heterosexual partnership for a period of at least 5 years'. I am referred by J. Cock, 'Engendering Gay and Lesbian Rights: The Equality Clause in the South African Constitution' (2003) 26 *Women's Studies International Forum* 35, 39; and M. T. Andenes and R. Wintermute (eds.), *The Legal Recognition of Same-Sex Partnerships: A Study of National, European and International Law* (Oxford: Hart, 2001), Appendix 1, p. 778.

The Special Pensions Act, however, was to feature in a different light in *National Coalition (1)*, reflecting the ambiguities of the ANC government's stance. As the Court there noted, the Act specifically precluded persons convicted of a criminal offense, including sodomy, from receiving pensions.[35] Parliament had thus recognized for the first time that a same-sex partner could be a 'spouse' sharing in a pension, but it had not acted to remove the disqualifying criminality of some of those spouses' sexual activity. Minister of Justice Dullah Omar also announced his intention to oppose *National Coalition (1)*, but formal opposition was mounted on 'very limited grounds' and the government withdrew its opposition before the first hearing.[36] The Court then handed down a decision that, like *Hoffman*, was bolder than necessary to dispense of the case. It employed the same tactic of skipping over the first rationality enquiry of the equality clause in order to invoke the explicit sexual orientation clause and make the stronger finding that the criminalization of consensual sodomy constituted unfair discrimination.[37] The judgment also included strong rhetoric in favour of LGBTI equality (including possibly the most quotable line in all of the Court's jurisprudence, from Sachs J: 'Only in the most technical sense is this a case about who may penetrate whom where').[38] As in *Hoffman*, the Court in *National Coalition (1)* could build on an existing policy trend (although this would become much more obvious in the National Coalition's second case, as we will see). As in *Makwanyane*, the Court could take a principled, counter-majoritarian stance to defend minority rights with confidence that it would not suffer backlash, albeit that the ANC's stance on the death penalty had been less equivocal. The Court was not just invoking the words 'sexual orientation' in the list of presumptively unfair grounds of discrimination, or an abstract philosophical idea of equality or dignity. It could instead feel itself to be articulating an idea of existing public status, with a track record of principled support among key political actors. This background should also affect the way we understand the government's stance in the case. The evolution of the ANC's views on LGBTI equality issues generally has been slow and uncertain, but it would be quite odd if the party had committed itself to the sexual

[35] Special Pensions Act, s 1(8) disqualifies from a pension any person convicted of an offense listed in Schedule 1 of the Criminal Procedure Act 51 of 1977 after 2 February 1990, which was true of sodomy prior to the *National Coalition (1)* litigation.

[36] *National Coalition (1)*, para. 5; Croucher, 'South Africa's Democratization', 328.

[37] *National Coalition (1)*, paras. 17–18.

[38] *Ibid.*, para. 107.

orientation clause in 1996 but opposed one of the most straightforward applications of that clause, the decriminalization of sodomy, in 1998. It is more plausible to understand the ANC's response to the case as a reaction to the issue being taken out of parliament and out of its control, part of what we have seen is a larger pattern of the party coming to terms with the fact that including so many issues in the *Constitution* was to place many issues within the potential power of the *Court.*

Both these points are still more clearly illustrated by the next step in the LGBTI equality litigation campaign. *National Coalition for Gay and Lesbian Equality* v. *Minister of Home Affairs* ('*National Coalition (2)*') is a more intricate exercise in institutional authority than is recognized when it is merely footnoted as the second LGBTI rights decision or filed as a simple case of principled minority rights protection.[39] The case concerned immigration rules for same-sex couples with one South African and one foreign member. The government initially accommodated these couples by means of special exemptions, but then decided that this practice could not continue.[40] When the National Coalition launched proceedings, the Cabinet chose at the last minute to oppose the litigation.[41] The government's chief concern appears to have been the institutional point that it should be the government, as sovereign, that controls the movement of non-citizens in and out of the country, and so this should not be subject to constitutional control. The government also argued that the issue was not ripe for hearing, on the grounds that it was possible to interpret the existing statute's reference to 'spouse' to include a same-sex life partner, and the applicants had not sought to have the section read that way by the relevant government officials before litigating.[42] The government had thus signalled that it would not welcome the Court deciding the issue, and its arguments offered two ways for a Bickellian court to have avoided doing so. The Court took neither. It held that whether or not the government enjoyed special deference in relation to foreign citizens, that would not stop the Court acting to protect the rights of the South African half of same-sex couples.[43] It also rejected the ripeness argument, which had much higher stakes than its framing as a technical jurisdictional issue can make it appear, on the basis that 'spouse' could not be read to include unmarried partners without

[39] *National Coalition for Gay and Lesbian Equality* v. *Minister of Home Affairs* 2000 (2) SA 1 (CC).

[40] *Ibid.*, paras. 18–20. [41] Ibid., paras. 5–6. [42] Ibid., paras. 21–25.

[43] Ibid., paras. 27–29.

doing violence to the statutory language.[44] Had it accepted this argument, the implications would have been large indeed. The state's ripeness argument amounted to a suggestion that references to 'spouse' in statutes clearly drafted with only married opposite-sex couples in mind could be read to include unmarried same-sex life partners. That could have decided most LGBTI equality issues at a stroke. The fact that the government advanced this argument reflects the uncertainties in its stance, because *National Coalition (2)* would *also* see the government offering the strongest substantive opposition it ever has to a LGBTI equality case. It not only argued against accommodating same-sex couples in immigration law on the basis that the state was obliged to protect (traditional forms of) marriage, but also put its name to the maddeningly formalist argument that the existing rules did not discriminate against LGBTI people because these people could avail themselves of the statute's protection by marrying someone of the opposite sex.[45] This is hard to reconcile with its accommodating ripeness argument, and supports the view that the state was just raising any argument that might allow it to keep control of the issue.

The Court's response to this government stance is instructive. A court driven by the desire not to antagonize the ANC might have been expected to be deferent in *National Coalition (2)*. The Court did not do this. It firmly rejected both the state's offensive formalist argument and the argument that the protection of the traditional institution of marriage provided a basis for excluding LGBTI couples from immigration law benefits, holding that this exclusion bore no rational relationship to protecting marriage. It found for same-sex couples in unequivocal terms.[46] As in *Makwanyane*, the Court was able to argue that the global trend is towards the formal legal recognition of LGBTI couples and to link its finding to that emerging global view.[47] However, in doing this, the Court was clashing much less with the government over a substantive issue than it may appear. The strongest evidence for this, in addition to what we have already seen, is that the Special Pensions Act was by no means Parliament's only step to extend legal protections to same-sex couples, nor even the only one enacted before *National Coalition (1)*. The Court in *National Coalition (2)* was able to rely on a growing list of enactments from the government itself supporting LGBTI equality. In an

[44] Ibid., paras. 21–25. [45] Ibid., para. 34. [46] Ibid., paras. 34–36, 38, 55–56.

[47] See esp. Ibid., para. 48; we will see this again in *Doctors for Life International* v. *Speaker of the National Assembly* 2006 (6) SA 416 (CC) in the next chapter.

exact parallel with *Hoffman*, the Court could offer a long footnote in authority for the propositions that 'a notable and significant development in our statute law in recent years has been the extent of express and implied recognition the legislature has accorded same-sex partnerships' and that 'this trend is significant in evincing Parliament's commitment to equality on the ground of sexual orientation'.[48] A government opposed to LGBTI equality would simply not have passed all these statutes, which are again invariably left out of legal scholarly accounts of the Court's decisions in this area. Once we include them in the picture, we can see why it makes much more sense to understand the state's stance in *National Coalition (2)* primarily as jurisdictional, not substantive.

National Coalition (2) also parallels *Hoffman* in its care in deciding what to decide. It did not take the opportunities for avoidance offered by the state's sovereignty and ripeness arguments, but it also did not exploit the state's position on the interpretation of the word 'spouse' to decide many LGBTI equality issues at a stroke. A Court intending to be a zealous defender of principles of justice, come what may, might have been expected to seize the opportunity, but the Court instead approached the issue on the basis that same-sex marriage was not at that point recognized in South Africa and confined itself to invalidating the exclusion of same-sex couples from the immigration law regime. We may explain its refusal to read 'spouse' broadly simply on the basis of standard principles of statutory interpretation, but we might also see a practical calculation of the sort I described in the last chapter about how best to give effect to LGBTI rights. The National Coalition had decided that the most effective approach was an incremental one that built up to the most controversial issues, and the Court may have agreed with this logic.[49] Certainly its accompanying use of bold rhetoric does not suggest judges personally reluctant or hesitant about the substance of LGBTI rights, and we will now see that such a calculation is the key to the same-sex marriage judgment.

[48] *National Coalition (2)*, para. 37 n. 42 cites the Special Pensions Act 69 of 1996, the Lotteries Act 57 of 1997, the Basic Conditions of Employment Act 75 of 1997, the Housing Act 107 of 1997, the South African Civil Aviation Authority Act 40 of 1998, the Employment Equity Act 55 of 1998, the Medical Schemes Act 131 of 1998, and the Road Traffic Management Corporation Act 20 of 1999.

[49] See also the discussion of the judgment in *Minister of Health* v. *Treatment Action Campaign (2)* 2002 (5) SA 721 (CC) and the TAC's strategy in Chapter 8.

The Two *Fourie* Decisions: Same-Sex Marriage

The first two LGBTI equality decisions are thus more subtle than they are usually taken to be: like *Makwanyane*, it is too simple to treat them as straightforwardly bold counter-majoritarian defences of rights, and like the voting rights cases, they are at least as much about drawing institutional lines as they are about the substance of rights. We will see at the end of this chapter how this pattern continued in subsequent cases, vindicating LGBTI equality in the context of pension benefits, guardianship, adoption and inheritance. But it will be useful to first discuss the same-sex marriage case, which was handed down after most of these other cases.

At first glance, it can seem as if the Court boldly enforced LGBTI equality right up until marriage, and then got cautious. In *Fourie* v. *Minister of Home Affairs* ('*Fourie (2)*'), it broke with the pattern of earlier cases and referred the choice about the ultimate form of legal recognition for same-sex unions to Parliament (although under a deadline; the Court made a suspended order simply extending the definition of marriage to include same-sex couples, which would come into effect if Parliament did not act within one year of the date of the order).[50] It had also earlier delayed deciding the same-sex marriage issue by declining to hear the matter on direct appeal from the court of first instance, holding in *Minister of Home Affairs* v. *Fourie* ('*Fourie (1)*') that the Supreme Court of Appeal should hear the matter first.[51]

However, we should start by noticing that while *Fourie (2)* did defer to Parliament, it did so to an exceedingly small degree. We are accustomed to a pattern in the global LGBTI equality story in which receptive legal systems choose between marriage or separate civil unions for same-sex couples, and so it can be deceptively easy to think that it is this decision that *Fourie (2)* left to Parliament.[52] It is not. In articulating 'guiding principles' for the legislature in making its decision, *Fourie (2)* calls the idea of a separate civil union for same-sex couples a 'separate but equal' solution. It then drives the point home by comparing the idea of a separate union to a notorious apartheid-era decision involving Godfrey Pitje, the clerk at the law firm of Mandela & Tambo, which had upheld

[50] *Minister of Home Affairs* v. *Fourie* 2006 (1) SA 524 (CC).

[51] *Fourie* v. *Minister of Home Affairs* 2003 (5) SA 301 (CC).

[52] For a pre-*Fourie (2)* framing of the South African debate in these terms, with reference to the global position at the time, see K. Williams, 'I Do or We Won't: Legalising Same-Sex Marriage in South Africa' (2004) 20 *South African Journal on Human Rights* 32.

racially segregated tables for legal counsel in court on the grounds that one table was functionally as good as the other.[53] *Fourie (2)* therefore effectively ruled out the approach adopted in several other countries of creating a special, separate civil union regime for same-sex couples. This was the interpretation of the decision subsequently adopted by the state law advisors and by Department of Justice officials testifying in Parliament, and it was this that led the government to abandon its first attempt at a response to *Fourie (2)*, which was indeed a draft bill creating a separate civil union regime for same-sex couples.[54]

Why then does *Fourie (2)* defer to Parliament while closing off almost all Parliament's room for choice? It is hard to explain this as avoidance of political conflict with the ANC. The path of least political resistance, apart from avoiding the issue entirely, would obviously have been to leave open the possibility of a separate civil union regime. That would have been reasonably progressive by international standards at the time, and consistent with the government's stance in the litigation; the fact that the government's first reaction to *Fourie (2)* was a separate civil union bill also strongly suggests this would have been its preferred option.[55] But instead of referring the issue to Parliament while leaving this way out carefully open, the Court referred it after explicitly comparing this route to Jim Crow and apartheid. In fact, the stance adopted in *Fourie (2)* created the largest possible political headache for the ANC, because it gave Parliament ownership of a controversial issue whilst also removing almost all its room for manoeuvre. If the Court had settled the entire issue itself, at least the ANC government would have had deniability.

The real reason for the Court's stance in *Fourie (2)* is not that it wanted to duck the decision about whether or not to recognize same-sex marriage, but that it wanted to involve Parliament in the decision to recognize it.[56] It is in this connection that we should understand its statements

[53] *Fourie (2)*, paras. 150–53. The earlier decision is *S* v. *Pitje* 1960 (4) SA 709 (A); the Court also refers here to *Brown* v. *Board of Education*.

[54] D. Bilchitz and M. Judge, 'For Whom Does the Bell Toll? The Challenges and Possibilities of the Civil Union Act for Family Law in South Africa' (2007) 23 *South African Journal on Human Rights* 466, 477, 479–81; De Vos and Barnard, 'Same-Sex Marriage', 803–06, 808–11, 819. The South African Law Reform Commission reached a similar conclusion in its March 2006 *Report on Domestic Partnerships* (Project 118), § 5.6.2–5.6.3.

[55] For its stance in the litigation see *Fourie (2)*, paras. 33, 35–36.

[56] See also Davis and Klare, 'Transformative Constitutionalism', 507–08; Roux, *Politics of Principle*, pp. 255–56.

about the value of legislative recognition as part of law's role as 'a great teacher' that 'establishes public norms'. Sachs J wrote for the majority:

> The claim by the applicants . . . should . . . be seen as part of a comprehensive wish to be able to live openly and freely as lesbian women emancipated from all the legal taboos that historically have kept them from enjoying life in the mainstream of society. The right to celebrate their union signifies far more than a right to enter into a legal arrangement with many attendant and significant consequences, important though they may be. It represents a major symbolical milestone in their long walk to equality and dignity. *The greater and more secure the institutional imprimatur for their union, the more solidly will it and other such unions be rescued from legal oblivion, and the more tranquil and enduring will such unions ultimately turn out to be* (emphasis added).[57]

The Court is not deferring to the legislature here because it has to, but because it thinks this is the best way to protect vulnerable rights going forward. This passage recognizes that, ultimately, members of the public are the crucial infrastructure for giving effect to LGBTI equality in its richer senses, and that if the symbolic legal milestone includes the legislature's 'imprimatur' as well as the Court's, the impact on the public mind will likely be greater, and the institution less vulnerable to later erosion by majority public prejudice. It is a decision about how to give effect to the constitution in the world based in part on social and political facts.[58]

This issue is also the point of internal disagreement in the case. *Fourie (2)* was not unanimous; O'Regan J was once again in lone dissent, and this is not a coincidence. Just as in *NNP*, the split is not about the substance of the rights issue itself, but the institutional decision about the constitutionally best way to give effect to it. On O'Regan J's view, which was shared by a majority of the earlier also-divided Supreme Court of Appeal bench, applicants had approached the courts to develop the common law (of marriage) so as to give effect to their constitutional rights (to equality and dignity). Courts are constitutionally obliged to conduct this development. Therefore, they should. It is irrelevant that action by a different institution might be preferable. O'Regan J states

[57] *Fourie (2)*, para. 137 (emphasis added).

[58] See also *National Coalition (2)*, paras. 82–83, referring to this kind of decision; Bilchitz and Judge 'For Whom Does the Bell Toll', 478 n. 69. It should be noted that Cameron JA, for the Supreme Court of Appeal majority, spoke of the trust judges are entitled to have in the South African public: *Fourie* v. *Minister of Home Affairs* [2005] 1 All SA 273 (SCA), paras. 23–25.

openly that 'it would have been desirable if the unconstitutional situation identified in this matter had been resolved by Parliament' and that 'an Act of Parliament conferring the right to marry on gays and lesbians might be thought to carry greater democratic legitimacy than an order of this Court'. But to her that is beside the point: it is not a good enough reason for a court to refuse relief to applicants who merit it.[59] By contrast, the rest of the Court felt obliged or at least entitled to take this into account and make the sort of effects-based institutional calculation I described in previous chapters. As Sachs J framed the point, 'What [earlier precedents] highlight is the need to look at the precise circumstances of each case with a view to determining how best the values of the Constitution can be promoted by an order that is just and equitable.'[60]

Fourie (2) again shows how the constitution-building account can capture the reality of South African practice. It also shows us that this approach is not confined to cases like *NNP* in which the rights violation is uncertain and prospective, but includes cases where the rights violation is an old one indeed. Both O'Regan J and Cameron JA (who wrote the SCA majority judgment) emphasize this fact, and they are hardly unreasonable to do so. But this argument is not decisive if a less court-centric approach might be able to do more to right the historical wrong – and the argument that a more multi-institutional remedy would best serve the interests of LGBTI equality was strong in South Africa in 2005. A good deal of change prior to *Fourie (2)* had occurred without a fight – indeed, without even being noticed very much, partly as a function of the silence from opposition religious groups noted earlier. That changed with the *Fourie* litigation, the first LGBTI equality case in which the litigation involved opponents from civil society. Doctors for Life International and the Marriage Alliance of South Africa, whose affidavit was deposed to by (Roman Catholic) Cardinal Wilfred Napier, Archbishop of Durban, were admitted as amici curiae, and the Court heard arguments from both. Even the way in which this opposition was conducted sometimes reflected the low profile of earlier developments. It was argued before the Court in *Fourie (2)* that marriage was centred on procreation and that same-sex marriage would undermine the institution, arguments which

[59] *Fourie (2)*, esp. paras. 170–71.

[60] *Ibid.*, para. 135. The decision would later be cited by the unanimous Court as authority for this proposition: see *Justice Alliance of South Africa* v. *President of the Republic of South Africa* 2011 (5) SA 388 (CC), para. 100. Note that Justice O'Regan had retired from the Court by this point.

the Court had firmly rejected nearly six years previously in *National Coalition (2)*.[61] Still more strikingly, later submissions before Parliament opposed same-sex marriage on the basis that recognizing it would open the way for same-sex couples to adopt – a right that same-sex couples had already held for three years at that point, following the Court's decision in *Du Toit* (discussed in the next section).[62] It is plausible that the *Fourie (2)* majority's attempt to bring in the legislature was informed by its concern about the public impact of its earlier LGBTI equality cases.

That decision, as in *NNP*, looks good in hindsight – and given the trajectory of the ANC's stance on the issue, we might at least owe it to the party to not find this particularly surprising. Having considered the possibility of a separate regime for same-sex couples, and rejected it in light of *Fourie (2)*'s comments, the legislature ultimately passed the Civil Union Act 17 of 2006. The Act permits the creation of civil unions between any two adults, who may chose to call their legal relationship a marriage or a civil union. Their choice determines how the state records the union, so same-sex couples that so elect are officially recorded as 'married'. Otherwise, the legal consequences are identical and mirror those of the old Marriage Act. Individual civil marriage officers may decline to solemnize same-sex marriages on grounds of conscience. Individual religious marriage officers may not marry same-sex couples unless the religious organization to which they belong opts in, via notification to the government. A provision explicitly excludes customary marriages, so same-sex couples remain unable to conclude customary marriages (except to the extent that customary law may already permit such unions, which is a subject of some contention).[63] The old Act, providing only for opposite-sex unions, is retained, so it remains possible for an opposite-sex couple to be married under either statute.

The Act is not perfect. It is odd that the old Act is retained, and this raises the possibility that the new Act might be used only by same-sex couples and become a de facto separate but equal regime. It is also worrying that the marriage officers of a state which may not discriminate on the basis of sexual orientation are afforded a personal right to refuse to

[61] *National Coalition (2)*, paras. 50–52.

[62] *Du Toit* v. *Minister of Welfare and Population Development* 2003 (2) SA 198 (CC), handed down on 10 September 2002.

[63] See e.g. J. Church, 'Same-Sex Unions: Different Voices' (2005) 9 *Fundamina* 49, 50–52; E. Bonthuys, 'Race and Gender in the Civil Union Act' (2007) 23 *South African Journal on Human Rights* 526; Bilchitz and Judge, 'For Whom Does the Bell Toll', 495–96; see also *Satchwell*, para. 12.

marry same-sex couples.[64] That said, however, same-sex unions now enjoy the multi-institutional symbolic protection that *Fourie (2)* spoke of. Those who criticize the Court on the basis that it could itself have done more to recognize same-sex marriage may make the mistake – one that will assume considerable importance in the following chapters – of asking the wrong question. If we ask not what bolder steps the Court could potentially have taken, but instead what step would protect rights best, we might be glad today that LGBTI equality does not rest only on a set of judicial pronouncements. Instead, South Africa has a legislatively enacted regime that has removed any necessary connection between marriage and a particular configuration of sexes. That is no small feat.

And it is significantly an ANC feat, though the party gets little or no credit for this in legal scholarship. David Bilchitz and Melanie Judge, who were involved in the public consultation process, record that 'the ANC Executive had to assert its authority and remind members of Parliament . . . of the deep commitment of the ANC to equality for all South Africans that was rooted in the Freedom Charter', and that the Act passed under an ANC three-line whip, 231–41, with three abstentions.[65] But they relegate these extraordinarily important facts to a footnote. What they signify is that the Court was not taking a lone counter-majoritarian stance. It was joined in that stance by the ANC leadership, among other parliamentarians, who were willing to defend the same vision of the Constitution as the Court.[66] As with *Makwanyane*, the Court was not enforcing a majority commitment, but that does not contradict the sense in which it was receiving into constitutional doctrine something with a broader, pre-existing public status. It is not merely

64 For criticism, including these objections, see Bilchitz and Judge, 'For Whom Does the Bell Toll', 487–96, De Vos and Barnard, 'Same-Sex Marriage', 813, 821–24; De Vos, '"Inevitability" of Same Sex Marriage', 462–63; generally Bonthuys, 'Race and Gender'.

65 Bilchitz and Judge, 'For Whom Does the Bell Toll', 482 n. 91. A three-line whip is one in which party members are obliged to be present and vote the party line. Other observers have been less admiring: see e.g. N. P. K. Masemola, 'Floor-crossing and Its Political Consequences in South Africa' (Electoral Institute of South Africa Occasional Paper No. 44, June 2007), 9, referring to 'the Civil Union Bill, which the ruling ANC bulldozed through Parliament despite massive objections from opposition parties'.

66 Roux's reading of *Fourie (2)* as a 'fully principled' decision based on confidence that Parliament would 'arrive at the position required by constitutional principle' comes closest to this argument, but *Fourie (2)* remains an outlier on his view, and in line with his general approach he gives the credit to the Court's strategy, with the ANC leadership's stance (which he notes) mentioned only because it could 'shield' the Court 'from the adverse public reaction to its decision' – Roux, *Politics of Principle*, pp. 258–59.

invoking the authority of the bare text, and as with the abolition of the death penalty a decade before, the celebrated constitutional outcome is one vindicated, despite resistance, by the ANC leadership in Parliament. In the wake of the interim Constitution's drafting, the National Coalition had acknowledged (no doubt partly strategically, but no less accurately for it) that the historic inclusion of the sexual orientation clause in the text was not based on the Coalition's size or strength, but 'on a commitment to human rights and a constitutional order by the ANC'.[67] That textual achievement is widely recognized; what is not is that this ANC commitment was still vindicating LGBT equality a decade later.

Pierre de Vos and Jaco Barnard, two other close observers of the same-sex marriage parliamentary process, note that while the issue is complex, the simple version is that 'the Constitutional Court's judgment left the ANC in a precarious position: it had to comply with the court judgment while aware that the vast majority of its voters were strongly opposed to it'.[68] This is in line with my argument that *Fourie (2)* was not an exercise in avoiding political conflict. But what is striking is that the authors take it for granted that the ANC chose, in this situation, to comply with the judgment. After all, the party could simply have failed to pass a statute by the Court's deadline, in which case the Court's default ruling would have come into force, the definition of marriage would have been extended, and the outcome could have been blamed on the Court. It could also have reacted more strongly, repudiating the judgment, attacking the Court, passing a separate civil union regime for same-sex couples and defying the Court to invalidate it, or pursuing a constitutional amendment protecting traditional understandings of marriage. In the hearings there were calls for such an amendment, or for a referendum.[69] Yet De Vos and Barnard do not consider the possibility that the ANC could have done these things, and they do not give the ANC credit for choosing not to, or for the stance it ultimately adopted.[70]

[67] Croucher, 'South Africa's Democratization', 325, citing National Coalition for Gay and Lesbian Equality 'We Must Claim Our Citizenship: Report of the Interim Executive Committee' (December 1994–December 1995), p. 9.

[68] De Vos and Barnard, 'Same-Sex Marriage', 820.

[69] See *Hansard*, 14 November 2006 (Minister of Home Affairs, N. Mapisa-Nqakula (ANC)); in the absence of an available official version I rely on the transcript available at https://pmg.org.za/hansard/18494/.

[70] See also J. Barnard, 'Totalitarianism, (Same Sex) Marriage and Democratic Politics in Post-Apartheid South Africa' (2007) 23 *South African Journal on Human Rights* 500; De Vos, '"Inevitability" of Same Sex Marriage'.

Among the reasons parliamentary leaders gave for acting was the jurisdictional one we have seen throughout this chapter: Parliament was seeking 'not to allow the Court itself to amend a piece of legislation' because 'Parliament should continue to be the one bearing the responsibility to pass legislation'.[71] The process was in some respects hasty as a result. But there was much more to it than that. Scholarly recognition is given, as noted, to the civil society organizations for their management of the litigation campaign leading up to the same-sex marriage judgment, something particularly important in *Fourie (2)* after the initial applicants had framed the legal issue in a troublesome way.[72] Strategic marks are awarded for their positioning of LGBTI equality in terms of the values of the struggle and the humiliations of apartheid.[73] But scholarship gives scant recognition to those on whose ears these arguments fell, unless those ears are judicial ears. Doubtless we would prefer a world in which the majority party and the country were free of prejudice against LGBTI individuals. But if we are handing out credit in the eyes of history, we may in the end be inclined to give more of it to those who heeded their principles even when the implications edged out over territory they found controversial and difficult. In an area where many in the ANC (and in other parties) were uncomfortable, where vociferous, hostile opposition had been registered during hearings,[74] and where this, unfortunately, was in all likelihood a fair representation of the public mind, we find many speakers defending principle. The Minister of Home Affairs rose to explain that:

> ... when we attained our democracy, we sought to distinguish ourselves from an unjust painful past by declaring that: 'Never again shall it be that any South African will be discriminated against on the basis of colour, creed, culture and sex.' This House, in passing the Constitution in 1996, recognised the fact that our nation's commitment to this noble principle of equality should be the cornerstone of the society we want to build. In breaking with our past, therefore, we need to fight and resist all forms of

[71] *Hansard*, 14 November 2006 (Minister of Home Affairs, N. Mapisa-Nqakula (ANC)); (also framing *Fourie (2)* as arising 'during' the process of a government which 'as far back as 1996 [had] recognized that the legal regime that regulates marriage in our country needs to be realigned with constitutional principles'.)

[72] See e.g. Budlender et al., *Public Interest Litigation*, pp. 25–34; Massoud, 'Evolution of Gay Rights', 301, 305–06.

[73] See esp. De Vos, '"Inevitability" of Same Sex Marriage', and see also the framing by Edwin Cameron referred to in note 22 of this chapter.

[74] Barnard, '"Totalitarianism', 515–17, 524–25; De Vos and Barnard, 'Same-Sex Marriage', 813–19.

> discrimination and prejudice, including homophobia. We also condemn violence against same-sex couples, fuelled by hatred, as recently observed here at home and in other countries. This commitment to our Constitution and in particular the principles of human dignity, equality and freedom of religion informed the drafting and refinement of this Bill. . . . We've decided to reject the calls to amend the Constitution. Whilst we understand that the Constitution can be amended from time to time to deal with practical arrangements, we are cautious of an amendment to the Bill of Rights, as it is the bedrock on which our Constitution and our democracy is based.[75]

The chair of the committee responsible for the bill, H P Chauke, continued:

> . . . the approach we took as Parliament was to recognise the very fact that whatever we do, we are guided by the Constitution. These rights that we talk about are not rights that are made by the ANC somewhere in the corner there. These rights are the rights that we ourselves, who have participated in compiling this wonderful document that we call the Constitution of South Africa which we all pride ourselves on, entrenched in it. These rights are rights that you cannot take away . . . in our deliberation as a committee, almost every top lawyer in this country, every constitutional expert that we have met in the committee agreed with us that there is no getting away from the rights of these individuals because it's entrenched in the Constitution. You cannot run away. It's something that is given and it's something that we have to live with. [Interjections.] So obviously, you gave it; you were part of the constitution-making process and you were part of the drafting of the Constitution. When we adopted that Constitution, all of us stood there – there is a nice picture outside, showing that you are there – confirming that we will respect and uphold the supreme law of the country which is the Constitution. . . . we believe that the work that was done by this committee confirms that this Bill will go through the Constitutional Court. In its findings, if it finds that this Bill is not constitutional, obviously, there will be a particular process that we must engage in with Parliament. [Interjections.] No, there is nothing wrong with doing that. It can be done all over again, but we have a responsibility as lawmakers, and we cannot run away from our responsibility. If the Constitutional Court finds that whatever we have made is still lacking, we will come back to Parliament again and engage and resolve whatever it is that is not in line with the constitutional requirements to make sure that these individuals that we want to cover, are in fact covered. . . . We will make sure that if you want to be unionised, you will be unionised. If you want to get married, we will make sure that you get married. That is our responsibility. As you go out as Members of

[75] *Hansard*, 14 November 2006 (Minister of Home Affairs, N. Mapisa-Nqakula (ANC)).

> Parliament, go and preach one gospel: These rights are rightly given and are rights that you cannot take away.[76]

Mosuia Lekota, after recalling gay and lesbian people who had fought in the struggle and risked their lives, and doubtless thinking of Simon Nkoli, asked:

> . . . as we stand here today, we can recall names and graves of comrades who resisted and refused to cave in the face of probable death sentences. How then can we live with the reality that we should enjoy rights that we fought together for, side-by-side, and deny them that? Today, as we reap the fruits of that democracy, it is only right that they must be afforded similar space in the sunshine of our democracy. We do them no favour, but reward their efforts in the same way that our own efforts are being rewarded. I have to remind the House that, after all, culture is not static. There was a time when voting was only for men. It was rejected that women should vote. There was a time when society would not accept that women should vote. Yet, in the 1890s, New Zealand led the world in granting her women the right to vote. Then, in 1918, Soviet Russia followed suit, and then, in 1921, Great Britain followed. In 1924, the Soviet Union extended the right to women. In this country, in 1930, white women, for the first time, were allowed to vote. Culture is not static. There was a time when you could not even talk about the possibility of a woman becoming a church minister. Today, denominations, one after another, are accepting that women may indeed become church leaders and church ministers. [Applause.] Oh yes, there was a time when being a homosexual meant imprisonment. Just by being a homosexual, you got locked up in jail. Oscar Wilde, in Victorian England, was locked up in jail, not for any crime, but simply because he declared his homosexuality. Today, Great Britain is a different society, because culture is not static. This country cannot afford to continue to be a prisoner of the backward, timeworn prejudices which have no basis. The time has come that we as this society, as this Parliament, on behalf of our nation, must lead. I therefore wish to urge members of the House to look past the prejudices of our time, and grant this right to those who have been pleading with us for so long now so that we may bequeath to succeeding generations a society democratic and more tolerant than the one that was handed down to us by those who preceded us. I thank you. [Applause.][77]

The process of enacting same-sex marriage was rocky, but then a mountain was being climbed. That the work is far from over, too, is sadly clear, not least from the rockiness of the climb. But this is an extraordinary moment, guided by an institutional argument that asserts Parliament's

[76] *Ibid.* (H.P. Chauke (ANC)). [77] *Ibid.* (Minister of Defence, M. Lekota (ANC)).

role and also respects the Court's, built on the Freedom Charter's promise of equality for all, now enshrined in the Constitution, which we can trace back through the ANC's evolution on LGBTI equality to its statements in the 1980s. That this moment receives so little attention – let alone acknowledgement, still less thrill – reflects just how much the constitutional quality of the post-1994 ANC government gets taken for granted.

Decisions to Decide, and Not to Decide: Family Law for Unmarried Couples

Part of the reason *Fourie (2)* is controversial is because its remedy looks different to those in the other LGBTI equality cases. But in fact it is closely consistent with them, once we understand the constitution-building logic they follow. *Fourie (2)* turns on views about the best institutional ways to defend rights, and this stance coheres with the approach of the remainder of the Court's LGBTI equality decisions: *Satchwell*, ending the exclusion of same-sex life partners from a pension arrangement; *Du Toit*, ending the exclusion of same-sex couples from adoption and guardianship statutes; *J*, ending the exclusion of one partner to a lesbian couple from parenthood and guardianship regimes where the other partner gives birth to a child via artificial insemination; and *Gory*, ending the exclusion of the surviving partner to a same-sex life partnership from inheriting where the other partner dies without a will.[78]

These cases are particularly important in understanding the Court's calculus of action and deference because, as with *Richter* and *AParty* in the voting rights context, each decides one issue and decides not to decide another. In each case, same-sex couple litigants sought admission to a particular legal framework, the state conceded the substance of the issue (which I shall refer to as 'the same-sex exclusion issue'), and the Court granted the relief sought by itself making changes in the relevant statutes, rejecting arguments that it should refer the matter to the legislature. The Court thus continues the approach we saw it adopting in vindicating LGBTI rights in the two *National Coalition* decisions. However, in each case (bar *Du Toit*) there were also issues which the

[78] *Satchwell* v. *President of the Republic of South Africa* 2002 (6) SA 1 (CC); *Du Toit*; *J* v. *Director General: Department of Home Affairs* 2003 (5) SA 621 (CC); *Gory* v. *Kolver NO* 2007 (4) SA 97 (CC). See also *Satchwell* v. *President of the Republic of South Africa* 2003 (4) SA 26 (CC), updating *Satchwell*'s finding to cover an overlooked statute.

Court declined to engage: most prominently, the fact that the Court's recognition of the rights of unmarried same-sex life partners raised the issue of the legal regime for unmarried *opposite*-sex life partners. In *Satchwell* and *J*, the state resisted the applicants' attempts to insert same-sex couples into the relevant statutory regimes on the sole basis that this relief was too *narrow* in applying only to unmarried same-sex life partners and not to opposite-sex ones, an issue also of concern in *National Coalition (2)*.[79] By *Gory*, decided just after *Fourie (2)* but before passage of the Civil Union Act, the changes benefitting same-sex couples had sharpened the point. It was clear that same-sex couples would soon be able to choose the legal rights of marriage in one form or another. The major difference between same- and opposite-sex life partners – that the former could not choose to marry – would soon fall away, at least in formal legal terms, yet unmarried same-sex couples would have rights in terms of the Court's earlier decisions that unmarried opposite-sex couples did not. The Court declined to engage this issue or to treat it as a reason to refuse relief to the same-sex couples.[80] The Court also declined to decide an important part of the same-sex couple issue: deciding that it is wrong to exclude all same-sex couples from pension regimes and the like does not decide which same-sex couples may be included in them. Must a same-sex relationship be 'marriage-like' for its members to avail themselves of these protections, and if so, in what respects, and how is this to be determined?[81] In *Satchwell*, the Court held that same-sex partners who had undertaken mutual duties of support would be eligible for pension benefits, but did not engage with how this is to be decided (or indeed even whether the couple before the Court had met this condition).[82] In *J*, on guardianship, it suggested a looser standard might apply and that mutual duties of support might not be required, but did not settle the issue.[83] In *National Coalition (2)*, it made yet another suggestion, offering a multi-factor checklist, but again ultimately left the issue undecided.[84]

What does the Court so firmly settle the same-sex exclusion issue and not any of the others? The lack of protections for members of unmarried

79 *Satchwell*, paras. 15–16; *J*, para. 11; the Court noted this issue in *National Coalition (2)*, paras. 36–38, 60, 87. The state did not oppose *Du Toit*; see para. 3.

80 *Gory*, paras. 29–31.

81 On these issues (implicated by the Court's tendency to talk in terms of marriage-like relationships), see esp. De Vos, '"Inevitability" of Same Sex Marriage'.

82 *Satchwell*, paras. 23–25.

83 *J*, paras. 23–26.

84 *National Coalition (2)*, para. 88.

opposite-sex couples certainly affects a vulnerable group in South Africa, given the social position of many South African women in long-term relationships who lack legal protections because their male partners decline to marry them.[85] Text is also likely not the difference. Excluding LGBTI life partners from the benefits of marriage implicates 'sexual orientation' on the list of presumptively unconstitutional grounds of discrimination in the Constitution's equality clause, but excluding unmarried opposite-sex life partners from these benefits presumably implicates 'marital status' on the same list. A textual argument is readily available in either case.

Instead, the key difference lies in the different degrees of newness that deciding each issue would require the Court to confront unilaterally, a point that also explains the reluctance to rule definitively on which same-sex couples count. The unconstitutionality of excluding same-sex couples from the regimes of family law was increasingly a foregone conclusion. *Du Toit* could footnote still further statutes and policy documents recognizing same-sex couples, and by *Gory*, the last case on the list, the Court disposes of that whole issue in four sentences.[86] Little debate, too, remained to be had about the remedy by the time of these later cases: either same-sex couples were included in these regimes or they were not, and there was statutory and now doctrinal precedent for the precise type of striking out and reading in to be used as a fix. What matters here is what this sense of a foregone conclusion represents. One issue is legitimacy. For a court to insert words into a statute or strike them out is for it to exercise legislative power, requiring justification.[87] A judge facing legal open-endedness and choosing to fill it in must have some legitimate basis for making *this* content part of the law of the land, rather than some other content that could have filled the space. Another issue is polycentricity. It is hard to be sure both of the effects that a small change might have on the existing workings of a system, and of whether the existing system can successfully regulate all aspects of the addition. The more political, statutory and doctrinal precedent the Court has to build upon, the more an issue has gone through institutional processes, and the more a solution has been adopted previously in similar cases, the less large

[85] See the discussion of *Volks NO* v. *Robinson* 2005 (5) BCLR 446 (CC) in Chapter 9.

[86] *Du Toit*, para. 32 nn. 33 and 34; Gory, para. 19.

[87] See the discussion of this issue in *National Coalition (2)*, paras. 65–76; see further Bishop 'Remedies', 9-97–9-110.

these concerns will loom. Both factors affect the Court's confidence in inserting itself decisively into an issue.

The Court raises considerations of this sort explicitly in *Fourie (1)*. The same-sex applicants in that case, which was framed differently to *Fourie (2)*, had sought an order declaring that they were 'married' for purposes of the Marriage Act. But they did not 'address all the consequences that would flow from the recognition of such a union' or how this would 'raise complex and important questions' for the 'common law of persons, family and succession' as well as 'labour law, insurance and tax.'[88] *Fourie (1)* therefore ruled that the case should be considered first by the SCA, at that time treated as having a special competence in common law issues. We can also see the relevance of such considerations in *Du Toit*, on adoption. The Court hesitated before simply reading same-sex couples into the relevant statute because of the lack of statutory provisions elsewhere to regulate the interests of the children in the event of a break-up of the relationship (since those statutes only provided for opposite-sex couples). However, it found that sufficient residual protection for the interests of the children existed, and so it was willing to order the reading-in.[89]

With an eye to the broader argument, it is worth adding here in parentheses that the reason the Court could make decisive orders on the same-sex couple exclusion issue, notwithstanding the presence of these sorts of polycentric concerns, is partly infrastructural. The Court could rule that same-sex couples could not be excluded from these legal regimes, without resolving issues like when mutual duties of support are required for certain rights and how to determine this, because it could take for granted the existing legal infrastructure for regulating pensions and wills and guardianship and adoption. It could implicitly rely on the existing legal professionals and officials to settle these issues as and when they arose, without having to try to decide them itself on limited information or exercise some form of ongoing supervision. This is crucial though unstated part of what gives the Court the confidence to afford same-sex couples immediate access to these legal regimes.

By contrast, the other questions in these cases were not foregone conclusions, in the sense discussed, to nearly the degree that the same-sex couple exclusion issue was. The Court did not have anything like the same political, statutory or judicial precedent to build on in deciding

[88] *Fourie (1)*, paras. 10–12. [89] *Du Toit*, paras. 33–34.

what to do about these issues, which concern the question of what do to about permanent relationships that are like marriages even if the parties have not chosen to get married. This is the crucial line running through the LGBTI equality cases between the issues the Court decisively resolves and the issues it declines to decide and leaves for the time being in the hands of other institutions.

The closest the *opposite*-sex couple issue came to offering support or precedent for the Court to build on was in *Satchwell*, on the inclusion of same-sex life partners in the pension scheme for judges. The state there submitted a draft bill that would include in the judicial pension scheme all life partners of judges, of whatever sex. The Court dismissed the relevance of the bill curtly.[90] This may seem surprising – isn't this just the sort of support that might have facilitated the judicial filling in of constitutional content? But having seen more precisely what the Court needs to be confident about, we can see why it acted as it did. An *incomplete* legislative process does not alleviate the legitimacy or polycentricity concerns, because it does not signify that other institutions have worked through a question and actually picked or tested a solution. Instead of offering a foundation for judicial action, the fact that a legislative process is ongoing is instead usually a reason to let that process finish.[91] In the LGBTI equality cases, this consideration was compounded by the way that the opposite-sex couple issue was invoked chiefly as a defensive pretext. Whereas the same-sex couple exclusion issue could count among its advantages a carefully designed litigation campaign, the opposite-sex couple issue could add to its drawbacks that the litigation did little or nothing to compensate for the paucity of political, statutory and doctrinal precedents available for the Court to build on. (The same consideration was important to the Court's decision in *Fourie (1)* to have the details of the same-sex marriage issue considered first by the SCA, as we saw.)

There is also a secondary institutional reason for the stark difference between the Court's assertive decision to resolve the same-sex couple exclusion issue by itself making the necessary changes to the relevant laws, and its refusal to decide the other issues. The Court's rejection of the draft bill in *Satchwell* did not follow only from the Court's views

[90] *Satchwell*, para. 28.

[91] This stance is consistent with the Court's later approach to this issue in *Doctors for Life* and *United Democratic Movement* v. *President of the Republic of South Africa (1)* 2002 (9) BCLR 986 (CC), both discussed in the next chapter, and *Glenister (1)*.

about proper institutional roles, but also from the need to reject the view of proper institutional roles implicit in the government's stance in the case. From the government's perspective, submitting the draft bill was another exercise in trying to retain control of the issue, telling the Court that a complete legislative solution for all couples was being prepared by the government and so the Court did not need to make the order sought by the same-sex couples before it. The Court's firm rejection of the bill's relevance to its decision on the same-sex couple exclusion issue is thus a rejection of the idea that the court should leave even an issue this conducive to judicial intervention to the legislature. This is perfectly compatible with its view that it should defer on the other less conducive, less squarely raised issues in the cases.

This brings us back to *Fourie (2)*. Critics sometimes see *Fourie (2)* as deferring to the legislature on the grounds that the Court did not itself feel able to make the policy choices about the particular form recognition of same-sex unions would take.[92] Seen in the context of the Court's treatment of the opposite-sex couple issue throughout these cases, they will object that the Court is adopting too weak a view of its own powers. But it is important here not to equate a decision not to settle an issue with a view that the Court cannot or should never settle issues of that sort. Instead, in each instance, an institutional judgment is being made about how the rights issue concerned should be dealt with – it is not a decision about what the Court *could* do, but about what it should do, as one institution among many, in response to particular cases. Thus, as we saw, *Fourie (2)* is not about policy deference, but about how best to vindicate the rights claim concerned. It refers a choice to the legislature as a way of involving it in the recognition process, on the grounds that this will protect rights better – but, as we have seen, it refers only a very small choice, and decides a great deal itself. To be fair to its critics, the Court sometimes signals its decisions not to intervene by invoking standard separation of powers arguments. This can not only make it look as if it is asserting a traditional restrained view, but also itself prompts the objection that the Court is not more firmly articulating a new separation of powers doctrine and dislodging the old one, which is sometimes the critics' main concern.[93] That is a perfectly fair point; it returns to the

[92] See e.g. Davis and Klare, 'Transformative Constitutionalism', 507–09. Davis and Klare are well aware of the majority's concerns with public processes, but consider this outweighed on the best understanding of the separation of powers: *Ibid.*, 508.

[93] See Davis and Klare, 'Transformative Constitutionalism', 507–09.

debate noted in Chapter 5 about how far a court should challenge the old tradition actively if its current legitimacy is partly seen to depend upon it. But the way in which the Court *does* sometimes decide more expansive issues, as we have seen and will continue to see, reflects the true substantive nature of its stance.

An implication of this argument is that the Court will do more or take more risks about open-ended policy questions when it feels this is necessary to protect rights or is the best way to do so. Some support for this can be seen in the way it was willing to settle the LGBTI equality claims we have seen it settle, notwithstanding the presence of some polycentric concerns and uncertainties, and in the way it was sometimes bolder than strictly necessary to decide the cases before it: skipping the first stage of the equality test to make the firmer unfair discrimination finding in *National Coalition (2)*, rejecting several ways to avoid issues in *National Coalition (2)*, *Satchwell*, *Du Toit* and *J*, and asserting the remedial power to make statutory changes itself instead of referring them to the legislature. The implication is also borne out by the neglected evidence of *Gory*, the decision on inheritance handed down a few months after *Fourie (2)* in which the Court offers its own interpretation of its earlier decision. In *Gory*, the effect of an order that the surviving member of a same-sex life partnership would inherit if their partner died without leaving a will was, inevitably, to rule that the previous intestate heirs, usually blood relatives, would *not* inherit the estate. It was therefore the first LGBTI equality case that had the effect of depriving third parties of vested rights.[94] A fully retrospective order would disrupt settled estates; a fully prospective one would afford no relief to the applicant before the Court. The Court therefore designed its own way to 'balance the potentially disruptive effects of an order' by providing that its order would not disrupt finalized transfers of inherited property 'unless the transferee was on notice that the property in question was subject to a legal challenge' on the lines of *Gory*.[95]

This is not uncontroversial, nor free from complications in its administration. A Court wary of resolving open-ended policy questions itself might have been expected to defer this decision to Parliament, and indeed the private defendants in *Gory* argued precisely this, relying on *Fourie (2)*. But the Court explicitly distinguished *Fourie (2)* on the basis that the couple in that case lost nothing permanently by being made to

[94] *Gory*, para. 38. [95] *Ibid*, para. 42 and the order in para. 66.

wait another year for what the Court saw as a more lasting vindication of rights. In *Gory*, by contrast, anything other than immediate relief would permanently preclude the applicant before the Court from inheriting – and so the Court unilaterally made the policy decision on the cut-off so that relief could be immediate.[96] (In line with the earlier infrastructure comments, we can also see the value in the Court being able take for granted an existing network of legal professionals administering estates who could deal with the need to decide about whether other heirs and executors in the estates affected by *Gory* were 'on notice' that the matter could be subject to constitutional challenge.) Nor is *Gory*'s stance an outlier, if we look to cases in other contexts raising equality concerns in the context of inheritance.[97]

If *Fourie (2)* is different to the other LGBTI equality cases, then, it is only because it takes a special multi-institutional route to vindicating the claim before it. It is interesting that the Court did not feel the need to do this in other cases, especially on the perhaps equally contentious issue of the right of same-sex couples to adopt, but there are a number of plausible explanations for this. The Court may have felt that same-sex marriage was the pinnacle issue of the litigation campaign, the most symbolic but also the most publicly controversial. That is how the strategy of gay and lesbian lobby groups viewed it and how I suspect most observers think of the issue. It may also be important that same-sex couple adoption, as the issue actually presented itself in *Du Toit*, was rather technical and attracted no opposition. It is worth remembering that the lesbian couple in *Du Toit* had been the joint caregivers of two adopted children since December 1994, when they had presented themselves to the agency concerned as a same-sex couple. One of them (since the law did not permit them to adopt as a couple) had been the children's adoptive parent since 1995. The target of *Du Toit* was therefore only the legal rule preventing the couple from adopting the children jointly. That was hardly unimportant, given what it is to be a parent but to not legally be a parent, but one can also see why one might think the main substance of the adoption issue was already water under the bridge.[98] By contrast, the degree to which *Fourie (2)*'s 'guidelines' to the legislature forced the government's hand suggests that the Court expected significant

[96] *Ibid*, paras. 21–31.

[97] See e.g. *Moseneke* v. *Master of the High Court* 2001 (2) SA 18 (CC); *Bhe* v. *Magistrate, Khayelitsha* 2005 (1) SA 580 (CC); *Gory* drew on both.

[98] *Du Toit*, paras. 3–7.

government and public resistance to same-sex 'marriage' in a way that it did not in the earlier LGBTI equality cases – an accurate perception, if so, given the government's apparent willingness to create a separate civil union but greater reluctance to go further and recognize same-sex marriage. And as noted earlier, the presence of visible opposition for the first time in *Fourie (2)* may have alerted the Court to the possibility that it might need to do more than it had in its earlier decisions to publicly vindicate the issue. Whatever our precise views about these explanations, it should not puzzle us that the Court felt that the issue of marriage equality merited a uniquely multi-institutional vindication.

This aspect of *Fourie (2)* deepens our understanding of the trust argument I discussed in Chapter 3. It shows how the trust argument serves the institutional argument, not the other way around. If trust were paramount, the Court would have deferred all the legislative fixes on all the issues throughout the LGBTI equality cases to Parliament. It would have deferred to the government's draft bill in *Satchwell*, and would have left the same-sex marriage issue much more open, in referring it to the legislature, than it actually did. As I have articulated it, however, trust is a way of building the institutional vision of the Constitution – and so it would make no sense to show trust when it would not serve that vision. The Court's decisive resolution of the same-sex couple exclusion issues in every case apart from *Fourie (2)* is a rejection of the traditional institutional view implied by the state's contentions that the Court should leave such matters to the legislature. *Fourie (2)* involves a more subtle trust calculation in which the protection of rights, not servility to the legislature or policy timidity, is paramount. Of course, it involves a measure of trust, since it would be self-defeating to refer the matter if one expected repudiation. But *Fourie (2)* also forces Parliament's hand considerably. It joins the other LGBTI equality cases in being a corollary to *NNP*: just as the institutional calculation sometimes implies that the Court should defer to others, so building the Constitution sometimes depends on the court asserting a power and on others accepting that. Though we can be sure this sometimes rankled in the LGBTI equality decisions, the government ultimately did just that in relation to every one of them.

That said, the cases also offer a concrete but overlooked illustration of how trust calculations do not always work out. The decision to involve Parliament in *Fourie (2)* may look good with hindsight, but the Court's repeated decision to leave the position of opposite-sex couples in the hands of other institutions has yet to bear fruit, though the Court has moved from simply not deciding the issue to actively calling for legislative action.[99] The bill introduced in *Satchwell* remains a bill at the time of writing, well over a decade later, and the family law regime for same-sex couples still contains the sorts of uncertainties side-stepped by the Court. The issue of deciding when to intervene will be central to the rest of the chapters of this book, and I will take it up in this specific connection in Chapter 9. I there discuss *Volks* v. *Robinson*, a case that raised the issue of opposite-sex couples squarely but was rejected by a majority of the Court. The constitution-building account has some light to shed on *Volks* as well. For now, however, it suffices for us to witness how the much-criticized decision in *Volks* has strong echoes in the institutional calculations of the celebrated LGBTI equality cases. The institutional calculations manifest throughout the LGBTI equality cases not only recall *NNP* but also belie an interpretation in line with the first *Makwanyane* story. Once we take account of the persistent decisions not to decide, alongside the decisive rulings of these cases, we can see why it is too simple to view the LGBTI equality cases as counter-majoritarian defences of text and abstract principle, and why *Makwanyane*'s closest descendants are in fact much like my retold version of the case. The famous findings the Court makes are the product of a substantial alignment of constitution-building pieces, once again ultimately vindicated by the government's stance. The issues raised most squarely for decision are those wholly or substantially conceded by the government, foreshadowed by political and increasingly also by statutory and judicial precedent, and supported by a legal infrastructure the Court could implicitly take for granted and often by a temporary infrastructure of legally sophisticated civil society coalitions. As with *Makwanyane*, to see what facilitated these decisions is not to diminish the Court's achievement in producing them in political waters choppier than *Makwanyane*'s, and it should not reduce our appreciation of their judicial craftsmanship. Instead, it is to see that the Court did not stand alone, that it had help, that there was something generous and principled of public status in South Africa stretching back through the years for it to build upon. The result is a more lasting public achievement. That its magnitude exceeds the effort the Court itself had to expend to produce it is quite the opposite of a cause for regret.

[99] Compare *National Coalition (2)*, para. 60, to *Fourie (2)*, para. 160, *Gory*, para. 27.

7

Democracy

It should come as no surprise that a post-apartheid society has a special concern with democracy, and in particular with democratic inclusion and participation. Rich democratic ideas have been identified in the South African Constitution, summed up in an influential contribution by Theunis Roux, and their influence has increased markedly since.[1] The Court's critics, however, have once again been dismayed by the apparent internal inconsistencies of the case law enforcing this idea, and indeed its decisions here can appear as self-contradictory as its voting rights decisions did.

There are two potentially troublesome patterns across the Court's ten decisions in this area. The first, commonly pointed out, is that the Court in *Doctors for Life International* v. *Speaker of the National Assembly* ('*Doctors for Life*') was bold and creative in articulating a new doctrine under which legislation is constitutionally invalid if the legislatures concerned do not do enough to facilitate public involvement in the legislative process. The decision is celebrated: on standard views, it joins the pre-*Fourie* LGBTI equality cases as one of the few true heirs of the first *Makwanyane* story. But while the Court invalidated two statutes on this basis in *Doctors for Life* and two more the same day in *Matatiele Municipality* v. *President of the Republic of South Africa ('Matatiele (2)')*, it has declined to invalidate legislation on this basis in any of the four attempts to invoke the doctrine since.[2] The second pattern presents a contrast that is starker still. In Chapter 3 I noted the Court's decision to uphold the introduction of floor-crossing in *United Democratic*

[1] Roux, 'Democracy'.

[2] *Matatiele Municipality* v. *President of the Republic of South Africa (2)* 2006 (5) SA 47 (CC); the subsequent four cases are *Merafong Demarcation Forum* v. *President of the Republic of South Africa* 2008 (5) SA 171 (CC); *Poverty Alleviation Network* v. *President of the Republic of South Africa* 2010 (6) BCLR 520 (CC); *Glenister* v. *President of the Republic of South Africa (No. 2)* 2011 (3) SA 347 (CC); *Moutse Demarcation Forum* v. *President of the Republic of South Africa* 2011 (11) BCLR (CC).

Movement v. *President of the Republic of South Africa* ('*UDM (2)*'). In this chapter, we will also see the Court's decision in the same year in *Democratic Alliance* v. *Masondo NO* ('*Masondo*'), where the Court declined to act to enforce minority party rights of participation in executive structures of local government.[3] How do we reconcile the restraint of these cases with the boldness of *Doctors for Life?* The point is not often framed this way, but as we will see, what the critics wanted the Court to do in *UDM (2)* looks a lot like what it actually did do in *Doctors for Life*. That *UDM (2)* was the more politicized case will only increase our suspicions of legal inconsistency. And can *UDM (2)* really be understood as another exercise in *NNP*-style trust when there can be no doubt that in supporting floor-crossing the ANC was acting for self-serving, narrowly political motives? Both this pattern and the one in *Doctors for Life*'s precedents are further complicated by two recent decisions that act quite boldly to review other internal parliamentary procedures on democratic grounds.

Once we know what to look for, however, we will see that the constitution-building logic of these cases is again tightly consistent. It is also deeply coherent with the account of the LGBTI equality cases in the previous chapter: the recognition that newness can arise in any context helps us to see similarities between cases whose divergent subject matter might otherwise keep them apart in the textbooks. In the democracy cases, however, the type of review itself displays rather more newness. Discrimination cases are familiar ground for judges, but judicial review of internal legislative activity is much more novel territory, globally speaking, and in South Africa it directly implicates the relationship between the legislature and the judiciary that had been so shaken up by the rapid post-apartheid switch from strong parliamentary supremacy to expansive constitutional supremacy. These features, and the Court's reaction to them, offer the key to *when* the Court has chosen to assert the rich ideas of democracy that are readily found in South Africa's post-apartheid constitutionalism. The very fact that they are so readily found means that the Court has never lacked for a potential constitutional basis for action in these cases, and it is because of this that critics find the apparent inconsistencies in its willingness to act so frustratingly perplexing. From the perspective of constitution-building, however, there is rather more to the question than that.

[3] *Democratic Alliance* v. *Masondo NO* 2003 (2) SA 413 (CC).

Doctors for Life

Let us start by noting the respects in which *Doctors for Life* – handed down eight months after *Fourie (2)* by a very similar bench – continues the line of the argument so far. It is one of the most important examples of a bold, internationally celebrated decision by the Court, and it is therefore important that this candidate for heir to *Makwanyane* too fits the third *Makwanyane* story best. But the concerns of *Doctors for Life* also provide the key to the other democracy cases.

Doctors for Life, and its sister case, *Matatiele (2)*, saw a majority of the Court accept challenges to the constitutional validity of specific statutes on the basis that the (provincial) legislatures concerned had not done enough to involve the public in the legislative process. The legislative processes in both cases were national ones, but the National Council of Provinces – the NCOP, the second, federal house of Parliament – had reasonably decided that public participation exercises would be conducted at the provincial level. (The role played by the NCOP, as we will see later in this chapter, is one of the more interesting, and interestingly neglected, features of *Doctors for Life*). Some provincial legislatures engaged effectively with the public; others made clear their intentions to do so but then made blatantly inadequate arrangements, such as announcing a public hearing with one day's notice or not getting around to doing anything at all, and it is these paltry efforts that the Court invalidated. The effect of *Doctors for Life* is to add to the constitutional requirements for the valid passage of a statute.[4] In addition to the usual manner and form provisions, a legislature must take steps to facilitate the involvement of the public. Exactly what is required is contextual, and assessed using a reasonableness standard, as in *NNP*. The threshold will be very low, for example, in relation to a technical statute in which there is little public interest, and higher as the public's desire for involvement rises. On the way to this doctrine, as we will shortly see, the majority recognized a fundamental right to political participation, even though the text of the Bill of Rights includes no such right – the first time the Court had even contemplated a doctrine of un-enumerated rights.[5]

[4] See also the interpretation of *Doctors for Life* in *Tongoane* v. *National Minister for Agriculture and Land Affairs* 2010 (6) SA 214 (CC), paras. 105–06.

[5] *Doctors for Life*, paras. 90–109 (fundamental right to participation, sometimes discussed in the judgment as an international law right); paras. 122–29 (flexible nature of obligations under it). I discuss the other example, to date, in Chapter 8.

As in *Makwanyane*, the Court in *Doctors for Life* was interpreting ambiguous text. There is certainly a textual basis for the majority's public participation doctrine, because the Constitution states that national and provincial legislatures have a duty to 'facilitate public participation' in their processes.[6] But the text is open-ended – it says no more than that – and the balance of textual arguments probably points away from the strong-form doctrine recognized in *Doctors for Life*, under which individual statutes can be invalidated for failure to comply with specific public participation requirements. The fact that the majority found it necessary to create a brand new right to public participation, and to work with so many international and comparative materials, is not unrelated to the paucity of the textual support. Justice Yacoob's dissent in *Doctors for Life* is a master class in textual interpretation, and it yields three conclusions: that the specific requirements for the passage of statutes are set out elsewhere in the text; that there are good reasons for not presuming to add to those requirements (such as that it is unwise to render the process of enacting legislation less certain and predictable); and that the relevant text is better read simply as a general obligation on the part of the legislature to have policies in place to facilitate the public involvement, without consequences for the validity of particular legislative acts. I shall return to the dissenting judges in a moment; first, we should see the extra-textual supports that existed for a more expansive finding.

If the ideas articulated by the Court might seem new in the abstract or in the context of global constitutional law doctrine, they rest on ideas of powerful public status in South Africa. If there is such a thing as an African idea of democracy, it is one reached by increasing the component of democracy that is about consultation and listening, and decreasing the part that is about resolving disputes by straight majoritarian voting.[7] If there is a South African idea of democracy, it is a post-apartheid conception that places a particular emphasis on inclusion, a conception that seeks to recover a pre-colonial idea of governance in which tribal decision-making was consultative, in which anyone could talk and the

6 1996 Constitution, s 59(1)(a) (in relation to the National Assembly); s 72(1)(a) (National Council of Provinces); s 118(1)(a) (provincial legislatures).

7 See esp. the work of Kwasi Wiredu e.g. K. Wiredu 'Democracy by Consensus: Some Conceptual Considerations' (2001) 30 *Philosophical Papers* 227. See also the recent survey of some African thinkers in this connection by G. T. Hessebon 'Some Major Themes in the Study of Constitutionalism and Democracy in Africa' (2013) 7 *Vienna Journal on International Constitutional Law* 28, 31–38.

rulers listened.[8] If one can speak of an idea of ANC democracy, it will be along the same lines: Oliver Tambo, the party's 'natural democrat' and long-time leader, is the symbol of this style of leadership.[9] Claims like these are, as ever, not free from romanticism, but that is to be expected: we are in the realm of ideals. They are also not necessarily unique to South Africa. The point is only that in invoking them, *Doctors for Life* is driving its taproot into some very deep local waters.

One would expect such deep ideas to have received concrete expression prior to 2006's *Doctors for Life*, and so they did. During the constitution drafting, the ANC emphasized the importance of involving the public in governance.[10] One of the party's larger legislative agendas on coming to power was to roll out wall-to-wall municipal government across South Africa, expressing a policy conviction that government should be closer to the people.[11] The party also supported the increased delegation of power to school governing bodies on similar democratic grounds.[12] These convictions also found expression in matters directly connected with legislative public participation. In 2005 – before the decision in *Doctors for Life* – the Second World Conference of Speakers of Parliaments in New York had been effusive in noting the 'whole range of activities' initiated by the South African parliament to involve the public.[13] Efforts to this end had also been made by provincial legislatures, although dogged by some capacity concerns.[14] Parliament and the

[8] As the Court articulated this idea in *Bhe*, para. 45: '[African c]ustomary law places much store in consensus-seeking and naturally provides for family and clan meetings which offer excellent opportunities for the prevention and resolution of disputes and disagreements', which inter alia facilitates 'the fostering of co-operation, a sense of responsibility in and of belonging to its members, as well as the nurturing of healthy communitarian traditions such as ubuntu'.

[9] Callinicos, *Oliver Tambo*, p. 17; the quoted phrase is Albie Sachs'.

[10] See S. Rose-Ackerman, S. Egidy and J. Fowkes, *Due Process of Lawmaking: The United States, South Africa, Germany and the European Union* (Cambridge University Press, 2015), p. 118 and sources there cited.

[11] Sisk, *Democratization*, pp. 190–91; N. Steytler and J. De Visser, 'Local Government' in Woolman and Bishop (eds.) *Constitutional Law*, 22–1; 22-3–22-4, 22-7–22-13; R. Simeon and C. Murray, 'Reforming Multi-level Government in South Africa' (2009) 43 *Canadian Journal of African Studies* 536, 547; Rose-Ackerman et al., *Due Process of Lawmaking*, p. 119 and further sources there cited; for the background and (more complicated) reality, see e.g. Klug, *Constitution of South Africa*, pp. 265–82.

[12] Woolman and Fleisch, *Constitution in the Classroom*, pp. 15–16.

[13] Inter-Parliamentary Union *Parliamentary Involvement in International Affairs* (Report to Second World Conference of Speakers of Parliaments, September 2005) available at www.ipu.org/splz-e/sp-conf05/involvement-rpt.pdf, 21.

[14] Rose-Ackerman et al., *Due Process of Lawmaking*, p. 119 and sources there cited.

provincial legislatures had also collaborated to develop the 'People's Assembly', which had gathered in 2005 – again, before *Doctors for Life* – to promote active participation in government, alongside a range of multimedia resources and outreach initiatives.[15] It should not therefore come as a surprise that in the particular legislative activity that came before the Court in *Doctors for Life* and *Matatiele (2)*, the parliamentary leaders had concluded of their own accord that they should and would engage in exercises to involve the public. Indeed, the most striking illustration of the pre-existing public status of the ideas with which the Court was working in *Doctors for Life* is that it was common cause between the parties that a legal duty to facilitate public participation existed.[16] It is novel – in South African or global terms – to contemplate that a court might engage in reviewing internal legislative activity of this sort, or impose specifically enforceable obligations in this context, and yet this fundamental point, details aside, was conceded by the government. The Court itself had to raise the question of its jurisdiction to conduct this sort of review prior to a law coming into force and call for argument on the point (displaying the concern for structural issues we have now seen repeatedly).[17] A sizeable fraction of the final judgment in *Doctors for Life* is concerned with questions of the Court's jurisdiction and the limits on it, including an explicit refusal, outside the most exceptional of cases, to consider bills that are still working their way through the legislative process (matching its approach to the draft bill in *Satchwell* we saw in the last chapter).[18] The Court also dealt at length with the legal basis of the duty in the right to political participation.[19]

Doctors for Life and *Matatiele (2)* are therefore further examples of bold cases where the Court is receiving pre-existing ideas into constitutional doctrine, rather than seeking to impose its own ideas on a government with sharply different views. Its reference to government activity as evidence for the idea is not conveniently gathered in one footnote as it was in cases like *Hoffman* and *National Coalition (2)* but it is there nevertheless. The Court makes reference to the World Conference of Parliaments Report just mentioned, quoting it as authority for the

[15] *Doctors for Life*, paras. 113–14, 132–34; see also the People's Assembly website, www.pa.org.za.

[16] *Doctors for Life*, para. 77.

[17] *Doctors for Life*, paras. 8–10; Directions issued by the Chief Justice dated 22 September 2005.

[18] *Doctors for Life*, paras. 13–72.

[19] *Ibid.*, paras. 79–146.

proposition that 'Parliament has done much to facilitate public involvement [in the law-making process'.[20] It also refers to the People's Assembly, noting that its Commission on Public Participation 'reiterated, through the voices of the people of South Africa' that 'one of the distinctive features of public participation processes in South Africa has always been that it is firmly grounded in the constitutional imperative of democratic participation and keeping society involved in legislative, policy and other decision-making processes'.[21] It quotes an NCOP member on the particularly democratic motivation – 'the people shall govern' – of the struggle against apartheid.[22] It invokes the gathering at Kliptown in 1955 that produced the Freedom Charter.[23] It cites statements in NCOP proceedings on the (extra-legal) public community structures that were developed during apartheid, and how they turned out to be 'crucial in laying the foundation for the future participatory democracy ... [t]his emphasis on democratic participation that was born in the struggle against injustice is strongly reflected in our new democratic Constitution and the entrenchment of public participation in Parliament and the legislatures'.[24] And it refers to the notion of a consultative, deliberative gathering, variously called imbizo, lekgotla and bosberaad – the terms cover most of South Africa's main language groups – not only as evidence of the 'traditional method of public participation' that 'was, and still is, followed within African communities', but as 'a tradition widely used by the government'.[25] This is undoubtedly another exercise in strategic, diplomatic judgment writing.[26] But it matters greatly that the ideas are really there to invoke.

The two cases are also further examples of decisions where the controversy is really about institutional questions rather than the substance of the underlying issue. The structural role of the NCOP is a central theme of *Doctors for Life*. The legislative processes in the case were national ones, and everyone accepted that the National Assembly, one of the two national houses of Parliament, had met *its* public participation obligations. Did that not suffice to meet the government's obligations in respect of the law-making process as a whole? The Court rejected this notion on the basis of arguments about the distinctive role played by the NCOP in the legislative process.[27] This is an institutional argument, akin to its

20 *Ibid.*, paras. 132–34. 21 *Ibid.*, para. 114. 22 *Ibid.*, para. 108.
23 *Ibid.*, para. 113. 24 *Ibid.*, para. 112. 25 *Ibid.*, para. 101.
26 See Chapter 2, where I refer to Roux's 'diplomacy' characterization.
27 *Doctors for Life*, paras. 5, 7, 29, 79–85, 151, 159–64.

findings in *NNP* about the proper relationship between Parliament, the Department of Home Affairs and the Electoral Commission, or the smaller-scale questions about the Court's relation to Parliament that we saw arising in the LGBTI equality cases. And just as in *Fourie (2)*, it is questions of this structural variety that were the source of the Court's split in *Doctors for Life*. None of the dissenting judges disputed the value of participatory democracy or public involvement in legislative processes. Instead, they were concerned about the model for judicial review being adopted by the majority. As in *NNP*, all the judges were keenly concerned with the institutional precedents being set. But here, the majority of the Court came down on the side of assertive action. Why?

It is at this point that we should return to the dissenters' views. Their structural argument, taking their separate judgments as a whole, runs as follows.[28] Introducing a new specific requirement for the passage of legislation, which is not capable of very precise determination – public participation must be 'reasonable', which varies with context – is structurally worrisome, given the importance of certainty and predictability in this context. It is still more worrisome because it is a standard that the Court will find difficult to apply in the longer term. The value of the doctrine lies in whether the people are genuinely consulted and listened to, whether the public is genuinely *involved*. But courts will struggle to assess whether legislators are really listening, or whether they are simply sitting through a tiresome charade, because it is not possible for judges to assess legislators' mental states. This is partly because reliable evidence of this will usually be hard to come by, and partly because legislators in a representative, multiparty democracy do not have to have objectively good reasons for their voting positions. They may vote, in principle, for any reason at all, including for purely party political reasons, because the primary check on them is that they are subject to election. This is the structural objection to applying administrative law-like standards to elected representatives.[29] The result is an uncomfortable dilemma. The more substance there is to the public participation requirement, the more judges are setting themselves up in the business of assessing legislators' intentions. That is a business they will find it practically hard to engage in, and it is also one that is intrudes on representative mechanisms.

[28] There were three dissents in *Doctors for Life*; see the judgments of Yacoob J, Skweyiya J and Van der Westhuizen J.

[29] Rose-Ackerman et al., *Due Process of Lawmaking*, esp. pp. 117, 125, 158; and post-*Doctors for Life* sources there cited.

This is the reason the dissenters object to the majority's claim to be harmonizing representative and participatory democracy, for they see these two ideas as being in tension here. On the other hand, the *less* substance is given to the idea and the less intrusively the Court reviews it, the more the requirement to involve the public risks becomes merely formal, and the greater becomes the danger that the Court will articulate a solemn constitutional obligation that can be met by a mere pretence and that it will find itself upholding empty charades as compatible with the rich ideas of democracy being articulated in *Doctors for Life*.[30] That would be bad for the ideas of stake, and bad for the credibility of constitutional review. And this rather unsatisfying result, the minority will remind us, is our only prize for introducing uncertainty into the passage of valid legislation.

However, just as the minority in *Doctors for Life* does not really disagree about the value of participatory democracy, so the majority does not really disagree about these structural concerns. They simply feel that a space for meaningful judicial review exists in the middle of these tensions. Judges do not have to engage in reviewing legislators' intentions to decide that some kinds of defective process are not meaningful – as the blatant defects on the facts before them showed. The majority judges' concern with the same structural arguments as the minority can also been seen in the attention they devote to establishing restrictions on their new ground of review. As noted, they impose strong jurisdictional boundaries so that, even if public participation is reviewed, the court will only intervene in a legislative process before its conclusion in extraordinary circumstances. They also articulate rules of standing to try and ensure that public participation does not become a general go-to ground for anyone seeking to overturn a law and is confined to those who sought to be involved in the legislative process, found themselves unreasonably excluded, and promptly sought to challenge this.[31] The intention is to counter the problems of uncertainty over the legislative process, since any statute not challenged on public participation grounds in its first years will become very hard to review on this basis (in just the same way that the majority in *NNP* held that the subsequent implementation of a statute would only briefly be a reason to review the legislature's decision to pass the statute, as opposed to a reason to review the subsequent implementation of the statute). The majority also seeks to articulate

[30] See esp. the judgment of Van der Westhuizen J, para. 244.

[31] *Doctors for Life*, paras. 216–20.

limits on when statutes will be subject to the drastic remedy of invalidation, using the flexibility of the reasonableness standard. The majority, in short, is engaging in longer-term calculations about institutional consequences and effects of just the sort I described in Chapter 5. But it sees these consequences as a concern to be managed, using the flexibility of its doctrine of separation of powers and the reasonableness standard, not a reason to refuse to exercise review in this area at all as the minority does.

The decision in *Doctors for Life* is thus readily reconcilable with the decision in *NNP*. Very similar structural considerations predominate in both cases. Both decisions contemplate that judicial intervention is appropriate to protect and promote democracy when necessary. The key to their different outcomes lies simply in the facts. In *Doctors for Life* and *Matatiele (2)*, the factual defects were blatant: as Van der Westhuizen J noted in dissent, it was not difficult to find a violation on those sorts of facts.[32] Furthermore, since the legislative process had ostensibly been completed, and there are no other relevant constitutional institutions in this area, it could only be the Court that could respond to this problem. Neither of these things was true in *NNP*. The constitution-building equation therefore came out differently.

Extending the Lines: The Later Public Participation Cases

The facts also explain the failure of most of the subsequent attempts to invoke the *Doctors for Life* doctrine, which have mainly been opportunistic challenges by applicants seeking any legal means to block a substantive policy choice they opposed. In one case, for example, the legislature concerned had received written submissions, including from the applicant organization, and held a number of meetings; when the applicant marched in protest on the grounds that a meeting had not been held in its area, the legislature held a further meeting there.[33] In another, an extensive process had been held and the applicant, who had participated in it, had complimented the committee at the time on the fair hearing he had received.[34] With the prominent exception of *Merafong Demarcation Forum* v. *President of the Republic of South Africa* ('*Merafong*'), which I engage with in detail shortly, the later cases were mostly just much less

[32] *Ibid.*, para. 244(6); see also Bishop and Raboshakga, 'National Legislative Authority', 17-72–17-73.

[33] *Moutse Demarcation Forum*, esp. paras. 52–60.

[34] *Glenister (2)*, paras. 34–37.

blatantly defective than *Doctors for Life* and *Matatiele (2)*.[35] But they offer several further insights into *Doctors for Life* and constitution-building.

Poverty Alleviation Network v. *President of the Republic of South Africa* ('*Poverty Alleviation Network*') may at first glance appear to confirm the concerns of the *Doctors for Life* minority. The case was effectively *Matatiele (3)*: in *Matatiele (2)*, the order invalidating the lawmaking exercise had been suspended to allow the legislature concerned to correct the public participation defect. When the legislature duly conducted a new process, the local residents concerned unsuccessfully objected in *Poverty Alleviation Network* that this was a simply an empty exercise in the service of a pre-determined outcome. This nicely illustrates the limitations of reviewing legislators for listening. Once it is established that hearings were held and submissions were received and incorporated into the legislative process – once it is established, in other words, that blatant failures such as those in *Doctors for Life* and *Matatiele (2)* have not occurred – there is usually little way for the applicants, the judges or anyone else to prove whether the legislators really listened and engaged. But on the reading of the case presented here, *Poverty Alleviation Network* in fact takes no skin off the nose of the *Doctors for Life* majority. That judgment was conscious of the practical limits on what judges can review, and was simply acting in the belief that there is useful review work to be done notwithstanding. It was not inevitable that the hearing in *Poverty Alleviation Network* would be something of a rote exercise – the legislators might still genuinely have learned something – but it was no doubt likely. That is an inescapable hazard of remedies in these cases, a point I return to later. The aim of *Matatiele (2)*, however, was mainly forward-looking: it sought to ensure that legislatures operate in a certain way by ruling that if they do not they will ordered back to repeat the process. *Poverty Alleviation Network* illustrates the concerns of the *Doctors for Life*

35 Rose-Ackerman et al., *Due Process of Lawmaking*, p. 118; M. Bishop, 'Vampire or Prince? The Listening Constitution and *Merafong Demarcation & Others* v. *President of the Republic of South Africa*' (2009) 2 *Constitutional Court Review* 313, 328; A. E. Psygkas, 'Revitalizing the "Liberty of Ancients" through Citizen Participation in the Legislative Process' (2010) 5 *Annuaire International des Droit de l'Homme* 720, 741. See also the successful invocation of the standard in the municipal context in *Democratic Alliance* v. *Municipality* 2012 (2) SA 151 (SCA), which much more closely resembled the breaches of *Doctors for Life* and *Matatiele (2)* on the facts; see further Rose-Ackerman et al., *Due Process of Lawmaking*, pp. 120–21.

minority, but it does not prove them right, nor does it show the Court retreating from the *Doctors for Life* majority's position.

Of much the greatest interest among the later public participation cases, however, remains the decision in *Merafong*, the immediate successor to *Doctors for Life* and *Matatiele (2)*. A majority upheld the public participation exercise in that case, but the facts give off a persistent sense that something had gone wrong, and the decision is very instructive in understanding the work of the constitution-building court.

Merafong was another case concerned with national legislation in the NCOP being acted on by provincial legislatures. The legislation sought to finalize South Africa's post-1994 provincial boundaries and thus had to place on one side of the line or the other several municipalities whose borders, for transitional reasons, had straddled provincial boundaries. Matatiele had been one such affected community. A provincial legislature had engaged with another of the affected communities, Merafong, and as a direct result decided to make a switch in policy in line with the community's wishes. Instead of supporting the national legislation unconditionally, it resolved to support it only if an amendment could be made accommodating Merafong's preferences. Legislative leaders in the NCOP, however, adopted the position that provinces could only vote yes or no on the whole statute and could not propose specific amendments. Under time pressure because of looming local government elections, the provincial legislature agreed to support the legislation without amendment. It did not go back to re-engage with the affected community about its re-reversal of position. The majority in *Merafong* ruled that this did not violate the constitution.

It is not difficult to see why finding a violation in *Merafong* would have involved a step beyond *Doctors for Life*. After all, the legislature in *Merafong* had made proper arrangements to engage with the people, and it had indubitably listened to them – to the extent of changing its mind and trying to enact their wishes. But if one wishes to see the Court simply acting to promote a rich idea of democracy, then it may seem natural to take this further step. It may seem natural to extend the lines of *Doctors for Life*'s efforts to inculcate participatory values into the way legislatures do business, and it may well seem anathema to ideas of participation, inclusiveness and consultation for a legislature to say it will do one thing, and then go off into the corridors of power and do another. It may therefore seem puzzling that the majority did not follow Justice Sachs' suggestion at the hearing that the legislature violated its public participation duties when it did not return to the people to re-engage with them about why it had reverted to its original position.[36] One may well end up concluding that *Merafong* is a failure to follow through on the promise of *Doctors for Life*'s rich ideas of listening and respectful, dignified engagement.[37] But *Doctors for Life* is qualified by its structural argument: it asserts a democratically-driven power of judicial review that aims to 'balance . . . the need to respect parliamentary institutional autonomy, and . . . the right of the public to participate in public affairs'.[38] Asking only whether something more richly democratic could have happened in *Merafong* will not suffice to understand the case.

From the structural perspective, the most striking thing about *Merafong* is the way in which the NCOP did not become the centre of the case (although as I read his dissent, Moseneke DCJ ended up reaching for an argument of this kind.)[39] The NCOP has also stayed on the margins in scholarly analysis, possibly because the focus on democratic values shifts attention away from structural issues.[40] But the underlying cause of the situation that arose in *Merafong* was the hasty legislative timetable adopted by the NCOP, which sought to complete the process before the scheduled local government elections, and by the NCOP's refusal, for the same reason, to consider specific amendments when the provincial delegations returned from engagement. In other words, the NCOP had adopted a legislative procedure that included space for the provincial legislatures to go and listen to the people but *not* space for that listening to have more than a ratifying impact on the legislative process itself. It was the NCOP process, far more than the provincial legislature's actions, that displayed a belief that public participation was merely a box to be checked off. But although these troubling features of the NCOP's process seem to inform some of the thinking in *Merafong*, the focus remains on what the provincial legislators did. Justice Sachs notes that the course of

[36] *Merafong*, para. 54.

[37] For this sort of reading, see e.g. L. Nyati, 'Public Participation: What Has the Constitutional Court Given the Public?' (2008) 12 *Law, Democracy and Development* 102, 108–09.

[38] *Doctors for Life*, para. 146; see also *Poverty Alleviation Network*, para. 35.

[39] *Merafong*, paras. 171–92.

[40] Choudhry adopts an explicitly structural approach, and as a result is also concerned about the national process. However, he understands the leadership of the provincial legislature 'were acting under orders of the ANC' and so the issue was 'dictation'; the details of the engagement did not matter because the provincial legislators 'were never open to persuasion in the first place': Choudhry, '"He Had a Mandate"', 63–64. The fact that the legislators did change their minds after the initial consultation, however, decisively rebuts this interpretation of the national problem in *Merafong*.

events 'gave rise to a strong perception, reflected in the papers, that the legislative process had been a sham because an irreversible political deal had already been struck at a political level outside the legislative process'.[41] If the whole exercise had been about legitimating a national decision by top leadership, then even the original consultation would probably seem like a charade to the people involved in it – and Justice Sachs thought it important for the provincial legislators to return to the community and correct this impression. But his proposal ultimately remains an answer to a question about the provincial legislators: what was democratically wrong with what *they* did? His concerns are hardly trivial, but one can also readily see why his proposal might seem no more than an apology, after the vote had been taken, which would not inform the lawmaking process and would only come afterwards to explain the ultimate result. One can therefore see why the majority of his colleagues thought the failure to do this 'possibly discourteous' but not unconstitutional, a matter that should be left to voters to punish in elections and which the Court should not be in the business of policing.[42] One can also see, applying the *Doctors for Life* participatory/representative balance, why Sachs J's suggestion in *Merafong* seemed to involve a smaller participatory gain than *Doctors for Life* for a greater intrusion into legislative autonomy. He himself said he would only require it in the sort of highly sensitive, fraught context of the case.[43]

Once we see this, we can see why *Merafong* in fact leaves open plenty of room for a re-engagement doctrine in cases where the participatory/representative stakes are more favourable: for example, where the underlying facts change significantly after an engagement such that people may well have different views, where different perspectives might now be valuable, and where relying on the earlier engagement process would mean that one had not actually consulted with the people on the real issue to a significant extent. That is not to say that participation is only to be judged instrumentally, in terms of how many facts are learned or mistakes avoided.[44] It is only that there are situations where engagement might have greater value yet trench less closely on the ultimate autonomy of political representatives to decide how to vote and how to relate to

[41] *Merafong*, paras. 292–93; see also the majority judgment of Van der Westhuizen J, paras. 43–47.

[42] *Ibid.*, para. 60; see also the concurring judgment of Skweyiya J, paras. 307–10; Woolman, *Selfless Constitution*, p. 460.

[43] *Merafong*, paras. 293–98.

[44] See Sachs J comment on this *Ibid.*, para. 299.

their constituents, to be judged by public opinion and voting. Re-engagement simply awaits facts as conducive as the facts in *Doctors for Life* were to the original introduction of the public participation doctrine.[45] But we may wonder if *Merafong* was not that case, had it been framed as a challenge to the NCOP's timetable. In *Doctors for Life*, the provincial legislatures' conduct had displayed the blatant defects and so had been the obvious target, but the majority there did consider the NCOP as well and held that '[w]hen it comes to establishing legislative timetables, the temptation to cut down on public involvement must be resisted' and that '[t]he timetable must be subordinated to the rights guaranteed in the Constitution, and not the rights to the timetable'.[46]

That *Merafong* was not framed this way can teach us something about how constitution-building can be difficult for Court and litigants alike when it requires them to confront significant newness. In trying to put a legal finger on the sense that something had gone wrong in *Merafong*, the Court twice asked for further evidence and argument in the run-up to the hearing. As it became clearer that the provincial legislature had reversed course based on what had happened in the NCOP, the directions focused on this.[47] Suggestions in the dissents reveal still further questions not fully explored; as noted, Justice Sachs raised a novel framing of the case during the hearing itself. What we are seeing here is the tension between the traditional idea of a court as a body which decides the legal issues brought by the parties, and the reality of what a court's job is actually like when questions of what the legal doctrines should be is a significantly open question. Constitution-building in the context of newness is significantly a learning exercise for everyone. It may take time for the legal issue to come into focus; the Court may also come to see the best line of doctrinal development differently to the way the parties have thought it best to bring it. Both forces will tend to pull against the traditional idea that a case is as it is framed by the parties in the pleadings, and that courts should not set off on their own enquiries, raise new issues, or drag out a costly litigation into something more like a law reform exercise or a

45 See, in a related local government context, the decision requiring re-engagement in *South African Property Owners Association* v. *Johannesburg Metropolitan Municipality* 2013 (1) SA 420 (SCA), which problematically does not consider *Merafong* or other relevant precedents; for discussion, see Rose-Ackerman et al., *Due Process of Lawmaking*, pp. 120–22.

46 *Doctors for Life*, para. 194; see also esp. paras. 86–88, 148–52.

47 Case CCT 41/07, Directions dated 6 December 2007 and 24 January 2008, available in the *Merafong* case file at www.constitutionalcourt.org.za.

commission of enquiry. *Merafong* pushes up against these restraints, and we will see it is far from unique in doing so.

The final points to be made concern *Merafong*'s epilogue. After the disputed legislation was upheld, the community continued to protest and boycotted the subsequent local government elections. The ANC responded by re-engaging with the community, seeking a solution and an end to the bad press, and ultimately passed further legislation that did give effect to the community's wishes.[48] This is a turbulent but working mechanism of representative democracy, which is why it mattered to the *Doctors for Life* majority to include deference to it, and why *Merafong* is consistent with *Doctors for Life* in so deferring. To say this is not to pretend that the democratic process always works out so neatly: the Merafong community may have got what it wanted in the end, but Moutse and Matatiele did not.[49] But *Doctors for Life* was never about giving the people what they want – hence much of the disappointment of those who have subsequently litigated in terms of the case who have unsurprisingly been more interested in the underlying policy issues than in the legal process questions they have sought to use as a means to halt that policy. *Doctors for Life* was about listening, not necessarily acceding.[50] What gives credibility to its concerns for the representative process is not, therefore, the outcomes, but the fact that in each of these cases the government continued to engage with the communities after the litigation had ended. Even if we assume uncharitably that this was only to avoid bad publicity, this is a system of elected representative democracy in operation.

It is also part of a broader pattern, of which the Court's public participation cases represent a truly tiny part (and so, we should bear in mind, represent a tiny sample from which to draw conclusions). Susan Booysen, a long time observer of the ANC, has noted the following about the ANC's response to the expanding service delivery protests (of which she treats the municipal relocation cases in Merafong, Matatiele

[48] Bishop 'Listening Constitution', 366–90; Rose-Ackerman et al., *Due Process of Lawmaking*, pp. 119–20.

[49] Matatiele remains in the Eastern Cape, whereas the community had sought to be located in KwaZulu-Natal; the municipality's website can be found at www.matatiele.gov.za. The two areas in Moutse, which had sought to be located in Mpumalanga province, are in the Elias Motsoaledi and Ephraim Mogale (at the time of the litigation, Marble Hall) local municipalities, which remain part of the Sekhukhune district municipality in Limpopo province, whose website is at www.sekhukhune.gov.za/local_municipality.html.

[50] See also Bishop, 'Listening Constitution', esp. 338–40; Woolman, *Selfless Constitution*, pp. 445–46.

and Moutse as a part, albeit as somewhat idiosyncratic variations on a theme):

> In the wake of the community protests, the residents of South Africa's township areas . . . witnessed (or learnt about) surges of community visits by municipal officials, councillors, members of provincial executives, even members of the national cabinet, and by 2009 the president himself, negotiating and promising improvements. Hitherto invisible councillors from several political parties, mayors and municipal managers emerged to address meetings . . . In the final run-up to the 2006 local government elections, many of the protest areas received izimbizo[51] visits . . . The 2009 protests confirmed the trend of protest bringing improved prospects for attention. The Zuma administration engaged on a high level and wide scale with communities . . . Protesting communities and social or political groupings had their belief reaffirmed that 'protest works' – at least in drawing the attention of authorities, including in many cases the ANC itself.[52] (internal citation added)

Booysen also notes survey evidence that this protest activity is often bound up with representative mechanisms: instead of straightforwardly signifying disaffection, it seems that those who protest are also often more likely to vote (and vote ANC).[53] In keeping with the idiosyncratic South African pattern in which much of what might conventionally be considered opposition activity happens within ANC structures, especially at lower levels, protests are often led by local ANC members, or are intra-ANC contests involving competing branches or organizations which are ANC partners at the national level, like the South African National Civics Organization (SANCO).[54] In keeping with the arguments of earlier chapters, then, the public participation cases are further instances where the Court is more restrained than it presumably could be in promoting a rich conception of democracy, yet the result is not necessarily a loss for democracy, because of how much other activity by other institutions and people is also in the picture. Once again, the ANC is central among these

[51] 'imbizo' (izimbizo is the plural) is an isiZulu word meaning a gathering or meeting for discussion, regularly used by the ANC government, among others.

[52] Booysen, *African National Congress*, pp. 136–37; for her view of the municipal relocation cases, see pp. 131, 157.

[53] *Ibid.*, pp. 129, 137–38, 149; drawing especially on her earlier study, S. Booysen 'With the Ballot and the Brick . . . the Politics of Service Delivery in South Africa' (2007) 7 *Progress in Development Studies* 21, which uses 2004–2006 data.

[54] See A. Harber *Diepsloot* (Johannesburg and Cape Town: Jonathan Ball, 2011), ch. 5; Booysen, *African National Congress*, esp. ch. 6.

other actors, following on a long and deeply held tradition of direct public contact occurring outside formal electoral mechanisms.

Court centrists may see in the fact that the ANC did, after all, re-engage after *Merafong* as evidence that the Court could feasibly have ordered this after all. Taken together with Justice Sachs' emphasis on the exceptional nature of his proposed step, thus restricting what might otherwise be an unwieldy precedent, they can offer this as a candidate for the constitution-building first prize. But how does it compare to the alternatives? I have already suggested that a legal finding targeting the NCOP's timetable might have been a better diagnosis of what had gone wrong in *Merafong*, though that raises complex concerns of what remedy might be offered without being hugely disruptive. But rather than this hypothetical, let us use the majority's actual approach as the basis for comparison. Granted that Justice Sachs' suggestion might imbue the doctrine with a richer idea of democracy, which approach is best for democracy? An important problem here is the evidence that the rise in public protest activity in South Africa signals, among other things, a degree of public dissatisfaction with formal public participation processes that are deemed mere rote exercises.[55] It seems eminently plausible that further formal processes in *Merafong*, like a return to explain, would have been seen as ritual and frustrating exercises by the community (just as the Matatiele community viewed the remedy in *Matatiele (2)*, as we saw in the follow-up litigation in *Poverty Alleviation Network*). It also seems likely that the informal cycle of political activity that ultimately resolved the situation would have gone ahead anyway. We will see a similar pattern in Chapter 9 in the *Joe Slovo* case, where informal political engagement continued after a court order and ultimately produced a superior result.[56] The conclusion of this argument is not that the Court should never intervene in these cases. (An order invalidating the legislation in *Merafong* might, for all we know, have contributed to the subsequent political resolution of the matter, for instance, and we will see in

[55] Booysen, *African National Congress*, ch. 5, esp. pp. 177, 181–82, 185–86; see also S. L. Robins, *From Revolution to Rights in South Africa: Social Movements, NGOs & Popular Politics After Apartheid* (University of KwaZulu-Natal Press, 2008), noting that political relations between the ANC government and townships are often a matter of street actions, violent protests and resorts to litigation that seldom resembles 'the kinds of deliberative democracy models of citizen participation promoted by NGOs, donors and democracy think-tanks': *Ibid.*, p. 83.

[56] *Residents of Joe Slovo Community, Western Cape* v. *Thubelisha Homes* 2010 (3) SA 454 (CC); I discuss the case in Chapter 9.

Chapter 9 how court-ordered engagement can itself be an important means of judicial intervention.) It is that there is a serious reason to ask *when* Court-ordered formal public participation processes are a superior substitute for ordinary political processes, and when not. This is the most important lesson of the *Doctors for Life* dissents, but it also the reason why the *Doctors for Life* majority is careful to respect representative institutions and electoral mechanisms, and why it is a mistake to read *Doctors for Life* more expansively than this crucial constraint implies. And while it is certainly possible that a richer democratic doctrine can contribute to richer democratic processes – the reason I interpreted the remedy in *Matatiele (2)* as heavily forward-looking – in the context of *Merafong* that would be about producing more engagement, and we have seen that a great deal of public engagement was already occurring in the years around *Merafong* under the Zuma administration. This is once again an instance in which the Court is one mechanism among others that are also doing constitutional work, and it is in such contexts that legitimate questions arise about whether or not Court intervention is really the best available option.

Seeing this as the key question is not only crucial to a proper assessment of *Merafong*, but also to understanding how the true precedent of *Doctors for Life* remains alive and well. Understanding that public engagement is a key part of ANC political activity that merits nuanced judgment as a component of South African democracy does not mean denying its flaws. The pathologies of public participation exercises under the ANC are many, and the fact that it has been 2006 since the Court invalidated a public participation exercise reflects only that the more problematic cases of subsequent years have not yet resulted in litigation.[57] For instance, first-hand documentation of public participation exercises in relation to the controversial Traditional Courts Bill records blunt flaws like obviously inadequate notice periods, inaccessible hearings and the privileging of certain voices, particularly those of traditional leaders.[58]

[57] See e.g. Booysen, *African National Congress*, ch. 5 and further sources there cited; C. Mbazira, 'Service Delivery Protests, Struggle for Rights and the Failure of Local Democracy in South Africa and Uganda: Parallels and Divergences' (2013) 29 *South African Journal on Human Rights* 251.

[58] See esp. T. Thipe, M. de Souza and N. Luwaya, '"The Advert Was Put Up Yesterday": Public Participation in the Traditional Courts Bill Legislative Process' (2015–6) 60 *New York Law School Law Review* 519; and for detailed summaries of the hearings and written submissions see N. Luwaya, 'Report on the Provincial Traditional Courts Bill Hearings: Exploring Rural People's Democratic Participation and Freedom of Expression' (2012) 2

Doctors for Life and *Matatiele (2)* provide plentiful grounds for challenging procedural defects like these.[59] The position of women in particular in this process fits *Matatiele (2)*'s idea of a 'discrete and identifiable group' whose participation may require special efforts from a legislature, an idea misapplied by litigants to date.[60] (That said, the fact that genuine disagreements have arisen in the NCOP and that the Bill has not been rammed through in the face of them reflects that the process, though troubled, is also no sham, in line with my broader arguments about political processes in South Africa.) A court-centric focus on the truly tiny sample of the six cases that have been challenged in litigation can make us over-read *Merafong* and its three less contentious siblings as retreats from *Doctors for Life* and *Matatiele (2)*, when in fact they really just rerelect that most objections to public participation are for various reasons playing out elsewhere.

Furthermore, once we recognize that *Doctors for Life* stands for both a democratic argument and an institutional one, and once we learn from *Merafong* the importance of keeping an open mind about the different institutional locations where its ideas of listening and participation might be vindicated, we can see that *Doctors for Life* symbolizes a great deal more than a requirement for the passage of valid national and provincial legislation. The ideas of public status in *Doctors for Life* flow into many different textual channels and into the spaces between them. As a four-judge concurrence has since observed, after quoting *Doctors for Life* on these ideas:

> This understanding of the inherent value of participation and engagement also underlies many decisions of this Court. Many provisions of the Constitution require the substantive involvement and engagement of people in decisions that affect their lives. This Court has recognized this in relation to political decision-making, access to information, just administrative action, freedom of expression, freedom of association, socio-economic rights, adequate housing and protection from arbitrary eviction or demolition of homes under the Constitution ... What is thus clear is that participation and engagement are central to our constitutional project.[61]

Issues in Law and Society 1; T. Thipe, 'Voices in the Legislative Process: A Report on the Public Submissions on the Traditional Courts Bill (2008 and 2012)' (2012) 1 *Issues in Law and Society* 1. These and further materials are available from the Centre for Law and Society at the University of Cape Town, www.cls.uct.ac.za.

59 Rose-Ackerman et al., *Due Process of Lawmaking*, p. 118; Thipe et al., 'Public Participation'.

60 *Matatiele (2)*, para. 68; see esp. *Poverty Alleviation Network*, paras. 50–53.

61 *Head of Department, Department of Education, Free State Province* v. *Welkom High School; Head of Department, Department of Education, Free State Province* v. *Harmony*

The true constitutional legacy of *Doctors for Life* is not a bold and creative judicial enforcement of abstract principle, or of a depressing failure to carry through on the rich excitement of those ideas, but the value of an institutionally sophisticated judicial incorporation of some of South Africa's deepest public ideas into the processes of constitutional government. These ideas are blurring traditional distinctions in the way judges review a range of administrative and legislative processes, as the same questions about listening and inclusion and engagement are levelled at a range of structures.[62] We will not be able to understand these developments or control their potential excesses unless we keep firmly in mind the institutional issues that occupy all the judges in *Doctors for Life* and which qualify its argument for a judicial role in promoting democracy. Once we do, we will see that far from proving more arid than hoped, the work of following through on the great post-apartheid tide that lifted *Doctors for Life* is only just beginning.

Promoting Democracy within Parliament and Local Government Structures

In drawing out the structural lines of *Doctors for Life* beyond the decision itself, it is useful to consider another set of three cases that concern minority voices in majoritarian representative institutions. Once again, the Court can appear to be inconsistent in its application of democratic values of participation and deliberation, until one takes into account the structural arguments that qualify that application.

Masondo saw O'Regan J dissent, once again on her own, in defence of an inclusive idea of democracy within structures of representative

High School 2014 (2) SA 228 (CC), para. 140, per Froneman and Skweyiya JJ, Moseneke DCJ and Van der Westhuizen J concurring. (Note that Moseneke DCJ was on the opposite side of both *Doctors for Life* and *Merafong* to Van der Westhuizen and Skweyiya JJ; this is the underlying agreement I spoke of in relation to *Doctors for Life*). See also the concurring judgment of Froneman J in *Albutt* v. *Centre for the Study of Violence and Reconciliation* 2010 (3) SA 293 (CC), paras. 90–92.

62 I and co-authors explore aspects of these developments elsewhere; see Rose-Ackerman et al., *Due Process of Lawmaking*, ch. 3. Another important area is the implications of the public participation doctrine for legislatures' oversight, as opposed to legislative, role: see L. Muntingh, 'The State of Civil Society Participation in Parliament' (2012) 16 *Law, Democracy and Development* 29. On challenges to effective public participation from a civil society perspective, see e.g. R. Calland and S. Nakhooda, 'Participatory Democracy Meets the Hard Rock of Energy Policy: South Africa's National Integrated Resource Plan' (2012) 19 *Democratization* 912.

government. As such, her position bears more than a passing resemblance to what *Doctors for Life* would argue four years later. This is sometimes seen as an ultimate vindication of her bolder ideas, just as *Richter* is sometimes seen as a validation of her stance in *NNP*.[63] In light of the discussion in Chapter 3, however, we should take more seriously the question of why O'Regan J was all on her own in *Masondo*, but part of a comfortable majority in *Doctors for Life*. Why did four other judges from the *Doctors for Life* majority (its author, Ngcobo J, and Justices Langa, Mokgoro and Sachs) not vote with her in *Masondo*?

The 2002 decision in *Masondo* is located in the intricacies of South Africa's new local government structures, initiated, as we have seen, by the ANC. Municipal government is seen as having mixed legislative and executive competence, and the framework legislation provides for several possible institutional structures to exercise the executive part of these powers. The elected municipal council itself may take all executive decisions, collapsing legislative and executive functions into one body. The council may also elect an 'executive committee', to which it delegates executive functions. The statute provides in so many words that representation on this executive committee must be approximately proportional to representation in the council itself. Or, finally, the council may elect an executive mayor, thus creating a unitary executive. In larger municipalities, the statute requires such a mayor to appoint a 'mayoral council', made up of members of the municipal council, to assist her in the fulfilment of her functions.[64] Amos Masondo, the ANC mayor of Johannesburg, had understood this to mean that an executive committee (the second option) had to include opposition members in proportion to their representation on the main council, but that a mayoral council (the third option) did not. The opposition Democratic Alliance (DA) had objected to this interpretation.

On the face of it, *Masondo* involves quite a simple question of legislative interpretation. The statute explicitly distinguishes the mayoral committee structure from the executive committee structure, and it explicitly requires proportional representation of minority parties only in executive committees, without making a similar provision for mayoral ones. The legislative intention about where minority parties have a right to be represented therefore seems clear, and requiring minority representation

63 See e.g. Woolman, *Selfless Constitution*, p. 288.

64 The relevant (somewhat intricate) provisions of the Local Government: Municipal Structures Act 117 of 1998 are set out in *Masondo*, paras. 12–14.

in mayoral councils involves doing at least some violence to the rules of statutory construction by removing an apparently intentional distinction. The DA, however, relied on s 160(8) of the Constitution, which provides that 'Members of a Municipal Council are entitled to participate in its proceedings and those of its committees', in a way that 'allows parties and interests reflected within the Council to be fairly represented' and 'is consistent with democracy'. The text provides that the issue may be regulated by national legislation. The DA argued that mayoral committees fell within s 160(8) and that this therefore required that minority party members be represented on them. O'Regan J, alone in accepting this contention, argued that local government is supposed to be particularly close to the community, so it is especially important for minority voices to be heard. Given that local government in South Africa is bringing together formerly white municipalities and black areas not formerly governed by municipalities, inclusiveness and consultation are especially important. The situation is structurally different to government at the provincial and national level, where we accept a situation in which minority parties are only entitled to representation in the legislature. Confirming that we are dealing with a sui generis institution here is the fact that while a mayor has the power to hire and fire members of the mayoral committee – as with a President and her cabinet – the council itself also the power to specify that the mayor must exercise particular powers in conjunction with the mayoral committee, unlike the President/Cabinet analogy. Faced with a novel institution, O'Regan J relies on s 160 (8) to argue for more inclusiveness rather than less, and reads the Act accordingly.[65]

If one reads *Doctors for Life* simply as the Court infusing representative institutions with a richer idea of democratic values, then it will be puzzling why O'Regan J's apparently similar efforts to do this in *Masondo* attracted no support. But her *Masondo* dissent is both more institutionally specific and more unilateral than the ruling in *Doctors for Life*. It does not tell municipal government that it has a duty to make space for the expression of opposition voices – 'be inclusive of minorities' – while leaving the details of precisely how and when to do this to the framework legislation and the individual local councils to decide. Instead, it decides that a certain sort of municipal government must do this in a particular committee, notwithstanding that opposition

[65] *Masondo*, paras. 56–82.

voices are already heard in another institution in that particular form of municipal government. O'Regan J's *Masondo* dissent is therefore more prescriptive than *Doctors for Life*'s reasonableness-based approach. It is also more unilateral. *Doctors for Life* received into law an obligation already accepted by legislatures and already in wide operation and so, as noted, the judges could be confident that it was feasible to make this into a constitutional obligation. In *Masondo*, by contrast, O'Regan J would have overridden the existing practice and the view of Parliament, whose choice of statutory language apparently accepted that local councils would have a choice in this area. This difference matters because of the uncertainty surrounding such questions. The reform of local government is very complex and contentious, but there was no evidence before the Court about whether Parliament might have had good reasons to give local municipalities the option of a more unitary mayoral executive (such as efficiency, a consideration recognized by all the judges in *Masondo*).[66] Nor, conversely, was there evidence about whether opposition voices were being sidelined in practice, such that a judicial intervention might be necessary to correct matters.[67] In *Doctors for Life* and *Matatiele (2)*, it was both much clearer that there was a problem and that there was a practicable and widely accepted solution the judiciary could feasibly order.

This difference between the *Masondo* majority and O'Regan J's dissent manifests itself in the different interpretative relevance they assign to the underlying statute. The majority gives weight to the fact that the legislature evidently thought councils should have some choice about how and where minority parties were to be represented.[68] O'Regan J, by contrast, rejects the significance of this legislative choice in firm terms. She states that '[t]he Structures Act must be interpreted in the light of the Constitution and not the other way round. The Structures Act can shed no light on the meaning of s 160(8).'[69] It is naturally true that it would reverse the logic of constitutional supremacy if one allowed a statute to dictate the meaning of the Constitution. But having seen how the Court works from statutes in cases like *Hoffman* and *National Coalition (2)*, we can see that looking at the legislature's views is instead simply about being less unilateral in constitutional interpretation.

[66] *Ibid.*, paras. 17, 19, 22 (majority), 44 (Sachs J), 76 (O'Regan J).

[67] A point emphasized by Sachs J in his separate judgment; *Ibid.* para. 50.

[68] *Ibid.*, para. 31.

[69] *Ibid.*, para. 52; see also the separate judgment of Sachs J, para. 39.

This is not, of course, a definitive rebuttal to O'Regan J's position in *Masondo*. As with *NNP*, she is hardly indifferent to institutional arguments. She is concerned to show that her ruling does not subvert representative democracy because the mayoral committee still ultimately decides by majority vote and because the mayor retains the power to dismiss its members.[70] She just occupies a position further along the spectrum than her colleagues: as in *NNP*, she is once again simply willing to act more quickly and more expansively to do what she believes will best promote democratic ideas. While some may welcome this approach, it should be readily explicable why not every judge who signed on to *Doctors for Life* would support her more expansive stance here, just as the other judges did not in *NNP*.

These features of *Masondo* are important for understanding its relationship to two more recent cases, which both *do* make assertive orders to promote minority-inclusive democratic practices within representative institutions. In *Oriani-Ambrosini* v. *Sisulu, Speaker of the National Assembly* ('*Oriani-Ambrosini*'), a member of parliament challenged parliamentary rules that prevented individual members from having bills considered by Parliament without approval by parliamentary organs controlled by the majority.[71] A similar issue arose in *Mazibuko* v. *Sisulu*, which concerned the majority's right to exercise control over when a motion of no confidence in the president could be tabled and debated.[72] In each case, a split Court upheld the challenges from the minority politician, and in each case, the basic logic is the same. The majority party exercises ultimate control, in the sense that no bill or motion can pass without majority approval. But this control should not preclude opposition members being able to offer constructive alternatives to majority party legislative proposals and to have them debated, nor should it preclude motions of no confidence being debated, as these are a vital check on the presidency. The decisions are both expansive, and not merely because they join *Doctors for Life* as interventions in internal parliamentary rules and procedures. The Court could surely have avoided deciding *Mazibuko* v. *Sisulu*: the opposition DA had launched a legal challenge the Court agreed was 'over-hasty', all the original

[70] *Ibid.*, para. 78. See Roux, 'Democracy', 10-42, noting the institutional concerns and concluding that O'Regan J's approach 'would arguably have contributed to the deepening of democracy in South Africa'; see also *Ibid.*, 10-72–10-75.

[71] *Oriani-Ambrosini* v. *Sisulu, Speaker of the National Assembly* 2012 (6) SA 588 (CC).

[72] *Mazibuko* v. *Sisulu* 2013 (6) SA 249 (CC).

challenges had fallen away by the time of the Court hearing, and a parliamentary committee was currently engaging the remaining issue. The Court nevertheless decided the issue, albeit suspending the order for six months to allow Parliament time to respond.[73] In *Oriani-Ambrosini*, it similarly rejected an argument by the Speaker that he was correcting the defects, and severed portions of the rules with immediate effect (while otherwise deferring on the final form the rules should take).[74]

These interventions, coupled with the decision not to intervene in *Masondo*, should recall the pattern of the LGBTI equality cases: either intervention is firm, decisively resolving issues and overriding parliamentary submissions that the issues can be left to it, or intervention does not happen at all. This resemblance between the two groups of cases reflects the similar causal factors at work. For one thing, compared to *Masondo*, the Court confronts much less newness in being asked to rule that a legislative body should not silence minorities, though it may ultimately subject their positions to majority votes. Both *Oriani-Ambrosini* and *Mazibuko* v. *Sisulu* effectively asked the Court to rule that the legislature is a forum for debate, and that a majority may win the debate but not preclude it. This idea resonates not only with ideas of democracy similar to those central in *Doctors for Life*, but also with classical ideas of parliamentary practice.[75] *Masondo*, dealing with minority involvement in sui generis municipal institutions of uncertainly mixed competence, has much less consensus and precedent to build upon. It also raised a considerably larger risk of unforeseen consequences, as an order about one municipality with implications for others made in the context of little or no broader evidence. By contrast, in *Mazibuko* v. *Sisulu*, the Court's only order was that the tabling of motions of no confidence for debate cannot be subject to majority approval, leaving it to Parliament to reform its rules accordingly. The Speaker himself had conceded that there was a gap in the rules in his oral submissions.[76] In *Oriani-Ambrosini*, the Court itself took steps to ensure that it could make a bold order safely, calling for further information from the parties about possible remedies. The Speaker's response, in identifying potential problems, helped the Court to design its remedy accordingly.[77]

[73] *Ibid.*, paras. 67–71, 77. [74] *Oriani-Ambrosini*, paras. 85–94.

[75] *Ibid.* paras. 43–51, 57–59; *Mazibuko* v. *Sisulu*, paras. 43–46; see also R. Venter, 'Motions of No Confidence: Parliament's executive check *and* checkmate' (2014) *Tydskrif vir die Suid-Afrikaanse Reg* 407, 415–16.

[76] *Mazibuko* v. *Sisulu*, para. 52. [77] *Oriani-Ambrosini*, para. 87.

In either case, the risk of unforeseen complexities that Parliament would be unable to deal with is far smaller than the uncertainties of a decisive order in *Masondo*. Both cases are conducive to judicial review, and as in the LGBTI equality cases on the same-sex couple issue, the Court decisively asserted its jurisdiction accordingly. It should be added here, however, that *Mazibuko* v. *Sisulu* is somewhat more pro-active in response to the degree of uncertainty that is present in the case. I noted the tensions of traditional litigation in *Merafong*, and how the Court there sought more from the parties of its own volition. *Mazibuko* v. *Sisulu* does the same in seeking the parties' input on what remedy it might feasibly be able to order. The scale of what it did not know in *Masondo* was vastly bigger, but with an eye to the later discussion, it is important to note the *Mazibuko* Court (11 years on) pushing out against the traditional common law idea that a court that is not usually self-informing.

Finally, the LGBTI equality cases are also an instructive parallel because of the dimensions of the trust argument they illustrated. Given that the Court could readily have been more restrained in both *Oriani-Ambrosini* and *Mazibuko* v. *Sisulu*, it is hard to explain either decision as showing trust for the sake of it, or as efforts to avoid antagonizing the ANC – especially since *Mazibuko* v. *Sisulu* inserted the Court into the contentious political issue of a motion of no confidence levelled at a troubled President Zuma. Here again we see that the institutional argument shapes the trust argument rather than the other way around, a point visible not only in the Court's decisive intervention but also in the careful lines of where it does *not* intervene. The Court declined on institutional grounds to grant the request of the minority MP in *Oriani-Ambrosini* to specifically order the Speaker to consider his bill or table it. *Mazibuko* v. *Sisulu* explicitly avoids prescribing the form that the rules for tabling motions of no confidence in the President must take beyond requiring that the process may not be subject to majority approval.[78] Again, adopting these institutional arguments involves a measure of trust. It would be naïve to defer on these matters, and to seek the constitution-building first prize of each institution fulfilling its assigned role, if one could not have some confidence in the other institutions. That trust, again, was vindicated by the Speaker's good faith engagement with the Court, the fact that a new Rule 102A on motions of

[78] *Oriani-Ambrosini*, para. 84; *Mazibuko* v. *Sisulu*, para. 71.

no confidence was duly inserted, and the fact that the motion of no confidence, in due course, was scheduled and voted on.[79]

But that said, *Oriani-Ambrosini* and *Mazibuko* v. *Sisulu* illustrate a facet of the argument that we have not yet seen, one that starts to shade into distrust (in Ely's sense). Both cases are interestingly expansive by the Court's standards, and again this applies especially to *Mazibuko* v. *Sisulu*. Given that we saw in *NNP* and *Doctors for Life* the Court's concern about permitting applicants to take a matter too readily out of the primary institution responsible and into the courts, the Court was quick, by its own standards, to permit the opposition DA to bring the political deadlock of the motion of no confidence to Court, and indeed made a rare grant of direct access to the applicants to raise the issue.[80] One explanation for this was the evidence of parliamentary deadlock on the issue, something that also explicitly informed the Court's decision to make a firm order instead of deferring to the parliamentary committee set up to reform the rules. The Court had asked for reports on the committee's progress; it appeared that after three months that process was still be mired in stalemate and owing to 'fundamental differences' that 'are likely to persist', the Court therefore held it was 'most improbable' that the problem in the rules would be corrected absent judicial intervention – with the important mechanism of the no-confidence vote left in limbo in the meanwhile.[81] The underlying issue also gave the Court more reason to think the status quo was concerning. I noted that in *NNP* the Court had little or no evidence to suggest that the ANC was acting from democratically untoward motives but that this had sometimes been different in later cases. The issue of a motion of no confidence arose in the context of the protracted public reaction to very substantial expenditure of public funds on President Zuma's personal residence at Nkandla, itself an episode in a series of long-standing concerns over the President's connections to corrupt activity and his accountability in this regard. This, together with the (Court-solicited) evidence of an apparently stalled process, made *Mazibuko* v. *Sisulu* a much less convincing case for deference. The more complicated nuances of trust and distrust

[79] The new Rule 102A in the National Assembly is available at www.parliament.gov.za/content/NA%20RULES%202014.pdf; it was inserted on 25 February 2014, according to the index of recent rules changes, available at www.parliament.gov.za/content/na.rules.changes.2014~2.pdf. The motion of no confidence was debated on 17 March 2015 and was defeated 221–113.

[80] *Mazibuko* v. *Sisulu*, paras. 67–72; see also the dissent, esp. paras. 132–36.

[81] *Mazibuko* v. *Sisulu*, para. 69.

on this issue and the actions of the Speaker reflect that even in this contested context, the stances of other actors are nuanced and so the institutional arguments must be too: it is not simply a matter of flicking from 'trust' to 'distrust'. This caution against simple explanations is also crucial in confronting this chapter's final case, arising from political fights eleven years earlier.

UDM (2) and the Brief Life of Floor-Crossing

The month before the Court decided *Masondo*, it handed down a decision that is usually placed right alongside *NNP* in the South African constitutional anti-canon.[82] *UDM (2)* unanimously upheld a package of legislation, including two constitutional amendments, that lifted the ban on floor-crossing which had been put in place during the constitutional negotiations. (It did find a technical problem with one of the statutes, but since it suspended that order of invalidity to give Parliament time to fix the defect this caused only a short delay in the introduction of floor-crossing).[83] The change applied to national and provincial legislatures and local councils. The ban would be re-imposed six years later, coming into effect in January 2009.[84] *UDM (2)* was handed down after an unusually extended three-day hearing that saw five political parties appearing before the court, together with the government and premier of the province of KwaZulu-Natal.[85] That hearing came after the court of first instance had ensured the judicialization of the issue by not only declaring floor-crossing constitutionally invalid but purporting to suspend the legislation before it could come into effect. The Court had therefore needed to deal with the issue on an interim basis, producing an earlier judgment ('*UDM (1)*') that was mostly concerned with articulating careful restraints on the judicial power to interfere with statutes before the whole process of enactment is complete. *UDM (1)* is entirely of a piece with the extensive discussion of the same issue nearly four years later in *Doctors for Life*.

[82] *United Democratic Movement* v. *President of the Republic of South Africa (No. 2)* 2003 (1) SA 495 (CC) was handed down on 4 October 2002, *Masondo* on 12 November.

[83] *UDM (2)*, paras. 77–118; Booysen, *African National Congress*, p. 274.

[84] Constitution Fourteenth Amendment Act of 2008; Constitution Fifteenth Amendment Act of 2008.

[85] In addition to the UDM, four other political parties (the ANC, IFP, ACDP and PAC) appeared before the Court.

The reason for legal scholars' concerns, and the reason that the court of first instance had acted so precipitately, was the fear that the ANC was introducing floor-crossing as a way to use its patronage and power to increase its strength artificially. *UDM (2)* is therefore understood as a case about the constitutional control of dominant party democracy, and the Court's response – upholding the legislation without even articulating a deeper theory of democracy with the resources to challenge dominant democracy's pathologies – is seen as a failure to assert that vital control. Some, like Samuel Issacharoff and Sujit Choudhry, explain this as a failure of doctrinal imagination; others, like Theunis Roux, as management of political risk.[86] These critics will also see *UDM (2)* as a powerful challenge to the constitution-building account. All the talk of trust and the public status of ideas and the readings of cases I have offered on the strength of them will be disingenuous or naïve if the Court does not, when it counts, stop trusting and start articulating its own content and enforcing it. Since critics see floor-crossing's introduction as threatening to subvert democratic mechanisms, they will see no way to miss the point more than by deferring to those democratic mechanisms, as *UDM (2)* did in holding that elections were the primary check on floor-crossing and that the Court should not intervene.[87] On this view, the later decisions in *Oriani-Ambrosini* and *Mazibuko* v. *Sisulu* offer some hope, but that does not make *UDM (2)* itself any less of a problem.[88]

In evaluating these arguments, it is important to be clear about the precise situation that arose in *UDM (2)*. Issacharoff understands floor-crossing heavily in terms of dominant party intent. He argues that the ban on floor-crossing was initially put in place to check the ANC, that in 2002 the ANC used its dominance to remove this check on itself for the purposes of expanding that dominance, and that it abandoned floor-crossing again once it had swallowed up the available political gains.[89] Choudhry similarly sees the ANC's support for floor-crossing particularly as an effort to seize control of the Western Cape, the only province

86 Choudhry, '"He Had a Mandate"', pp. 37–48; S. Issacharoff, 'Constitutional Courts and Democratic Hedging' (2011) 99 *Georgetown Law Journal* 961, 996–1001; S. Issacharoff, 'The Democratic Risk to Social Transitions' (2013) 5 *Constitutional Court Review* 1, 6–7, 22–23; Roux, 'Principle and Pragmatism,' 128–30; Roux, *Politics of Principle*, pp. 351–62; Roux, 'Democratic Rights Jurisprudence', 66; see also Roux, 'Democracy', 10-54–10-55, 10-69, 10-77.

87 See e.g. Choudhry, '"He Had a Mandate"', 33–34.

88 Issacharoff, 'Democratic Risk', 29–30 sees *Oriani-Ambrosini* in this light.

89 Issacharoff, 'Democratic Hedging', 996–1001; Issacharoff 'Democratic Risk', 2, 6–9.

the party did not control at the time, and more generally as a means to secure its position. He also argues that the Court initially understood the floor-crossing ban as a check on the ANC.[90] Both view *UDM (2)* as a case about a dominant party trying to manipulate and abuse the democratic system to entrench its position at the head of 'an increasingly one-party state'.[91] From this perspective, it will seem highly problematic that the Court discussed floor-crossing in rather abstract terms as consistent in principle with multiparty democracy, proportional representation and the right to vote, and not in the particular context that made it a concern. It will seem necessary to articulate not merely richer standards but ones that are insulated even from dominant political power. Both accordingly support much stronger doctrinal checks targeted at this problem and advise consideration of a basic structure doctrine.[92]

This argument draws support from the claim, which is perfectly true, that the ANC benefitted more from floor-crossing than any other party. It also sees as telling that, after the first floor-crossing window in which any member could cross the floor, 10 per cent of a party's members in a particular legislative chamber would have to wish to cross the floor before any member could. That would obviously make it harder to co-ordinate a departure from a party as large as the ANC while giving individual members of smaller parties with ten seats or less an effective unilateral power to cross the floor.[93] But the argument, even when it comes to this apparently blatantly self-serving threshold, ultimately rests on an inadequate account of floor-crossing in South Africa.

Floor-crossing was prohibited under the original negotiated arrangements, partly to protect the minority parties the new proportional representation system aimed to make space for, and partly in the interests of

[90] Choudhry, '"He Had a Mandate"', 37–44.

[91] The quoted text is from Issacharoff, 'Democratic Risk', 7–8; see also Choudhry, '"He Had a Mandate,"' esp. 10–13.

[92] Issacharoff, 'Democratic Risk', 13–22; Choudhry, '"He Had a Mandate"', 45–48. Devenish, who also seeks richer content, nevertheless believes *UDM (2)*'s approach to the basic structure issue was correct: G. E. Devenish 'Political Musical Chairs: The Saga of Floor-crossing and the Constitution' (2004) 15 *Stellenbosch Law Review* 52, 56; *UDM (2)*, paras. 15–17.

[93] C. M. Fombad, 'Challenges to Constitutionalism and Constitutional Rights in Africa and the Enabling Role of Political Parties: Lessons and Perspectives from Southern Africa' (2007) 55 *American Journal of Comparative Law* 1, 32; Issacharoff, 'Democratic Risk', 7; Issacharoff, 'Democratic Hedging', 997; T. Hoeane 'Floor-crossing in South Africa: Entrenching or Undermining Democracy? (2008) 27 *Politeia* 70, 76–77; Devenish, 'Political Musical Chairs', 57–58.

stability during the transition.[94] The ban on floor-crossing was resisted by the DP's Colin Eglin, who thought that the post-1994 political landscape would be fluid and that the ban would inhibit natural political re-alignments. Dawie de Villiers of the NP favoured the ban in the interests of stability, but also anticipated realignments and 'suggested that the provision be made less rigid with a view to allowing substantial party factions to break away' – an opposition party view we should connect to the 10 per cent threshold ultimately adopted in 2002. That a straight ban was imposed was due above all to ANC *opposition* to floor-crossing; all but the DP and another smaller party came round to the ANC view, but it remained unclear how many supported the ban only as a transitional measure.[95] This floor-crossing ban was retained in the 1996 text and ruled compatible with the Constitutional Principles in the *First Certification* judgment.[96] That it was an uncertain and transitional arrangement is however reflected in the fact that the drafters of the 1996 Constitution also granted Parliament the power 'within a reasonable period' after the 1996 Constitution took effect to lift the ban by ordinary legislation. They did so by inserting a provision to that effect into a schedule of interim arrangements, including what would happen if parties dissolved or otherwise ceased to exist, that was imported from the 1993 interim text. The Court upheld transitional arrangements of this sort, subject to important restrictions protecting the Constitution from amendment by ordinary legislation, in the *Second Certification* judgment.[97] The regulation of floor-crossing was therefore the uneasy combination of a negotiated arrangement, locked in like other such arrangements by its constitutional status in the 1993 text and carried over in that form into the 1996 text; and a back-door transitional arrangement, deferring the issue to the ordinary majority judgment of Parliament once the 1996 text was passed. This background is important,

[94] Hoeane, 'Floor-crossing in South Africa', 71; Spitz, *Politics of Transition*, p. 111.

[95] Spitz, *Politics of Transition*, pp. 111–12. Spitz's own view (in 2000) was that while the ban on floor-crossing reflected strong party control, as a party without a distinct ethnic base 'the anti-defection provision would serve to bolster the ANC as majority party while preventing political realignments within Parliament' – *Ibid*., p. 112.

[96] 1993 interim Constitution, ss 43(b), 133(b); 1996 Constitution, ss 47(5), 106(3), 157; *First Certification*, paras. 180–87.

[97] 1996 Constitution, Sch. 6, Annexure A, Item 13; 1993 interim Constitution, Sch. 2, Item 23, as amended by the insertion of Item 23A (Sch. 2 was incorporated into the 1996 text); *Certification of the Amended Text of the Constitution of the Republic of South Africa, 1996* 1997 (2) SA 97 (CC), paras. 90–95; see also *UDM (2)*, paras. 77–113.

not only because this was the source of the technical problems noted earlier, but also to qualify what is otherwise the natural first impression that *UDM (2)* is about a dominant party amending the constitution to suit its short-term political aims. There is something of that, but the fact that the dispute had constitutional stakes at all was at least partly due to the Constitutional Assembly's failure to decide in 1996 whether floor-crossing needed to be constitutionally prohibited beyond the transition, or whether it could be left as a matter for ordinary politics.

The background is also important to see how the regulation of floor-crossing was a multiparty story, something that continued to be true after the constitution-drafting phase. In 1998 the DP, in keeping with its stance during the negotiations, moved that the lifting of the ban be reconsidered, and a committee was formed accordingly.[98] The ANC was still opposed to permitting floor-crossing, as was the IFP, while the NNP and two other small parties besides the DP all supported floor-crossing. Two professors consulted by the committee both favoured the introduction of a qualified freedom to cross the floor, with one proposing that it be permitted where 20–25 per cent of a party wished to cross the floor and the other where 5–10 per cent did. (Here we see the specific origin of the 10 per cent threshold in the 2002 arrangements, again not an ANC proposal). The committee, however, ultimately concluded that in the interests of stability floor-crossing should not yet be introduced, and proposed reconsideration of the issue after the 1999 elections. There the issue might well have rested had it not been for the political opportunity presented by the slow death of the NNP. The other parties now reran their floor-crossing calculations in light of their prospects in picking up former NNP members. The DP again made the first move, forming an electoral alliance with the NNP to create the Democratic Alliance (DA). Candidates from both parties contested the 2000 local government elections under the united banner of the DA. Then the largest faction of the NNP broke with the leadership of the DA, and formed an alliance with the ANC. NNP members at the local level, however, had been elected as DA local councillors and so would lose their seats if they left the DA and joined the ANC. In these circumstances, it is easy to see why the ANC and the NNP would favour the introduction of floor-crossing. The DA also judged that it stood to benefit from the mêlée, and stuck to its 1998 position in support of floor-

98 Booysen, *African National Congress*, p. 268; Hoeane, 'Floor-crossing in South Africa', 74–75; Devenish, 'Political Musical Chairs', 59.

crossing. Thus it was that the package of floor-crossing legislation passed with 86 per cent support in Parliament. The IFP continued to oppose floor-crossing, while the PAC and the ACDP switched from their earlier position and also opposed it: neither party stood to gain from the NNP's collapse. Floor-crossing, then, was no unilateral ANC scheme.[99] The party also did not ram through its original version of the bill, under which the President would have had the discretion to declare floor-crossing periods, presumably when they suited the ANC. After opposition resistance, it instead accepted a system of fixed windows whose dates were established in advance.[100] Seeing this multiparty background also makes sense of the fact that after floor-crossing's 2008 repeal, the party most trying to get around the re-instated ban was the DA, something that may otherwise seem 'paradoxical', as it does to Issacharoff.[101]

Recognizing all this, however, does not rebut more nuanced criticisms of *UDM (2)*. If floor-crossing would serve to strengthen an already very strong party, it is reasonable to worry about its introduction on democratic grounds regardless of specific intentions or events at the time of its introduction. In addition, the original concern about floor-crossing that appears in the *First Certification* judgment is not about the dominance of the ANC so much as that floor-crossing would threaten the smallest parties, reducing the representation of minority views. If so, the fact that two of the larger opposition parties joined the ANC to pass the legislation is not necessarily reassuring. One might want a richer democratic argument from the Court, less to head off a specific threat and more to defend a certain structure of government. Once again, on this view, the fact that the Court not only upheld the legislation but did not articulate any such richer theory is

99 Much of this background is summarized in the *UDM (2)* judgment; see also S. Booysen, 'The Will of the Parties versus the Will of the People? Defections, Elections and Alliances in South Africa' (2006) 12 *Party Politics* 727; E. McLaughlin, 'Electoral Regimes and Party-switching: Floor-crossing in South Africa's Local Legislatures' (2012) 18 *Party Politics* 563, and further sources cited later.

100 R. Southall, 'The State of Party Politics: Struggles within the Tripartite Alliance and the Decline of Opposition' in J. Daniel, A. Habib and R. Southall (eds.), *State of the Nation: South Africa 2003–2004* (Pretoria: Human Sciences Research Council, 2003), pp. 70–71.

101 Issacharoff, 'Democratic Risk', 9 n. 40, referring to the DA's dual-membership arrangement with the Independent Democrats; see further Booysen, *African National Congress*, pp. 269, 284.

cause for regret or, at best, is something to be explained as a strategic response to its political position.[102]

The argument that floor-crossing would strengthen the ANC was, however, by no means uncontested. The matter has been a subject of disagreement among political scientists, although constitutional lawyers do not usually recognize this. While floor-crossing's scholarly critics have raised the nuanced concerns just noted,[103] its scholarly supporters have seen it as a way to empower individual representatives and lessen the strict party discipline that generally prevails in South African legislatures, and also as a possible step towards producing greater competition in the political system by facilitating the breakaway of factions from the ANC's broad coalition.[104] The various parties' shifting positions also reflect that the political effects of floor-crossing were not seen as straightforward by them, either. *UDM (2)* was about these more contested questions, rather than about a judicial response, or non-response, to a clear threat to South African democracy. The judgment is thoroughly aware of the background and the debates. Thus it concludes: 'What is apparent from this is that there were conflicting views within Parliament as to whether or not floor-crossing was appropriate for South Africa.' It adds that 'the

102 See esp. the richer account in Roux, 'Democracy'; his political account of the case is prompted by his need to explain what he sees as *UDM (2)*'s failure to articulate any such account.

103 Opponents include V. T. Maphai, 'A Season for Power-sharing' (1996) 7 *Journal of Democracy* 67, 75; T. Koelble and A. Reynolds, 'Power-sharing Democracy in the New South Africa' (1996) 24 *Politics and Society* 221; D. Atkinson, 'Taking to the Streets: Has Developmental Local Government Failed in South Africa?' in S. Buhlungu et al. (eds.) *State of the Nation: South Africa 2007* (Pretoria: Human Sciences Research Council Press, 2007), 64; Hoeane, 'Floor-crossing in South Africa'; Devenish, 'Political Musical Chairs'; N. Misra-Dexter and J. February (eds.), *Testing Democracy: Which Way Is South Africa Going?* (Cape Town: IDASA, 2010), 174: 'Floor-crossing undermined the electoral system in three ways. First, it disrupted or distorted proportionality as expressed by voters; second, it distorted the public financing of parties; and finally, it interrupted the internal functioning of political parties.'

104 See e.g. C. Jung and I. Shapiro, 'South Africa's Negotiated Transition: Democracy, Opposition, and the New Constitutional Order' (1995) 23 *Politics & Society* 269, 277; I. Shapiro and C. Jung, 'South African Democracy Revisited: A Reply to Koelble and Reynolds' (1996) 24 *Politics & Society* 237, 239–40, 244–45; R. B. Mattes, 'South Africa: Democracy Without the People?' (2002) 13 *Journal of Democracy* 22, 24; A. Gouws and P. Mitchell, 'South Africa: One Party Dominance Despite Perfect Proportionality' in M. Gallagher and P. Mitchell (eds.), *The Politics of Electoral Systems* (Oxford University Press, 2005), 366; see also Booysen, 'The Will of the Parties', 729–31 (noting these arguments and that floor-crossing, internationally, has sometimes been destabilizing and sometimes not); Choudhry,'"He Had a Mandate"', 38 (noting these arguments).

differing views were each supported as being consistent with democracy' and so ultimately the issue was resolved by 'a political decision'.[105] The Court sees the matter as up for reasonable constitutional debate and thus leaves it to the realm of majoritarian politics. Its *First Certification* finding was that a ban on floor-crossing was compatible with basic constitutional principles; its *UDM (2)* finding was that a ban, while 'possibly desirable', is not constitutionally required either.[106] Seen this way, *UDM (2)* in no way rules out the future possibility of a stronger doctrinal position along the lines sought by its critics, any more than *NNP* rules out stronger action against threats to elections. The Court's real disagreement with its critics is not about whether constitutional ideas of democracy could be found to guard against threats by a dominant party or protect the smallest members of pluralist multiparty democracy – clearly they could. Instead, as in *NNP, UDM (2)* is a decision about *when* to act, about whether the facts require the Court to insert itself into the situation and into the operations of other mechanisms. The Court simply does not think it should intervene, though doubtless it *could* do so.

What, then, informs the decision not to intervene? Deciding about floor-crossing meant making a judgment call. The manoeuvres prompted by the break-up of the NNP were a matter of ordinary electoral politics. Though the outcome of that specific interaction was too uncertain for the Court to be making findings about it, it was a good bet that floor-crossing in general would lead the ANC to gain some seats. But that too is, in itself, a matter of ordinary party politics: sometimes parties succeed in attempts to poach each others' voters, and sometimes they do not, and majority parties everywhere try to leverage their governing position to their advantage. Whether *UDM (2)* was a case for judicial intervention does not turn on whether floor-crossing was or was not going to lead to some political advantages for some parties, likely including the ANC. It turns on whether these advantages would represent a structural threat of some kind to South African democracy. That might be the destruction of smaller parties, if their members left wholesale for larger parties and thus destroyed those parties before the next election such that voters would have no chance to respond and save them. It might be that the ANC would use its dominant position to take more control at local level or in the two provinces where it faced significant electoral competition,

[105] *UDM (2)*, esp. paras. 60–67; the quoted text appears at para. 67.

[106] *Ibid.* paras. 32–25. The two judgments are therefore not 'clearly' in 'contradiction', as argued by Devenish, 'Political Musical Chairs', 63–64.

KwaZulu-Natal and the Western Cape, though since the ANC was already dominant and since floor-crossing would not stop it from having to stand for election, the potential for structural damage here is less clear. But both points were speculative, and the debates among parliamentarians and political scientists, to say nothing of the DA's calculated support for the legislation in 2002 when the party was in competition with the ANC over floor-crossing's fruits, show that it was far from one-sided speculation either.

Whether one believes the *UDM (2)* judges should nevertheless have pulled the trigger of intervention, then, depends a good deal on one's starting assumptions. The general trends already noted – court centrism, the judiciary as guardian against the looming ANC, better safe than sorry – will predispose one towards intervention. Indeed, there is a strong sense in which legal scholarship on *UDM (2)* is about these general ideas more than the case itself, one reason why the details of exactly what threat floor-crossing posed sometimes seem less important than the fact that the critics are looking for signs that the Court will stand up to the ANC and therefore worry when *UDM (2)* does not show those signs. Different starting assumptions make the case look very different.[107] The ANC's leadership, after all, has shown little if any sign of intent to violate electoral rules or otherwise break the electoral game, as opposed to playing it to win by means dirty and clean. One also has to make some rather craven assumptions about South Africa's opposition parties to think their members would cross the floor in sufficient numbers that portions of the opposition spectrum would actually be destroyed. Floor-crossing may then well seem insufficiently concerning to warrant judicial intervention. And as with *NNP*, if one is not of the view that Rome is on fire, than other considerations will come into focus. For one, it was no doubt appealing for the Court to stay out of the political fight if it thought it could. This is easily seen as a purely strategic decision, but *if* one does not think that the Court had to intervene to protect democracy, we can see its constitutional logic. Party politics, and its realignments, are a key democratic mechanism for adjusting to shifting patterns in the electorate.[108] In the events leading up to *UDM (2)*, political actors were responding to the demise of a party that had been a fixture of the

[107] See further Fowkes, 'Right After All', 165–68.

[108] On party realignments, see J. L. Sundquist, *Dynamics of the Party System: Alignment and Realignment of Political Parties in the United States* (Washington, DC: Brookings Institution, Rev. Ed., 1983).

South African political scene for decades. This party competition is a key part of the constitutional democratic mechanism, and it does something different to the judicial mechanism, by different and often more expedient means. Deferring to this mechanism, *if* one does not think there is a structural threat to head off, is consistent with an appealing constitutional allocation of tasks. For another thing, it was also appealing to avoid the issue of the precise legal basis on which a judicial intervention should be mounted. A finding that floor-crossing was inconsistent with democracy in principle was always going to be implausible in a world where many democracies permit floor-crossing. Being more specific on the facts, for example by ruling that floor-crossing was unwise in the context of dominant party democracy, could not be done without saying provocative things about the ANC and treating it explicitly as a threat.[109] And more specific *abstract* findings, such as for that floor-crossing is incompatible with closed-list proportional representation systems featuring small minority groups, would require the Court to settle unilaterally issues displaying quite significant newness, in the substantial absence of the sorts of evidentiary consensus or other support we have seen underpinning bold findings in other cases.

All of this, to repeat, is conditional on whether one thinks South African democracy was under threat, for if it was then the risks of unilaterally resolving newness or confronting the ANC might have to be borne, or strategically ducked in a way that could not be reconciled with a defensible reading of the text. The post-*UDM (2)* trio of *Oriani-Ambrosini, Mazibuko* v. *Sisulu* and especially *Doctors for Life* are reason to think that the Court can make more expansive democratic findings when it decides it needs to do so. *Mazibuko* v. *Sisulu*, in turn, joins a set of cases on other topics that offer reason to think the Court is also willing to make bold, creative findings in response to political threats when necessary.[110] But if South African democracy was not under threat in *UDM (2)*, and if the Court therefore did not need to do something extraordinary, than *UDM (2)* would be consistent with the pattern of the Court's earlier decisions – indeed, so consistent that we might not be at all surprised at the outcome. After all, if we do not depart from the premise that floor-crossing posed a clear threat to South African democracy, then the application in *UDM (2)* effectively asked the Court to assert a particular idea of democracy in a contested, uncertain context in

[109] See also Roux, 'Democratic Rights Jurisprudence', 66.
[110] See the recent cases cited in *Ibid.*, 69–71.

order to overturn a majority parliamentary decision – something every judge in *Masondo* except O'Regan J declined to do. (All the judges who sat in *Masondo* also sat in *UDM (2)*). It also asked the Court to act at the instance of an opposition party, which had found itself on the wrong side of a majority vote in parliament, to forestall an anticipated threat to democracy for which the opposition party could offer only speculative evidence – something every judge in *NNP* and its sister *DP* decision, again except O'Regan J, had declined to do. (All the judges who sat in *NNP* and *DP* also sat in *UDM (2)*). And in light of these split decisions, it should be particularly striking that *UDM (2)*'s unanimous result included O'Regan J's vote. This might reflect only the internal pressure of the Court's customary preference in politically sensitive cases for a unanimous judgment issued only in the name of 'the Court'. But O'Regan J had been a lone dissenter in sensitive cases before, and if we are willing to look beyond bluntly political explanations for her vote, her position might lead us to take seriously that possibility that *UDM (2)* was a less convincing case for judicial intervention than its democratic predecessors. We might think, for example, that *NNP* concerned rather more classical grounds for judicial intervention in democratic processes than *UDM (2)* did and that, if one is operating from the perspective of potentially excluding 20 per cent of the electorate from an election, that *NNP* also concerned a more serious problem. We might also consider that ruling floor-crossing inconsistent with the Constitution (or making one of the more specific versions of this ruling that I outlined) is a more drastic step than merely reading a statute in a more democratically inclusive direction, as in *Masondo*. From this perspective, it might in fact have been surprising if the result in *UDM (2)* had been anything other than an 11–0 loss for the applicant's argument.

Finally, it is worth addressing the tone of *UDM (2)*, which can make it seem more worrying than it is. Tone merits careful consideration given the care the Court devotes to such matters (and it will be an important issue in the next two chapters, too). A good deal of concern about *UDM (2)* seems to stem from the way the judgment declines to engage with floor-crossing except at the abstract level of its general compatibility with democratic principles and, even then, does so in a way that gives quite a strong sense of trying to tick off the arguments raised by the applicant in order to be able to dismiss the case.[111] This will strengthen the

[111] See e.g. Issacharoff, 'Democratic Hedging', 998, describing *UDM (2)* as 'formalist'; Devenish, 'Political Musical Chairs', 57, describing parts of the judgment as 'weak, superficial and unconvincing'.

appearance that the Court was just trying to get rid of a politically tricky matter and so declined to engage with its substance as a legal adjudicator should, at least if it is not being bluntly strategic. It makes it easy to see the Court as taking a parsimonious view of its role, as an adjudicator of a legal case rather than a defender of democracy. It also means that the Court certainly does not actually set out all the arguments I have raised to explain its judgment, which is why *UDM (2)* is not seen as reassuring or useful with an eye to future threats, and which may also give rise to legitimacy objections based on transparency.

This tone, however, reflects its own constitution-building logic. *If* one feels that intervention was essential to safeguard democracy, then the style of the judgment and the associated concerns just set out will simply add to the list of serious problems with *UDM (2)*. But if one does not think that, then some of the reasons for not intervening will also be reasons for not articulating content. We have seen the difficulties associated with various possible legal findings in the case. The uncertainty also matters. Given reasonable arguments that floor-crossing might serve to counter ANC dominance or South Africa's strong party discipline, for example, there are risks to setting up precedents against it in advance even (indeed, especially) for those who see the ANC as a dominant party threat. The usefulness of a stronger finding as a signal or a precedent, if one wants the Court to involve itself in policing the ANC as a political player, is that this strategy might backfire in ways that would make it self-defeating. Claims like these are arguable. The point is only that in light of them, the approach to judgment-writing adopted by the decision has stakes just as its eventual findings do. *UDM (2)*'s tone is a logical function of its decision not to intervene – implying that it stands for little in itself and that matters would be different if the context were different, something the Court's later more expansive decisions in democratic and politicized situations tend to confirm. This is the expansive-or-not-at-all pattern we saw in previous chapters, and we will see it again in Chapters 8 and 9, a fact which in itself tends to rebut the idea that *UDM (2)*'s tone is a product of its particularly politicized context.

Epilogue to *UDM (2)*

UDM (2)'s judgment call, like *NNP*'s, is by its nature debatable, but it is once again worth noting that *UDM (2)*'s epilogue bears out many of the features of the Court's approach. Criticism in legal scholarship generally goes no further than noting that, as predicted, the ANC benefitted more than any other party from floor-crossing.[112] And so it did. But there is more to the picture, especially at provincial and local level where most of the action took place. The primary product of floor-crossing was not ANC dominance, although it certainly increased the ANC's overall strength in various ways, but increased political instability, one reason why parties across the spectrum supported its rebanning six years after *UDM (2)*. Perhaps its most important damaging effect was interfering with the functioning of political parties and legislatures. It certainly left some small parties scrambling to retain members. The United Democratic Movement (UDM), as the eponymous litigation reflects, sought to head off defections by litigation and, when that failed, by suspending members; the IFP and the Independent Democrats also suspended members.[113] The ANC made a particular point of tempting away the DA's black African Members of Parliament.[114] Legislatures and municipal councils became preoccupied with politicking instead of service delivery.

But if this shows the ANC engaging in political tactics, and doing so successfully in the sense of becoming stronger at the expense of its political rivals, the first point of central importance is that the party showed little sign of subverting democracy. Floor-crossing did assist the ANC to take control of the Western Cape in 2003 (after the DP's deal with the NNP had helped *it* take over the province as the DA, though at that time the DP was the junior partner in the deal).[115] This was one of the ANC's key aims in supporting floor-crossing. But it accepted the DA's outright election victory in the province in 2009, and has acquiesced in the DA's control since (while engaging, unsurprisingly, in an array of the strategies of ordinary politics to try and retake the province). The ANC also acquired a majority in the KwaZulu-Natal provincial legislature as a result of floor-crossing, part of its long-term aim to control that province. But it continued to govern in a (troubled) coalition with the IFP in the interests of stability in a province historically plagued by political violence, and indeed, it did so even after winning control of KwaZulu-Natal outright in the 2004 elections.[116] These are not the actions of a party seeking to subvert the multiparty system or shut others out of as much political power as possible by any means.

[112] See e.g. Choudhry, '"He Had a Mandate"', 44.
[113] Booysen, *African National Congress*, pp. 259–60, 262, 284.
[114] *Ibid.*, p. 278.
[115] See e.g. Hoeane, 'Floor-crossing in South Africa', 71–72.
[116] Booysen, *African National Congress*, pp. 227, 261–62.

The record also does not support the concern for a democratic distortion.[117] Dampening the common assertion that floor-crossing distorts democratic will, most of the ANC's gains (and most of the gains generally) were *ratified* by the election that followed them. The principal exception came in 2009, when the ANC's 293 seats in the national parliament, increased by floor-crossing from its 2004 election tally of 279, was cut to 264 seats as part of the swing against the ANC that year. The ANC accepted that loss, and indeed redoubled its ordinary political efforts in response to it. Insofar as floor-crossing's threat is interpreted in terms of the demise of smaller parties, the facts are still more unequivocal. Every smaller party represented in the national parliament in 1999 was still there after the 2009 elections (with three new parties being added during that period).[118] Parties with less than 5 per cent of the vote collectively held more seats in 2004, after floor-crossing's introduction, and in 2009, at the end of the floor-crossing era, than such parties did in 1999.[119] Even if we go down to the provincial level – where quite a lot of party-forming and re-forming took place, where some single-member parties existed, and where the story has it that at times more than one provincial legislator had to check at roll call which party he belonged to – the smaller parties that existed in 2002 were mostly still in existence when floor-crossing ended. And it may be worth adding that insofar as these parties were swallowed up, it was more often by the DA than the ANC.[120]

The thesis that floor-crossing principally caused instability relies especially on its record at the local level. Care must be taken when examining figures here, since some scholarly writing quotes only the net losses and

[117] Issacharoff recognizes that *UDM (2)*, while interesting jurisprudentially, proved not to be a watershed in terms of ANC consolidation of power: Issacharoff, 'Democratic Risk', 22; see also Issacharoff, 'Democratic Hedging', 996.

[118] The Afrikaner Eenheidsbeweging, the Federal Alliance, and the Vryheidsfront/Freedom Front merged to form the Freedom Front Plus (FF+) during this period, but since the concern is with representation of minority voices this is not a relevant change; the FF+ continued to win seats.

[119] Parties with less than 5% of the vote collectively won 34 seats in the 1999 election, 43 seats in 2004 and 39 seats in 2009. (The 2009 figure includes the IFP, which dropped below the 5% threshold in that election, but excludes the newly-emerged COPE, which won 7,4% of the vote. I exclude parties with less than the 0,25% of votes needed for a seat in the National Assembly.)

[120] Smaller parties originating from floor-crossing splits were often eliminated, however; see Booysen, *African National Congress*, p. 283.

gains, which show the ANC to be the outright winner.[121] That it was, but without the gross figures, we will miss that many councillors also left the ANC. It is important here that in small local councils with 15 or 30 seats in total, the 10 per cent threshold offered far less protection for larger parties than it did in the 400-seat National Assembly. The fact that the NNP joined the DA before floor-crossing began must also be kept in mind. The numbers reflect, for example, that the DA lost 417 municipal councillors in 2002, but one must remember that the DA had gained fully 612 councillors from its original merger with the NNP.[122] It still controlled more councils after the 2002 floor-crossing than it had before the merger. Furthermore, the ANC's gain in councillors does not mean it was the only beneficiary at local level. In 2002, power shifted in 21 municipalities as a result of floor-crossing (out of 284), but the ANC was the new controlling party in only 8 of the 21.[123] This reflects the fact that 217 of the 555 local defections in 2002 were not connected to the NNP.[124] These were wild cards, responding to different, unpredictable political incentives, and only 77 of these 217 non-NNP councillors defected to the ANC.[125] Floor-crossing produced a complex political interaction, not a mass departure for the ruling party. This pattern persisted in subsequent years, though matters settled down somewhat. In 2004, the ANC continued to reap the NNP windfall, receiving another 195 councillors from the dying party, and 141 further councillors from other parties. The DA was also a net beneficiary, losing 44 councillors but gaining 67.[126] (The disparity between it and the ANC shows that the DA lost its floor-crossing gambit decisively. The DA's position in the Western Cape is due to its success in attracting former NNP voters in elections, and a high turnout amongst those voters, not floor-crossing).[127] The IFP lost

[121] See e.g. R. L. Muriaas, 'The ANC and Power Concentration in South Africa: Does Local Democracy Allow for Power-sharing?' (2011) 18 *Democratization* 1067, 1077–78; Hoeane, 'Floor-crossing in South Africa', 73, 82, who blurs the claim that the ANC has benefitted most from floor-crossing with the claim that 'it has been immune to the negative effects of floor-crossing'.

[122] Southall, 'State of Party Politics', 71. [123] Booysen, 'Will of the Parties', 740.

[124] P. Graham, 'Opening the Door to Crossing the Floor' (2003) 11 *Democracy in Action* 1, 6–7.

[125] The ANC gained a total of 128 councillors in 2002, of which 51 came from NNP members leaving the DA coalition.

[126] Southall, 'State of Party Politics', 71.

[127] Z. Jolobe, '"Things Fall Apart, Can the Centre Hold?" The State of Coalition Politics in the Cape Metropolitan Council' in Buhlungu et al. (eds.), *State of the Nation 2007*, p. 83; Booysen, *African National Congress*, p. 230.

25 councillors and gained 8. Power shifted in ten municipalities, with the ANC gaining eight of them. In 2007, with the NNP's demise complete, the ANC gained 77 new councillors and majorities in five new councils, all in the Western Cape or KwaZulu-Natal. But it also lost 23 councillors and three majorities that it had previously held. By comparison, the DA gained 19 councillors and lost 21, ending up controlling one more council than it had before the floor-crossing period, while the IFP gained 14 councillors and lost 7, and ended up one municipal council worse off.[128]

Finally, the circumstances of floor-crossing's demise are also of significance. There is truth to the claim that the ANC turned against floor-crossing when its political advantages decreased – as other parties did and as any party would. But floor-crossing was already broadly unpopular within the ANC. Those fearing that floor-crossing would permit the ANC to use its patronage power to tempt members away from smaller parties do not factor in the internal costs of diverting that patronage away from loyal members who are displaced by opportunistic newcomers on the electoral lists. It is also likely that floor-crossing was seen as a threat to the ANC's traditionally rigid system of party discipline and the strong control exercised by the party leadership over parliamentarians and councillors.[129] It is also surely not coincidental that the ANC voted to re-introduce the ban on floor-crossing at the same conference where Mbeki lost his bid for a third term as party president and a large section of the party suddenly found its internal prospects a great deal bleaker. The ANC was generally zealous in limiting the potential fall-out from this episode when the actual split occurred with the formation of the Congress of the People (COPE) the following year.[130] The likelihood that

[128] Independent Electoral Commission '2007 Floor Crossing Results: Summary Reports' available at www.elections.org.za/content/WorkArea/DownloadAsset.aspx?id=1324, 14.

[129] Roger Mattes notes that the ANC had shown 'steadfast opposition' to floor-crossing before 2002, and links its prior support for constitutional anti-defection provisions to its internal discipline. The NNP's collapse caused an about-turn out of 'naked political opportunism': Mattes, Democracy Without the People?', 25–26, 27, 34–35. Gouws and Mitchell 'South Africa', 366, argue that floor-crossing restrictions served to enhance party discipline. Muriaas, 'ANC and Power Concentration', 1077, notes the disagreement among ANC members about the issue. McLaughlin, 'Electoral Regimes and Party-switching', 577, traces this discontent to the way that 'defectors to the ANC could bump older, more senior members off the top of party lists'; Booysen, *African National Congress*, pp. 259, 282, 284–85, describes the swing against floor-crossing within the ANC.

[130] On the conference and subsequent reaction to COPE, see Booysen, *African National Congress*, chs. 2 and 9.

repealing floor-crossing was motivated in part by this effort offers support to the scholarly arguments that floor-crossing might create greater political competition by facilitating the breakaway of factions from the ANC's broad coalition.[131] And finally, there is the non-trivial fact that floor-crossing by 2007 had become a squalid spectacle, which politicians inside and outside the ANC feared would be bad for their public image. That this mattered says something important about the ruling party and about the nature of its relationship with the public. It is also a reason why having some faith in South Africa's party processes and in ordinary electoral mechanisms is not necessarily naïve.

Floor-crossing certainly affected South African democracy, but it did not significantly distort it. When the ANC got outside the mid-60 per cent share of the national vote it has made its own since 1994, it suffered an electoral correction. The instability affected the functioning of opposition parties in particular, but small parties mostly survived, and at the national level they all did and indeed increased their collective share of the vote relative to pre-floor-crossing days. With these results in the back of one's mind, it can be easier to understand why the Court at the time did not feel it vital to intervene, and why it did not feel it necessary for it and the Constitution to regulate this sort of ordinary, if hardly inspiring, politics. There are solid reasons to think that *UDM (2)* was a case like *NNP*, in which the argument for judicial intervention at the time of the hearing was speculative (though important and hardly far-fetched), and in which the subsequent evidence, which again is generally neglected by scholarly critics, does not bear out either that argument's speculations or the critics' main fears.

[131] For a similar suggestion that the ANC's rejection of floor-crossing was related to the COPE split, see Muriaas, 'The ANC and Power Concentration', 1077–78; for the scholarly views, see sources cited in note 104 of this chapter.

8

Socio-economic Rights

Two of the most contested areas of the Court's case law are its socio-economic rights decisions, which have generated more scholarly discussion than any other area of its jurisprudence, and a set of equality decisions, on areas such as sex work, Sunday closings and Rastafarianism, which are criticized as widely as *Makwanyane* and the LGBTI equality decisions are applauded. In this chapter and the next, I will argue that the Court's stance in both areas continues the lines of the constitution-building argument, although these are cases where the balance has sometimes been harder to strike and, I will argue, the Court has not always found the best balance available, especially in the equality context. In both areas, its stance is something of a work in progress. But we will see that the two sets of cases share important features with each other, reflecting the institutional thinking we have already seen. We will also see the Court grappling with problems key to its future work.

Rights and Newness

At the outset, however, this way of approaching the problem deserves brief comment, for these two areas of the Court's case law are seldom analyzed together.

It is a standard though usually implicit assumption of writing on socio-economic rights in South Africa (and elsewhere) that they are a separate kind of right with its own special features and challenges, to be analyzed by its own discrete branch of scholarship.[1] This assumption is

[1] Thus the scholarship cited in this chapter is invariably subject-specific. For example, South Africa's constitutional law treatise, Woolman and Bishop (eds.), *Constitutional Law*, has separate chapters for 'Interpretation' and 'The Interpretation of Socio-economic Rights'. Significant exceptions arise only when the meaning of the rights is not taken as the starting point of the discussion: see esp. Woolman, *Selfless Constitution*, and also Roux, *Politics of Principle*. Of course, scholars differ on the nature and degree of differences they perceive between kinds of rights claims and which they consider relevant in making decisions about

often the starting point for defenders and sceptics of socio-economic rights alike. By contrast, my claim is that the same constitution-building logic that I have applied in previous chapters, and in particular the same newness-based thinking, is similarly illuminating in both the equality and socio-economic rights contexts. I elsewhere defend the strong-form conclusion of this view, which is that it is a mistake to treat socio-economic rights as a different kind of right and that the controversial features they sometimes display, which can cause us to think of them as different in kind, are due to newness rather than anything inherent to the nature of the right.[2] Here, however, it suffices to offer some brief illustrations of why it might make sense to use the same lenses across these different areas and why the current area-specific approaches may mislead us, before turning to individual cases.

I should emphasize at the outset that my arguments do not serve to *rebut* these more area-specific explanations, and indeed I think some of them do have some explanatory power. Socio-economic rights scholarship, for example, is often focused on rebutting socio-economic rights scepticism, the view that socio-economic rights are unsuitable or significantly less suitable for enforcement by courts. This was and is a perfectly real view in South Africa, as elsewhere, and this area-specific scepticism has doubtless had an effect on how these rights are litigated and adjudicated.[3] It is possible, however, to take the concern to rebut it too far. The point is similar to the one I made about transformative constitutionalism: there is a risk that we will see anything other than a bold and creative enforcement of socio-economic rights as evidence of socio-economic rights scepticism, and thus respond with arguments aimed at rebutting that view, showing that socio-economic rights are important and that

the enforcement of these rights, but at most only suggestive traces of the strong-form conclusion that they are in all significant respects the same can be found; see further Fowkes, 'Normal Rights, Just New'.

[2] See Fowkes, 'Normal Rights, Just New', from which several points made here are drawn and which engages more fully with relevant scholarship; I do not repeatedly cite it in what follows.

[3] Some of the most important interventions in the South African socio-economic rights debate have been arguments against scepticism: see E. Mureinik, 'Beyond a Charter of Luxuries: Economic Rights in the Constitution' (1992) 8 *South African Journal on Human Rights* 464; M. Pieterse, 'Coming to Terms with the Judicial Enforcement of Socio-economic Rights' (2004) 15 *South African Journal on Human Rights* 383; Bilchitz, *Poverty and Fundamental Rights*. See also the later discussions of *Mazibuko* v. *City of Johannesburg* 2010 (4) SA 1 (CC) and *Prince* v. *President Cape Law Society of the Cape of Good Hope* 2002 (2) SA 794 (CC).

courts can actually do a great deal to enforce them – which will be beside the point in relation to judges who know that and are deciding *whether* to do those things in a particular case. This risk arises especially because so much commentary on all sides is framed in exclusively socio-economic terms, with problems treated as peculiar to that context. This naturally leads those who engage with socio-economic rights, including justices writing judgments, to frame what they say in the same way – thus reinforcing impressions that the judges are treating socio-economic rights differently and feeding the cycle of anti-sceptical criticism. In this context, it can be very important to pay attention to the substance of what judges are actually doing.

A striking illustration of these points is the Court's reasonableness test, commonly taken as the symbol of what is wrong with its socio-economic rights jurisprudence and a symptom of its failure to take these rights as seriously as other kinds of rights. But this criticism often does not consider the fact that the Court uses the reasonableness test in a number of other contexts besides socio-economic rights, which the focus on socio-economic-specific explanations seems to have kept from view.[4] We have seen it already in relation to the right to vote in *NNP* and *Richter*, and in *Doctors for Life* and the other public participation cases, and the Court has also used it to assess state-provided security on trains, in terms of the s 12(1)(c) right to freedom from public and private harm, and in applying the general s 7(2) duty to 'respect, protect, promote and fulfill' rights.[5] This usage across types of rights sharply questions the ubiquitous assumption that the Court's reasonableness approach reflects something specific about its attitude to

[4] Some scholarship compares reasonableness in the socio-economic context and reasonableness in the administrative law context (where it is used somewhat differently, though there are some signs of convergence: see Rose-Ackerman et al., *Due Process of Lawmaking*, pp. 144–54). Though it crosses disciplinary boundaries, however, this scholarship joins the broader argument that the Court has adopted a particularly administrative law approach to socio-economic rights, as opposed to other rights. It therefore remains focused on explanations specific to socio-economic rights framed in contrast to how other, more traditional rights are enforced. See recently Quinot and Liebenberg, 'Narrowing the Band'; M. Pieterse, 'Procedural Relief, Constitutional Citizenship and Socio-economic Rights as Legitimate Expectations' (2012) 28 *South African Journal on Human Rights* 359; S. Wilson and J. Dugard, 'Constitutional Jurisprudence: The First and Second Waves' in M. Langford et al. (eds.) *Socio-Economic Rights in South Africa: Symbols or Substance* (Cambridge University Press, 2014) and earlier sources there cited.

[5] *Rail Commuters Action Group* v. *Transnet Ltd. t/a Metrorail* 2005 (2) SA 359 (CC), paras. 84, 86–88; *Glenister (2)*, paras. 189, 194. For the other cases see Chapters 3 and 7.

socio-economic rights adjudication.[6] Indeed, if the complaint is that the Court is often not bold or creative enough and does too little, then we have seen throughout that this is a standard *general* complaint about the Court's case law – suggesting that the general explanations offered for it in other contexts may well be important in the Court's socio-economic rights cases as well.

Such arguments offer an important rebuttal to socio-economic rights sceptics because they reflect similarities rather than differences across types of rights, but they should also lead supporters of socio-economic rights to test their assumptions. For example, it is an article of faith among many critics of the Court's socio-economic rights cases that the Court should have articulated more of the content of socio-economic rights and that this omission holds back their enforcement and enjoyment. Yet in the equality context the Court early on articulated one of its most maximalist and detailed rights tests, and we certainly know a great deal about the content of the equality right – and we still have many cases where the Court is seen as having failed to do enough, including those I discuss in the next chapter.[7] Some will again reach for area-specific explanations, such as the argument that the Court's equality test is problematically grounded in dignity rather than equality itself. But memories of *NNP* should warn us that restraint in a case is not necessarily due to a weak understanding of the right concerned and that an easy tendency to assume that it must be can cause us to miss other explanations, which I will suggest provide the real key in the equality context as well.[8] Or, to take another crucial example, if the degree of newness and not the kind of right is the crucial factor, then scholars who argue that socio-economic rights claims must be treated the same as civil-political rights claims need to be careful about the basis of comparison. If they are asking that *new* socio-economic rights claims are treated the same as *settled* civil-political ones, they will be asking judges not for the same treatment

[6] It is still, however, consistent with the key factor being not newness but a positive rather than a negative rights claim, or a claim that takes resources to fulfill: for analysis and reasons for thinking newness is indeed the crucial factor, see Fowkes, 'Normal Rights, Just New'.

[7] For the early test, see *Prinsloo* v. *Van der Linde* 1997 (3) SA 1012 (CC) and *Harksen* v. *Lane*.

[8] For the argument that the equality right test should be based on equality as a value rather than dignity as a value, see originally C. Albertyn and B. Goldblatt, 'Facing the Challenge of Transformation: Difficulties in the Development of an Indigenous Jurisprudence of Equality' (1998) 14 *South African Journal on Human Rights* 248.

(in one important sense) but for *much more* in the socio-economic context. It is not implausible to think judges could do much more, but we should recognize what is really being asked of them and calibrate our arguments accordingly. Since civil-political rights claims can also display newness, as we have seen, this point can also be crucial when comparing equality rights cases, such as the celebrated examples already discussed in this book where the court enjoyed considerable support, to those in the next chapter that displayed much more newness.

Finally, for present purposes it is particularly important to note an implication of this argument for aspirational constitutionalism and socio-economic rights analysis. Everyone, I think, accepts that some aspects of a text like the 1996 Constitution are not enforceable immediately. The examples we usually give to illustrate this are about resources – it will take time and money to build everyone a house – and so we commonly associate this point with the standard view that socio-economic rights are an especially resource-intensive kind of right that is less amenable to judicial enforcement as a result. But newness can help us to see that the point actually holds across types of rights, and not merely because of the widely recognized point, which has been acknowledged by the Constitutional Court, that all rights can cost money.[9] We *say* that a socio-economic right stops being enforceable at the point where the state cannot afford it, but as defenders of these rights know, in real life socio-economic entitlements usually start being considered aspirational well before the point where the state could not possibly pay for them. What claims run up against is not the limits of available resources, but a variably entrenched status quo consisting of ideas about redistributive taxation and spending priorities and global economic realities and so on. The real limit, then, is usually the same in socio-economic cases as it is in relation to, say, a controversial equality claim: we run into the gap between the text and the society, whether that refers to the currently distribution of concrete goods or more intangible ones like acceptance of one's lifestyle or beliefs.

Recognizing this sort of equivalence is again important in rebutting socio-economic rights sceptics, since it implies that judges should be expected to do the same in protecting people who are made vulnerable by any kind of entrenched social status quo, whatever type of interest is at issue. But it also serves to highlight how we may well be demanding more

[9] See *First Certification*, paras. 77–78; *TAC (2)*, para. 99; see further the sources cited in Fowkes, 'Normal Rights, Just New'.

of our judges in socio-economic rights claims than we do in civil-political claims. Suppose, for example, we learned that the couples who headlined the later LGBTI equality cases were still subject to discrimination in their daily lives notwithstanding their legal victories. (I am making this up, but unfortunately it is a perfectly real possibility, and a certainty in relation to more vulnerable LGBTI people in South Africa.) We would regret this, certainly, and recognize that much more remained to be done. But I doubt we would think less of the LGBTI equality cases themselves just for this reason. Yet we will still labour under the sense that there must be something wrong with the famous housing rights decision in *Grootboom* because Ms Grootboom passed away, some years later, still without a house.[10] We have a stubborn sense that socio-economic rights are not being taken seriously as rights until they represent a concrete, socially real right to be free from a state of homelessness that shapes one's existence, yet we will think equality rights are being taken perfectly seriously even though they may represent far, far less than a concrete, socially real right to be free from a state of stigmatized otherness that can be equally existence-defining. Indeed, as we will see, the Court has arguably done more in response to socio-economic rights in the context of newness than it has done in relation to traditional rights claims in the context of comparable newness, contrary to the standard view that the Court is weaker in its socio-economic rights cases.

Part of what this reflects is that it is easy to think of claims in terms of very traditional rights that display more newness than many socio-economic rights claims currently do in South Africa, and that is because, in some important senses, socio-economic rights claims are not actually that new in South Africa, in my sense.[11] The idea that people have socio-economic entitlements against the state has significant public status. That the state should be working to better the socio-economic situation of its

[10] *Government of the Republic of South Africa* v. *Grootboom* 2001 (1) SA 46 (CC). Ms Grootboom died in August 2008. Some members of the community had been gradually moved to more permanent accommodation in the years since the judgment – Liebenberg, *Adjudicating Socio-economic Rights*, p. 401. Three hundred houses were provided to the *Grootboom* community in July 2008, although it is unclear how many of those involved in the litigation were among the beneficiaries. Ms Grootboom's family received a house in September 2008, one month after her death – Budlender et al., *Public Interest Litigation*, p. 44.

[11] See also R. Dixon, 'Creating Dialogue about Socioeconomic Rights: Strong-Form versus Weak-Form Judicial Review Revisited' (2007) 5 *International Journal of Constitutional Law* 391, 414.

citizens is a standard assumption of South African public talk and is taken for granted by public officials. Judges will not usually lack confidence in making pronouncements about this. The extensive government activity in these areas also means that the Court often has considerable work by other institutions to build on. It is true that much more disagreement exists about the means that should be adopted to these ends, but that is a debate about how to achieve what the socio-economic rights in the text require. The basic idea that the Constitution requires the building of an effective welfare state is a staple of ANC politics (and that of other parties) as much as of constitutional text.[12]

The question that then arises is why it is, if socio-economic rights are quite well entrenched in at least this sense, that the Court has been restrained in its socio-economic rights cases? (And why, by the same token, do I suggest that newness is important to understanding these cases?) Part of the answer, as we will see, is that if we zoom out from the scholarly preoccupation with the concrete content of the socio-economic rights themselves, the Court has often *not* been very restrained in articulating content in socio-economic rights cases. A decision not to articulate the content sought by the critics is not the same as a decision not to articulate content. Another part of the answer is that the government has

[12] Dennis Davis has argued that the rightward shift in the ANC's economic policy in the mid-1990s produced a situation in which the text's commitment to social democracy is more progressive than the government's, prompting a pragmatic judicial caution that partly explains the Court's restraint on socio-economic rights. See D. M. Davis, 'Adjudicating the Socio-economic Rights in the South African Constitution: Towards "Deference Lite"?' (2006) 22 *South African Journal on Human Rights* 301, 314–17; D. M. Davis, 'Socioeconomic Rights: Do They Deliver the Goods?' (2008) 6 *International Journal of Constitutional Law* 687, 697–98; on the shift itself, see sources cited in Chapter 4, note 57. The difficulty with this argument is similar to the one raised about transformative constitutionalism. It is only the simplest versions of neo-liberalism, such as the idea that the socio-economic welfare of the population should be left to the market, that are indubitably ruled out on the plain face of the text, and this is not the ANC government's position. Conversely, the more specific neo-liberal strategies it *has* tried, such as privatization or seeking to promote foreign investment by slashing tariffs, cannot be ruled out by simple textual arguments (a point Davis recognizes: see Davis, 'Socioeconomic Rights', 691 n. 9). They stand or fall, instead, on their success or failure as *means* to fulfill the state's constitutional duties, a question which the text itself cannot answer. See further Fowkes, 'Transformative Constitutionalism'. For present purposes, this means tensions between the letter of the text and the ANC government's economic positions should not be overstated. The more important tensions arise simply from the exercise of judicial power in areas where the government also claims authority, which is certainly an implication of Davis' argument and important to Roux's political account of these cases – see Roux, *Politics of Principle*, ch. 7, discussed later in this chapter.

been much more receptive to the idea that it has socio-economic duties to its people than that judges should be reviewing their performance of these duties. And finally and most importantly of all, the greatest reasons for restraint have lain where the greatest newness does: not in relation to the idea that citizens have socio-economic entitlements against the state, but in relation to issues of implementation. State incapacity is often the largest obstacle to the delivery of socio-economic goods, and this is very important to evaluating judicial action. It is when the state denies that it has an obligation that the scope for judicial intervention is most obvious, and some expansive cases have indeed arisen in response to stances of this sort: *Khosa*, ordering that permanent residents are entitled to welfare benefits in the context of an initially unresponsive government actor,[13] and *TAC* and most of the eviction cases, which I discuss later in this chapter and in the next. When the obstacle, instead, is the problem of getting state machinery to function, it is often much less obvious how and where judicial intervention will assist. This point can be neglected by scholarship focused on bearing witness to the presence of a social injustice and showing that there are things the Court *could* do, or could at least try to do, in response. But for those who wish to argue that the Court should have done more in socio-economic rights cases, this is usually not the true burden of proof. It often seems to be taken for granted that more aggressive judicial action would have been good for the enjoyment of socio-economic goods in South Africa, but this is not at all a point that can be assumed (although the reverse cannot be assumed either, as it is often is by socio-economic rights sceptics). Instead, in a context where the government is also often active on socio-economic matters, this is usually the most critical issue for decision: will judicial intervention be an improvement on other institutional options, such that it would be a good thing for the court to take the issue out of the hands of the institutions currently responsible for it (to some extent)? If this is the question, then neither the fact that there are things the Court *could* do, nor that there are problems with what other state actors are doing, can be decisive, though of course both would be of central importance. The decisive question, instead, is whether adding judicial intervention to what is already going on would be *better* than not doing so, something that is often far from obvious if the problem is a skills shortage or a

[13] *Khosa*, paras. 6–7, 12–25; see e.g. K. Young, 'The Avoidance of Substance in Constitutional Rights' (2013) 5 *Constitutional Court Review* 232, 235, describing *Khosa* as 'a stunning work of non-avoidance'.

dysfunctional department. We will see that no point is more important to understanding the Court's stance, or what critical scholarship about it misses.

The constitution-building account can therefore offer a fresh perspective on the Court's socio-economic rights cases and its extensive accompanying literature. The discussion here cannot possibly due full justice to either; I seek only to draw the conclusions this perspective affords us. It is particularly important here that the *general* nature of this perspective allows us to draw links between socio-economic rights cases and decisions in other areas, something not usually done. This is especially valuable considering that the level of scholarly interest in South African socio-economic rights has for a long time been inversely proportional to the number of cases, and it is crucial to bear in mind this methodological constraint. For the first seven years of the life of the 1996 Constitution, there were just three cases – *Soobramoney, Grootboom* and *TAC* – and so a good deal of scholarly writing on socio-economic rights in South Africa, in addition to its potentially misleading preoccupation with rebutting socio-economic rights scepticism, has been drawing big conclusions from a truly tiny sample. Even as the number of cases has risen in recent years, the fact that the state tends to offer settlements in the cases it feels itself most likely to lose further biases the sample of judgments. (*Grootboom*, where the state's tender of concrete goods was not a settlement conditional on terminating the case, was an important exception in this regard).[14] The constitution-building account's ability to expand the sample would therefore be important in any case, and it is especially vital because this is not just a tiny sample of a settled pattern but a tiny sample from what is, for government, courts and litigants, a work in progress. Deputy Chief Justice Moseneke, addressing the sharp criticism directed at the Court's socio-economic cases, recently noted that '[m]y personal take is that socio-economic rights jurisprudence is in many ways embryonic'.[15] That the cases do not fit the pattern of what the critics want might reflect that the Court has the wrong pattern, but it might also reflect that as yet we only have glimpses of the whole.

[14] Budlender et al., *Public Interest Litigation*, pp. 40–41 (on *Grootboom*), 78–94 (on more recent settlements).

[15] D. Moseneke, 'Striking a Balance between the Will of the People and the Supremacy of the Constitution' (2012) 129 *South African Law Journal* 9, 21.

Maximalism in Socio-economic Rights Cases: *Grootboom*, *PE Municipality*, and *Joseph*

The famous decision in *Grootboom* v. *Government of the Republic of South Africa* ('*Grootboom*') arose, as is well known, out of the eviction of a poor community who, faced with a long wait for government housing, settled in desperate conditions on a public sports ground. But what is seldom noted about *Grootboom* is that the Court did not necessarily need to write it. A court simply seeking to avoid engaging with the right to housing had at least three ways to take a much narrower approach.

First, the Court could simply have addressed the way the local municipality had related to the community in *Grootboom*. The community members' first move in search of better living conditions had been to leave the heavily waterlogged area where they had been living and settle, apparently unknowingly, on private land. After an unsuccessful attempt at mediation, the municipality evicted the community from this land, with a callously heavy hand that destroyed many of their belongings. The community then moved to the sports ground.[16] It was in that context that the court of first instance heard the case and made an order against the municipality that the community was entitled to certain very basic concrete socio-economic goods. These were tendered by the government and, after they were initially not supplied for several months, were made a detailed order of the Constitutional Court two weeks before the main judgment was handed down.[17] A court cautious of engaging socio-economic issues might simply have held that the municipality was obliged to engage with the community properly, criticized its earlier behaviour, held that the offer of concrete goods as a good first step that should have happened much earlier and ordered that the process continue. The case would then have petered out into a mundane exercise in enforcement, and its major lesson might have been the failed experiment in using the South African Human Rights Commission to monitor the remedial stage.[18]

[16] Budlender et al., *Public Interest Litigation*, pp. 36–37; *Grootboom*, paras. 88–90.

[17] Constitutional Court Order, CCT 38/00, in fact dated both 21 and 26 September 2000; the judgment gives the date as the 21st: *Grootboom*, para. 5. Liebenberg has also noted that critics often fail to take account of this concrete agreement: Liebenberg, *Adjudicating Socio-economic rights*, p. 400; for her views, see notes 90 and 91 of this chapter.

[18] Budlender et al., *Public Interest Litigation*, p. 126; see further note 90 of this chapter.

The evolution of the legal argument offered a second opportunity for avoidance. The applicants in fact abandoned the right to housing argument in the Constitutional Court, after the court of first instance had rejected it. An amicus successfully broadened the argument to re-include it, but the Court has resisted this sort of broadening in other cases; this, too, represents an avoidance route not taken.[19] And thirdly, the case started out with a local focus. That *Grootboom* happened at all was initially significantly due to the efforts of local ANC actors, who sought (at least in part) to use the case to embarrass the opposition-controlled municipal and provincial governments.[20] By the time the Court took up the issue, those authorities had begun implementing a plan in the metropolitan area concerned, the Accelerated Managed Land Settlement Programme, which the amicus conceded was constitutional and appropriate in response to short-term housing needs.[21] This, too, would have offered a way for the Court to decline to engage broader issues and defer to the evolving local response. That it took none of these ways out, and instead wrote a long and famous judgment, reflects something important.

Due both to the government's concrete offer of goods to the local community and the amicus' successful broadening of the case in the Constitutional Court, primary attention in *Grootboom* was focused on the national government's general housing policies. Those policies were and are extensive, involving the building of hundreds of thousands of houses.[22] The question was whether the Court should say anything about this programme or simply let the government carry on, and this implicated a contentious issue. The justiciability of socio-economic interests had been contested within the ANC for some time. The 1993 interim Constitution omitted socio-economic rights, and it may seem surprising

[19] *Grootboom*, para. 18; Budlender et al., *Public Interest Litigation*, p. 40. For resistance to such broadening, see e.g. *Campus Law Clinic, University of KwaZulu-Natal, Durban* v. *Standard Bank of South Africa* 2006 (6) SA 103 (CC), and *Nokotyana* v. *Ekurhuleni Metropolitan Municipality* 2010 (4) BCLR 312 (CC), discussed later in this chapter.

[20] Budlender et al., *Public Interest Litigation*, pp. 38–39.

[21] *Grooboom*, paras. 60–69.

[22] The Court in *Grootboom* accepted figures of 362 160 houses built or under construction (March 1994–September 1997) and 637 190 subsidies allocated for projects by October 1997. By the end of March 2014, the government (on its own figures) had subsidized the construction of 2 835 275 houses and 903 543 serviced sites: Department of Human Settlements *Celebrating 20 Years of Human Settlements: Bringing the Freedom Charter to Life* (2014), 27. Notwithstanding significant problems, including corruption and poor build quality, this is quite a total in a country of about 52 million people. See also Woolman, *Selfless Constitution*, pp. 321–22.

that the ANC accepted this, given how this omission would appear. As Albie Sachs had put the point in a 1991 lecture:

> There is much to be said for leaving the question of legislation on social and economic questions solely to the wisdom of the electorate and Parliament. Unfortunately, in South Africa there is no possibility at all that that will be done . . . The very first clause that the presently privileged will search for, long before they look at voting rights, will be that dealing with property. Once the economic rights of those who are property-ful are on the agenda, the economic rights of those who are property-less cannot be ignored.[23]

The clue as to why the ANC would nevertheless accept their omission, despite the symbolism problems, is contained in Sachs' first sentence. The ANC wanted to assert the importance of socio-economic interests and redistribution, but it was internally divided about making these interests enforceable in the courts. Factions favoured more direct democratic means of enforcement to which Sachs alluded his lecture; a little time before, he had proposed creating a special Social and Economic Rights Commission as the primary enforcer of socio-economic rights, while also suggesting that decisions about how best to give effect to these rights should be left to Parliament.[24] In light of uncertainties like these, the ANC preferred to defer the decision on socio-economic rights to the elected Constitutional Assembly that would write the 1996 Constitution. That body would decide to include them, but the uncertainties in the ANC's attitude towards these rights persisted.[25]

It is in this light that we must understand the government's resistance to the Court's exercise of jurisdiction in *Grootboom* (and, as we will see, again in *TAC (2)*). And it is because of this resistance that *Grootboom* is so concerned with articulating the basic features of the Constitution's socio-economic rights standards and how they can be enforced by courts

[23] A. Sachs, 'The Third Ernie Wentzel Memorial Lecture: "Watch out – There's a Constitution about" Preparing Ourselves for the Era of Constitutionalism.' 8 May 1991 (CALS Pamphlet, 1991), 9.

[24] A. Sachs, *Protecting Human Rights in a New South Africa* (Oxford University Press, 1990) 21, 32. For a similar suggestion in broader contexts see Ackerman, 'New Separation of Powers', 696.

[25] F. Haysom, 'Constitutionalism, Majoritarian Democracy and Socio-economic Rights' (1992) 8 *South African Journal on Human Rights* 451, 453; Spitz, *Politics of Transition*, p. 367; Mark S. Kende, 'The South African Constitutional Court's Construction of Socio-Economic Rights: A Response to Critics' (2003–2004) 19 *Connecticut Journal of International Law* 617.

in a manner consistent with the separation of powers and respect for other branches. The Court's decision to say much more than it could have reflects a desire to speak on socio-economic rights, in light of their extraordinary public relevance but also of the government's discouraging signals. *Grootboom* happened around the same time as the early LGBTI equality cases, and like them it is an exercise in resisting the restrictive vision of its own jurisdiction in rights cases implicit in the government's stance. And *Grootboom* has had an important impact in this regard. It is widely noted that the decision led to new policies on emergency housing needs, ultimately in the form of revisions to the Housing Code.[26] But it is at least as important that *Grootboom* has 'impacted significantly on government's attitude to socio-economic rights'. There is evidence that, in the wake of its findings, 'parts of government began factoring these issues into budget processes and became far more responsive to lawyers letters pointing out flaws and requesting information', notwithstanding continued 'misgivings'.[27] In my terms, this is an instance of infrastructure not accustomed to working in close relation to the courts starting to adjust to the implications of justiciable socio-economic rights.[28]

While the comparison between *Grootboom* and the LGBTI equality cases is instructive, the analogy to *Doctors for Life* is still more striking. *Grootboom* and *Doctors for Life* both engaged in a novel, controversial kind of judicial review, which both chose to assess by means of the reasonableness standard. Both used this standard to invalidate government conduct on this novel basis for the first time, in ways that have turned out to have pervasive effects on law and governance, albeit sometimes slowly. Both accompanied this assertion of jurisdiction with

[26] An emergency housing policy announced in August 2003 was followed by a new Chapter 12 of the Housing Code in 2004, and see currently National Housing Code (2009), Vol. 4, Part 3. See Budlender et al., *Public Interest Litigation*, p. 45; K. McLean, 'Housing' in Woolman and Bishop (eds.), *Constitutional Law*, 55–14; Socio-Economic Rights Institute of South Africa, *A Resource Guide to Housing in South Africa 1994–2010: Legislation, Policy, Programmes and Practice* (2011), www.urbanlandmark.org.za/downloads/SERI_Housing_Resource_Guide_Feb11.pdf, 94–96.

[27] Budlender et al., *Public Interest Litigation*, pp. 46, 66. *Grootboom* merited a separate subheading in the government's own chronology of the first two decades of its housing program; see Department of Human Settlements, *Celebrating 20 Years*, 20. The shift in the Housing Code also laid the foundations for important developments in eviction law; see Wilson, 'Breaking the Tie', 275–76 and later discussion.

[28] See the discussion of infrastructure in Chapter 5, and contrast, for example, the familiarly legal infrastructure the Court relied on in *Gory* and *Du Toit* in the LGBTI equality context; see Chapter 6.

careful and diplomatic discussion of the limits of judicial authority and the importance of the competence of other branches. And apart from the controversial issue of the details of the judicial review power itself, both relied heavily on ideas already articulated or conceded by government actors. The order in each case represented an adjustment to an existing government approach, leaving that existing approach substantially intact, and was in each case based on existing commitments and ideas of strong public status: as noted, the idea that the state has obligations to provide housing enjoys very substantial public status in South Africa, while conversely the act of eviction has similarly strong apartheid associations to practices of political exclusion and disrespect. Given these similarities, the fact that *Grootboom* has received a more equivocal scholarly response than *Doctors for Life*, particularly inside South Africa, is telling, and may reflect the tendency to demand more of socio-economic rights already noted.

I will return to *Grootboom* later in this chapter; first, we should see that it is not alone in its decision to articulate content in this way. Its most direct descendant is *Port Elizabeth Municipality* v. *Various Occupiers* ('*PE Municipality*'), which is much less globally famous but also of central importance to subsequent developments.[29] *PE Municipality* was another eviction case, but one that reached the Court earlier as part of an effort to obtain permission to evict in the first place. *PE Municipality* was therefore concerned with what was required before an eviction order could be granted, and once again it would have been easy for the Court to say a lot less on this issue than it chose to. Where *Grootboom* could have gone no further than ruling that the local authorities should have engaged with the community much more respectfully and much earlier to work out a solution, *PE Municipality* could simply have told the parties to go away and do just that. Instead, on the way to declining to issue the eviction order sought by the local authorities, it announces far-reaching changes to property law and articulates significant content about the judicial role in eviction cases.

In formal terms, the Court was engaging for the first time with the very open-ended provisions of s 26(3) of the Constitution, which state that evictions from homes may not occur 'without an order of court made after considering all the relevant circumstances.' This provision is so open-ended that one can even read the apartheid-era approach into it,

[29] *Port Elizabeth Municipality* v. *Various Occupiers* 2005 (1) SA 217 (CC).

by treating 'relevant circumstances' to mean only whether someone is occupying someone else's property without permission (as several early High Court judgments more or less did, although one must ignore a good deal of law outside s 26(3) to reach this result).[30] What *PE Municipality* is doing is receiving into s 26(3) the radical post-apartheid changes in eviction law, encapsulated most importantly in the 1998 Prevention of Illegal Eviction Act ('PIE'), but as we will see, also going somewhat beyond that Act. *PE Municipality* articulates 'humanized procedures' in the eviction context, and in doing so is consciously articulating the rejection of apartheid's approach to eviction, in which anyone established to be on land without the permission of the owner was treated as a criminal liable to immediate, forceful removal without notice.[31] *PE Municipality* explicitly takes PIE as providing guidance to courts in exercising their new discretion, but the judgment goes beyond just requiring that judges exercising their s 26(3) discretion must look to the Act. Two examples will suffice. PIE treats the issue of whether alternative accommodation is available for the evictees merely as a factor 'the court must have regard to', and *PE Municipality* therefore accepts that there is 'no unqualified constitutional duty' to provide it. But it rules that a court should generally be reluctant to grant an eviction 'unless it is satisfied that a reasonable alternative is available', at least on an interim basis.[32] And while PIE mentions 'mediation' as a device a municipality 'may' try, *PE Municipality* elevates 'whether mediation has been tried' to a factor relevant to whether an eviction order would be just and equitable.[33] (The Court has subsequently extended both lines of reasoning, at least blurring PIE's and *PE Municipality*'s distinction in relation to

[30] See T. Roux, 'Continuity and Change in a Transforming Legal Order: The Impact of Section 26(3) of the Constitution on South African Law' (2004) 121 *South African Law Journal* 466; S. 'Breaking the Tie: Evictions from Private Land, Homelessness and a New Normality' (2009) 126 *South African Law Journal* 270, 271–72. For recent decisions outside the Constitutional Court emphasizing owner's rights see e.g. the cases discussed by D. Bilchitz, 'Avoidance Remains Avoidance: Is It Desirable in Socio-economic Rights Cases?' (2013) 5 *Constitutional Court Review* 296, 303–05.

[31] Prevention of Illegal Eviction from and Unlawful Occupation of Land Act 19 of 1998; *PE Municipality*, para. 13; *Jaftha* v. *Schoeman; Van Rooyen* v. *Scholtz* 2005 (2) SA 140 (CC), para. 27; C. O'Regan, 'No More Forced Removals? An Historical Analysis of the Prevention of Illegal Squatting Act' (1989) 5 *South African Journal on Human Rights* 361; Van der Walt, *Constitutional Property Law*, pp. 521–28; Wilson, 'Breaking the Tie', 275–76 and later discussion.

[32] PIE, s 6(2); *PE Municipality*, paras. 28–29; see also Liebenberg, *Adjudicating Socio-Economic Rights*, pp. 275–76.

[33] PIE, s 7; *PE Municipality*, paras. 39–46.

alternative accommodation between short- and long-term occupiers, and turning meaningful engagement into a standard requirement.)[34]

This is bold stuff. Obligations to provide alternative accommodation can have significant implications for budgets, private owners' exercise of their property rights, and the design of urban housing programs, as we will see in the next chapter. That the Court was confronting uncertain points can be seen in the way that, continuing the pattern we saw it repeatedly in the last chapter, it sought further argument on the mediation question, with both parties accepting it as a possibility the Court could feasibly order.[35] The Court's confidence in imposing these non-trivial burdens, however, is not based only on this acceptance by the primary actors involved in the issue. Nor is it based only on PIE – as we have seen, its goes beyond the text of the statute. *PE Municipality* draws strongly on the public status of the idea that a post-apartheid state seeking to realize the right of access to housing should not be in the business of casting people out on the street. This is also reflected in the Court's approach in the related but distinct context where homes are sold in execution of debt, where the Court has overseen comparably far-reaching changes to the prior legal property regime that make it much harder to collect a debt at the cost of homelessness, especially when this would simultaneously serve to undermine a government scheme for the provision of housing.[36]

In understanding the broader changes wrought by *PE Municipality*, it is highly significant that the Court in that case refused to grant the eviction order sought by the municipality even though the municipality *had* offered the occupiers an alternative place to live, which they had rejected as inadequate.[37] The key thing that *PE Municipality* is articulating here is the importance of treating occupiers as independent agents instead of as a problem to be humanely managed. Thus the most decisive

[34] *Occupiers of Portion R25 of the Farm Mooiplaats 355 JR* v. *Golden Thread Ltd.* 2012 (2) SA 337 (CC), para. 16: 'while [PIE's distinction between short- and long-term occupiers] is important, I do not think it is decisive to the justice and equity enquiry'; see also B. Ray, 'Evictions, Aspirations and Avoidance' (2013) 5 *Constitutional Court Review* 172, 224, describing this finding as 'functionally eliminating the distinction between short- and long-term occupation'. *PE Municipality*'s earlier findings about the relevance of alternative accommodation had referred to 'relatively settled occupiers': see para. 28.

[35] *PE Municipality*, para. 44. Both parties expressed only qualified enthusiasm in the context of the case and the Court ultimately did not order mediation: see para. 47.

[36] *Jaftha* v. *Schoeman*, and *Gundwana* v. *Steko Development CC* 2011 (3) SA 608 (CC); see further Fowkes, 'More Power than Pact'.

[37] *PE Municipality*, para. 2.

consideration in its decision not to grant an eviction order was the fact that the municipality had completely failed to engage with the occupiers.[38] In this, the Court is drawing on PIE, but also receiving into s 26(3) the broader post-apartheid themes of inclusion, consultation and listening that we saw in the previous chapter.

The Court is also quite expansive, finally, in discussing its own role in the eviction context. It is true that s 26(3) is unusual in the constitutional text in making it quite clear that *courts* must exercise a particular role, and so the Court does not have to decide the institutional question of *whether* to insert judges into eviction cases as a routine matter. PIE also offers guidance. But the Court nevertheless has to make decisions of its own here on *how* to insert courts, and it articulates a vision as expansive as its substantive findings. It holds that courts should adopt a 'managerial role' – still a new idea in South Africa – in eviction cases, acting in inquisitorial fashion and going beyond the parties' pleadings if need be.[39] While later cases (discussed in the next chapter) have prompted the Court to make a number of further findings on these issues, *PE Municipality* is the most detailed discussion of these ideas anywhere in its case law – and again, these general comments, obviously aimed at providing future guidance to litigants and judges, goes far beyond what was necessary to dispose of the case.

This attitude to articulating content may also be observed in a final example of maximalism, the 2009 decision in *Joseph* v. *City of Johannesburg* ('*Joseph*'). Its place in a sequence of *Grootboom* (2000) and *PE Municipality* (2004) offers some evidence against suggestions that the Court has become less inclined to articulate content over time. I noted that *Doctors for Life* is one of only two cases in which the Court has invoked a doctrine of unenumerated rights; *Joseph* is the other.[40]

Joseph raised a situation in which the City had cut off electrical power to a building. The tenants had duly paid their electricity bills to the landlord, but the landlord had not in turn paid the City and had accumulated huge arrears.[41] Instead of taking action against the

38 *Ibid.*, para. 58.

39 *Ibid.*, para. 39; see further Fowkes, 'Managerial Judge', Fowkes, '*Maphango*'.

40 *Joseph* v. *City of Johannesburg* 2010 (4) SA 55 (CC). There may now be three such cases, depending on how one reads the rather more uncertain reference to an opposition MP's 'right' to introduce motions of no confidence by the majority in *Mazibuko* v. *Sisulu*; see esp. para. 45 and the dissent's objections, paras. 90, 141, 156.

41 These are common types of problems. See J. Dugard, 'Urban Basic Services: Rights, Reality, and Resistance' in M. Langford et al. (eds.) *Socio-Economic Rights*, p. 284.

landlord, the tenants argued that the City had a legal relationship with them, and that the City was accordingly obliged to give them (and not only the landlord, the contractual customer) notice of the cut-off, and potentially to engage with tenants who responded to that notice. Access to electricity is not a textual right under the 1996 Constitution, and the tenants suggested several possible grounds for this legal relationship, including the rights to housing and dignity. The Court, however, chose to ground the obligation on a new fundamental right to service delivery. Just as in *Doctors for Life*, however, this new right is hardly created out of thin air. The Court can refer to constitutional text on the duty of municipal government to supply services, to similar obligations recognized in the government's municipal framework legislation, and to the government's service culture philosophy of Batho Pele ('People First').[42] It links the new right to ideas of participatory democracy, and while *Joseph* does not cite *Doctors for Life* the connection is obvious. It is no accident that the Court's two unenumerated rights cases concern overlapping sets of ideas of deep public status, and once again illustrates how the presence of such ideas can be more important to the constitution-building court than what it is the text.

The Court in *Joseph* was also concerned with the institutionally polycentric consequences of its decision. However, it could be confident that it was not imposing an unsustainable administrative burden on the municipal authorities concerned because these authorities conceded that the procedurally fair action sought by the tenants – written notification in advance of a cut-off of power – was practically feasible. The authorities also expressed their willingness to engage with the applicants.[43] The Court could therefore again take its cue from the actors primarily responsible for the issue. Indeed, such was the Court's confidence in *Joseph* that it not only created a new right, but also settled the issue across areas of law not directly implicated by the case. The Court itself severed words from the relevant by-laws in order to make it clear that it is mandatory to provide notice to 'customers' before disconnection of electricity – notwithstanding that the whole point of *Joseph* was that the

[42] *Joseph*, paras. 34–45; C. Hoexter, *Administrative Law in South Africa* (2 edn., Cape Town: Juta & Co., 2012), pp. 402–04; Rose-Ackerman et al., *Due Process of Lawmaking*, pp. 133–34.

[43] *Joseph*, paras. 60–61.

applicants before the Court were *not* 'customers' for the purposes of that by-law, as the Court confirmed.[44] Once again, the Court is far from minimalist when support for confronting newness is present. And once again, it was also careful not to resolve unnecessary issues where the support for doing so did *not* exist. The Court scrupulously avoided deciding the issue of whether a cut-off was an appropriate action in the case or in basic service delivery cases in general, which is a much more contested issue, and also one in respect of which there had been no helpful concessions from the relevant state authorities involved in the case.[45]

Grootboom, *PE Municipality* and *Joseph* are powerful evidence against suggestions that the Court's socio-economic rights cases can be generally understood as an exercise in restraint or minimalism. But why, then, is the Court restrained about articulating the actual concrete content of socio-economic rights, as opposed to the largely procedural issues we have seen in this trio of cases? The distorting focus on socio-economic rights scepticism can make us look only at this concrete content, and so discount all the rest of what is being said, but it is still true that this concrete content is generally absent, and the central question of existing scholarship in this area is to want to know why. I do not deny that socio-economic rights scepticism may have played a role in this absence. But the three cases just discussed followed from a decision to articulate content, and that implies the possibility that the same logic might, in different circumstances, entail a decision not to do so. In both the previous chapters, we saw the quite sharp divide between decisions to act, which often meant acting boldly including in articulating content, and decisions not to act at all. I now turn to consider the second kind of decision in the socio-economic rights context.

[44] *Ibid.*, paras. 71–76. The applicants had unsuccessfully raised the by-laws, but having found that the applicants were not customers for the purposes of the by-laws, the Court did not have to say anything more about them.

[45] *Ibid.*, para. 55. The organization behind the litigation in *Joseph* had intended that it would be preceded by *Mazibuko*, a case on water cut-offs discussed at the end of this chapter, presumably in the hope that *Mazibuko* would underpin findings on this question in *Joseph*; as it happened, *Joseph* reached the Constitutional Court first and *Mazibuko* in any event did not turn out as planned: see J. Dugard and M. Langford, 'Art or Science? Synthesizing Lessons from Public Interest Litigation and the Dangers of Legal Determinism' (2011) 27 *South African Journal on Human Rights* 39, 42.

Non-Intervention Decisions: *Soobramoney*, *Nokotyana* and *Grootboom*

It is again helpful here to begin with the very familiar. *Soobramoney* v. *Minister of Health, KwaZulu-Natal*, as the Court's first socio-economic rights case and for nearly three years its only one, was always going to be much discussed.[46] The case concerned a man seeking state-funded dialysis treatment, without which he would die. It saw the Court accept, with little interrogation, the statements from provincial hospitals officials that they had established fair protocols for allocating access to publicly funded dialysis, that this dialysis was limited in light of already overspent budgets, and that the applicant did not meet the protocols because he was too sick.

The first thing to note about *Soobramoney*, in line with the preceding discussion, is that it too cannot be described as minimalist. Indeed, Frank Michelman criticized the decision at the time for its lack of restraint in going beyond what the case required it to say. The case was brought in terms of the right to emergency healthcare in s 27(3), and so the Court perhaps did not need to engage in interpreting the main, non-emergency part of the right to health in 27(1).[47] And indeed this argument may understate the point: the separate judgments of both Madala J and Sachs J in *Soobramoney* engage freely with issues of life and death in the context of modern medical treatment.[48] Conversely, as Roux has pointed out, the prospects of success were so low that a Court keen on avoidance could easily have simply declined to hear the case at all.[49] Instead, *Soobramoney* decides to decide that s 27 must be interpreted in light of s 27(2)'s provision that the state's obligation is 'to take reasonable . . . measures, within its available resources, to achieve the progressive realization' of the

[46] *Soobramoney* v. *Minister of Health, KwaZulu-Natal* 1998 (1) SA 765 (CC).

[47] F. Michelman, 'The Constitution, Social Rights and Reason: A Tribute to Etienne Mureinik' 14 *South Africa Journal on Human Rights* (1998) 499, 502–05; see also D. Moellendorf, 'Reasoning about Resources: *Soobramoney* and the Future of Socio-economic Rights Claims' (1998) 14 *South Africa Journal on Human Rights* 327, 328–29 (making a similar point); and Roux, *Politics of Principle*, pp. 273–76, 279–80 (agreeing with Michelman). The argument that it was not necessary to look beyond s 27(3) may be questioned, since the Court's reasonable view was that s 27(3) had to be understood in terms of the section as a whole. However, it is certainly true that a court trying to say less about s 27(1) and (2) could easily have done so.

[48] Madala J even engaged with the horizontal application of the right to health: *Soobramoney*, para. 48; M. Pieterse, 'Indirect Horizontal Application of the Right to Have Access to Health Services' (2007) 23 *South African Journal on Human Rights* 157, 164–65.

[49] Roux, *Politics of Principle*, pp. 276–77.

right. In this, it set a precedent for approaching socio-economic rights cases through the internal qualifier – Is the state taking reasonable measures to progressively realize the right, given resource constraints? – instead of articulating what concrete things people are entitled to in terms of these rights and *then* asking if the government is doing enough to provide those things. Michelman's concern was that *Soobramoney* engaged this question too rapidly and expansively, and indeed it turned out to set a pattern that *Grootboom* and later cases continued.

Apart from this, however, *Soobramoney* decided not to intervene, without even determining whether the state's obligations under s 27 should be evaluated using a rationality standard or one of reasonableness.[50] It does, however, make it clear why it is deciding not to act. The Court does not see any good reason, on the facts, to take decisions about the distribution of health resources out of the hands of the institutions primarily responsible for them, whether at the micro level of dialysis allocation at a particular hospital, or at the levels of allocating various health goods or of budgetary allocations to health in general.[51] It does not see any reason, on the facts, to prefer its own jurisdiction to the standard mechanism. It is a now-familiar judgment about when to intervene, and when to leave matters to others. *Soobramoney*, like *NNP*, is an attempt to secure a constitution-building first prize. It seeks to have budgetary and healthcare decisions made by the institutions primarily responsible for them, which are usually better suited to making them than the Court is. Once again, that is not to say that the Court *cannot* or *should not* make those decisions, just as *NNP* hardly means that the Court cannot or should not intervene to protect elections and voting rights. (It is important not to read *Soobramoney*, just one case with unpromising facts, as standing for more than it does; later comments by the Court tend to confirm its willingness to examine general budgetary allocations when it deems this necessary.)[52] It only means that ideally it will not make those decisions when that is a feasible option, which it will be where non-intervention is compatible with the Court's other constitutional responsibilities, and in particular its duty to protect rights. I argued that decisions

[50] See *Soobramoney*, para. 25 ('unreasonable', 'fairly and rationally'); para. 29 ('rational decisions taken in good faith').

[51] *Ibid.*, paras. 24–36. Liebenberg, *Adjudicating Socio-economic Rights*, pp. 140–44 notes the lack of evidence before the Court on this point but argues that a greater justificatory burden should nevertheless have been placed on the state.

[52] See esp. *City of Johannesburg Metropolitan Municipality* v. *Blue Moonlight Properties 39 (Pty) Ltd* 2012 (2) SA 104 (CC), paras. 71–74.

like *NNP* and *UDM (2)* were only free to seek the optimal constitution-building outcome, and take into account an array of institution-building imperatives, because the evidence did not show that judicial activity was immediately necessary to stave off a serious threat to rights. In *Soobramoney*, the Court's ability to leave healthcare and budgetary decisions in the hands of the primary institutions is again conditional on a judgment that the evidence did not show that it was necessary for the Court to intervene in the circumstances – a decision which most observers accept was tragic but also correct.

Soobramoney also recalls the structural concerns of *NNP* in its implicit precedent that the right to health does not permit a citizen to trigger a sweeping examination of the relevant budgetary decisions just because those decisions have the effect of depriving him or her of treatment at state expense.[53] This, of course, comes at the price of potentially not discovering a real problem, but this price must be weighed against the cost of such a low threshold for a searching review. *Soobramoney*, therefore, is once again the result of a constitution-building calculation that is heavily about the consequences of particular models of review – that it would be better if the Court does not re-evaluate budgetary decisions every time someone is denied a benefit from the state, that it would be better if the Court does not second-guess professionals or elected officials in the absence of any evidence that anything other than good faith activity has occurred, and that it is therefore better for the Court to do less than it could in such a case and to take the accompanying risk of not discovering unconstitutional conduct that a more searching enquiry might reveal.

If we apply the traditional picture of judging to *Soobramoney* and simply place the right down next to the conduct, we might well get the same result, which, as we saw, is generally accepted.[54] But the most important thing the constitution-building picture allows us to see is that the Court's calculation is not just a matter of weighing a right against an abstract doctrine of separation of powers or some other argument for judicial restraint. Nor is it bluntly about the political costs and benefits of

[53] For criticism of this, see Moellendorf, 'Reasoning about Resources', 330–33; M. Pieterse, 'Health Care Rights, Resources and Rationing' (2007) 124 *South African Law Journal* 514; Bilchitz, *Poverty and Fundamental Rights*, pp. 227–30; Liebenberg, *Adjudicating Socio-Economic Rights*, pp. 143–44.

[54] Although it is also true that judicial intervention in a case like *Soobramoney*'s is far from inconceivable, as developments in Latin America show. I am grateful to Daniel Bonilla for initially pointing this out to me.

particular stances, although among the consequences of a more interventionist stance in other institutions would, presumably, be an increased risk of irritating the ANC government and generating opposition. As in *NNP*, I am in no position to rebut explanations of such deference as the product of a strategic decision not to vex powerful political actors. But I can argue that such considerations, if they are in play, are compatible with a powerful constitutional argument and so do not have to be seen as coming at the cost of legal interpretation properly so called.[55] Instead, the calculation is a richly constitutional judgment about competing institutional ways to realize the right. I argued that the Court's decision in *NNP* ultimately protected the right to vote better by contributing to more stable and trusted electoral arrangements going forward. Similarly, in *Soobramoney* one can argue plausibly that the right to health was overall better protected by a decision not to intervene than by a potentially disruptive decision setting a precedent that many subsequent medical and budgetary decisions would have to go through the courts, or could be made to do so at the instance of a litigant armed with no evidence of wrongdoing or error.

This point is very important to see in the socio-economic rights context because the standard argument is not just that the Court's refusal to articulate socio-economic rights content is a sign of reactionary scepticism. It is also often an argument that separation of powers arguments in this context are equally outmoded, that these are *rights* we are talking about, and that if their enforcement requires courts to consider policy or budgetary matters than that is what must happen, because that is what a rights commitment means.[56] Sometimes, as we saw generally in the discussion of transformative constitutionalism, that is an important argument to make, with a perfectly real South African target. But seeing the constitution-building calculation going on in *Soobramoney* is crucial to see that a decision not to do very much with a socio-economic right might equally reflect a decision that the right might be better protected another way, rather than a decision to leave it unprotected in the name of some traditional doctrine. (And seeing the parallel to *NNP* is crucial to

[55] For a political account of *Soobramoney*, see Roux, *Politics of Principle*, pp. 273–80; see also the support for such explanations (with reference to Roux's early work) expressed by D. Brand, 'The Proceduralisation of South African Socio-economic Rights Jurisprudence, or "What Are Socio-economic Rights for?"' in H. Botha, A. J. Van der Walt and J. Van der Walt (eds.) *Rights and Democracy in a Transformative Constitution* (Stellenbosch: Sun Press, 2004), p. 51; and Wilson and Dugard, 'First and Second Waves', p. 37.

[56] See esp. Pieterse, 'Coming to Terms'.

see that this result does not have to have anything to do with socio-economic rights scepticism). Arguments that the Court should articulate the content of the right, measure the state against it, and announce the result may themselves be operating with too traditional a conception of rights enforcement.

These arguments are also crucial to understanding the decision in *Nokotyana* v. *Ekurhuleni Metropolitan Municipality* ('*Nokotyana*'), a second non-intervention decision which in turn helps to explore the argument further. *Nokotyana* was handed down within a few weeks of *Joseph* by an almost identical bench.[57] Critics have been puzzled as to why the Court in *Joseph* was so expansive as to create an entirely new right to service delivery, and yet was simultaneously restrained in relation to service delivery in *Nokotyana*.[58]

Nokotyana dealt with an informal settlement that was awaiting an upgrade to a township, and which had been waiting for three years: the municipal authorities had made the relevant determinations, but the provincial actors were lagging.[59] Under the relevant policies, service delivery upgrades and the associated investment in permanent infrastructure are conditional on the formal declaration of township status. The case was about what service provision the community was entitled to in the interim, especially in light of the long delay. The residents claimed water and refuse removal, which the municipality conceded and which, as in *Grootboom*, was made an order of the Court. But they also claimed one toilet per family where the municipality offered one per ten families, and high-mast lighting which the municipality claimed it could not provide.[60] The Court declined to order the municipality to do more than it had offered and did not seek to articulate what the applicable rights might require. It did, however, require an apology from the government's

[57] *Nokotyana* was handed down on 9 October 2009; *Joseph* on 19 November 2009. The only difference in the bench was that Chief Justice Langa sat in *Nokotyana* but not *Joseph*; both decisions were unanimous.

[58] D. Bilchitz, 'Is the Constitutional Court Wasting Away the Rights of the Poor? *Nokotyana v Ekurhuleni Metropolitan Municipality*' (2010) 127 *South African Law Journal* 591, 596–97; D. Bilchitz, 'Citizenship and Community: Exploring the Right to Receive Basic Municipal Services in *Joseph*' (2010) 3 *Constitutional Court Review* 45, 71–72; Dugard, 'Urban Basic Services', 304, referring to *Nokotyana* and *Joseph* (and *Mazibuko*, discussed later) as 'seemingly erratic judicial outcomes'.

[59] *Nokotyana*, paras. 55–57; Budlender et al., *Public Interest Litigation*, p. 73.

[60] This was a new policy, prompted by the litigation: Wilson and Dugard, 'First and Second Waves', pp. 50–51; on this dynamic, see the later discussion of *Mazibuko*. On earlier conditions, see Dugard, 'Urban Basic Services', pp. 284–85.

counsel to the residents at the hearing. It also put the relevant official on terms to decide on the township's status (although it took the deadline from the government's own statements about how long the process would still take.)[61]

Nokotyana therefore does indeed say rather less than *Joseph* did. However, the two cases in fact run on quite similar lines. On the one hand, in both cases the Court acts to remove the thing blocking enjoyment of the government's normal service delivery efforts. In *Joseph*, that meant establishing that the residents had a legal relationship with the service provider, and so meant quite a creative new legal finding. In *Nokotyana*, it only required getting the government to make a decision about whether the area was to be designated a township and thus not leave the residents in service delivery limbo. The Court responds to this obstacle just as it did in *Joseph*, but in *Nokotyana* that response required much less creative articulation of novel law. There was, after all, no real legal dispute in *Nokotyana* that government should be making this decision, nor that it was unreasonable to condition permanent service infrastructure on the decision; the only problem was the delay in the process. On the other hand, both decisions also decline to make a different sort of finding. *Joseph* keeps away from the substance of the City's electricity distribution plans and the issue of whether cut-offs are an appropriate sanction for non-payment, as noted; it is confined to creating a legal relationship between the City and the tenants in this regard. *Nokotyana* similarly declines to second-guess the City's claims about what level of services it provides pending declarations of township status, and after them. It simply insists that the authorities end the delays in taking a decision in terms of the process envisaged by that policy.[62]

Since the applicants in *Joseph* were focused on their procedural rights, that decision did not require much engagement with this second sort of issue. But the applicants in *Nokotyana* did make specific concrete demands, and so the Court needed to give reasons for not making an

[61] *Nokotyana*, para. 57 (taking the provincial government's submitted time-frame and adding a month).

[62] Thus critics attack both *Joseph* and *Nokotyana* on the basis that they did not articulate the specifically socio-economic rights content relevant to this point: see M. Murcott, 'The Role of Administrative Law in Enforcing Socio-economic Rights: Revisiting *Joseph*' (2013) 29 *South African Journal on Human Rights* 481 (for *Nokotyana*, see 484 n. 19); Bilchitz, 'Citizenship and Community', although Bilchitz also comments that 'this "new" right, articulated in *Joseph*, is an exciting development in South African jurisprudence' – *Ibid.*, 77.

order accordingly. The reason the Court gives is *not* that the applicants are asking for more than the Constitution entitles them to, an issue about which *Nokotyana* says little at all. The Court says that a 'detailed analysis [of the socio-economic rights provisions] is *not required* in the circumstances of this application' (emphasis added).[63] Critics find this infuriatingly wrong and frankly perplexing. They will want to know how it is possible to find that the government is meeting its obligations in terms of the socio-economic rights without first saying what those socio-economic rights require of the government – as Bilchitz puts the point, 'even if one accepts the virtues of minimalism' it does not 'allow the court to ignore constitutional provisions that clearly exist.'[64] But what the Court is deciding is that there is not sufficient basis to take the issue out of the hands of the government and start dealing with it itself, and that includes a decision that the Court does not need to start elaborating the details of what service delivery the applicants are entitled to.

Bilchitz's objection lies at the centre of the critical scholarly reaction to the Court's socio-economic rights cases: how can one answer the question of whether the government is providing what a right entitles people to unless one first says what the right entitles people to?[65] It is therefore crucial to see that it is not the only possible question to be asking. Another question might be this: what judicial action, in this situation, would best give effect to the right, and the Constitution, as a whole? We should not miss the way in which these two possible questions resemble the two different approaches of the Court in *Fourie (2)*, which had been decided a few years before by a similar bench.[66] O'Regan J, dissenting in *Fourie (2)*, asked simply whether the applicant had established a rights violation, and would have awarded judicial relief on the basis of that answer alone. The majority in *Fourie (2)* asked the broader question of what would best advance the cause of LGBTI equality and same-sex partnerships, and was willing to consider what blend of action by the Court and other institutions might best advance that goal. *Nokotyana*

63 *Nokotyana*, para. 46.

64 Bilchitz, 'Wasting Away', 597; see also Bilchitz, 'Citizenship and Community', 52, noting that the minimalist explanation is also implausible because 'developing a "new" right' as the Court did in *Joseph* 'appears to be more activist than minimalist'.

65 See also the important statement of this argument in Brand, 'Proceduralisation'.

66 Seven of the nine judges sat in both cases, and six joined the majority both times. The seventh is O'Regan J, who joined *Nokotyana* but dissented in *Fourie (2)*; on her position, which is also interesting in light of her authorship of the *Nokotyana*-like unanimous decision in *Mazibuko*, see note 162 of this chapter.

decided that, in context, the best answer to this question was to leave the issue in the state's hands, apart from the order to remove to administrative logjam and take the decision on township status. The fact that the Court does not start deciding what lighting and sanitation arrangements are owed to people living in areas awaiting upgrades to township status follows from this decision, since to start deciding these things is in itself a very substantial intervention in the government's processes.

Given that it is not based on the concrete content of rights, then, what is the decision not to intervene based on? The answer might be thought to lie in the Court's decision not to engage the broader substance of the government's policy in relation to settlement upgrades or the provision of basic services prior to declarations of township status on the grounds that the issue was being raised for the first time in the Constitutional Court to a significant extent. *Nokotyana* – fanning the flames of criticism that it does too little – declined even to hear new argument and evidence concerning details of the policy, on the grounds that it should not act as a court of first and last instance. It concluded that '[a]ll that this Court should do with regard to the Municipality's new policy is to note it and record the Municipality's intention and undertaking to act speedily.'[67] This has at least something to do with problems in the way the case was brought, with relevant evidence not being adduced in the court of first instance and the provincial government, the body actually failing to take the decision, not joined as a party.[68] But the Court's stance will still attract the standard objection that it is too reluctant to act as a court of first and last instance, and it may also seem inconsistent when compared with the more creative and flexible approaches we saw in cases like *PE Municipality* and *Joseph*.

The decision not to hear the additional evidence, however, is not a reason for the Court's decision not to intervene, but a result of it. The procedural creativity discussed in a case like *PE Municipality* is the result of a decision that the Court should actively articulate content about its role. *Nokotyana* is consistent with this, and with the creativity of *Joseph*, because it is simply a decision not to do that sort of thing in a context where the Court does not feel it should intervene. Witness the fact that

[67] *Nokotyana*, para. 52. For criticism of this, see S. Wilson and J. Dugard, 'Taking Poverty Seriously: The South African Constitutional Court and Socio-economic Rights' (2011) *Stellenbosch Law Review* 644, 680–81.

[68] Budlender et al., *Public Interest Litigation*, pp. 73–74; see also Wilson and Dugard, 'First and Second Waves', pp. 51–52.

although *Nokotyana* declined to hear the new evidence on appeal, it by no means stuck stubbornly to the traditional role of appeal court. In fact, the Court acted in a managerial fashion by actively encouraging the parties to seek a settlement before the hearing, a step consistent with a view that it should not intervene in the case but also an act traditionally considered unacceptable for common law judges.[69] (The provincial government duly offered a pre-hearing settlement that was more generous than what had been offered by the municipality, but the applicants rejected it.)[70] In response to the applicant's failure to join the crucial provincial defendant, the Court ordered the joinder itself.[71] This is significant, because a Court merely seeking to avoid the case could have used this serious defect to dismiss it. That the Court instead effected the joinder, proceeded with the case, and sought a better settlement for the applicants is consistent with my claim that its non-intervention in other areas of the case is part of a broader calculation about what would best give effect to the rights and other constitutional interests at stake.

This answer means, however, that mere procedural inflexibility is also not the basis for the decision not to intervene, and so we still seek the basis for that decision. The reasons given in the judgment may seem all too familiar to those dedicated to opposing socio-economic rights scepticism. *Nokotyana* notes that, for the approximately 1000 families in the informal settlement whose members were before the Court, there are 109 other such settlements in the jurisdiction of the municipality, with another 139 000 families living in them. These numbers were part of an estimated 1,8 million such families, or between 7 and 8 million people, nationally. If the decision to upgrade the settlement at issue were taken, it would join 502 other informal settlements that were being upgraded at the time of the judgment.[72] In this context, the Court was no doubt concerned about the sustainability of any broader precedent it might set by second-guessing the decisions of a government that denied it was able to do more at present.

To those used to opposing socio-economic rights scepticism, the natural response is that polycentricity is not an insuperable obstacle to judicial intervention, and that there were surely creative ways to try and improve the situation without imposing unsustainable immediate

[69] On traditional common law and continental views of settlement, see Fowkes, 'Managerial Judge', 242 and sources there cited.

[70] Budlender et al., *Public Interest Litigation*, p. 74.

[71] *Ibid.*, pp. 73–74.

[72] *Nokotyana*, para. 9.

obligations on the government.[73] But note that this jumps straight to showing what the Court *could* do, which presupposes that it *should* intervene, the real issue the Court needs to decide about. It was clear that the government's delay in declaring the township, thus delaying service upgrades, was unreasonable and the Court duly intervened in this regard (and the township has subsequently been declared, though its size is now a new issue; the desired high mast lighting and some additional toilets have also been installed).[74] But should the Court have intervened more broadly to review the policy itself, as opposed to this particular delay in implementing it? The answer that the Court's critics will give is that the situation was deplorable. But however true this is (and it is), this answer argues straight from the undoubted presence of need and injustice to the claim that the Court should be acting boldly in response, again jumping over the real question, which is whether judicial intervention will improve on the existing efforts to combat that injustice.

Nokotyana is a good illustration of how this question can confront the Court with the dilemma we began to see in *Soobramoney*. For the Court to be able to decide to intervene with confidence, it will want to know not only that there is something constitutionally objectionable about the existing level of service delivery, but also that judicial intervention (and what kind?) would be the best way to improve the situation, or at the very least that it would be an improvement on the status quo and would not make things worse. But aside from the obvious defect in the government's activities in relation to this particular community – the delay in making the township decision – it did not look possible to make any further finding that the government constitutionally owed the community more without addressing the general service delivery policies for all similarly situated communities. It was partly as a result of this implication that the dispute had started to become about these broader policy issues by the time it reached the Court, producing the applications from both sides to raise new issues and lead new evidence.[75] The Court's difficulty was about what to do in response. It could follow the applicants' lead and launch a full-scale enquiry into the government's broader

[73] See e.g. Bilchitz, *Poverty and Fundamental Rights*, esp. pp. 197–207, noting the sustainability and other concerns of broad precedents, but arguing that general standards are still feasible.

[74] Budlender et al., *Public Interest Litigation*, p. 75; Wilson and Dugard, 'First and Second Waves', p. 51; Dugard, 'Urban Basic Services', p. 304.

[75] *Nokotyana*, paras. 19–20.

policies, and that might identify some deeper problem that it could remedy. But there was no reason to think that it would – indeed, the most likely conjecture was that service delivery delays were due to mundane bureaucratic difficulties, incapacity and the sheer scale of the problem, none of which judicial intervention could likely do very much about. A broader enquiry, therefore, would have been a purely investigative exercise, and ostensibly not a very promising one at that. *Nokotyana*'s decision not to embark on this step follows from the same logic as the non-intervention decisions in *Soobramoney* and *NNP*, and reflects the same concern with how readily applicants are to be permitted to trigger potentially quite expansive reviews of government policy. (We should recall here that *DP*, the sister case of *NNP*, similarly rejected arguments about the hearing of further evidence, as part of a decision not to intervene.)

There is a chicken-and-egg problem here for litigants, of course, since it can seem as if they need the results of the investigation into the government's policy in order to be able to prove to the Court that the investigation should be conducted – or must do at least some of the investigative work themselves, at potentially prohibitive cost and effort, and with the obstacle that much of the information will likely lie in government hands.[76] This is a perfectly real and reasonable concern. What is seldom acknowledged is that to the extent that litigants do not do this work beforehand, understandably or not, the Court will face a similar chicken-and-egg problem. It will have to decide whether to launch a large-scale review, in the full knowledge that unless there is quite an obvious problem that the applicants have failed to raise, a great deal of investigation and interrogation of the government's decisions might be necessary before a responsible Court might be in any position to second-guess the choices that were made and thus to be able to do anything other than limply end a costly and intrusive exercise of jurisdiction.[77] While such choices will inevitably be debatable, we can see why the *Nokotyana* Court might not have been confident enough that it was worth launching a wider judicial intervention.

This is why *Nokotyana* sometimes shows the same terseness that we saw in *UDM (2)*. Having decided that this is not a case for intervention,

[76] See e.g. Bilchitz, *Poverty and Fundamental Rights*, pp. 206–07; Wilson and Dugard, 'First and Second Waves', pp. 44–56; Brand, 'Proceduralisation', pp. 52–53; see also, in light of the present argument, *Ibid.*, p. 53 n. 133, on the potentially sweeping enquiries latent in the Court's approach.

[77] Fowkes, 'Managerial Judge', esp. 243–46.

the judgment turns to tick off the points the applicants had managed to raise on their own to show why they are not enough to show a violation. Those focused simply on the content of rights naturally again find this approach highly objectionable: if one is rejecting legal challenges, then there is no excuse for doing so on the basis of a thin and hasty analysis of the legal provisions in question. They will also see the obvious response to be to try to show the Court why its interpretation is too thin – which is why so many scholars react to the Court's socio-economic rights cases by trying to come up with thicker interpretations that might find favour with the judges. But once we recognize that the Court has made a judgment call about whether to intervene and decided not to, the tone of the judgment will look less puzzling, and we will understand that the Court is not offering a thin account but instead, as it says in so many words, deciding that it is not necessary in the context of the case to offer any account at all. Once we recognize that the decision not to articulate content follows from the decision not to intervene, instead of the other way around, this approach will also look less worrying as a precedent. And again, the parallels to cases like *UDM (2)*, *NNP* and *DP* help us to see beyond simple explanations from socio-economic rights scepticism.

These parallels can also help us to see a final, special reason for *Nokotyana* to be cautious about starting down the road to review the government's service delivery upgrade policy. In Chapter 3, we saw the Court being very cautious of threatening the integrity of elections, and there is an important analogy to the service delivery context here. A persistent theme of the Court's jurisprudence on housing and land is the concern to guard against queue-jumping: to try not to allow people to skip to the head of the waiting list for houses or land just because they litigated, or because they occupied property.[78] The basis for this concern is that if the Court permits this, it will threaten the system of waiting lists and progressive realization put in place by the government – and this is the same concern not to undermine a mechanism with considerable implications for public order that we saw in the electoral context. We should recall that in *Richter*, one of the pair of 2009 cases on the right to vote of citizens who were overseas on election day, the Court was willing to not decide an equality issue, even though it was before the Court and the rights of many citizens to vote in provincial elections depended upon it. It took this stance because if people overseas had the right to vote in

[78] See e.g. *Grootboom*, paras. 81, 92; *PE Municipality*, para. 55; *Blue Moonlight*, para. 93.

their provincial elections then people inside South Africa, but outside their province of residence, should also have that right, but the Electoral Commission claimed it was not in a position to provide this and there was no evidence before the Court to prompt it to second-guess the Commission about this. The full implications of such an order thus risked being disruptive to the general system, and so the Court did not make it, even though this had the effect of depriving some people properly before the Court of something to which they had at least a plausible constitutional claim. A decision was being made that non-intervention was the best way to uphold rights generally.

Richter is a particularly striking analogy here because in *Nokotyana* the embarrassed provincial and national government had offered to make special funds available to provide the community with the service infrastructure they sought. They emphasized, however, that they could not afford to do this for any other similarly situated communities. The municipality strongly opposed this offer, and the Court declined to order it.[79] This may seem surprising, but it reflects the broader stakes of the case for social order: giving one community special treatment is potentially exceedingly destabilizing and difficult to justify politically.[80] We would surely reject out of hand a suggestion that the applicants in *Richter* should have had special entitlements to vote in provincial elections just because they had gone to Court, or because the government was embarrassed, notwithstanding that it is clearly good if even a few more people get to exercise their right to vote, because of its implications for the integrity of the more generally beneficial voting system. The same holds for the fundamental rights at stake in the context of service delivery in *Nokotyana*.

This analysis of *Soobramoney* and *Nokotyana* brings out the other half of *Grootboom*, to which we can now return. For of course alongside *Grootboom*'s decision to assert jurisdiction and articulate an approach to socio-economic rights is a decision in that case to mostly leave housing policy in the hands of the government.[81] Once again, this stance is often

[79] *Nokotyana*, paras. 53–54.

[80] Bilchitz, 'Wasting Away', 602–04 criticizes the decision to reject the offer. Striking the balance between a possibly destabilizing special privilege (a concern he has recognized elsewhere; see Bilchitz, *Poverty and Fundamental Rights*, pp. 203–05) and a simple act of alleviating suffering naturally produces debatable cases; the Court went the other way on the (arguably distinguishable) concrete offer in *Grootboom*.

[81] Mark Tushnet thus treats *Grootboom* as a paradigmatic example of judicial use of socio-economic rights as weak substantive social rights: M. Tushnet, *Weak Courts, Strong Rights: Judicial Review and Social Welfare Rights in Comparative Constitutional Law*

attributed to a weak understanding of socio-economic rights and is therefore met with proposals for stronger ones. But the indubitable fact that Court certainly *could* have taken this larger task upon itself to a greater degree than it chose to is not decisive in a context where the government actors involved were making housing efforts that were very far from trivial, their flaws notwithstanding. *Grootboom* intervened more than *Soobramoney* did, in light of the national government's resistance to the Court's jurisdiction and to the idea that a short-term housing policy was needed to supplement its existing longer-term efforts. But otherwise the two decisions are similar, combining maximalism where the decision is made to articulate content with a non-intervention decision on other issues.

The standard objections to this approach in *Grootboom*, as in *Soobramoney*, are in fact all conditional on certain assumptions, and the assumptions usually receive rather less attention than the supervening objections. There is again the argument that the Court's stance, focusing on the reasonableness of the government's housing policy, cannot be reconciled with the way the text of the socio-economic rights grants entitlements and only then subjects them to the limits of available resources and progressive realization.[82] But that argument is less powerful if the decision is only that the Court should not articulate these entitlements *here*, for it is then a reading that the Court should not yet spell out the full implications of the text, not that the text lacks those implications or that the Court lacks the power to spell them out. (The Court, of course, does articulate some content in *Grootboom* that is not purely procedural, such as the short-term housing policy point.)[83] The debate is not about whether the Court can articulate such content, but when it should do so, and so arguments for articulating more concrete content are conditional on it being true that doing so would give best effect to socio-economic rights and the Constitution as a whole in a particular context – something the text of the right itself does not answer.

(Princeton University Press, 2008), p. 243. Brian Ray has recently argued in this direction, though he remains sympathetic to a number of the standard criticisms I discuss here: see B. Ray, 'Evictions, Aspirations and Avoidance'; his work to date has focused on the eviction cases in particular, which I discuss in the next chapter.

[82] See esp. Bilchitz, *Poverty and Fundamental Rights*, ch. 5; Brand, 'Proceduralisation'; Liebenberg, *Adjudicating Socio-economic Rights*, ch. 4; Roux, *Politics of Principle*, ch. 7; Davis, 'Socioeconomic Rights', 696–97, 699–700.

[83] See Pieterse, 'Procedural Relief', 360–61 and earlier sources there cited.

Something similar is true of the argument that the Court should articulate a minimum core conception of socio-economic rights, which *Grootboom* declined to do.[84] That, too, was a refusal to articulate content on the facts of the case rather than a more general rejection – '*In this case*, we do not have sufficient information to determine [it]' (my emphasis),[85] – though such refusals have been repeated in later cases. In light of the broader arguments of this book, we can now better understand the Court's resistance to the minimum core argument. The minimum core represents a bid to respond to socio-economic scepticism and to the conviction that socio-economic rights will not be enforceable or enforced the same as civil-political rights until they have concrete content. It is also often an example of how this expectation can demand much more from courts than is demanded in relation to traditional rights, because a unilateral court-established minimum core is a manufactured substitute for an idea of more settled content and public status, and setting it can require a court to confront a great deal of newness.[86] Polycentric uncertainties arise because a standard designed in one case has precedential implications for all the other, potentially different, cases as well. Sophisticated accounts of the minimum core recognize these risks, and respond by making the standards more general and basic.[87] It *is* convincing to argue that courts can set standards like this without vast amounts of information: setting a basic amount for daily water needs is a particularly good example. But while this may be decisive if we are debating whether a Court could possibly set a minimum core, it is not decisive if we are debating whether it should have done so in a particular context.

If we are asking the latter question, we can see that the real objections may not lie in the difficulty of setting the standard, but in something like

84 See esp. Bilchitz, *Poverty and Fundamental Rights*, ch. 6; Liebenberg, *Adjudicating Socio-economic Rights*, esp. pp. 148–41, 163–73.

85 *Grootboom*, para. 33.

86 See further on this argument Fowkes, 'Normal Rights, Just New'.

87 Danie Brand has raised detail concerns of this sort in relation to the minimum core; Bilchitz's reply deliberately side-steps engaging such details: D. Brand, 'The Minimum Core Content of the Right to Food in Context: A Response to Rolf Künneman' in D. Brand and S. Russell (eds.) *Exploring the Core Content of Socio-Economic Rights: South African and International Perspectives* (Pretoria: Protea Book House, 2002); and see also D. Brand, 'The Right to Food' in D. Brand and C. Heyns (eds.), *Socio-Economic Rights in South Africa* (Pretoria University Law Press, 2005) and the critique by Liebenberg, *Adjudicating Socio-economic Rights*, pp. 168–73 and sources there cited; for the reply, see Bilchitz, *Poverty and Fundamental Rights*, pp. 197–207.

the reverse. Broad conceptual standards, like 'access to accommodation that involves, at least, protection from the elements in sanitary conditions with access to basic services, such as toilets and running water', are so intuitively easy to set that we might wonder what difference setting them would make.[88] For one thing, this sort of basic claim that government should be meeting basic needs and delivering services to poverty-stricken communities is often not what is in dispute in South Africa: the problems usually lie in the details and delays in implementation. More decisive action in *Nokotyana*, for example, would have required putting concrete figures to what 'sanitary conditions' and 'access to . . . toilets and running water' entails; everyone involved accepted that the government had the basic obligation to provide these things. It is hard to see what difference, if any, an interpretation of the relevant rights in the form of this sort of broad conceptual standard would have made in the case. Furthermore, as one might expect given the broad consensus about the government's service delivery obligations, the government itself often already sets basic standards in legislation and policy documents that can effectively amount to a minimum core. The Court's intervention in *Grootboom* yielded new general standards for housing – just in the form of changes to the government-written Housing Code instead of judge-written changes to the interpretation of the s 26 housing right. (We will see something similar in this chapter's two final case studies). Nor is it necessarily true that judicial standards are better: litigating on the basis of the government's own standards is a very powerful tactic, and any attempt by government to repeal or roll back its own standards will be both conspicuous and ripe for challenge as a retrogressive step. Of course, the government might fail to set such standards, but even then the plausible judicial response might simply be to order it to do so – as has happened in a recent successful litigation and lobbying campaign in the education context[89] – rather than for the judiciary to take that task upon itself. And since the argument in the first place is only about when to set standards, rather than whether to do so, nothing precludes the Court from

[88] The quoted standard is offered as an example by Bilchitz, *Poverty and Fundamental Rights*, p. 198.

[89] Equal Education School Infrastructure Campaign, materials available at www.equaleducation.org.za/campaigns/minimum-norms-and-standards; see also C. Mcconnachie and C. Mcconnachie, 'Concretising the Right to a Basic Education' (2012) 129 *South African Law Journal* 554; Budlender et al., *Public Interest Litigation*, pp. 81–84.

articulating more content when judicial content is needed – as the examples of selective maximalism already considered illustrate.

The final standard argument calls for bolder action at the remedial stage. Critics note that local authorities were very slow to deal with short-term housing needs in the wake of *Grootboom*. The Court is blamed for awarding only declaratory relief, and for its deference to the South African Human Rights Commission's offer to monitor implementation of its order, which produced a report but was substantially ineffective.[90] Such criticism is made in hindsight. As an argument about what the Court should have done in response to the facts before it at the time, calls for supervisory jurisdiction in *Grootboom* are arguments that the Court's default starting premise should be one of distrust in relation to the other constitutional actors involved.[91] While it is true that problems in short-term housing persisted in the municipality concerned, the argument that *Grootboom* did not do enough about these general problems is an argument for a sweeping judicial intervention indeed, to be launched despite the fact that the evidence before the Court at the time was that the local authorities were evolving their policies to respond to the problems revealed by the case. It also rests on an assumption, which usually goes unquestioned, that such intervention would have been a good thing for housing. We will see in the two final case studies to follow how such assumptions are often far from straightforwardly valid.

To identify these assumptions in the arguments for bolder approaches to content and remedies in *Grootboom* and elsewhere is not to prove that they generally do not hold, nor do I believe that to be the case. The point is not to establish that bolder strategies are generally a bad idea in socio-economic rights cases. It is to note that the standard arguments rest heavily on surprisingly untested assumptions that bolder strategies would be a *good* idea. For example, the argument for bolder remedies is quite

[90] *Grootboom*, para. 97; on subsequent events and criticism of *Grootboom* on this basis, see K. Pillay, 'Implementing *Grootboom*: Supervision Needed' (July 2002) 3 *Economic Social Rights Review* 16; Bilchitz, *Poverty and Fundamental Rights*, pp. 151–53; K. McLean, *Constitutional Deference, Courts and Socio-Economic Rights in South Africa* (Pretoria University Law Press, 2009), p. 200; McLean, 'Housing', 55-20 - 55-24; Davis, 'Socio-economic Rights', 701; Liebenberg, *Adjudicating Socio-economic Rights*, pp. 400–09, 429–31; Budlender et al., *Public Interest Litigation*, p. 126.

[91] Liebenberg, while criticizing *Grootboom*'s approach and suggesting 'a more robust remedial attitude in future', also argues that the Court's 'confidence' in the state 'may have been warranted in light of the fact that it was the first major test case' on the right to housing – Liebenberg, *Adjudicating Socio-economic Rights*, p. 409.

straightforward if one departs from the assumption that judicial action is the only thing that will help, since it will then usually be enough to show that there is a problem and that there is something judges can do about it. Similarly, the argument for more content is often defended on the grounds that this will make litigation easier. That is perfectly plausible, but begs the question about whether that should be the priority, something that again will seem much more obvious if one is focused on court-centred strategies to the exclusion of other institutional options.

If we strip away these court-centric biases, what remains is a question about socio-economic governance that is often much more complex and open-ended and usually implicates serious empirical questions. The mechanics of realizing socio-economic rights, including the effects of judicial intervention into the activities of other institutions via popular devices like structural interdicts, often implicates issues of bureaucracy and the mechanics of regulation. Such subjects receive much less attention in South African than questions of the bolder content socio-economic rights might potentially be given or the bolder action courts could potentially take to enforce them.[92] Comparative examples are also very valuable in this context, but while existing work does sometimes consider them, they are usually invoked to show that bolder judicial action is possible.[93] That is important as a response to scepticism, but if we are trying to decide *when* to try bold things, it too leaves the key debates to be had.

In this, the position in the socio-economic rights context is the same as in other examples considered in the book. *NNP* was not just about how to interpret the voting right and *Doctors for Life* was not just about how to understand democracy; both were also about institutional arguments over how and when courts should intervene, and in neither case were the constitutional issues surrounding this straightforward. *Grootboom*

[92] I have benefitted here from work including T. K. McCraw, *Prophets of Regulation: Charles Francis Adams, Louis D. Brandeis, James M. Landis and Alfred E. Kahn* (Harvard University Press, 1984); J. Q. Wilson, *Bureaucracy: What Government Agencies Do and Why They Do It* (New York: Basic Books, 1989); J. L. Mashaw and D. L. Harfst, *The Struggle for Auto Safety* (Harvard University Press, 1990); and C. R. Epp *Making Rights Real: Activists, Bureaucrats, and the Creation of the Legalistic State* (University of Chicago Press, 2010). For studies of bureaucracy in South Africa, see esp. the work of Ivor Chipkin, e.g. I. Chipkin, 'Transcending Bureaucracy: State Transformation in the Age of the Manager' (2011) 77 *Transformation* 31.

[93] See e.g. the references to Indian developments in the South African context, admiring but largely in passing, cited in Fowkes, 'Indian PIL', 435 n. 1.

and its descendants are of the same mould, and this should not surprise us. The key underlying question of how to get the world to change in the direction required by the Constitution is the same across the different types of claims, and the difficulties of answering it similarly dependent on newness and support and not the kind of right at stake. Now armed with a sense of how this general insight affects our view of the socio-economic rights cases in general, I conclude this chapter with more detailed studies of its workings in two important cases that are enduring subjects of controversy. One is the much-criticized 2010 decision in *Mazibuko* v. *City of Johannesburg* ('*Mazibuko*', not to be confused with *Mazibuko* v. from the previous chapter). But first I discuss the famous decision in *TAC*, without which no discussion of socio-economic rights, or decisions about when to intervene, or the ANC and its political relations to the Constitutional Court, can be complete.

Minister of Health v. *Treatment Action Campaign*

The story of HIV/AIDS in South Africa will never be anything other than a tragedy, and the notorious denialism of Thabo Mbeki and his faction of the ANC quickly became beyond defence. *TAC*, then, is not a case whose substance is underpinned by an admirable stance from the ANC government, although (as is widely recognized) it is particularly misleading to treat the ANC as a monolith here. In keeping with its central importance in South African public life, ANC actors were important on both sides of the case. But it is also true that the ANC government was remarkably respectful of the Court in the context of so serious a disagreement, a point that has gone unacknowledged due to a live TV interview whose significance I will argue is exaggerated. Court centrism is once again highly misleading here, notwithstanding that the greatest problem in *TAC* was the stance of the government. The two HIV/AIDS cases in *TAC* and *Hoffman* represent the only two moments in which a long line of public activity on HIV and AIDS briefly spiked up into the Court, before continuing on its way outside it. The response to the pandemic has mostly played out in other institutions: in the Competition Commission, the Advertising Standards Association of South Africa, NEDLAC (the bargaining forum for government, labour and business) and the Medicines Control Council; in legislation and regulations and administrative decisions; in the Presidency and the Cabinet and the Ministries of Health and Finance; in political parties and trade unions; and in the activities of doctors and nurses and traditional healers and quacks and a range of

NGOs, among which the Treatment Action Campaign has already entered legend.[94] As with *Makwanyane*, it is crucial to tell the legal story in *TAC* alongside the political one, and the chronology here is particularly important. Aspects of the story are well known, but not all are, and some of the details are of underacknowledged significance, so it is important to offer a brief but complete sketch.

Mbeki's denialism had generated serious opposition well before the *TAC* litigation. He himself had begun to acknowledge the need for him to step back from the issue as early as October 2000, reflecting the growing internal pressure, as well as his own recognition of the damage his stance was causing to South Africa's image among global leaders and investors. Stubbornly convinced of the correctness of his suspicion of antiretroviral drugs (ARVs), however, he had been slow to retreat. Journalists with high-level access have argued that many senior ANC members did not dare to take on Mbeki, but were deeply worried about his stance on HIV/AIDS.[95] As a result of his weakening but still stubborn stance, the government agreed to make the drug Nevirapine available at state hospitals for the first time, but only on a trial basis and only at two pilot sites per province. Two doses of Nevirapine dramatically reduce the chances that an HIV-positive mother will infect her baby during the birth process, when most mother-to-child transmission occurs (although today other treatments are now usually used). Mothers outside the two pilot sites would remain unable to get the medication at state hospitals. In this context, the Treatment Action Campaign launched proceedings seeking to compel the government to roll out Nevirapine beyond the pilot sites. Considered in the abstract, the order sought was rather interventionist: asking a court to order the roll out of a particular drug, in the face of various policy-laden objections including concerns about the drug's safety and the risk of producing drug-resistant strains if taken incorrectly, and overriding the government's stated preference to test Nevirapine at

[94] See generally N. Geffen, *Debunking Delusions: The Inside Story of the Treatment Action Campaign* (Johannesburg: Jacana, 2010); N. Nattrass, *Mortal Combat: AIDS Denialism and the Struggle for Antiretrovirals in South Africa* (University of KwaZulu-Natal Press, 2007).

[95] Gevisser traces Mbeki's first mention of the possibility of his withdrawing to an ANC NEC meeting in October 2000, but reports that 'to the exasperation of many of his colleagues, he found himself unable to do so'. Gevisser, *Dream Deferred*, pp. 753–54. Gumede notes that at a January 2001 Cabinet meeting Mbeki acknowledged the damage his stance was doing to South Africa's international image: Gumede, *Thabo Mbeki*, pp. 208–09.

pilot sites first.[96] However, as with *Hoffman*, the Court enjoyed considerable support in confronting these questions and so the real task it faced was very different.[97] Just as South African Airways' own expert essentially conceded the medical points in *Hoffman*, so in *TAC* the government's own officials had signed off on the safety of Nevirapine (a fact so predictably crucial to the Court's willingness to make the order sought by the Treatment Action Campaign that they had delayed the litigation for five months to wait for the Medicine Control Council's decision).[98] Because the government itself had launched pilot sites, its concerns about dangers were also diluted in the same way that SAA's argument in *Hoffman* that it was not safe to hire HIV-positive people for flight duties was undermined by the fact that it had taken no steps to screen HIV-positive people out of its existing flight crews. Several provinces had also already initiated much more extensive roll-outs by the time of the litigation, and this fruit of competitive federalism undermined the government's arguments still further. In addition, the company concerned had agreed to supply the drug for free for five years.

In this context, TAC succeeded in the court of first instance on 18 December 2001.[99] Mbeki's biographer Mark Gevisser writes that this decision meant that 'Mbeki's campaign against ARVs ... had been lost. Most ANC leaders understood this, and more than a few heaved a sigh of relief.'[100] (We should note the significance these leaders attached to a judicial decision.) Among those internally arguing for Mbeki's withdrawal from the issue at this time were Nkosasana Dlamini-Zuma, former Minister of Health and at that time Minister of Foreign Affairs, and Joel Netshitenze, Mbeki's chief advisor and at that time de facto the

96 See also McLean, *Constitutional Deference*, p. 131.

97 See e.g. Davis, 'Socioeconomic rights', 694–95, K. Lehmann, 'In Defense of the Constitutional Court: Litigating Socio-economic Rights and the Myth of the Minimum Core' (2006–2007) 22 *American University International Law Review* 163, both noting that *TAC (2)* was a relatively easy case. This is an important qualification to arguments such as Mark Tushnet's that the Court's 'examination of the government's justifications ... was quite searching and nothing in [the judgment] indicates that the Court was giving any real deference to the government's judgments': Tushnet, *Weak Courts*, p. 246.

98 M. Heywood, 'Preventing Mother-to-Child HIV Transmission in South Africa: Background, Strategies and Outcomes of the Treatment Action Campaign Case against the Minister of Health' (2003) 19 *South African Journal on Human Rights* 278, 286, 298; Roux, *Politics of Principle*, pp. 294–96.

99 *Treatment Action Campaign* v. *Minister of Health* 2002 (4) BCLR 356 (T).

100 Gevisser, *Dream Deferred*, p. 754.

second most powerful person in the country.[101] Those opposing Mbeki openly included ANC parliamentarian Pregs Govender, and after a slow start, Nelson Mandela. (Among the latter's acts of dissent was to sign off on the award of the Kaiser Foundation's new Nelson Mandela Prize for Health and Human Rights to two of Nevirapine's pioneering doctors in February 2002, right in the middle of the *TAC* litigation. The following year's Nelson Mandela Prize would go to the Treatment Action Campaign itself.)[102] At a January 2002 cabinet meeting, Mbeki had 'conceded that, despite the state's appeal on the Nevirapine case, plans should be put into place to roll out ARV treatment for HIV-positive pregnant mothers'.[103] The first public signs of the shift came in his State of the Nation address on 8 February 2002, where he spoke (rather equivocally) of the possibility of new sites for ARVs to prevent mother-to-child transmission.[104] Shortly thereafter, he stated in a television interview that 'provinces with the resources to extend the [mother-to-child transmission] programme should not be delayed by provinces that did not have the resources.'[105] Ten days later, Mbhazima Shilowa, the ANC's Premier of wealthy Gauteng, reacted to these signals by announcing a large-scale roll-out of ARVs in his province.[106] Health Minister Tsabalala-Msimang attacked him for this, but her zeal overshot her master's: in line with his televised remarks, Mbeki 'apparently had no problem with Shilowa's decision', and the Gauteng roll-out proceeded.[107] At a March 2002 ANC National Executive Committee (NEC) meeting, a notorious confrontation took place in which Mandela was criticized for his public challenges to the government's AIDS policy, while most NEC members

[101] *Ibid.*, p. 419; R. Calland, *Anatomy of South Africa: Who Holds the Power?* (Cape Town, Zebra Press, 2006), pp. 8–9, 22, 49–50.

[102] Gevisser, *Dream Deferred*, pp. 722–23. [103] *Ibid.*, p. 754.

[104] 'At the same time [as efforts to combat AIDS by poverty reduction and appropriate nutrition] continuing work will be done to monitor the efficacy of anti-retroviral interventions against mother-to-child transmission in the sites already operational and any new ones that may be decided upon'; the speech also mentioned positive talks with pharmaceutical companies: State of the Nation Address by the President of South Africa, Thabo Mbeki, 8 February 2002, available at www.sahistory.org.za/archive/2002-president-mbeki-state-nation-address-8-february-2002.

[105] Heywood, 'Preventing Transmission', 303.

[106] *Ibid.*, 303–04; Gevisser, *Dream Deferred*, p. 756. Shilowa's announcement was made in a speech on 18 February 2002; available at www.polity.org.za/polity/govdocs/speeches/2002/sp0218.html.

[107] Gevisser, *Dream Deferred*, p. 756, who reports that Tshabalala-Msimang's action was described to him by insiders as typical of how insecure subordinates would attempt to anticipate President Mbeki's wishes rather than consult him.

stayed quiet. Mandela, dismayed, interpreted this as evidence of Mbeki's suppression of dissent. But a question mark is placed against his interpretation by the fact that the Cabinet (of which Mandela was no longer part) had disagreed with Mbeki so strongly in January and would do so again in April. This supports what Gevisser's sources told him: 'other ANC leaders at the NEC felt exactly the opposite about the meeting: that by remaining silent, the majority were signalling their agreement with Mandela, and that this represented a real breakthrough on AIDS.'[108]

On 11 March, the court of first instance ruled that its order to start rolling out Nevirapine across the country should be implemented pending the government's appeal to the Constitutional Court. The government took the decision to appeal this ruling to the Court as well – a potentially controversial step because interim orders pending appeal are not usually themselves appealable. The fact that the government did this has been described as a strategic misstep because it gave the Constitutional Court an opportunity to signal its view in advance of the main litigation.[109] This is a standard remark, but one that of course contradicts the general claim that the Court is restrained and cautious of getting involved in socio-economic matters, or politicized ones. It would have been open to the Court to avoid saying anything on the grounds that interim orders should not be appealable (which would have left the roll-out to proceed by default). Instead, the Court took less than 24 hours to deny the interim appeal and put its own stamp on the interim roll-out. This order, subsequently justified in a judgment ('*TAC (1)*') handed down at the same time as the judgment on the main appeal ('*TAC (2)*'), is important to remember when assessing the Court's actions on socio-economic matters.[110] Finding the state inexplicably not acting to roll out a free life-saving drug whose safety had been cleared by its own experts, the Court acted overnight. *TAC (1)* offers important counter evidence to claims that the Court will never intervene decisively in socio-economic matters, or that it shrinks away from political risk and confrontation.[111] Its stand gets obscured, however, because less than two

108 *Ibid.*, p. 755.

109 Heywood, Preventing Transmission', 306–07; Roux, *Politics of Principle*, p. 298.

110 *Minister of Health* v. *Treatment Action Campaign (1)* 2002 (5) SA 703 (CC).

111 It is plausible to argue, as Roux does, that the micro-politics of *TAC* offered enough signs of the government's weakening stance for the Court to detect that political space existed for its intervention: Roux, *Politics of Principle*, pp. 293, 297–99, 303. It was undoubtedly, however, a very high profile political contest to enter, and so the real question is whether this boldness is consistent with explaining deference in *other* cases, with much lower

weeks later the Cabinet sounded a retreat from denialism – continuing the trajectory of the political trend, but also presumably taking some note of the clear signal of intent sent by the Court in *TAC (1)*. On 17 April, the Cabinet issued a statement rejecting the denialist position and accepting the role of ARVs in government policy to combat HIV/AIDS.[112] As Roux has pointed out, this effectively meant that the political battle was over even before the Court's main hearing, held on 2, 3 and 6 May.[113]

What is often missed is that this made *TAC* rather a lot like *Grootbooom* in becoming substantially about the proper role of the judiciary in such contexts. *This* was still a live issue because the government made it one. The Cabinet's effective concession on ARVs on 17 April did not include a concession about the jurisdiction of the Court to make the order sought by the applicants in *TAC (2)* – which is why the case did not peter out into mootness after the Cabinet's statement but instead continued to be contested to the degree of requiring what is for the Court an exceptionally long hearing. It is not especially surprising that the government resisted the Court's authority, notwithstanding the Court's firm assertion of jurisdiction in *Grootboom*. If one is worried about the implications of a judicial position in one case, then one obvious thing to do in the next one is to continue to raise the same concerns in the hopes that the Court will realize its mistake, or at least qualify its earlier remarks. Proponents of more generous interpretations of socio-economic rights have, after all, done much the same thing for rather longer in asserting more concrete interpretations of socio-economic rights on three further occasions after *Grootboom* opted instead for the reasonableness test.[114] It is also worth recalling that the order sought in *TAC* could plausibly be thought to go beyond what the Court had decided in *Grootboom*. At least one independent observer took this view at the time, and I have noted the fact that the order sought in *TAC* is rather expansive, at least on paper.[115] Finally, and reflecting less well on the government, it

political stakes, on the grounds of the Court's unwillingness to risk any confrontation with the ANC government.

112 Statement on Cabinet meeting of 17 April 2002, available at www.gcis.gov.za/content/newsroom/media-releases/cabinet-statements/statement-cabinet-meeting-17-april-2002-1.

113 Roux, *Politics of Principle*, p. 299.

114 In *TAC (2)*, *Nokotyana*, and *Mazibuko*.

115 K. Hopkins, 'Shattering the Divide – When Judges Go Too Far' (March 2002) *De Rebus* 23; see also K. Hopkins, 'Democracy in a Post-TAC Society' (November 2002) *De Rebus* 14.

seems clear that its lawyers were reaching for any basis to convince the Court not to make an order, as we saw in several of the LGBTI equality cases. Given the degree of effective concession on the merits, separation of powers arguments were all that was left.

The Court's response is consistent with the approach we have seen up to now. The judgment spends time addressing the government's separation of powers concerns. It firmly asserts the Court's jurisdiction while showing the familiar scrupulous concern with institutional boundaries. As in *Hoffman*, its findings on policy matters are confined to areas of effective consensus: it is able to state that '[t]he essential facts, as we see them, are not seriously in dispute'.[116] Thus, for example, it rejects the government's concerns about drug safety in light of the government's own decision to roll it out to test sites, the finding by the government's own body that the drug was safe and the World Health Organization's recommendation.[117] Conversely, a subsidiary question in the case was whether the order to provide Nevirapine should be accompanied by an order to provide formula (so that the use of Nevirapine to prevent transmission during the birth process would not be undone by subsequent transmission in breast milk).[118] The sort of consensus present in relation to points such as the safety and efficacy of Nevirapine was absent here, and so the Court declined to make a finding on this point, just as it had declined in *Hoffman* to decide whether HIV should be considered a disability for the purposes of employment legislation.

Many scholars, however, will not consider it much of a defence that the Court approached *TAC (2)* as business as usual. Admittedly the argument for consistency is important given how politicized the case was, offering further support for the reservations I have expressed about bluntly political explanations. But for many, *TAC (2)* was a case of unusually egregious government failure – and defiance. On 24 March 2002, a week before the Court's hearing on the interim order pending appeal, the Minister of Health had been asked during a live interview about her attitude to the Court ruling on the Nevirapine matter. She replied that 'my own view is that the judiciary cannot prescribe from the bench,' a line that would be heard again from the government's lawyers in the Court. The interview then continued as follows:

[116] *TAC (2)*, para. 21. [117] *Ibid.*, paras. 12, 60–64. [118] *Ibid.*, para. 128.

Interviewer: Mmm, so you think it's inappropriate that this is in court, but nevertheless it's there. Will you stand by whatever the Court decides?

Minister: No, I think the Court and the judiciary must also listen to the regulatory authority, both of this country and the regulatory authority of the US.

Interviewer: So you're saying no?

Minister: I say no. I am saying no.[119]

It is very easy to see why this interview provoked anger and concern (and led the Minister to be dubbed 'Dr No' in the press). But because the interview tends to colour all perceptions of *TAC*, it is important to note several points about it. Most importantly, we should pause for a moment and reflect on the fact that this not unequivocal exchange, live and unscripted, is the *high water mark* of public resistance to the Court's authority by senior members of the ANC in at least the first decade of the Court's life. One suspects there are other young constitutional democracies that would dearly love such a record. Furthermore, the government moved swiftly after the interview to rebut any suggestion that it would not comply with the Court's order. The Minister of Justice, Dr Penuell Maduna, promptly disavowed any intention to circumvent the Court's authority.[120] Two days after the interview, the Health Minister herself issued a statement saying 'I would like to emphasize that we have no intention of circumventing the courts or simply delaying matters by endless litigation. We stand ready to abide by the final decision of the courts', adding that '[w]e have turned to the highest court in the land precisely because of our belief in the judicial system'.[121] The speed of the retraction may reflect the growing control that the rest of Cabinet was taking over the issue, but it is also perfectly possible that the Minister had once again overshot in her zeal to give voice to Mbeki's views, as she had in attacking Premier Shilowa the previous month. Whatever his views on AIDS, it is doubtful that Mbeki would have looked with favour on any statement that would make South Africa appear the stereotypical dysfunctional African democracy.[122] Finally, although South Africans will

119 Quoted by Heywood, 'Preventing Transmission', 308. 120 *Ibid*., 308–09.

121 Department of Health, 'Minister Approaches Constitutional Court on Nevirapine Order' Press Release in the name of Dr Manto Tshabalala-Msimang, 27 March 2002, available at www.doh.gov.za/show.php?id=208.

122 After finalization of this manuscript, I encountered the following in Edwin Cameron's recent memoir: 'In December 2012 ... I asked [Minister of Justice Maduna] if it was President Mbeki himself who had mandated him to state that government would abide

not be inclined to extend this particular Minister much interpretative charity, it is worth considering the point she was actually making, because she is often understood to have been expressing an intention to defy any Court order. Her comments in fact followed an announcement that Nevirapine's manufacturer was withdrawing its application for clearance from the US Food and Drug Administration. This was in fact merely due to technicalities, and the government's attempt to use this to raise concerns about Nevirapine's safety was disingenuous – something that Justice Kriegler would openly state during the hearing in *TAC (1)*, and which confirms that by this point the government was reaching for anything that might persuade the Court not to intervene.[123] But it also means that the point the Minister was making, in bad faith or good, is that 'the Court and the judiciary must also listen to the regulatory authority, both of this country and the regulatory authority of the US', and should not overrule these bodies on the safety of medicines – a proposition with which the Court and most if not all constitutional lawyers would likely agree, at least absent special circumstances. The statement was careless at best. But we should really wonder how seriously or generally to take it as defiance of the Court's authority.

The Court, at least, does not seem to have taken it that seriously, and it is here that we come to the issue of *TAC (2)*'s remedy. The Court declared the government's policy on Nevirapine invalid, and ordered the government to make the drug generally available, where prescribed, for preventing mother-to-child transmission. But it declined to issue any form of supervisory order to monitor compliance, simply stating that 'the government has always respected and executed orders of this Court. There is no reason to believe that it will not do so in the present case.'[124] The Minister's TV statement is usually Exhibit A in the argument for a stronger order.

Both *TAC (2)*'s approach and my interpretation of the Minister's interview may seem naïve, especially since we now know that the Minister would use her office to lead opposition to ARVs for a number of years

by the court's decision. He confirmed that it was. In bowing to the courts when they disclaimed his own dogma, President Mbeki, more signally even than President Nelson Mandela, ensured a victory for the rule of law in South Africa.' – E. Cameron, *Justice: A Personal Account* (Cape Town: Tafelberg, 2014), pp. 199–200.

123 Heywood, 'Preventing Transmission', 308–09.

124 *TAC (2)*, para. 129. For this criticism, see e.g. Pieterse, 'Coming to Terms', 415; Bilchitz, *Poverty and Fundamental Rights*, p. 163.

after *TAC (2)*.[125] As a result, one might be inclined to see the TV interview as the one moment of unguarded candour that revealed the truth. One might therefore be inclined to dismiss the careful press statement that followed the interview – as well as the series of other, equally respectful, Department of Health press statements that had greeted each stage of the *TAC* litigation – as so much cheap talk, and wish that the Court had reacted to the one candid danger signal that slipped out.[126] But it would be a mistake to be so quick.

Suppose we assume that all these press statements were nothing more than rote language put out by the departmental press office as a matter of course. Even if that were so, the Court would have had a strong reason to take them at their word. When a government uses rule of law talk, and expresses faith in the Court's wisdom and respect for its authority, it is using language that constitutes a tender of trust. It is a statement that this is a government that understands the importance of maintaining the judiciary's authority, and the dangers of impairing that authority. That is the point of using the sort of respectful language that appears throughout the Minister's of Health's press statements: it is a ritual, performed using the ritual phrases. The choice before the Court was what step to take next in the context of this ritual. Having taken a firm stand against the government's policy in its 4 April ruling and watched the general retreat soon thereafter, it could have taken the position that the government had broken these rules and could not be trusted, and issued a supervisory order (whose symbolic effect, we should recall, would have been all the greater for it being the Court's very first such order). Alternatively, it could send a signal that it was not going to act expansively merely because the government was politically embarrassed. It could accept the government's tender of trust, as recently reinforced by the two Ministers' confirmations of the government's intention to accept the Court's ruling – while recalling, perhaps with a meaningful glance, the broader rule of law ritual that they had built up: 'The government has always respected and executed orders of this Court' – and we are confident this time will be no different. This would speak to the sense that we saw the senior ANC leaders attaching to the first order against the government in

125 For an account of subsequent events, see Geffen, *Debunking Delusions*; see also Treatment Action Campaign, *Fighting for Our Lives: The History of the Treatment Action Campaign 1998–2010* (2010), available at www.tac.org.za/files/10yearbook/index.html.

126 The press statements are available from the Department of Health website's media resources, available at www.health.gov.za/ps.php#.

December 2001 by the court of first instance. Just as the *NNP* Court had a reason to play the trust game, and just as President Mandela had a reason to play it in saying that he welcomed the decision in *Executive Council* whether he did or not, the *TAC (2)* Court had a reason to take this rule of law talk at its word. The only way to build the institution of obedience to the law is to rely on it.

Of course, this strategy will break down if the Court places its faith and then finds that faith betrayed. The Department of Health had indeed given the Court some reason to mistrust it, and Justice Kriegler's statements in the hearing make it quite clear that the Court was aware of this. The minister's TV interview, furthermore, at least raised an area of concern, however interpreted. So why did the Court still express trust in the government? Fear of political backlash is one possibility.[127] But an important question mark is placed against this explanation by the fact that the Court's most proximate response to the Minister's interview was its interim order of 4 April – where, as we saw, the Court did not take an available way out and instead quickly affirmed the interim roll-out, sending a strong signal. There is also little reason to think that the government would really have defied a supervisory interdict, given its respectful public statements, the extent to which Cabinet was in full damage control mode (and also – in hindsight – the fact that the government has since accepted structural and supervisory interdicts in a number of other cases).

Instead, if these more intrusive interdicts are supposed to be used in the context of government recalcitrance, or where it seems the relevant authorities might need assistance in complying, *TAC (2)* may not have appeared to the Court to fit the bill very well. Instead of a recalcitrant government, Cabinet had waved a white flag. The roll-out was already well underway in a number of provinces, and indeed there was no

[127] Roux has revised his earlier understanding of *TAC (2)* in terms of the avoidance of shorter-term political conflict (see Roux, 'Pragmatism and Principle', p. 171). He now understands the Court to have been intervening in a shifting political context that got conducive enough in time – see note 111 of this chapter – but limiting that intervention with a pragmatic eye to the future. On its choice of remedy, he writes, the Court was 'evidently thinking of its longer-term relationship with the ANC and the need, even in this most pressing of cases, to engage the political branches as partners in the constitutional project.' – Roux, *Politics of Principle*, p. 303. This would mark a point of agreement with the broader argument presented here. Roux still, however, seems to understand this decision in strategic terms only. He views the socio-economic rights cases in general as compromises that do not adopt the best legal reading of the text, and explicitly agrees with a number of the standard criticisms I have discussed.

evidence at the time that the interim roll-out was not proceeding everywhere. The picture painted in *TAC* was of the medical mechanism revving desperately against the denialist foot on the brake, and so signs that the foot had finally lifted implied that the battle was won. The Treatment Action Campaign, too, seem to have thought that Mbeki's retreat signalled victory, one reason that it initially did not focus closely on monitoring *TAC (2)*'s order.[128] And finally, the presence of such an effective organization was surely crucial.[129] Just as the Court in *NNP* could place credible reliance on the Electoral Commission and the suspicious opposition parties to monitor election preparations in 1999, so the Court could reasonably rely on the very high quality temporary infrastructure offered by South Africa's most effective social movement. Critics sometimes raise, as evidence that a supervisory interdict was needed, the fact that the Treatment Action Campaign subsequently found it necessary to launch contempt proceedings in the province of Mpumalanga due to the failure of authorities there to begin the roll-out. (The province conceded before the matter got to court.) But while this confirms that the threat of non-compliance was not illusory, it shows equally that reliance on the Treatment Action Campaign for monitoring was not misplaced – and recall that doing so permitted the Court to make the additional trust-building gains already discussed. Again, a careful constitution-building balance is being struck.

Even if the argument for a more intrusive remedy was debatable at the time, however, doesn't the subsequent history suggest that, in hindsight, it would have been better if the Court had gone further? We know now that President Mbeki retained his denialist views well beyond 2002, and that Minister Tshabalala-Msimang continued to oppose ARVs and frustrate their roll-out. We know now that it would only be in September 2006, more than four years after *TAC (2)* was handed down, with Mbeki politically weakened and Tshabalala-Msimang in hospital, that activists would be able to speak of a 'sea change' in the government's policy on ARVs – and even then, only because of the stand taken by the Deputy Minister of Health, Nozizwe Madlala-Routledge, to exploit the absence of

[128] J. Berger, 'Litigating for Social Justice in Post-Apartheid South Africa: A Focus on Health and Education' in V. Gauri and D. M. Brinks (eds.), *Courting Social Justice: Judicial Enforcement of Social and Economic Rights in the Developing World* (Cambridge University Press, 2008), p. 80.

[129] See also e.g. Liebenberg, *Adjudicating Socio-economic Rights*, pp. 426–27.

her boss to act.[130] More somberly, we also know that the number of children born with HIV/AIDS *increased* substantially after *TAC (2)*, and that many thousands of children whose infection (and likely death within a few years) could have been prevented by Nevirapine still did not receive the drug after the Court's order. Many may thus be inclined to agree with Stu Woolman that 'part of the responsibility for this failure surely lies with the Court itself' and that things might have been different had it retained jurisdiction.[131]

However, the fact that lives are at stake is all the more reason to take a careful look at the arguments: it is too simple to move straight from tragic deaths to a claim about more expansive judicial action without considering what the effects of a supervisory order would have been and whether it would have improved the situation. The roll-out of Nevirapine would have faced enormous obstacles even if no-one senior in the government had been a denialist, because of enormous capacity problems in the healthcare system and because even if the stance of Mbeki and his faction surely exacerbated fatal suspicion of ARVs, it can hardly be said to have created what is a common reaction to 'Western medicine' in colonial and post-colonial settings.[132] A supervisory order would have been able to do little to change either of these things, since an order piggy-backing on government action is constrained by the same limits that the government action is. Furthermore, the hard reality is that (we now know) South Africa had a silenced but stubbornly, unrepentantly denialist President with diminished but nevertheless considerable influence in many parts of the government and society, and a rather less silenced unrepentantly denialist health minister. In these circumstances, the reality is that the South African ARV roll-out faced some tough years regardless of what the Court did. The argument, therefore, must be that supervisory jurisdiction might have brought to light problems that the Court could have helped to solve, or that it could have focused attention on problems which others could solve – in some way that would not already be done by the very effective temporary infrastructure offered by the Treatment Action Campaign and its multifaceted efforts. We will,

130 Gumede, *Thabo Mbeki*, pp. 212–13.

131 Woolman, *Selfless Constitution*, pp. 433–34; see also K. Roach and G. Budlender, 'Mandatory Relief and Supervisory Jurisdiction: When Is It Appropriate, Just and Equitable?' (2005) 122 *South African Law Journal* 325, esp. 333–34, 347–48.

132 J. Steinberg, *Three Letter Plague: A Young Man's Journey through a Great Epidemic* (Johannesburg: Jonathan Ball Publishers, 2008); J. Steinberg, *AIDS and AIDS Treatment in a Rural South African Setting* (Pretoria: Institute for Security Studies, 2008).

of course, never know for sure, but this is already probably quite a slim hypothetical benefit.

If the benefits are slim, what about the costs? If judicial action is the only possibility, and lives are at stake, then difficulties and drawbacks are usually outweighed. But if others are acting, then one is not weighing lives against institutional considerations, but competing institutional options for saving lives, and then no court can discount the possibility that its intervention might not be the best one and, worst still, might interfere with a better one if launched. The risks of structural interdicts in theory are familiar. Exerting judicial control over bureaucracies risks replacing bureaucratic authority with judicial authority. Orders from superior officials are replaced by, or become tangled up with, orders from courts and officials must spend time and effort appearing and reporting in court, in addition to their existing obligations. Such judicial intervention therefore risks confusion, duplication of effort, and the hampering of the primary mechanisms for giving effect to rights. Another potential cost is that a court which exercises jurisdiction on the basis that it must act until a problem is solved, rather than until an application can be said to have been heard and legally resolved, may find it hard to *stop* exercising jurisdiction.[133] As noted in discussing *Nokotyana*, a Court that is not to retreat feebly will need a basis on which to claim that a situation that was unconstitutional is now constitutional such that the case can be brought to a credible end, which can be difficult when the problem is stubborn or evolving. A monitoring exercise in *TAC (2)* that sought to ensure the roll-out was completed, or even that it was underway with no more than the inevitable practical problems, would have stretched on for a number of years in several provinces before the Court could have claimed enough success to terminate its jurisdiction credibly. This raises questions of legitimacy and institutional capacity, and to the extent that the missed opportunities for trust- and institution-building are not compensated for, such long exercises of jurisdiction can erode other institutions that exist to protect rights.

But these arguments are rather theoretical: do they have concrete stakes? The subsequent history of action on HIV/AIDS and ARVs, often taken to be a reason why the Court should have done more in *TAC (2)*, in fact offers quite a good illustration of the potential pitfalls to which these theoretical arguments should alert us. The Cabinet's concession

[133] See further Fowkes, 'Managerial Judge'.

statement of 17 April talked about a *general* ARV roll-out, across the spectrum of people with HIV and AIDS, not confined to preventing mother-to-child transmission as the roll-out at issue in *TAC (2)* was. If the Court had appointed itself supervisor of the Nevirapine roll-out, how should it have responded to this broader initiative? Should it have required all concerned to focus on Nevirapine, in accordance with the Court's incentive to get its own order enforced? Should it take into account that doing so might interfere with the broader roll-out and might have consequences for broader live-saving efforts, or not? A similar problem arises from the fact that a good deal of the post-*TAC (2)* obstructionism would take the form of rival advocacy, with Minister Tshabalala-Msimang casting public doubt on ARVs by promoting alternative treatments including quack remedies and not taking effective action against exploitative private actors doing the same. This would be the focus of much of the TAC's energy and anger in the years after *TAC (2)*. But is this behaviour contrary to an order to make Nevirapine available? Even if discouraging people from using ARVs by promoting other alleged treatments is contrary at least to the spirit of the *TAC (2)* order, that order certainly did not go as far as ordering the government to offer *nothing but* Nevirapine, or similar ARV medication. The Court would therefore have faced the choice between swallowing what was a very real threat to its order, or trying to expand the order into territory that would become harder and harder to substantiate and trench further and further into the ordinary rights of political leaders to speak on policy. It is at least somewhat significant here that although *TAC (2)* did not preclude a subsequent challenge if something further did go wrong, just as *NNP* did not, this challenge never came. An underacknowledged datum in evaluating ongoing judicial supervision in *TAC (2)* is that while the Treatment Action Campaign possessed the means to litigate again, it mostly chose not to, and certainly not on anything like the scale of the Nevirapine litigation.[134] Some of the country's most effective activists do not seem to have thought it strategically best to invoke the Court's power again. It is perfectly fair to reply that, had the Court said and done more in *TAC (2)*, it might have been easier to litigate HIV/AIDS issues again, and that might have altered the activists' calculations. But it is still significant that the Treatment Action Campaign and

[134] See Geffen, *Debunking Delusions*; see also Friedman and Mottiar, 'Rewarding Engagement?', 533 n. 138, 537, noting that the TAC considered litigation among their options if the promised roll-out did not materialize.

its legal team, who so astutely designed their case to be one in which the Court could act, do not seem to have thought that a similarly conducive case could be brought again on HIV/AIDS. This reflects, I suggest, the fact that countering the absurdities that arise from stubborn denialism at the top is a problem much more conducive to judicial action than the different problems that became the main focus in the years after 2002.

The point of these arguments is not to raise a long list of problems and doubts in order to show that supervisory interdicts can be troublesome. Problems and doubts are inevitable and so are not decisive if intervention is necessary. It is simply to note that it would be plainly irresponsible to take on such risks and costs unless there is a good reason to think they will be worth it – and having seen the troubles more expansive intervention after *TAC (2)* would likely have encountered, it becomes doubly important that the value such an intervention might have added is quite doubtful. The Court has to consider such questions in deciding when to put its authority on the line, and its critics must confront these questions too, but seldom do. As with *UDM (2)*, showing that more expansive action was possible and looking for signs that the Court will stand up to the government is not the same as proving that more expansive action is the best constitutional response to a particular set of facts.

The final point to be made about *TAC (2)* is that its epilogue again offers some reason to think that a judicial stance that makes space for other institutional action is not naïve or foolish, even in hindsight. Critics offer the now-familiar objection that *TAC (2)* said very little about the content of the s 27 right to health, as opposed to the details of the judicial role in this context. However, court-centrism should not prevent us from noting that a great deal of evolution in the meaning of s 27 has taken place, just not in the courts. The most important component of the meaning of the right to health here is in the government's HIV/AIDS plans, often drawn up with civil society involvement, including members of the Treatment Action Campaign.[135] These have been steadily ramping up what the public sector is expected to provide: from single-dose Nevirapine to pregnant mothers to prevent mother-to-child transmission, to ARVs for all HIV-positive persons with low CD4 counts, to a more effective dual-dosage regime for mothers, to medications like fluconazole for associated conditions, and so on. The extent of

[135] M. Heywood, 'South Africa's Treatment Action Campaign: Combining Law and Social Mobilization to Realize the Right to Health' (2009) 1 *Journal of Human Rights Practice* 14.

geographical coverage of the program has also been expanding all the time.[136] While the standard of care varies from province to province and is often significantly lower in rural areas, we are at or are close to the point where some aspects of this drug regime would constitute individually enforceable entitlements, should it come to that. It would now be very hard to justify the lack of availability of basic medication against mother-to-child transmission, and it would be almost as hard in the case of ARV medication for a patient with a low CD4 count. The issue of HIV/AIDS, in my terms, is becoming rapidly less *new*, with an expanding public status and infrastructure. Of course, any potential judicial orders about such entitlements would be subject to an array of qualifications about facilities and medical advice and substitute medications and so on, but shining through this is the fact that s 27 means a great deal more to an HIV-positive person than it did in 1998 when the Treatment Action Campaign was formed or in 2002 when *TAC (2)* was handed down. This tends to be overlooked because courts have not articulated this content in the form of an interpretation of rights. But public content is judicial content when necessary, as we have seen. What is being built is the content that constitutionally matters, partly because it can underwrite judicial intervention, but also because it means there is less need for it. And it is content being built within the institutions that must act upon it, a gap that more unilateral judicial interventions invariably have to struggle to close. In the long arc of the story of HIV/AIDS in South Africa, we have reached a point where the largest ARV program in the world is being run by the mechanisms primarily responsible for it. A very powerful party boss took a wildly unreasonable stance, and suffered political defeat partly because of it. These are no small feats of democracy, of federalism, of civil society action. The whole saga, so corrosive of Mbeki's image and so destructive to millions, is also a testament to the strength of South Africa's constitutional politics, turbulent as they

[136] See e.g. *National Strategic Plan on HIV, STIs and TB 2012–2016*, www.doh.gov.za/docs/stratdocs/2012/NSPfull.pdf, 14 (mother-to-child transmission target 2% at 6 weeks and 5% at 18 months), 48 (anti-retroviral treatment, 80% coverage target, with 70% of that figure 'alive and on treatment at the end of five years'), 49 (anti-retrovirals for all HIV-positive infants). See also e.g. E. Wouters, H. C. J. van Rensburg and H. Meulemans, 'The National Strategic Plan of South Africa: What Are the Prospects of Success after the Repeated Failures of Previous AIDS Policy?' (2010) 25 *Health Policy and Planning* 171, 172, noting that the previous 2007–2011 Plan was 'greeted with general acclaim, even by the government's most strident critics'.

inevitably will sometimes be.[137] Constitutions need to be built, and this is how it is done. That it took place in the context of a partly preventable pandemic will forever be a reason for everyone to ask if they could have done something differently. There will be the impulse to throw institutional arguments to the wind and want the Court to just do the boldest thing it can. That it is by no means clear that South Africa would be better off today if the Court had done so, however, is a sober reminder that moral logic in the real world is seldom that simple – and a heartening confirmation of how many other institutions and people are assisting with the work of constitution-building.

Mazibuko v. *City of Johannesburg*

The final case to be discussed in this chapter is the 2010 decision in *Mazibuko*, which many have viewed as a setback for socio-economic rights.[138] The Court confronted a policy that had been the subject of plausible, demonstrated constitutional concerns, and still decided to do nothing. To make matters worse, *Mazibuko* appears to articulate a generally restrained role for courts specifically in socio-economic rights cases. Criticism of the decision has been sharp and also, I think, sometimes sincerely perplexed about how the Court could have done what it did. As with *NNP*, however, I see the standard conclusion that *Mazibuko* is plainly flawed as revealing in the context of a judgment whose correctness is again much more debatable.

Mazibuko concerned the ongoing tale of attempts to creating a functioning water provision system in the context of a number of challenges.[139] These include poverty and need, especially in a rapidly

[137] A. Butler, 'The Negative and Positive Impacts of HIV/AIDS' (2006) 23 *Journal of Contemporary African Studies* 3, and R. Calland and C. Oxtoby, 'Machiavelli Meets the Constitution: Mbeki and the Law' in Glaser (ed.), *Mbeki and After*, p. 76, make similar observations.

[138] Although the extent of the setback is a matter of debate. See e.g. Liebenberg, *Adjudicating Socio-Economic Rights*, pp. 467, 469–70, 480; D. Roithmayr, 'Lessons from *Mazibuko*: Persistent Inequality and the Commons' (2010) 3 *Constitutional Court Review* 317, esp. 320–24; Wilson and Dugard, 'Taking Poverty Seriously'; M. Wesson 'Reasonableness in Retreat? The Judgment of the South African Constitutional Court in *Mazibuko v City of Johannesburg*' (2011) 11 *Human Rights Law Review* 390; M. Langford, R. Stacey and D. Chirwa, 'Water' in Woolman and Bishop (eds.) *Constitutional Law*, 56B-3; J. Sinclair 'Poverty: Giving Meaning to the Right to Social Assistance' (2012) *Stellenbosch Law Review* 191, 209, 213; Ray, 'Evictions, Aspirations and Avoidance', 173, 182, 193; Wilson and Dugard, 'First and Second Waves', pp. 54–58.

[139] Much of this background is set out in *Mazibuko*, paras. 2–3, 7, 10–18.

expanding urban area such as Johannesburg in which thousands of people do not even have access to the City's most basic water provision level of a tap within 200 m of their dwelling; the persistent culture of non-payment for services, mostly left undisturbed during the transition, that can be traced to the anti-apartheid movement's very successful efforts in the 1980s to make townships ungovernable; the decay of poor quality or simply ageing apartheid-era township infrastructure; and South Africa's general need for careful water management. The neighbourhoods in question in *Mazibuko* accounted for between a third and a quarter of the water supplied by the City (partly due to leakage), and 1% of its revenue, a situation everyone including the applicants accepted was unsustainable. In response to this complex situation, the City of Johannesburg was trying out pilot programs, attempting to respond to problems and conducting extensive engagement. In the neighbourhoods in question, which had a level of water provision well above the communal tap level, it had (in the face of some community protest, stifled after an interdict was obtained against the organizers) replaced a deemed consumption policy with prepaid meters.[140] Under the deemed consumption policy, consumers paid a flat rate no matter how much water they used. With prepaid meters, consumers received an initial free allocation of water and also paid a lower rate for water thereafter than users with credit meters, but were (unlike credit meter users) subject to immediate cut-off if they did not pay for water above their initial allocation. In response to the legal challenge, the City had come to Court in apparent good faith and with extensive disclosure of its efforts. The judges were impressed by what they saw as a government actor engaging seriously with a difficult problem.[141] They were thus reassured that the issue could be left in the City's hands and declined to order any intervention.

Though *Mazibuko* was a complex case and the applicants raised many different challenges, at the outset one can readily see the basic reason the Court had for thinking it did not need to act. *Mazibuko* displays the now-familiar features of a decision not to intervene. In order to reach that decision, the Court did not need to engage extensively with what the right

[140] On the protest action, see J. Dugard, 'Civic Action and Legal Mobilisation: The Phiri Water Meters Case' in J. Handmaker and R. Berkhout (eds.) *Mobilising Social Justice in South Africa: Perspectives from Researchers and Practitioners* (The Hague: ISS and Hivos, 2010), pp. 88–89.

[141] See also Ray, 'Evictions, Aspirations and Avoidance', 187.

to water concretely requires, beyond the reasonableness test – a statement that, once again, may sound outrageous until we see it as an answer to the question of whether the Court needs to start intervening, by articulating standards or otherwise. And again, the decision can give the impression of briskly ticking off the arguments raised by the applicants, compounding its error in the eyes of those seeking more content, but in a way that makes sense once we see this follows from a decision not to intervene.[142]

However, *Mazibuko* is a more intricate (and instructive) instance of a decision not to intervene, for several reasons. We can start with the fact that the City's policy, as it stood at the time when the litigation was launched in the court of first instance, may well have been unconstitutional. The Constitutional Court itself hints at this, and both the previous courts that heard the case had concluded that the City's policy was unconstitutional.[143] The most important reason for thinking this was that the free allocation, in terms of the government's Free Basic Water Policy, was 6 kiloliters per month per stand, irrespective of the number of people living on the stand.[144] In relation to the average City household, this amounted to a per person allocation exceeding even the applicants' definition of a sufficient free water allowance. But in relation to more densely populated stands such as those common in the areas in *Mazibuko*, it often fell short, meaning larger households might be without even such a limited water supply for half of every month.[145] The City had recognized this problem nearly three years before the Court's hearing, but five months after the litigation began, and made adjustments its policies (in ways discussed shortly). The City sought to lead new evidence of these adjustments. New evidence is seldom received in the Constitutional Court, but *Mazibuko* held that it would be appropriate to hear evidence concerning government attempts to respond to ongoing problems, including the problems that were targeted by the litigation itself.

[142] Liebenberg, *Adjudicating Socio-economic Rights*, pp. 478, 480 describes the decision as 'a-contextual', 'formalist', 'deferential' and 'normatively thin'; see also L. A. Williams, 'The Role of Courts in the Quantitative-Implementation of Social and Economic Rights: A Comparative Study' (2010) 3 *Constitutional Court Review* 141, 189, referring to the judgment's 'terse, conclusory language' and 'lower and more cursory . . . level of attention to the evidence.'

[143] *Mazibuko*, para. 95; *Mazibuko* v. *City of Johannesburg* [2008] All SA 471 (W); *City of Johannesburg* v. *Mazibuko* 2009 (3) SA 592 (SCA).

[144] For further details of the policy, see Langford et al., 'Water', 56B-29; as the authors there note, this is an example of the situation noted earlier in which the government has effectively adopted a minimum core approach to the right to water.

[145] *Mazibuko*, paras. 86–88.

As it happened, it also held that enough of this development had occurred by the close of pleadings in the court of first instance that it did not actually need to admit new evidence on appeal in order to uphold the government's efforts.[146] But this was simply a technical coincidence. If the evidence of the policy evolution had come a little later one can be confident that the Court would have made the exception it took the trouble to propose and describe. This may seem unfair: if the applicants had shown unconstitutionality on the case they had brought, are they not entitled to a finding to that effect? If one understands the Court's task to be to apply the right to water to the facts established by the applicant and announce the legal result of that enquiry, it may seem obvious that they are. But the *Mazibuko* Court, in line with the pattern we have seen elsewhere, did not see its task that narrowly. It felt free to weigh the costs and benefits of announcing an interpretation of the right. The litigant's wishes are subject to the general duty to do what best upholds the text, even when the litigant has a good claim to have raised a constitutionally valid objection.[147]

Mazibuko's controversial status as a decision not to intervene goes further, however, because the Court was not just declining to make a declaration of invalidity that had been superseded by a policy evolution. It also declined to make one in respect of at least three legal concerns which, on the version of the facts the decision itself set out, were still very much alive notwithstanding that evolution. The first of these requires some background. The measures the City had introduced five months after the litigation began, in terms of its indigency policy, offered 4 more free kiloliters of water per month per stand on demonstration of indigence.[148] But that supply provided even the government's definition of a basic water supply – 25 liters per person per day – only for stands occupied by 13 or fewer people, and some of the stands in the *Mazibuko* areas were more densely populated than this. That policy was followed on 1 July 2009, two months before the Constitutional Court heard *Mazibuko*, by the Expanded Social Package, which provides for another 5 free kiloliters a month to indigent persons.[149] That sufficed to provide

146 *Ibid.*, paras. 36–41.

147 See generally Fowkes '*Maphango*'. Thus *Grootboom*, having decided to articulate content, made an order 'as of the date of the *launch* of this application' (*Ibid.*, para. 69, my emphasis), notwithstanding the subsequent local policy evolution during the case, while *Mazibuko*, having reached the opposite view on intervention, did not.

148 *Mazibuko*, para. 81.

149 The package is also known as Siyasizana ("we help each other"); see Statement by the Executive Mayor of Johannesburg, Clr. Amos Masondo, at the media briefing on the

the government's basic supply even to very densely populated stands, and the applicant's desired amount (double that) to most of them. But what is important is that, while the Court was aware of both evolutions, the judgment itself only takes note of the first of them – yet it is only the second that gives solid reason to think larger households will not face perennial water cut-offs that deprive them of even the most basic definition of an adequate water supply for portions of each month.[150] The fact that the Court took the first evolution as sufficient means it was declining to intervene in a situation in which the City had introduced a scheme, which deliberately limited the access to water, of a non-trivial number of households, to a level below the government's own definition of the basic amount of water it should be seeking to supply.

How can non-intervention be justified in these circumstances? We have in fact seen such decisions before. Cases like *NNP* and *UDM (2)* were decisions not to deploy available constitutional arguments in situations where the Court felt able to leave the primary mechanisms to deal with a situation, but where constitutional concerns were certainly present and it was far from certain things would turn out well. *Mazibuko*'s decision to uphold the policy in light of evidence of only the first 4-kiloliter increase is not, in other words, a finding that the policy had evolved to the point where it was constitutional, but a finding that the City's evolving policy effort sufficed to meet the constitutional threshold.[151] That view certainly gains credence from the fact that the City continued to evolve its policy, resulting in the second increase, but this detail is not, in principle, required for the finding that the City's action were constitutional and that a court charged with making the Constitution work should not intervene.[152]

City of Johannesburg Expanded Social Package Programme, available at www.joburg.org.za/index.php?option=com_content&task=view&id=4012&Itemid=114; see also City of Johannesburg 'Social Package', available at www.joburg.org.za/index .php?option=com_content&task=view&id=3432&Itemid=168 and further materials there provided.

150 The evolution of the government's policy was set out extensively in the papers; for a convenient summary, see First and Second Respondent's Heads of Argument, paras. 33–37, available in the *Mazibuko* case file at www.constitutionalcourt.org.za.

151 Although I cannot do full justice to them here, this is the most important answer to the careful questions Lucy Williams raises about the Court's approach to analyzing details of the City's policy – see Williams, 'Role of Courts', 175–81, 189–97 – namely, that it is a decision not to start interrogating the policy. See also the discussion of reframing of cases by the Court in the next chapter.

152 The applicants in *Mazibuko* were aware of the importance of exhausting political remedies before litigating. However, they were focused on prepaid water meters, and it was much more apparent that political engagement on this issue was exhausted than was

This sort of non-intervention argument is, however, inapplicable to the other two legal objections that remained alive. An important problem with prepaid water meters is that they permit disconnection of an essential service without notice, something that the Water Services Act appears to be preclude.[153] Even if a temporary monthly interruption is not a 'termination' of service, as *Mazibuko* rules, it does seem like a 'limitation', and the Act requires notice in both situations. Furthermore, this concern also raises an important equality argument, since consumers in richer, formerly white suburbs with credit meters *do* enjoy this notice period. Neither problem would evolve away, at least any time soon. To understand the Court's treatment of *these* issues, we need to understand not the evolution of the City's policies but their national roots. In the early 2000s, the national government moved towards reducing its subsidies to local municipalities and thus required them to raise more of their own revenue (while also introducing the Free Basic Water policy which provided the basic 6-kiloliter allocation).[154] This shapes the whole situation in *Mazibuko*: the decision to introduce prepaid water meters, the reason the City was more worried about water loss in a poor area for which it was not being paid than about lavish water use in rich areas for which it was being quite handsomely paid under a progressive pricing system, the reason why it was seeking to create a culture of payment for services, and the reason it was using means tests and giving additional free water only to those who could not afford to pay for it.

This background has important implications for what the relief sought in *Mazibuko* was actually asking the Court to do. Water policy is an area of significant newness, for the Court and government alike. The Court was not merely being asked to rule on several large, open-ended issues in this context – about the constitutionality of means tests, prepaid water meters and requiring payment for basic services – but was being asked to do this in a context where the desired rulings flew in the face of years of

true for possible improvements to the water policy of which the meters formed part. Hence the terms of the debate between Dugard and Langford, 'Art or Science', 50 ('activists and residents only resorted litigation after resisting *the roll-out of PPMs* in every possible political forum') and Budlender et al., *Public Interest Litigation*, p. 111 n. 208 ('political engagement in relation to [the City's] *indigence measures regarding water* had not occurred at all') (both my emphasis).

153 Water Services Act 108 of 1997, s 4(3); see Liebenberg, *Adjudicating Socio-Economic Rights*, pp. 473–74, 478–79; Wesson, 'Reasonableness in Retreat?', 12–13; Langford et al., 'Water', 56B-51 – 56B-53; Wilson and Dugard, 'First and Second Waves', pp. 56–57.

154 See Dugard, 'Urban Basic Services', p. 276 and further sources there cited.

the government's efforts to confront these issues and build an infrastructure. Means tests are embedded in many of the government's anti-poverty programs. More than 80 000 prepaid water meters had been installed when the Constitutional Court heard *Mazibuko*.[155] And given the national government's stance and its reductions of subsidies to local authorities, overturning the City's payment-orientated approach to basic services might have had very significant implications for its service delivery plans. Given what we have seen of the Court's reaction to newness, that it unanimously declined to rule that prepaid water meters or means tests are unconstitutional is no surprise, and we will not feel the need to reach for any specifically socio-economic reason to explain why.

Arguments about prepaid water meters look very different when considered in this context as opposed to when considered in the abstract, and the same goes for the otherwise powerful-looking legal objections that surround them. Unless one is willing to rule that the government cannot use prepaid water meters, it is hard as a practical matter to rule that they require the government to give notice and opportunity for representations before each automatic cut-off, whether on the basis of the Water Services Act or of the inequality relative to credit meter users. In that situation the force of the argument can reverse direction, and become a positive reason *not* to accept that prepaid meters entail notice requirements, due to the impracticable consequences. This is a familiar-looking administrative law rationale, although it is undoubtedly concerning that the important problem of notice is sidelined in this way.[156] But we would be wrong to conclude from this that *Mazibuko* is indifferent to these arguments (a suggestion which is, on reflection, quite unlikely, especially considering the administrative law reputation of the author, O'Regan J). Rather, the situation is one where no available option is without its constitution-building defects. For instance, it is very possibly true that the Water Services Act, which preceded the national government's shift in approaches to subsidy and revenue in local service delivery, simply was not drafted with prepaid meters in mind and is therefore unsurprisingly awkward to reconcile with them.[157] But that point is not

[155] See also Budlender et al., *Public Interest Litigation*, p. 65.

[156] For criticism, including reference to English cases that upheld similar objections to prepaid meters, see Langford et al., 'Water', 56B-20–56B-21, 56B-51–56B-54; Wesson, 'Reasonableness in Retreat?', 6; see also *Mazibuko* (SCA), para. 55. On the existing practice of disconnections, see Dugard, 'Urban Basic Services', p. 282 n. 25.

[157] The Act does not mention prepaid meters. On the interpretation of s 4(3) in light of changes in national policy, see Langford et al., 'Water', 56B-47–56B-51.

decisive in a context where reading the Act to apply to prepaid water meters has the awkward implication of making 80 000 existing meters hard to practically use.

In this situation, the matter becomes a question of striking the best balance one can. That is not to say that the Court picked the only available balance. In its earlier judgment in the case, the Supreme Court of Appeal had declared prepaid water meters unconstitutional but suspended the order, giving the City time to amend its by-laws (thus likely giving it time to try and establish a firmer legal footing for prepaid meters, though burdening their use with the finding that the meters' automatic cut-offs required greater notice of some kind).[158] But note that, given the escalation in the City's allocation of free water, the most worrying feature of prepaid meters – that the more densely populated stands were regularly deprived of water mid-month without the administrative protections afforded richer consumers – is substantially alleviated. The Court's decision in this context to strike the balance by upholding the use of water meters might be arguable but is hardly indefensible.

These arguments are not intended to deny that the situation in *Mazibuko* was troubling, but only to focus the enquiry not on the fact of the troubling situation but on the options the Court had in responding to it. If so, we can see succinctly the reason for the failure of the litigation in *Mazibuko*. Judicial action will make sense if there is some way in which the Court can contribute to realizing rights and alleviating hardship that improves upon what is happening or would otherwise happen. But where the *Mazibuko* litigation proposed the Court make modest interventions, such as raising water quotas somewhat to cover more densely populated stands, the City was doing this already. Conversely, insofar as the litigation asked the Court to do things that would not otherwise happen, like invalidating prepaid water meters, it asked the Court to confront very substantial newness, unsupported, and in the face of considerable contrary state efforts.[159] This framing of the case is therefore important in explaining the result, and we shall see in the next chapter that some of the controversial equality cases have suffered from a similar problem.

[158] *Mazibuko* (SCA), paras. 55–60; Budlender et al., *Public Interest Litigation*, p. 65.

[159] *Mazibuko*, therefore, is not as serious a bar to future water rights challenges as it may appear, provided they avoid these problems. See also Budlender et al., *Public Interest Litigation*, pp. 64–65. For some promising possibilities for future challenges, see Langford et al., 'Water', 56B-59–56B-61.

This perspective can also help us to see that *Mazibuko* is not a retreat from *Grootboom* and *TAC (2)*, which presented more conducive opportunities for intervention. The view that it *is* a retreat follows only from perspectives that make *Mazibuko* look more straightforward than it was by focusing simply on the fact of the hardship and not on the question of how and whether to intervene. Indeed, if *Grootboom* is like *Doctors for Life*, *Mazibuko* is rather like *Merafong*, and not just in being the scion of a famous case from which it is seen as a backward step but which is heavily just to be explained on the facts. *Mazibuko* is also like *Merafong* in that those who focus only on the concrete issue at stake – water and cut-offs, richly democratic participation – neglect the institutional arguments central both to these cases and their famous forbears. And in both cases, in hindsight, the litigation ran into trouble by targeting a set of local officials who had acted imperfectly but apparently quite sincerely and in good faith, where the real source of the problem was the broader national framework in terms of which the local officials were operating: the national government's stance on increasing local revenue for services in *Mazibuko*, and the NCOP's legislative timetable in *Merafong*. *Grootboom* and *TAC (2)* demonstrated hardship, but they *turned* on revealing fixable problems with national policies. They showed the Court how and where it, as one institution among many, could usefully intervene, and that is what the Court felt it lacked in *Mazibuko*.

An important objection to this reading of *Mazibuko* arises because of what the decision itself says about socio-economic rights litigation. As in *PE Municipality*, the *Mazibuko* Court chose to say quite a lot about its role in cases like the one before it, and the judgment ends with a section headed 'Litigating social and economic rights'. The Court sought here to respond to the applicant's frustrated contention, in line with the scholarly position seen throughout this chapter, that if the Court is not willing to articulate the concrete content of socio-economic rights and remains deferent to government programs then 'litigation in respect of positive obligations imposed by social and economic rights would be futile'.[160] The Court's response is that *Mazibuko*, which yielded extensive disclosure and apparently policy evolution from the City, illustrates how 'litigation concerning social and economic rights can exact a detailed accounting from the government' and 'impact beneficially on the policy-making process'.[161] For critics, this limited and mainly procedural

[160] *Mazibuko*, para. 159. [161] *Ibid.*, para. 163.

vision of litigation in this context shows the Court is still failing to take socio-economic rights seriously.

There are three things to say about the Court's argument and these conclusions about it. First, it is possible that the main reason the Court replies in these specifically socio-economic terms is that the applicants, understanding themselves to be battling socio-economic rights scepticism, cast *their* arguments in those terms. If so, this would be an example of how the focus on socio-economic rights scepticism can create its own target, as noted earlier. Second, however, it may well be that the Court *does* think of socio-economic rights as a separate category of rights with special challenges, as indeed is the standard view among its critics and in discussions of these rights in general. In that case, I think the Court is as incorrect as its critics to depart from this assumption.[162] But in keeping with my general argument, it is then very important to recognize that whatever the labels, what the Court actually did in *Mazibuko* is hardly unique to its socio-economic rights cases. We have seen that its approach is consistent with a much more general pattern, and the specific logic of what *Mazibuko* said in socio-economic terms also finds obvious application outside that context. This is particularly obvious in relation to the evidentiary exception the Court mentioned. It articulated this in specifically socio-economic terms, but the phenomenon of an ongoing, evolving government policy response is hardly unique to that context. The story of preparations for the 1999 elections, for example, is a case study in evolving government responses to an obligation. It is easy to imagine an *NNP*-like case in which evidence of that evolution could only be produced on appeal, and it is easy to see why the Court would view this evidence as crucial and be willing to admit it, just as *Mazibuko* was.

The third and final point is that, however else we read this section of the *Mazibuko* judgment, it cannot be correct to read it as setting hard limits on the judicial role. If the Court envisions a model in which the

[162] O'Regan J's position is suggestive here: she authored *Mazibuko* and joined, inter alia, *Soobramoney*, *Grootboom*, *TAC (2)* and *Nokotyana*, but was also a lone dissenter in favour of bolder judicial action in both democratic contexts (*NNP*, *DP*, *Masondo*) and equality ones (*Fourie (2)*, and see also cases discussed in the next chapter). She also framed several points in *Mazibuko* in specifically socio-economic terms. This should, however, be read in light of *Rail Commuters* on the state's duty to provide security on trains, which she also authored and which argues in terms of positive obligations rather than socio-economic rights, and possibly also in light of the fact that textually socio-economic rights are qualified in ways that the relevant text in the democracy and equality cases is not. See also the discussion of *Prince* in the next chapter.

government comes forward and discloses the plan that it is implementing, what happens if the government has no plan, or is not implementing it, or makes an inadequate disclosure? It would be highly uncharitable to read *Mazibuko* to mean that the Court in any of these contexts would do no more than call on the state to disclose its plan, and in fact the judgment explicitly leaves open further possibilities in such scenarios.[163] The *Certification* judgment's statement that the Court could 'at least' enforce the negative aspects of socio-economic rights hardly precluded the more expansive things the Court has indeed gone on to do.[164] Similarly, *Mazibuko*'s talk about the meaningfulness of socio-economic rights litigation, even in the context of serious government activity to realize socio-economic interests, is setting a floor, not a ceiling. This is why the judgment uses conditional language: '*ordinarily* it is institutionally inappropriate' for a court to defer on these issues because the political branches are '*best* placed' and because it is '*desirable* as a matter of democratic accountability' (all emphasis added).[165] This is talk of optimization and preferable defaults, not about things the Court will never do even when the primary mechanisms go wrong.[166] In this, *Mazibuko*'s language actually makes important concessions towards a greater role for itself compared to the Court's statements in *TAC (2)*, which are facially more restrictive:

> courts are ill-suited to adjudicate upon issues where court orders could have multiple social and economic consequences for the community. The Constitution contemplates rather a restrained and focused role for the courts, namely, to require the state to take measures to meets its constitutional obligations and to subject the reasonableness of these measures to evaluation.[167]

[163] See also *Mazibuko*, para. 71, noting that, once disclosed, 'if the process followed by the government is flawed or the information gathered is obviously inadequate or incomplete, appropriate relief may be sought'.

[164] *First Certification*, para. 78.

[165] *Mazibuko*, para. 60.

[166] Wilson and Dugard, 'Taking Poverty Seriously', 664, argue that the Court 'suggested that it is precluded from' developing 'a substantive account of the positive obligations socio-economic rights place on the state' as a result of 'the particular formulation of the separation of powers doctrine it has adopted', but it is the qualified text of para. 60 that the cite for this proposition. See also Wilson and Dugard, 'First and Second Waves', pp. 57–59, and Liebenberg, *Adjudicating Socio-economic Rights*, pp. 466–80, for a similar reading to theirs.

[167] *TAC (2)*, para. 38.

Such language, in *TAC (2)*, needs to be read in light of its diplomatic function in the context of that case, and also in light of my remarks at the beginning of this chapter about the possibly misleading terms of socio-economic debates. But it is nevertheless significant that the Court's statement eight years later in *Mazibuko* is in fact more open – and open along the lines I have suggested in this chapter. What *Mazibuko* is in fact embracing is one possible way out of the problem we saw in *Nokotyana*. If it is often difficult for judges to know when and where judicial intervention would be useful absent a good deal of information about the government's policies, and if it is often difficult for applicants to assemble all that information themselves, a model of litigation that encourages the government to come to court and make extensive disclosure of its efforts will not always achieve this and will not always suffice even if it does but might nevertheless regularly be a very useful thing.

Mazibuko will remain a valid subject of argument, because while it presented a much less conducive opportunity for judicial intervention than is usually acknowledged, the question of what the Court should do in less conducive cases is and will remain a difficult and vital area of debate – especially in cases where the government is doing less than was the case in *Mazibuko*, and when the arguments for deferring to that effort are accordingly weaker. I will say something about this in the next chapter. But here, at the end of a long argument, we should pause to reflect on the unrecognized successes of the approach the Court chose in *Mazibuko*.

As argued, the fact that intervention would have to confront newness, with the difficulties and risks that involves, is relevant but never decisive if judicial intervention is needed to protect rights and uphold the Constitution. But, by the same token, it would be foolish to take on these costs unless one needs to. It is with this in mind that we should read the comments made a year after *Mazibuko* by Malcolm Langford and Jackie Dugard (involved in the litigation). They note that under the expanded free water allowances noted earlier, most households in the areas at issue in *Mazibuko* now receive 50 liters per person per day, as the litigation sought. They also note that the City had softened its stance on prepaid meters in several ways. They conclude that 'in effect, this means that the applicants and community have received the relief they litigated over, but through legal mobilization rather than the judicial process.'[168] This sees

[168] Dugard and Langford, 'Art or Science', 58. Dugard, 'Urban Basic Services', p. 301, comments to similar effect: 'despite the judicial defeat, there have been some

success as having been achieved *despite* the Court's attitude, as a result of the broader activity surrounding the case and by the fact of the litigation having been brought. It does not acknowledge that it was precisely this sort of incrementally positive action by the City and other actors that *Mazibuko* left space for, nor that these effects of the legal mobilization are just what *Mazibuko* said such litigation could achieve: to 'exact a detailed accounting from government and, in doing so, impact beneficially on the policy-making process', and, by 'shining a bright, cold light on the policy that undoubtedly revealed flaws', to prompt its revision.[169] According to one City official, 'the mere existence of the Mazibuko litigation gave progressive bureaucrats in the City a lever with which to effect policy changes', and the 'threat of an adverse order . . . made the expansion of the indigent persons and social benefits programmes politically possible'.[170] At the same time, the Court had sent a signal that it would trust sincere, responsive efforts from the City, and that the City could trust *it* not to interfere merely because a policy needed adjustment, incentivizing the City and other state actors to make usefully extensive disclosure in future cases.

Amidst all the criticism and the calls for more boldness, therefore, it is not recognized that *Mazibuko* may well have struck the best constitution-building balance available. It also not recognized that, as in *Merafong*, the mechanism to which the Court deferred ended up responding substantially to the litigants' concerns (though not entirely: the use of prepaid water meters themselves continues, though the City seems to have decided to turn a blind eye when users bypass them).[171] *Mazibuko* is no backward step in the Court's socio-economic rights jurisprudence, and it is no retreat from *TAC* and *Grootboom*. Indeed, as an effort to make the Constitution work that is meaningfully underwritten by government efforts; as a decision which, at least on the substantive matters

unanticipated outcomes of the case that confirm the analyses of legal mobilization as being about more than simply the judicial outcome'; see also pp. 294–97, 305.

169 *Mazibuko*, para. 167.

170 Budlender et al., *Public Interest Litigation*, p. 66; see also T. Coggin and M. Pieterse, 'Rights and the City: An Exploration of the Interaction between Socio-economic Rights and the City' (2012) 23 *Urban Forum* 257, 270. On the way litigation can strengthen the internal position of progressive officials, see e.g. Rosenberg, *Hollow Hope* (whom Budlender et al. cite); Epp, *Making Rights Real*. Thus socio-economic rights adjudication can have significant impacts on government policy even if the Court's approach is not boldly substantive, contrary to the argument on rights as 'policy-structuring devices' in Brand, 'Proceduralisation', pp. 53–54.

171 Dugard and Langford, 'Art or Science', 58; Dugard, 'Urban Basic Services', pp. 301–02.

where it counts, reflects a general institutional pragmatism rather than scepticism about socio-economic rights; and as an exercise of institutionally nuanced judgment which goes largely un-appreciated by scholars intent on rebutting socio-economic rights scepticism and focused on how the system should work instead of how it does, *Mazibuko* is as good a representative as any of a body of socio-economic rights cases that undoubtedly represents a work in progress but deserves far more critical appreciation than it gets.

9

Equality, Eviction and Engagement

In the context of rights more traditional than socio-economic rights, we tend to be highly suspicious of newness as a reason to enforce rights differently or to some lesser degree. The newness of civil-political rights claims often relates to the public status of the idea concerned, and so the idea of being cautious in the face of it looks uncomfortably like the idea of giving in to majority prejudice. We are therefore often inclined to be more suspicious of judicial concessions to newness in this context than in the context of socio-economic rights, where newness is commonly understood in terms of practical resource constraints. This is what produces the sharply negative reaction to the equality cases I will consider in the first half of this chapter. *NNP* and *UDM (2)* are certainly part of the standard anti-canon, but the decisions we will consider here, such as *Volks* v. *Robinson* on domestic partnerships and *S* v. *Jordan* on sex work, are probably the ones scholars find hardest to stomach. Once again, observers see objectionable and puzzling inconsistencies when the Court's restrained, curt unhelpfulness in these cases is compared to the (standard understandings of the) LGBTI equality cases or *Hoffman* or *Doctors for Life* – or, of course, to the first *Makwanyane* story, which sees its greatest betrayal in this context.[1]

Recognizing that the concerns of newness apply in similar ways across all types of rights, as argued in the previous chapter, helps us to recalibrate our judgments. Any rights claim can display newness, and it presents an obstacle to the judicial enforcement of the claim whenever it arises. We are more alive to this in the context of socio-economic rights claims, but we already accept it to some degree in the context of more traditional civil-political rights: we recognize that an equality claim

[1] See e.g. D. Meyerson, 'Does the Constitutional Court of South Africa Take Rights Seriously? The Case of *S v Jordan*' (2004) *Acta Juridica* 138, 154: 'If one compares [*Jordan*'s approach to *Makwanyane*'s] it is difficult to avoid the impression that the Bill of Rights is being applied selectively.'

brought by a black person facing racial discrimination is likely to be a much more straightforward prospect for judicial enforcement in South Africa than an equality claim brought, for example, on behalf of a non-human animal. Even those who would wish to see the courts vindicate both sorts of claim recognize that even a pro-animal rights judge would today likely have to treat the non-human animal claim differently.[2] In turn, the appreciation we have gained of the support the Court has enjoyed in its bolder decisions can help us understand what is going on in these more restrained ones. Whereas existing critics fall back on attitudinal explanations to explain the inconsistencies they perceive, we will now be able to see that these are cases where the Court simply enjoyed less support in confronting newness. Part of this lack of support, in turn, is because these claims were sometimes litigated without sensitivity to this point, as if they were any other equality claim. The parties bringing them thus did not always do enough to assist the Court to act in the face of the newness-related challenges they presented, especially when compared to socio-economic rights litigation where these challenges, though incorrectly understood as the product of that special rights context, are nevertheless for that reason often taken much more seriously.

This offers an explanation. Whether it also constitutes a justification depends on how much we think judges actually can do in response to newness when support from other actors is limited. What happens in a case like *Hoffman* when the foundations in legislation and policy and civil society work that the Court could build on there are absent? As noted in previous chapters, the argument for judicial intervention gets stronger when other actors cannot be relied upon because the problems and risks of unilateral judicial action often count for less when the alternative is no action at all. By the same token, the argument for judicial creativity to respond proactively and try and manage those problems and risks is also strengthened. The equality cases in this chapter sometimes show the Court being slow to be creative when the need has arisen, and this represents *the* key respect in which its own understanding of its institutional role is a work in progress. That said, the Court has shown this sort of creativity in other contexts: its emerging engagement remedy, originally developed in the eviction context, is the foremost example to date. Recognizing that this creativity is a response to newness, and that

[2] See Bilchitz, 'Recognition of Animal Rights?', discussed in Chapter 2.

this newness arises across types of rights, will help us to see in the second half of this chapter how these developments in the socio-economic context might be instructively cross-applied to equality rights and allow the Court to improve its handling of such cases.

The Promise of Legislative Action: *Masiya* and *Volks* v. *Robinson*

Masiya v. *Director of Public Prosecutions, Pretoria* ('*Masiya*') offers a helpful way into the more controversial equality cases. It is seen as an exercise in pedanticism that is indicative of a more general stance. *Masiya* concerned the definition of rape.[3] A female had been anally penetrated without consent, but the common law definition of rape existing at the time was confined to non-consensual vaginal penetration. The Court duly extended the definition of rape to include non-consensual anal penetration of a female. But a majority declined to decide whether rape should also include non-consensual anal penetration of a male. It did what was necessary to decide the case, while declining to redefine rape as a gender-neutral crime.[4] *Masiya* is attacked because of the self-perception of the Court's role that it is thought to represent. The concern is now no longer with socio-economic rights scepticism; here, the blame is placed on the Court's minimalist understanding of its powers to develop the common law in line with the Constitution. Critics see it interpreting this power in a modest, incremental way that leaves larger changes to the legislature.[5] They prefer the approach of the *Masiya* minority, which would have ruled that non-consensual anal penetration counts as rape regardless of the sex of the victim.

Masiya follows the now-familiar trend of the Court choosing not to act where it demonstrably possesses the ability to do so. As in other non-intervention decisions, it would be a mistake to treat the decision as evidence that the Court does not think it could intervene in this sort of case, if necessary. Indeed, *Masiya* hints strongly that it would do so if a case were to reach it whose facts required the question to be settled.[6]

[3] *Masiya* v. *Director of Public Prosecutions (Pretoria)* 2007 (5) SA 30 (CC).

[4] *Ibid.*, paras. 30, 46, 61.

[5] See e.g. H. Botha, 'Equality, Plurality and Structural Power' (2009) 25 *South African Journal on Human Rights* 1, 30–31: 'The majority [in *Masiya*] is happy to affirm the difference between male and female survivors; the minority, by contrast, is looking to transform it'; Woolman, 'Amazing Vanishing Bill of Rights', 766–72.

[6] *Masiya*, e.g. para. 46.

This, too, infuriates critics – why not just decide the point now, then, instead of waiting for another costly litigation? They see this simply as pedantic minimalism, deciding only what is very strictly necessary. But the fact that the Court is regularly quite maximalist, as we have seen throughout, should make us suspicious of any diagnosis of reflex minimalism, of restraint for restraint's sake. Instead, as in several of the LGBTI equality cases, the *Masiya* Court faces both a question it must answer to resolve the case, the answer to which is also more or less constitutionally inevitable (like the same-sex couple exclusion issue in the LGBTI equality cases), and a question it does not have to answer to resolve the case, the answer to which is rather less constitutionally inevitable (there, like the opposite-sex couple issues and the question of which same-sex relationships qualify for inclusion in legal regimes for married couples). As a matter of constitutional principle, it *is* less obvious that rape should be a gender-neutral crime than that the rape of a female should not depend on where she is penetrated, especially given South Africa's extremely high levels of gender-based violence.[7]

Critics will reply, reasonably, that the Court has broader law reform responsibilities, and to that end should have confronted the broader gendered issue as well. It is thus significant that the issue was also the subject of an ongoing statutory process, which had proposed a gender-neutral definition of rape. As in *Satchwell*, the *Masiya* dissenters consider it of limited relevance, in making the argument for a gender-neutral definition of rape, that an ongoing legislative process seems to be coming to the same conclusion.[8] The majority similarly does not see the presence of the legislative process as a reason why it should not deal with the claim before it and extend the definition of rape to include anal penetration of a female. But on the broader question of making rape gender-neutral, the legislative process encouraged the majority to think that it could have the constitution-building first prize of the elected legislature speaking on the issue. That is not, as before, an argument that the Court should not or cannot make such decisions, only that it might be thought ideal if this sort of decision is made by the full law reform mechanisms, where that is an option. It is another choice about when to intervene, yielding a

[7] See *Ibid.*, paras. 36–37; see further C. Albertyn, 'Substantive Equality and Transformation in South Africa' (2007) 23 *South African Journal on Human Rights* 253, 263–65 (noting these concerns, though preferring an approach that acknowledges them but seeks to transcend gender categories).

[8] *Masiya*, para. 91; see also the majority judgment, para. 40–45.

decision that the optimal institutional calculus favoured action on one point and restraint on another.

As in the other cases we have seen, that decision involves some risks. Should a case involving a male victim arise before the legislative law reform process was finalized, it would of course be possible to approach the Court again, but the barriers to that are significant. In fact, the constitutional challenge in *Masiya* only arose because a magistrate, boldly and very probably without legal authority, decided to raise the constitutional point of the definition of rape of his own motion.[9] Waiting for the legislature implies the possibility that a case with a male victim might occur in the meanwhile but not come to the Court's attention, resulting in a lower sentence for the perpetrator and potentially less vindication of rights. If this risk were being taken purely out of engrained adherence to some traditional concept of the separation of powers, it would be easy to see the objection. But *Masiya* is a decision between institutional options for protecting and promoting rights, and as in *Fourie (2)* the majority prefers a legislative route where that is an option. And as things turned out, the legislature indeed passed a statute, a few months after *Masiya*, instituting the new gender-neutral definition of rape sought by *Masiya*'s critics.[10]

But how far can we follow the tracks of such arguments? Even if we accept the constitutional value of what the Court is seeking by not itself intervening we will worry about how much risk to rights might be swallowed in the name of an uncertain prospect of a possibly only theoretically optimal institutional solution which might not work out as neatly and promptly as *Masiya*'s did. What happens if judges defer to a legislature that does not act or does not act satisfactorily? Or if the harm in question becomes more serious or less remediable in the meanwhile, or if the issue, given the high barriers to access to justice, struggles to return to the Court? These problems arise because a court that confronts both a non-trivial problem and an imperfect government response will find constitution-building imperatives harder to align. In that position, the Court cannot avoid risk: either the risk of judicial intervention in challenging circumstances, including the risk of precluding a better institutional response, or the risk of leaving a right unprotected. The Court will also usually have to make the choice about which of these risks to run

[9] *Ibid.*, paras. 8–10. Magistrates' courts are not courts of constitutional jurisdiction in South Africa; see further *Ibid.*, paras. 65–69.

[10] Criminal Law (Sexual Offences and Related Matters) Amendment Act 32 of 2007, s 3.

in conditions of significant uncertainty about the effects of the various possible courses of action. While many of these judgment calls will be reasonably debatable, the first thing to see is simply that there is a judgment call to be made, and I hope it will now be clear why, although there are sometimes easy answers in particular cases, there is no easy *default* answer here. This is crucial to bear in mind as we confront more difficult cases than *Masiya*; what is also crucial, however, is that the Court has some ability to restructure cases in a more active fashion and so adjust the judgment calls it has to make or the support it has in making them. It has some ability, in other words, to alter the terms of the constitution-building equation.

This recognition is important in confronting the much-lamented decision in *Volks* v. *Robinson* ('*Volks*'). At first glance, *Volks* can look like a *Masiya* where we are still waiting for the rights-defending action from the other institution. As we saw in Chapter 6, the interests of unmarried opposite-sex life partners were raised in the LGBTI equality cases as a side-argument against judicial intervention, but *Volks* raised the issue squarely. The applicant was the surviving (female) partner to a permanent relationship, whose male partner had made some provision for her in his will (but not necessarily enough for her to live on), while leaving the home they had shared to his children. Had their relationship been formalized as a marriage, a statute would have precluded this result by giving her a claim against the estate for maintenance. She argued that her exclusion from this statutory protection merely because she had not been married violated the right to equality.[11] Her position stood for that of many partners, mostly women, in South Africa, where forced patterns of migrant labour and geographical segregation have created many relationships of mutual support that exist alongside a marriage to someone living elsewhere, or which are relationships of convenience in some sense. Well over two million people in South Africa were in this position at the time *Volks* was decided (although of course in a wide variety of circumstances, not necessarily rooted in historical injustices or patterns of gendered subordination).[12] The majority in *Volks* rejected the applicant's claim and took no action in response to the problem.

[11] *Volks*, paras. 1–7; Maintenance of Surviving Spouses Act 27 of 1990.

[12] B. Meyersfeld, 'If You Can See, Look: Domestic Partnerships and the Law' (2010) 3 *Constitutional Court Review* 271, 274, giving a rough figure of 2.3 million people based on 2001 census figures (which is also the figure used by O'Regan and Mokgoro JJ in *Volks*, para. 118); for the lower figure of 1 268 964 people based on 1996 census figures drawn on

Critics draw unflattering comparisons between the Court's restrained approach in *Volks* and the more assertive stance taken by the court of first instance.[13] That court accepted the applicant's claim and made the order she sought, inserting surviving unmarried opposite-sex life partners into the same statute that protected surviving spouses. But this criticism misses an important difference in what was before each court. In the court of first instance in *Volks*, the government indicated that it would abide the court's decision – a signal that it was not planning to act in response to the issue and an implicit invitation for the court to do so if it felt it necessary, which that court duly accepted.[14] In the Constitutional Court, however, the government altered its stance, indicating that it was preparing legislation on the issue and asking the Court to leave it to do so.[15] *Volks*, therefore, is another decision not to act because another institution is acting – but here, the other institution did not act. The legislative process raised in *Volks* in May 2004 was the same as the one raised in *Satchwell* in February 2002, and the issue surfaced again in the 2006 hearings on the Civil Union bill. Members of the public at these hearings apparently voiced strong opposition to imposing legal consequences on unmarried partners, and at least partly due to the rush to get the bill passed in time the draft provisions on life partnerships were removed from it (an interesting footnote to the majority's decision to impose as short a deadline as possible so as to hasten the vindication of same-sex couples' rights, and to arguments about the polycentric consequences of judicial intervention in other institutions in general).[16] At the time of writing, more than a decade after *Volks*, the bill is still in limbo – and in its present form, it has legal consequences only for parties who 'register' their relationships, meaning that if it passed, South Africa would have no less than four different voluntary ways for couples to formalize their relationships, while still providing no protection for those, like the

by Sachs J, *Ibid.*, para. 194, see B. Goldblatt, 'Regulating Domestic Partnerships: A Necessary Step in the Development of South African Family Law' (2003) 118 *South African Law Journal* 610, 610 n. 1, who also notes the lack of precise data on the point.

13 See e.g. L. Wildenboer, 'Marrying Domestic Partnerships and the Constitution: A Discussion of *Volks v Robinson* 2005 5 BCLR 446 (CC)' (2005) *SA Publiekreg/SA Public Law* 459, 460–61; H. Kruuse, '"Here's to You, Mrs Robinson": Peculiarities and Paragraph 29 in Determining the Treatment of Domestic Partnerships' (2009) 25 *South African Journal on Human Rights* 380, 383.

14 *Robinson* v. *Volks NO* 2004 (6) SA 288 (C), 294A.

15 *Ibid.*, paras. 28, 67; see also the minority judgment of Sachs J, paras. 237–39.

16 *Hansard*, 4 November 2006; see esp. the speech of H. P. Chauke (ANC).

applicant in *Volks*, whose partners enjoy relationships of mutual support while controlling all or most of the partnership's resources, and who decline to formalize the relationship legally.[17] Seen this way, we may be inclined to criticize not only *Volks* itself but also the earlier LGBTI equality decisions which we saw applying a similar logic. But *Volks* was not just a *Masiya* gamble that didn't come off, and seeing why is important to our broader understanding of the constitution-building account.

Volks raised a difficult question: how far should the state go in attaching automatic consequences to relationships that pass a certain factual threshold of permanence? We saw the Court offering only tentative answers to this question in the LGBTI equality cases, making different suggestions for immigration, pensions and adoption, and *Volks* reflects similar concerns.[18] It is therefore easy enough to see why the Court preferred Parliament's tender of action. The framing of *Volks* also contributed to this result. Because the case was presented as an unfair exclusion from the statute protecting married persons, it did not ask the Court to find it unconstitutional that there was no legal protection for persons in the position of the applicant. It asked it to find that it was unconstitutional that the protection was not the same as the protection afforded to married persons. In other words, it asked the Court to find that the Constitution *requires* that the decision to marry should have *no* significance to maintenance obligations after the death of one partner to a permanent relationship, and that the state can have *no* legitimate reason to treat the situations differently *in any way* on this issue. We might not be surprised that the whole Court had reservations about this finding: all the judges accepted that it was problematic that there was no protection for vulnerable partners to permanent relationships not formalized as marriages, but not even the dissenters were willing to making an unqualified ruling that this situation *had* to be resolved by including them in the protections for married persons.[19] *Volks* should therefore

[17] Domestic Partnerships Bill (2008), Notice 36 of 2008, *GG* 30663, 14 January 2008; the other three being marriage under the Marriage Act and marriage or civil union under the Civil Unions Act, as discussed in Chapter 6. For a recent update, see B. S. Smith, '*Parker*, Life Partnerships and the Independent Trustee' (2013) 130 *South African Law Journal* 527.

[18] *Volks*, see e.g. paras. 27, 67 (main judgment), 138–39 (dissent of Mokgoro and O'Regan JJ), 213–20, 226, 236 (dissent of Sachs J).

[19] The majority's position is summed up by Ngcobo J, *Ibid.*, para. 94: '[Contextual evidence] points to the need to regulate permanent life partnerships. This does not mean that a law

strongly recall *Mazibuko*, in which a significant South African problem with very real human consequences arrived in Court as a rather more particular and troublesome challenge for the constitution-building court. As in *Mazibuko*, the majority in *Volks* declined to take up the applicant's invitation to intervene in these circumstances, and the result is another clipped non-intervention decision. Critics once again react very negatively to this tone, and see in it the Court's indifference to the position of vulnerable people in such relationships.[20] The proximity of *Volks* to cases like *Fourie (2)* and *Bhe* v. *Magistrate, Khayelitsha* suggests that such simple attitudinal explanations, though possibly of some effect, have limited explanatory power. Every single member of the *Volks* majority, around the same time, would vote to intervene boldly in *Bhe*, a case about the vulnerable position of women in the context of inheritance under customary law.[21]Instead of personal indifference to the issues at hand,

designed to regulate marriage is unconstitutional because it does not regulate permanent life partnerships.' Sachs J would have invalidated the statute for its failure to provide any protection for life partners without being prescriptive about what protection had to be offered or whether it had to be the same as the protection for married persons: *Ibid.*, esp. paras. 237–41. Mokgoro and O'Regan JJ would have gone furthest, ruling that life partners should be read into the statute but suspending the order to give the legislature time to conduct reforms of its own and noting that the protection did not have to be the same as for marriage: *Ibid.*, esp. paras. 133–34, 136, 140. All three dissenting judges would also only have extended protection to a certain category of permanent life partners who had undertaken mutual duties of support, a curtailment of the relief ordered by the court of first instance that was conceded by Ms. Robinson's counsel in oral argument: *Ibid.*, paras. 27, 138–39, 213–20, 226, 236. And even the dissenters held that she had received an equitable share of the estate under the will and was not entitled to the greater share a married person would have received under the statute: *Ibid.*, paras. 141, 240.

20 See e.g. Albertyn, 'Substantive Equality', 265–68; C. Lind, 'Domestic Partnerships and Marital Status Discrimination' (2005) *Acta Juridica* 108; S. Jagwanth, 'Expanding Equality' (2005) *Acta Juridica* 131.

21 *Volks* was heard on 20 May 2004 and decided on 21 March 2005. *Bhe* was heard on 2–3 March 2004 and decided on 15 October 2004. Justices Chaskalson, Langa, Moseneke, Skweyiya, Van der Westhuizen and Yacoob voted the same way in both cases. Ngcobo J wrote a separate judgment both times and did not concur with the majority in *Bhe*, but his dissent there only concerned the manner of intervention. Apart from Chaskalson CJ, all the *Volks* judges also sat in *Fourie (2)* later that year. The subsequent admired decision in *Hassam* v. *Jacobs NO* 2009 (5) SA 572 (CC) was also joined by every member of the *Volks* majority who sat in the later case. (Chakalson CJ had retired; Ngcobo J did not sit.) *Hassam* was a case about the position of women in polygynous Muslim marriages, which until recently were not recognized in South African law. For criticism of *Volks* based on its substantive similarities to *Hassam*, see Meyersfeld, 'If You Can See, Look'; D. Meyerson, 'Who's In and Who's Out? Inclusion and Exclusion in the Family Law Jurisprudence of the Constitutional Court of South Africa' (2010) 3 *Constitutional Court Review* 301. In contrast to *Volks*, the state supported judicial intervention in *Hassam*; see

the Court's position in *Volks* has much more to do with institutional considerations: it prefers the possibility of an answer by elected representatives on a difficult, contested issue.

Volks, then, is not such a puzzle, but we should still wonder whether the Court struck the best constitution-building balance available. Non-intervention in *Volks* comes with a strong set of bad consequences. Each day that surviving partners are not protected, estates are wound up and vulnerable people permanently lose any claims they might have had. Non-intervention in *Volks* therefore has more final legal consequences than non-intervention in a case of only potential harm, like *NNP*, or a case of ongoing harm with a less obvious point after which it can no longer be remedied. *Fourie (2)*'s applicants could more readily be expected to wait; among the same-sex couple cases, *Volks* is much more like *Gory* v. *Kolver*, but it reaches the opposite result.[22] The resulting inconsistency, in which same-sex unmarried partners are now protected in ways that opposite-sex unmarried partners are not, is the natural consequence of the law's jerky evolution to accommodate same-sex couples. We might therefore see in *Volks* a reason to think that the Court was wrong in its LGBTI equality decisions to treat marriage as irrelevant in the same-sex couple context while declining to address the position of opposite-sex couples. But the real significance of these earlier decisions is that they should have made it quite clear how long the legislative process in response to the position of unmarried life partners was taking. It was clearly a much less actively evolving state response than the City's water policy in *Mazibuko*, for example – and this is a further problem with *Volks*' non-intervention decision. Even if one accepts that a judicial solution was not the ideal option, the strength of that consideration weakens as inaction by other institutions persists.

The arguments against making the strong prescriptive ruling sought by the litigants, as noted, are not trivial. But this is only a reason not to make *any* finding or issue any relief if we accept the argument that the Court should adhere to the traditional role of an appeal court and rule only on

para. 3. For similarly directed comparisons to some earlier cases, see also A. Cooke, 'Choice, Heterosexual Life Partnerships, Death and Poverty' (2005) 122 *South African Law Journal* 542.

22 For criticism on this basis, see Kruuse, '"Here's to You, Mrs Robinson"'. This problem is presumably part of what prompts the dissenters to find that the person before the Court had in fact received an equitable share and so was not herself unfairly treat by the delayed effect of their orders: *Volks*, paras. 141, 240; for criticism of this finding, see Cooke, 'Heterosexual Life Partnerships', 555.

the legal issues as raised by the parties. There are non-trivial constitutional reasons to value adherence to expected procedural forms, including fairness and the need for proper ventilation of issues, but these considerations are, of course, not necessarily decisive.[23] In light of the costs of non-intervention, why did the Court not reframe the legal enquiry in *Volks*? Instead of asking whether it was constitutionally acceptable for the state to exclude unmarried permanent partners from the marital maintenance regime, why did it not ask whether it was constitutionally acceptable for the state to provide *no* legal protection for unmarried permanent partners in the position of the applicant? The majority recognized this as the true question but confined itself to finding that this broader omission was not a reason to think the protection for married people was unconstitutional, thus using the framing of the case as a way out. Both dissents, particularly Sachs J's, do some reframing of the issue. But Mokgoro and O'Regan JJ are unwilling to engage the promising common law routes for offering protection because 'development of the common law . . . was not the relief sought in this litigation', and even Sachs J's more open-ended approach does not entirely escape the awkwardness of the litigation's framing. His objection is to the lack of a legal response to the broader issue, not to the exclusion of life partners from the protection from married persons. But it is the marriage protection statute he invalidated as a basis for requiring that response.[24]

More thoroughgoing reframing offers readier routes to the real legal problems in ways that meet the majority's perfectly accurate objection: nothing was actually necessarily wrong with the statute being challenged, in itself. One option is via the underlying common law on testamentary freedom. In the absence of any sort of legislative intervention, that common law gives people complete freedom to exclude from their estates the person with whom they have formed a long-term partnership with reciprocal duties of support, even if this leaves the surviving partner destitute and even if, for gendered and other reasons, the financial fruits of South African partnerships are usually mainly controlled by only one of the partners. One might therefore conclude that this common law position violates the Constitution. Even if one prefers a legislative solution to the problem, this would provide a basis for finding a violation and referring the issue to the legislature under a

[23] See further Fowkes, '*Maphango*', esp. 313–18.

[24] See *Volks*, paras. 139 (quoted text), 146–52, 186, 190–95, 207–08, 237–41.

deadline without having to take a definite position on the required fix. Another option (which I will return to later) is to see the government's persistent lack of response to the situation as a violation of its s 7(2) duty to take positive steps to promote rights, which would also not dictate precisely what steps it has to take. This reframing of the case would not introduce substantially new issues, so it has limited costs in fairness to the parties or in prompting the need for new evidence. And insofar as either option might involve a delay in relief to give the legislature time to act – something even the dissenters in *Volks* saw as unavoidable – it would be possible to protect the applicant's claims and others like it by precluding the winding up of estates where executors were aware of the constitutional challenge, as was done in *Gory*.

Volks, then, is a case where the constitution-building elements were hard to reconcile, partly because of the way the case was framed, and ultimately because of the persistent failure of the legislature to act on an important issue. But it is also a case where the Court, with limited costs to itself or the parties, could have reframed the issue in a way that would reduce the constitution-building difficulties. As reframed, the case would require the Court essentially only to find that the entirely unprotected status of a group with some very vulnerable members could not constitutionally continue, a proposition which every judge in *Volks* seems to have accepted was clearly true. That the Court did not do this is the real objection to *Volks* – and it is an objection that is entirely consistent with upholding other non-intervention decisions, like those already discussed. For those seeking bold action to remedy injustice, *Volks* is wrong because it did not act in the face of injustice. For the constitution-building account, *Volks* is correct to see the challenges in a relatively difficult case for judicial action. But it is wrong because it did not take a feasible way to respond to significant rights concerns consistent with being sensitive to those challenges, and so did not adopt the institutionally best route to protect rights.

Deferring into Space: *S* v. *Lawrence* and *S* v. *Jordan*

The other pair of controversial equality cases I consider here take the argument a step further. They bear similarities to *Masiya* and *Volks* but did not involve the explicit prospect of an ongoing legislative process. One is *S* v. *Jordan* ('*Jordan*'), which scholars might well label the Court's least admirable decision. The other, *S* v. *Lawrence* ('*Lawrence*'), is like

Masiya in raising its own concerns but in serving, for my purposes, principally as a helpful way into the more controversial case.[25]

Decided under the interim Constitution, *Lawrence* was the Court's first freedom of religion case, and it saw a majority upholding restrictions on the right to sell liquor, including in relation to the ban on holders of grocers' licenses selling on Sundays and on two obviously Christian holidays, Easter Friday and Christmas Day. (Holders of other kinds of liquor licences, including restaurants and bars, could sell on those days.)[26] Three grocery store owners had been accused of selling liquor in violation of the conditions of their licences, one of them (the focus here), for violating the Sunday trading restriction. All raised no defence except that the licence conditions were unconstitutional. Their challenges might therefore be thought opportunistic, and the Court did not confront a story of personal religious harm so much as an abstract challenge in an attempt to avoid prosecution for illegal commercial activity.[27]

If we approach these arguments on the basis of setting the constitutional rights down next to the statute and asking if they match, there is no doubt that some concerns arise. Most obviously, the fact that restrictions apply on Sundays and the two most important Christian holidays (and only those days) blatantly reflects that the 1989 legislative scheme had, at least, its origins in Christianity, the state-sponsored religion during apartheid. Four judges downplayed the significance of this symbolism, on the grounds that Sundays had since acquired a largely secular significance as rest days.[28] Two others, Sachs J joined by Mokgoro J, held that this symbolic favouring of Christian days violated the right to freedom of religion, belief and opinion, but that this was justified under the limitations clause. This latter finding was based on arguments that

[25] *S* v. *Lawrence; S* v. *Negal; S* v. *Solberg* 1997 (4) SA 1176 (CC); *S* v. *Jordan* 2002 (6) SA 642 (CC).

[26] Liquor Act 27 of 1989.

[27] P. Farlam, 'The Ambit of the Right to Freedom of Religion: A Comment on *S v Solberg*' (1998) 14 *South African Journal on Human Rights* 298, 305–08, 325; J. E. Buckingham, 'Religious Freedom and Wine Sales on Sunday' (1999) *Stellenbosch Law Review* 117, 119, 124; and A. Gouws and L. M. du Plessis, 'The Relationship between Political Tolerance and Religion: The Case of South Africa' (2000) 14 *Emory International Law Review* 657, 681, note among the case's defects as a vehicle for the issue its commercial nature (and see also the judgment of Sachs J, *Lawrence*, paras. 140, 154), its poor factual record and the fact that no religious groups presented argument.

[28] *Lawrence*, paras. 91–106; for criticism of this approach, see e.g. A. Stein, 'Constitutional Jurisprudence' (1997) *Annual Survey of South African Law* 45, 61–63; Gouws and Du Plessis, 'Political Tolerance and Religion', 682–83.

these were days when the government had a particular interest in curtailing drinking, arguments which were both tenuous – why not on Friday evening or Saturday? Why not on other holidays? – and speculative.[29] Finally, a three-judge dissent written by O'Regan J would have invalidated the restrictions.

My interest in *Lawrence* here lies not in the debates about religious freedom tests that dominate scholarly discussion of the case, but in the respects in which the case resembles a non-intervention decision. In a case that has much to do with factual questions about the effects of the licence restrictions on non-Christians and on limiting alcohol consumption, there are concerns about the limited factual record but no moves to supplement it.[30] What creates the effective six-judge majority in *Lawrence*, above all, is the common decision not to disrupt the status quo by inserting the Court into the issue. That is partly informed by a view that the harm is not particularly severe: the main judgment looks for harm but does not find much indication of it, while Sachs and Mokgoro JJ see the harm as more serious but nevertheless hold it to be outweighed by their tenuous speculations about reducing alcohol consumption. But it is also informed by a sense that society is secularizing on its own. Christian days used to be firmly favoured by the state and that *would* be problematic, but South Africa is changing into a different society that often views Sundays simply as days off. Like *Masiya* and *Volks*, then, there is a sense in which the Court is preferring a course of action on an issue other than firm judicial intervention. But unlike those two cases, what the Court is deferring to is not a specific legislative process or some other particular institutional response as much as the broader, informal social process of a largely Christian country, which had before 1994 had a state-sponsored but racist religious stance whose opponents included religious groups, coming to terms with the new place of religion in a far more open, pluralistic society that is in some respects secularizing and in others becoming more religious. It is again helpful to imagine the majority contemplating speaking out to society on the issue, but turning away with the feeling that on Sunday liquor trading it might be best to say nothing firm at all. And while the effects of bolder options are hard to speak about with much precision, one can appreciate why the judges

[29] *Lawrence*, esp. paras. 175–78; see Farlam, 'Ambit of the Right to Freedom of Religion', 303–04; Buckingham, 'Religious Freedom', 122, 124, criticizing the degree to which Sachs J here relies on judicial notice to make findings without evidence.

[30] *Lawrence*, paras. 9–25, 97–98 (Chaskalson P); 130–32 (O'Regan J); 140, 175–76 (Sachs J).

might feel that the cause of a pluralistic society in which religion has some place in state activity might be best advanced by this approach.[31]

It is not without interest, therefore, that Parliament has since taken a similar view. As a serious constitutional actor in its own right, it has engaged of its own accord with the difficulties that arose in *Lawrence.* And rather than attempt to settle the issue definitively, it has delegated it to the provincial level, while retaining the 1989 statute that was at issue in *Lawrence* as the default if provincial legislatures do not act. Seven of the nine provinces have legislated to date, and the majority of them have chosen to remove the restrictions on Sunday liquor sales (while one has chosen to replicate the arrangements of the 1989 statute). In a further decentralization, three provinces have permitted local municipalities to adopt their own rules on the matter.[32] We should, I think, see this as a virtuous process, an appealing approach to a perennially contested issue with important personal issues on all sides. And insofar as we think this, we should acknowledge that the approach in *Lawrence* enabled it by not imposing a more abrupt answer.

[31] Currie and De Waal, *Handbook*, p. 330, suggest that the state should perhaps not legislate on Sunday closings and leave the issue to union negotiations.

[32] New national legislation, passed in 2003, provides for the passage of provincial laws to regulate, inter alia, liquor sales, providing that the old legislation upheld in *Lawrence*, the Liquor Act 27 of 1989, will apply in provinces until they pass such laws – Liquor Act 59 of 2003, s 46 read with Schedule 1, s 2. Seven provinces out of nine have passed such laws to date; Limpopo and North West being the two that have yet to legislate. One province has re-enacted the 1989 Act's prohibition on holders of off-consumption licenses, which includes the grocers' licenses at issue in *Lawrence*, from selling alcohol on 'closed days', meaning Sundays, Easter Friday and Christmas – Northern Cape Liquor Act 2 of 2008 (entry into force on 1 April 2010), s 17(5) read with s 17(2) and the definition of 'closed day' in s 1. It gives the relevant MEC limited powers to declare exceptions to this in the public interest – see s 17(7). Three more provinces, the Eastern Cape, Gauteng and the Free State, have passed legislation providing for liquor sales on 'any day' within the prescribed hours: see Eastern Cape Liquor Act 10 of 2003 (entry into force 12 May 2004), s 42(a); Gauteng Liquor Act 2 of 2003 (entry into force 1 November 2004), ss 53, 55, 57, 59, 62, 64, 66, 68, 70, 72, 74, 76, 78, 82, 85, 88, 93 and 96 (s 93 applies to the grocer's license at issue in *Lawrence*); Free State Gambling and Liquor Act 6 of 2010 (entry into force 11 June 2010), s 48(1). The Western Cape Liquor Act 4 of 2008 (entry into force 1 April 2012) gives individual municipalities the power to determine opening days and times, but provides that licensees may otherwise sell on 'any day' – see s 59(1), 59(3). Both Kwazulu-Natal and Mpumalanga have established liquor authorities with the power to set trading hours and also provide for the possibility of municipal restrictions, but permit Sunday liquor sales – KwaZulu-Natal Liquor Licensing Act 6 of 2010 (entry into force 28 March 2014), ss 5, 78(1), Sch. 3; Mpumalanga Liquor Licensing Act 5 of 2006 (entry into force of relevant sections 30 August 2014), ss 4, 24 and Ann. 14 to regulations issued in terms of the Act.

As with *Masiya*, however, we might be less concerned with this approach on the particular facts of *Lawrence* than about where the tracks of such arguments lead. *Jordan* may be the least admired of all the Court's decisions, and is also, it seems, the one most regretted by O'Regan J, whose partially dissenting minority judgment co-written with Sachs J was apparently a vain attempt to win a majority by moderating her own views.[33] Like *Lawrence, Jordan* confronted an apartheid-era statute enacted to enforce a certain version of public morality by criminalizing prostitution. The statute applied only to those who sold sexual services, and not to those who bought them, although buyers could be found guilty as accessories, with equivalent penalties, in terms of other law.[34] The majority rejected an equality challenge to this arrangement, as well as arguments against the criminalization of sex work based on the rights to dignity, privacy, freedom of person, and freedom of profession, and took no action. On the way to this result, the majority ruled that no kind of gender discrimination occurs when a statute criminalizes those who sell sex but not those who buy it (at least when there is a legal basis for prosecuting buyers, too, even if only in principle), leaving the gendered differentiation in the statute's approach undisturbed.[35] The whole Court, including the minority judges, also ruled that criminalizing sex work does not violate the right to dignity of sex workers because any impairment follows from the apparently inherently undignified fact of being a prostitute.[36] These are broad findings: *Volks* poses a much smaller obstacle to the future constitutional claims of vulnerable women in non-formalized relationships than *Jordan* does to the future constitutional claims of sex workers.

All this makes *Jordan* so easy to criticize that we may not take the time to try and understand it. The constitution-building account can help us see that whatever else *Jordan* is, it is not inexplicable, and there are things to learn from it. The case's problems again begin with its framing.

[33] Woolman, *Selfless Constitution*, p. 34 n. 17 reports a personal conversation with O'Regan J to this effect. Three other judges joined the O'Regan/Sachs JJ minority.

[34] Sexual Offences Act 23 of 1957, s 20(1)(aA); possible accomplice liability in terms of the common law and under the Riotous Assemblies Act 17 of 1956, s 18.

[35] It was accepted that in practice only sex workers were charged: *Jordan*, para. 42. On the symbolism, see esp. *Ibid.*, paras. 63–73, 97; N. Fritz, 'Crossing Jordan: Constitutional space for (un)civil sex?' (2004) 20 *South African Journal on Human Rights* 230; E. Bonthuys, 'Women's Sexuality in the South African Constitutional Court' (2006) 14 *Feminist Legal Studies* 391.

[36] *Jordan*, paras. 8–19 (gender equality); 1, 74 (dignity).

We have seen the difficulties that arose in other cases when litigants raised a general area of plausible concern but sought a more specific, ambitious order. *Volks* sought, in the context of a general area of gendered vulnerability, a specific order that the Constitution required equality of treatment between unmarried and married survivors of life partnerships. *Mazibuko* raised the general issue of the government's water provision policy, but sought a specific ruling that prepaid meters are unconstitutional. In the same way, *Jordan* confronted a generally troubling gendered statute and issue, but the general points raised were bound up in arguments seeking the decriminalization of sex work. Decriminalizing sex work is an issue likely displaying not merely newness but entrenched contrary public status. The Court would also have had to resolve it quite unilaterally: the state took the opposite view, and much of the authority and evidence either way is contested or inconclusive.[37] The added twist in *Jordan*, moreover, was that the part of the argument the Court was most likely to uphold, and on which the hearing in *Jordan* was chiefly focused, was the gendered differentiation in the statute.[38] Such a finding would have represented much less of a stretch for the Court, and it is on this basis that the dissent would have invalidated the statute. But its links to the broader decriminalization issue created problems. The most natural response to an underinclusive provision is usually not to remove the provision, but to extend it: we would hardly have taken the gender problems with the definition of rape in *Masiya* as a reason to invalidate the crime of rape.[39] *If* one has already come down in favour of the decriminalization result, then the statute's gender problems provide a way to reach that result by striking down the criminalization. But if one has decided not to confront such newness so unilaterally, then the argument much more clearly shows a problem (most obviously, the gendered differentiation) than dictates the preferred solution (decriminalization).

And thus we might start seeing why the majority chose not to act at all on the problem. The immediate stakes of invalidating the statute or not were only some nuisance-level criminal convictions: the applicants in *Jordan* had been fined R200 (less than $20).[40] In addition, the only

[37] *Jordan* repeatedly treats issues as contested and thus as subjects of legitimate legislative discretion – see paras. 30, 45–46, 55–56, 86–89, 90–94, 119, 123–28.

[38] *Ibid.*, para. 8. [39] See *Ibid.*, paras. 45–46.

[40] See Appellants' Heads of Argument, paras. 4, 106, available under the *Jordan* case file at www.constitutionalcourt.org.za.

outcome of a judicial invalidation which referred the statute to Parliament might be that the client's technical liability would be altered from accomplice to co-principal, which would not affect the criminal liability of sex workers and might well have little or no impact on the litigants' broader concerns about sex work's regulation.[41] From here, we might be able to see why the gendered differentiation in the technical details of the criminalization of sex work, which most South Africans were doubtless entirely unaware of, could have seemed like the liquor laws in *Lawrence* in not being worth the jolt of a judicial invalidation. The *Jordan* majority's tone on this point, downplaying the seriousness of the issue, certainly squares with this reading. And as it happens, the parallel goes further: *Jordan* is also like *Lawrence* in that legislative action turned out to follow the judicial decision not to act. The same 2007 statute that introduced the gender-neutral definition of rape also introduced a new offence of engaging sexual services, while retaining the separate offence of providing those services at issue in *Jordan*.[42] Parliament has therefore responded to what the *Jordan* majority did not by ending a situation in which the criminal liability of the buyer of sexual services is only subsidiary to that of the seller.

But the *Jordan* majority, as in *Lawrence*, had no particular reason to think that Parliament would act, and given that South Africa has a much greater problem with gender discrimination and with sexual and gender-based violence than it does with religious discrimination or religious-based violence, and given that sex workers are among the groups most exposed to this harsh state of affairs, the stakes were rather higher in *Jordan*. We therefore reach the most stubbornly difficult question about *Jordan*, which is why six justices, including Chief Justice Chaskalson, were apparently not persuaded by such considerations, and were willing to hand down a judgment that not only did not react to these issues but set substantial contrary precedents. It is easy to reach for attitudinal explanations, and they may have purchase here: such suggestions are in any event impossible to rebut definitively, as usual. But as with *Volks*, other decisions of the Court count against at least simple attempts to

[41] The minority accepted criminalization was a legitimate legislative response and thus that in principle its objection to the statute would be removed if both buyer and seller were criminalized equally: see *Jordan*, esp. para. 69; R. Krüger, 'Sex Work from a Feminist Perspective: A Visit to the *Jordan* case' (2004) 20 *South African Journal on Human Rights* 138, 149; Meyerson, 'Does the Court Take Rights Seriously?', 148.

[42] Criminal Law Amendment Act, s 11.

explain *Jordan* away as the product of insensitivity to gender claims or social context.[43] The constitution-building account, instead, will see another non-intervention decision, underpinned above all by an institutional argument rather than a flawed conception of equality. It will see as significant both the briskness of the decision – the majority disposes of all the constitutional arguments in just 19 paragraphs – and the way that *Jordan* recalls a case like *Nokotyana* in identifying several important disputes of fact but declining to take steps to engage them.[44]

If there is an unarticulated premise in *Jordan*, I suspect it has as much or more to do with the role of the Court and a certain appellate court irritation about the litigation before it than assumptions about gender and sex work. An analogy to an earlier scenario can help us understand the point. In 1998, before any of the Court's LGBTI equality decisions, a foreign same-sex couple contemplated launching a legal bid for the recognition of same-sex marriage in South Africa. In what is usually understood as a crucial intervention, their lawyer referred them to the National Coalition for Gay and Lesbian Equality, which persuaded the couple not to disrupt its careful incremental strategy and risk setting a contrary precedent.[45] Given what we saw in Chapter 6, even a 1998 challenge seeking same-sex marriage might have succeeded, but the point here is to see the senses in which *Jordan* was the sort of case, with the sort of result, that the National Coalition was worried about in 1998. Such cases cause worries because they are instances where the textual status of rights that are in principle applicable to an issue diverge significantly from the public status of that issue. Sex work, both as a gender equality issue and more broadly, is a good example of such a situation. Such cases therefore raise the prospect of a hard, zero-sum choice between sidelining textual status and sidelining public status, and neither side of that choice is appealing for judges. The more textual status wins, the more a court risks a backlash from the government or alienating the public from the text. Conversely, the more public status wins, the more the court is threatening its status and obligations as an adjudicator according to law and the more it is leaving vulnerable people to fend for themselves. The more we adopt the abstract, majority-transcending picture of the first *Makwanyane* story, the more we will think the idea of a choice here is precluded in principle, and that textual status must prevail, be the consequences

[43] See cases discussed in note 21 of this chapter.

[44] See note 37 of this chapter.

[45] Budlender et al., *Public Interest Litigation*, p. 30.

what they may.[46] But having seen what cases like *Makwanyane* really rest on, we can see the importance of ANC power in finessing divergences between textual and public status in such contexts, and we can see why judges might feel much more exposed telling South Africans what they have committed themselves to without that kind of support. The litigation in *Jordan* put the Court in this position, but it did little to offer the Court a way to finesse or respond to the tensions of that position, or even to provide it with information about it: in assessing the consequence of possible actions, the *Jordan* Court is driving in a fog, unsure whether there are cliffs around or how close or precipitous they might be.[47]

Finding itself in this position, how should the constitution-building court respond? None of the judges were willing to go as far as ordering that sex work should be decriminalized, or to make broader general findings about sex work's regulation. The minority wished to leverage the limited finding of unconstitutionality of the gender differentiation in the statute into a broader referral, 'giving Parliament a fair opportunity to undertake a comprehensive review of the matter, producing a balanced and well thought-through approach to the manner in which commercial sex can and should best be regulated in contemporary South Africa'.[48] It sought to have Parliament engage with the general issue of sex work's regulation without finding the existing general regulation unconstitutional – recalling the *Volks* minority's effort to prompt engagement with the regulation of domestic partnerships by invalidating a statute for married people it did not think was necessarily problematic in itself. Some of the *Jordan* majority's likely reasons for not taking this route also recall *Volks*, including *Jordan's* awkward legal framing, and the concern over confronting everyone with what risked being a choice between the commitment to constitutionalism and their commitments on the

[46] The argument from newness thus again offers a reply to those who, in another example of the first *Makwanyane* story's prevalence, make the now familiar kind of inconsistency objection, comparing the treatment of sex work in *Jordan* to the approach to issues such as abortion, and to LGBTI equality and gender equality in other Court cases – see e.g. Krüger, 'Sex Work from a Feminist Perspective', 145–49; Meyerson, 'Does the Court Take Rights Seriously?', 144–47, 150, 153; Albertyn, 'Substantive Equality', 269–70; C. Boudin and M. Richter, 'Adult, Consensual Sex Work in South Africa: The Cautionary Message of Criminal Law and Sexual Morality' (2009) 25 *South African Journal on Human Rights* 179, 190–93.

[47] See the discussion of newness in Chapter 5; see also Fritz, 'Crossing Jordan', 230 and n. 3, 235–36.

[48] *Jordan*, para. 126.

underlying issue. If a 1998 same-sex marriage referral might have been a risky prospect, we can certainly see why this might be riskier still on an issue with much less pre-existing political and legal support behind it. This concern, obviously applicable to the idea of ordering the decriminalization of sex work, extends to the gender differentiation issue chiefly because of appearances. If critics worry about the symbolic effects of retaining a gendered provision in a statute, the majority may have been more worried about the symbolic effects of invalidating it, especially in the form of un-nuanced newspaper headlines. It is significant here that the court of first instance in *Jordan*, which upheld the gender equality challenge, had (improperly) not then ruled on the other challenges – and instead of avoiding a decision on these arguments for this reason, the *Jordan* majority ruled on them anyway as a court of first and last instance, something it is usually reluctant to do. *Jordan* was thus an unusually firm decision that the Court would not act on the issue.

It is also important, in assessing the *Jordan* majority, that the minority's preference for criminalizing the conduct of buyers equally to sellers, generally approved by scholars and subsequently given effect to in legislation, is apparently opposed by sex workers themselves. Equal criminalization may have increased the risks faced by sex workers by making buyers nervous and thus driving the industry further underground.[49] This reflects, once again, the perils of unilaterally resolving newness, in the absence of the sort of factual consensus so important to decisions like *Hoffman* and *TAC (2)*. Returning to my speculations about the real unarticulated premise in *Jordan*, I suspect the result has something to do with the justices' mental reactions to rights claims presented without heed of their newness, which sought for the judges to make very sweeping findings while doing little to assist with the risks and magnitude of the unilateral decision the Court was apparently being expected to take. I would speculate that all this led the majority to do what appellate courts have felt entitled to do for centuries when they encounter litigation that seems to them irritatingly ill-conceived and to ask too much, and to dismiss it in blunt terms.

[49] See N. Fick, 'Well Intentioned but Misguided? Criminalizing Sex Workers' Clients' (2007) 22 *SA Crime Quarterly* 33, 34–35; I am referred to this concern by Boudin and Richter, 'Adult, Consensual Sex Work in South Africa', 193–94. Of course, the same criticism potentially applies to the legislature's subsequent decision to install equal criminalization, reminding us that legislative routes are of course not immune to newness-related difficulties either.

This offers an explanation for a decision that is otherwise puzzling; it also offers some comfort to those of us who find it concerning. If *Jordan* was about dismissing a litigation and declining to intervene in an issue, we should not expect it to be a strong precedent on general issues of gender or statutory stereotyping – as indeed looks accurate. A foreign observer unschooled in South African constitutional law who was only handed *Jordan* would not draw reliable conclusions about the Court's more general response to gendered issues before or since.[50] For the same reason, seeing the sense in which *Jordan* is a non-intervention decision also suggests it might be weaker as a precedent against future action on the issue of sex work than it might appear, if a more conducive case could be framed (a point I return to shortly).

Whether this explanation also constitutes a justification is harder to accept. As in *Volks*, better constitution-building options seem to have been available. If a majority was unwilling to take even the route offered to them by O'Regan and Sachs JJ, the solution may have been reframing of the case. The s 7(2) route suggested in *Volks* might be promising here. After all, the ban in *Jordan* came from an apartheid-era statute, strongly stamped with that state's view of morality, and so by letting the gendered statute remain on the books, the legislature was failing to fulfil its positive duty to promote equality – just as it would if it had left a race-based provision on the statute books without a good, likely transitional, reason. In the words of another ANC MP, MR Sikakane, talking about *Fourie (2)* during the Civil Union Act debates, the Court would be saying: '"Parliament, you have repealed all discriminatory laws, but I think you have overlooked this one. Just go and repeal this law so that everybody is equal." So, it is not actually the court that told us what to do. It reminded us of our duty, of our function, to change and repeal this discriminatory law.'[51] Such framing might have gone some way to deal with the diplomatic hazards of the judgment.

Section 7(2) also offers a way to confront the broader issue of sex work that is less legally awkward than the minority's leveraged approach. One does not need to adopt any particular constitutional construction of sex work – a job, an inevitability, a crime, a sin – to recognize that the state should respond in some way to the harms associated with it. The chief

50 See e.g. Bonthuys, 'Women's Sexuality', 392, noting the contrast between *Jordan* and the Court's prior 'series of enlightened judgments' on gender equality, and note 21 of this chapter.

51 *Hansard*, 4 November 2006 (M. R. Sikakane, ANC).

response the state had adopted, however, was the criminal ban, and it did not appear that this was being enforced with any zeal. The sex workers charged in *Jordan* had raised the pettiness of their R200 sanction as evidence that that the state was not seriously enforcing the criminal ban that it claimed was important.[52] (This trend has continued since. In 2009, one of the civil society groups involved in *Jordan* even succeeded in interdicting police officers in the Western Cape from arresting sex workers for exploitative purposes. A key reason the judge in that case was willing to make the truistic order that arrests should only be made for valid legal reasons was that he accepted that police officers knew that no cases would actually be prosecuted and so their arrests had to be for other, ulterior purposes.)[53] If one believes a quiet de facto decriminalization is the best that sex work advocacy groups were likely to get at the time, then as in *Lawrence* this is an outcome enabled by the Court's non-intervention in *Jordan*. And on this line of thinking, the problems of *Jordan* are importantly to be explained by the fact that if de facto decriminalization is the best available outcome, the issue is probably not best pursued in an institution defined by its obligations to uphold the law. As with the party realignments and cross-boundary municipalities discussed in Chapter 7, the Court is likely to prefer action by other constitutional mechanisms on such issues.

Alternatively, if one is more optimistic about the prospects of government reform if prompted, then the s 7(2) argument suggests that the lessons of newness should be heeded, and that the issue of sex work should have been approached in the way other attempts to review large-scale government policies have been attempted: via reasonableness. *Makwanyane* or the LGBTI equality decisions might not be the best precedents to have in mind, and the socio-economic rights cases, as well as other reasonableness cases like *NNP*, *Doctors for Life*, *Rail Commuters* and *Glenister (2)*, would offer a surer guide to understanding and litigating the issues in *Jordan*, although the way our conventional understandings are divided up by types of rights tends to obscure this. And if so, the starting point would be to find and emphasize tensions within the government's positions – for example, between its policies on gender-based violence or, at least in recent years, on HIV/AIDS, and a criminalization policy on sex work which could only be a response to these

[52] Appellant's Heads of Argument, para. 106.

[53] *Sex Workers Education and Advocacy Taskforce* v. *Minister of Safety and Security* 2009 (6) SA 513 (WCC).

problems if it were reducing sex work's prevalence, which it likely could not be doing if it were not being seriously enforced.[54]

Each of these possible routes involves risk: doing too little, doing too much, avoiding decisions by relying on Parliament to make them, or insisting that all such strategic considerations should be treated as irrelevant – which is its own tacit reliance on Parliament and social and political actors more broadly, as I argued in Chapter 5. Whether bolder judicial action in *Jordan* would have had good outcomes for sex workers is a debatable question whose answer we will never know. Whether one thinks the various possible strategies for action in *Jordan* compatible with legal commitments will also be a debatable point: certainly the majority's response is hard to accept as the best option available, as in *Volks*, and some observers will have more difficulty than others with the degree of strategic consideration implied by the other routes to resolving the case. But the upshot is that if one expects more judicial action, then the Court needed more useful support from the litigants or, finding that support missing, needed to do more itself to reshape the case into one on which it could take that further action consistent with constitution-building imperatives. It is this institutional point that links these equality back to the Court's response to newness in socio-economic rights cases, the topic of the rest of this chapter.

But before we leave *Jordan*, whatever we ultimately think about the optimal response to the case, we should see the broader argument. The reason the case raises the issues it does is because of its constitution-building imperatives: aligned in the Court's celebrated cases, we see them here pulling apart. We have come full circle from *Makwanyane*. The degree of newness (indeed, in all likelihood, contrary entrenchment) is high, both in relation to the public status of the issue and in relation to the Court's own institutional position as an enforcer of significantly aspirational civil-political rights. The degree of support is low: the government's stance is unhelpful, and as argued, so was the litigation in important respects, perhaps most importantly because the Court lacked information about its options. If *Jordan* is the Court's most problematic

[54] The papers in *Jordan* reflect that such issues were among the arguments raised; the argument here is about emphasis and framing, not that the *Jordan* litigants were unaware of the significance of such considerations. In the wake of *Glenister (2)*, arguments based on international obligations are also promising; on such arguments in the related context of domestic violence, see B. Meyersfeld, *Domestic Violence and International Law* (Oxford and Portland, Oregon: Hart Publishing, 2010).

decision, it happens where the constitution-building account would expect problems to arise. It lies at or beyond the fuzzy boundary where the constitution-building account begins to break down as an interpretative account. It arises in the difficult territory we saw being acknowledged by Dworkin's strategic reasons judges might have for altering their statements of the law, illustrated in *Jordan* by the decision of O'Regan J (and perhaps other of the minority judges) to moderate her own views. It raises the problem engaged by Bickel's avoidance devices, illustrated in *Jordan* both by the possibility of using s 7(2) as a democracy-forcing approach to refer the issue to the legislature and, negatively, by the majority's decision *not* to avoid ruling on the substance. One may imagine Bickel arguing that if the Court wanted not to engage such a controversial issue, actual avoidance would have been better than concrete contrary findings. I believe the alternatives to the *Jordan* majority's routes are legally defensible, and the largest strike against it is therefore its failure to explore them, something I would trace above all to the fact that the Court's re-imagination of its own role is a work in progress. Others may prefer to see this as a compromise on principle, a decision in which judges see the best legal reading but choose not to adopt it on political grounds. Given that an openly strategic court seeking to preserve its legal reputation had more moderate options than the concrete stance the majority took, I see the explanation based on the Court's wrestling with the legal details of its role as more convincing, but these are matters of debatable detail. I argued in Chapter 1 that I did not see accounts like Roux's as implausible accounts of possible constitutional worlds, but simply saw less need to reach for them to explain the South African case to date. If *Jordan* comes closest to the point where one might need to reach for such explanations, then its outlier status in the Court's jurisprudence supports my claim that this sort of situation has been rare.

Meaningful Engagement: Adjusting the Constitution-Building Equation

Cases like *Volks* and *Jordan* show the limitations of a traditional approach driven by the first *Makwanyane* story: a principled rights claim backed by civil society groups nevertheless fails because it is insufficiently alive to the newness-related problems for the judicial enforcement of that claim in a particular society at a particular time. They also show the incompleteness of the Court's response to situations of real concern where credible action by other branches is uncertain or fails to transpire.

In fact, to date the Court has come closer to grappling with this situation in the socio-economic context – where, as noted, traditional legal views can be more receptive to the impact of newness-related considerations in rights cases. It is true that the kind of newness at issue is not always the same, but while that must be kept in mind there are lessons to be learned nonetheless. For example, even the *Mazibuko* idea that litigation might (at least) prompt a useful disclosure of government's policy efforts in a particular area, disdained by scholars in the socio-economic context, represents a novel and interesting option for a case like *Jordan*, and challenges conventional understandings of such cases. But my principal interest here is with the device of meaningful engagement, widely discussed as the Court's most creative socio-economic rights intervention to date. My discussion of it serves the limited purposes of the argument of this chapter and is not comprehensive. Because the device is used to do more than one thing, and because it is crucial for analytic purposes to distinguish these differences, we need to start by understanding meaningful engagement as it currently operates.

Engagement arose in cases on eviction, and thus in the context of what has often been one of the clearest systemic violations of socio-economic rights the Court has encountered. Many of the eviction cases to date have concerned the City of Johannesburg (and what can be said about the City's policy also holds, for present purposes, for some important examples in other places).[55] The term 'neo-liberal' is used often and loosely in talk about South Africa, but the City's approach to urban development prior to the eviction cases has a strong claim to fit the label. Seeking to improve areas of the inner city where many buildings had been abandoned, the City would have liked to clear the buildings, attract private investment and establish a functioning housing market in which developers upgraded the buildings against the rents the market could be expected to bear. This, of course, meant evicting the people currently living in those buildings. The insights of the law and geography movement are helpful in describing the result, because the implication was not just that people would be forced to leave the place where they lived. Low-cost inner city housing is in very short supply (and is in any event not

[55] See esp. *Abahlali Basemjondolo Movement SA* v. *Premier of the Province of KwaZulu-Natal* 2010 (2) BCLR 99 (CC), a successful challenge to the KwaZulu-Natal Elimination and Prevention of Re-emergence of Slums Act 6 of 2007, whose blunt title accurately reflects its attitude towards those trying to live in the areas concerned; and *Pheko* v. *Ekurhuleni Metropolitan Municipality* 2012 (2) SA 598 (CC).

that low-cost), and other low-cost housing options are separated from the inner city by kilometers of urban sprawl traversable only by expensive transport options. In this context, the occupied buildings in the inner city often represented the only place where people from the least well-paid parts of its economy could live. The City's policy would therefore effectively make certain lives legally impossible – it would no longer be possible to hold the lowest wage jobs in the inner city and live in a home. The efforts of the civil society bodies resisting the policy represent a campaign to keep open a legal space for these lives.[56]

Engagement therefore arose in a context with importantly conducive features. As noted in the discussion of *PE Municipality*, section 26(3) provides a rare explicit mandate for judicial involvement in eviction cases, and the justices could feel confident announcing out to South Africa that the government should not be in the business of creating misery and homelessness by heavy-handed evictions.[57] Eviction is also traditionally closely associated with courts: as I argued was important in cases like *Gory* v. *Kolver* and *Du Toit* in the LGBTI equality context, key parts of the associated infrastructure are accustomed to working with judicial structures. Finally, the City's stance has also contributed, partly because it has sometimes (ultimately) made important concessions, but mainly because it has adopted some implausibly rigid stances – not engaging with people facing eviction at all despite the lessons of *Grootboom* and *PE Municipality*, or claiming sharply fewer responsibilities in evictions sought by private actors – while usually being unable to offer serious showing that it was necessary to adopt these stances – that it could not afford to provide alternative accommodation, for example, or that concerns about safety and sanitary conditions really

[56] For influence of the movement in South Africa, see esp. recent work on the 'right to the city' by Coggin and Pieterse, 'Rights and the City', esp. 259–62; M. Pieterse, 'Development, the Right to the City, and the Legal and Constitutional Responsibilities of Local Government in South Africa' (2014) 131 *South African Law Journal* 149. On the situation and the campaign, see esp. S. Wilson, 'Litigating Housing Rights in Johannesburg's Inner City: 2004–2008' (2011) 27 *South African Journal on Human Rights* 127; G. S. Dickinson, 'Blue Moonlight Rising: Evictions, Alternative Accommodation and a Comparative Perspective on Affordable Housing Solutions in Johannesburg' (2011) 27 *South African Journal on Human Rights* 466, esp. 487–89, 491–93; S. Wilson, 'Curing the Poor: State Housing Policy in Johannesburg after *Blue Moonlight*' (2013) 5 *Constitutional Court Review* 279, 279–81 and further sources there cited, and see also *Blue Moonlight*, paras. 6–7.

[57] See e.g. *Blue Moonlight*, paras. 34–36; *Machele* v. *Mailula* 2010 (2) SA 257 (CC), para. 25.

did require evictions without engagement or alternative accommodation and without considering upgrading buildings instead.[58]

The question of *how* to intervene, however, has not been as straightforward. There are many other occupied buildings in inner city Johannesburg, and of course anything the Court might rule would also apply to municipalities not enjoying the resources of the country's largest economic centre.[59] The Court thus faced the sort of concerns about the broader implications of its order that we saw in a case like *Nokotyana*. The interests involved were complex, and the disputed nature of how urban development should proceed also meant that judicial intervention raised the prospect of having to confront significant newness unilaterally.[60] In the eviction cases, however, the City's stance gave the Court strong reasons to think it needed to intervene, and in line with my claims in the previous chapter, it did. But that did not alter the challenges, and so the question of how to intervene loomed large.

The expansive institutional discussion in *PE Municipality* provided a blueprint. Meaningful engagement requires the parties to an eviction – the tenants or occupiers, the landlord or owner, and the relevant authorities – to negotiate over the details and consequences of an eviction order. The content articulated in *PE Municipality* and its successors means that it is a negotiation conducted with some sense of what outcomes will not be constitutionally acceptable. For example, as noted in the last chapter, provision for alternative accommodation will now usually be required and that will usually imply some concessions from the municipality about providing it and from the owner about letting the occupiers remain on her property until the municipality does indeed provide another place

[58] The City failed entirely to engage those who would be evicted by policies in the seminal decision in *Occupiers of 51 Olivia Road, Berea Township and 197 Main Street, Johannesburg* v. *City of Johannesburg* 2008 (3) SA 208 (CC), paras. 13, 22, 44. It did, however, later make important concessions in that case: see *Ibid.*, paras. 24–26, 34, resulting in an agreement that 'arguably went further than an order which even a sympathetic court would have granted': Liebenberg, *Adjudicating Socio-economic Rights*, p. 420. For the City's stance on private evictions and cost, see *Blue Moonlight*, paras. 68–75, 91–95. The resistance to alternatives to blunt eviction is a general theme in these cases; see also, in a different municipality, *Pheko*. See also e.g. Ray, 'Evictions, Aspirations and Avoidance', 217, noting that the City's implausible legal stance made a case like *Blue Moonlight* quite easy, in this respect.

[59] In *Olivia Road*, para. 19, the Court accepted a figure of 67 000 as the number of similarly situated occupiers in the area of the Johannesburg municipality (a substantially larger area than the inner city).

[60] On some aspects of the complexities of intervention in Johannesburg's inner-city housing situation, see Dickinson, 'Blue Moonlight Rising'.

to go. But engagement is nevertheless a heavily procedural device, which can seem like another exercise in deference in a socio-economic rights context, avoiding or delaying setting the substantive rules for evictions that the Court should ultimately be articulating, and it has been the subject of scholarly concern and criticism accordingly.[61]

As noted, however, 'engagement' is a multi-faceted tool, and different applications need to be distinguished if we are to understand it. As the Court often talks about it, engagement is a standard procedural duty that government actors must comply with in every eviction, and municipalities, or at least the larger ones, should develop a dedicated, qualified staff to conduct it.[62] It has obvious links to ideas of listening and inclusion and participatory democracy, as the standard procedural duty established in *Doctors for Life* does, and is rooted in dignity and respect.[63] Engagement in this form does not necessarily have to have anything to do with the courts, except in the sense that conducting it is now a requirement for a court to grant an order of eviction. *If* the government acts appropriately, then engagement from the Court's perspective is substantially a non-intervention device, and in line with the argument of other chapters it should be evaluated as an exercise in trying to pick the best institutional response to the issue of eviction rather than as a judicial abdication.

However, that *if* is of course crucial, and as noted the eviction cases have often seen government actors failing to satisfy this condition. In *that* situation, the Court's reaction has been far from confined to developing new procedures. As we saw in the previous chapter, it has expanded alternative accommodation requirements, imposed obligations and

[61] See e.g. B. Ray, '*Occupiers of 51 Olivia Road v City of Johannesburg*: Enforcing the Right to Adequate Housing through Engagement' (2008) 8 *Human Rights Law Review* 703, 709–10; Davis, 'Socioeconomic Rights', 706; L. Chenwi, 'A New Approach to Remedies in Socio-economic Rights Adjudication: *Occupiers of 51 Olivia Road and Others v City of Johannesburg and Others*' (2009) 2 *Constitutional Court Review* 371, 389–92; B. Ray, 'Engagement's Possibilities and Limits as a Socioeconomic Rights Remedy' (2010) 9 *Washington University Global Studies Law Review* 399, 417; K. McLean, 'Meaningful Engagement: One Step Forward or Two Back? Some Thoughts on *Joe Slovo*' (2010) 3 *Constitutional Court Review* 223, esp. 240–41; B. Ray, 'Proceduralisation's Triumph and Engagement's Promise in Socio-economic Rights Litigation' (2011) 27 *South African Journal on Human Rights* 107, 111–12; S. Liebenberg, 'Engaging the Paradoxes of the Universal and Particular in Human Rights Adjudication: The Possibilities and Pitfalls of "Meaningful Engagement"' (2012) 12 *African Human Rights Law Journal* 1; Ray, 'Evictions, Aspirations and Avoidance', 178, 181–82, 185–87, 197–98, 217–20, 228–31; Bilchitz, 'Avoidance Remains Avoidance'; Woolman, *Selfless Constitution*, esp. on this point pp. 441–42; Wilson and Dugard, 'First and Second Waves', pp. 46–47.

[62] *Olivia Road*, paras. 15, 19, 44.

[63] See esp. *Ibid.*, paras. 10, 16.

burdens on private owners, weakened if not eliminated the statutory distinction in this context between short- and long-term occupiers, and showed significant resistance to budgetary and capacity objections. We saw in the LGBTI equality cases how the Court, when it decided to intervene, directly read words into statutes instead of referring the matter to Parliament, and the Court has done the same thing in this context in reading engagement directly into the National Building Regulations and Building Standards Act, the City's key statutory pretext for evictions.[64] But that said, the engagement cases have nevertheless certainly seen the Court articulate much less content than it might have. In this regard, engagement is being used as a different sort of tool, for use by judges during litigation as opposed to as a standard procedural duty binding on government actors (and others) before litigation. If the parties before the Court can be induced to work out a solution, then this permits a court to manage substantive aspects of an eviction without having to take on the task of trying to set an acceptable general standard applicable to all evictions on that point. And even if the parties are unable to work everything out by themselves, their engagement may yield partial agreements or simply information that may assist the Court to make a ruling if it ultimately needs to do so. Thus the engagement cases, alongside the emphasis on listening and dignity, also emphasize the relevant authority's subsequent duty to place relevant information including details of the engagement before the court.[65] Whereas engagement as a procedural duty of the government is a respectful requirement whether or not it yields any new information, engagement as a device for judicial use can have much more to do with substantively assisting a court to design a 'just and equitable' eviction order. On the strength of the argument of this book to this point, we can see what meaningful engagement, in this guise, can represent to the Court: it is a way for the Court to confront a situation where a conventional legal response would require it to resolve a good deal of newness unilaterally, and *not* have to choose between doing that and doing nothing.

[64] National Building Regulations and Building Standards Act 103 of 1997; *Olivia Road*, paras. 50–51. Chenwi, 'New Approach', 377, notes how the Court chose an 'intrusive' remedy here.

[65] *Olivia Road*, para. 21; *Occupiers of Mooiplaats*, paras. 12–13; see also e.g. Liebenberg, *Adjudicating Socio-economic Rights*, pp. 286–90; Ray, 'Evictions, Aspirations and Avoidance', 226–27. See also Michael Bishop's (pre-*Olivia Road*) analysis of different forms of supervisory orders; Bishop, 'Remedies', 9-179–9-181.

Although my interest in the context of the argument of this chapter is particularly in these latters aspects of the engagement device, the general picture of its usage is important for taking the measure of the concerns and criticisms that have been directed at it, including the objection that engagement is an evasion of the Court's responsibility to set broader substantive legal standards for evictions. The questions I have raised throughout in this book – the question of when, the question of assessing bold judicial options in comparison to other institutional possibilities and taking seriously the idea that there often are some – are once again crucial. For example, if it seems predictable that the relevant authorities are not going to act constitutionally, then a participatory democratic procedure is going to seem just as inadequate to critics (and to the people facing eviction) as the participatory democratic understanding of socio-economic rights litigation did in *Mazibuko* – which is why here, as there, the issue cannot be answered in the abstract, and may well look different to the extent that government is genuinely responsive. Similarly, engagement may represent an intervention that is less content-rich than other possibilities, but the claim that it represents an evasion of the Court's standard-setting responsibilities rests partly on an assumption that comprehensive standards are the ultimate regulatory goal here. We do not always hold this assumption: labour law is a good example of a regulatory context where we certainly expect a set of minimum standards and framework rules, but we also expect that a good part of the terms and conditions of particular employment contracts will be the result of an ongoing cycle of conflict and co-operation and compromise. In this context, mechanisms like mediation and arbitration, or more combative ones like strikes and lock-outs, are not necessarily devices to postpone or avoid deciding on substantive rules, but are permanent institutions designed to deal with an enduring area of tension between important interests in a way that is rule-guided but far from rule-determined. Courts would be remiss not to play their part in setting framework standards, but we do not necessarily think it illegitimate if, some of the time, judges do not do this and instead defer to processes between the parties involved. Treating engagement as an abdication, without more, therefore risks begging important questions about how eviction should be legally regulated.

For my purposes here, however, it is two further points of this more nuanced institutional variety that are key. The first is that, from the perspective of the constitution-building account, the engagement cases are an exercise in creating an institutional mechanism to which the Court then partly defers. As in other non-intervention cases, the Court sees itself as deferring to the primary actors responsible for the issue: it is the Court's view, tracing back to *PE Municipality*, that the parties to an eviction have primary constitutional responsibility for resolving that situation in accordance with rights. The judicial responsibility in terms of s 26(3) is one of ultimate, managerial oversight of this process.[66] As a result – again, as in other non-intervention cases – the Court may have responsibility to do more if things go wrong, but it will decline to do so if it does not yet feel the need to take the issue out of the hands of the actors primarily responsible for it. The key difference in the eviction context, however, has been that the infrastructure for these other actors to act was not already in place. The Court could have responded to this gap by articulating a more comprehensive set of rule-based standards itself, thus making the judiciary the primary constitutional mechanism for resolving evictions. It could also have shied away from acting. But engagement instead seeks a middle course: it proactively creates the infrastructure for judges to then (partly) defer to, while exercising ultimate oversight. This is consistent with the Court's general approach to subsidiarity, with the key difference that the Court does an unusual amount here to create the primary mechanism in question.[67] The superficial paradox that the engagement cases are therefore quite an expansive exercise in facilitating restraint is an important reason why they can require careful analysis. And since the Court is seeking to establish a new mechanism, there is a non-decisive but nevertheless important reason for it to then let that mechanism resolve matters instead of the Court doing so itself. This is an important reason for the contrast between the firm legal findings in a case like *Blue Moonlight* – municipalities cannot avoid engagement or their other eviction responsibilities by leaving it to private actors to seek evictions or by failing to budget for all of an eviction's consequences – and the follow-up case's curt decision to defer to processes between the parties and to lower courts. Once again, this is not the product of a puzzlingly inconsistent attitude to rights.[68] It reflects different aspects of

66 *PE Municipality*, paras. 38–39.

67 On subsidiarity, see esp. A. J. van der Walt, 'Normative Pluralism and Anarchy: Reflections on the 2007 Term' (2008) 1 *Constitutional Court Review* 77; K. Klare, 'Legal Subsidiarity and Constitutional Rights: A reply to AJ van der Walt' (2008) 1 *Constitutional Court Review* 90; and in this context in particular Ray, 'Evictions, Aspirations and Avoidance', 190–209; Fowkes, '*Maphango*'.

68 For criticism seeing a problematic inconsistency between *Blue Moonlight* and the follow-up litigation in *Occupiers of Saratoga Avenue* v. *City of Johannesburg Metropolitan*

the effort to build an institution: articulating it, on the one hand, and letting the now-standard mechanism establish itself by operating, on the other.[69]

Institution-creation may be an alternative to a principally standards-setting approach when confronting newness, but that does not mean it avoids the risks. Engagement had things to build on – s 26(3), PIE, the democratic ideas of listening and inclusion we saw in Chapter 7, the constitutional idea that private actors can have horizontal rights responsibilities to other members of society – but it is nevertheless quite a unilateral judicial construction. This is further evidence that the Court does act, even in the context of newness, when it has to, but it is also further evidence of the potential costs of doing so. The Court has not overruled the City's decision that an inner-city rejuvenation would best serve Johannesburg's interests, but it has placed non-trivial constraints on the City's initial view that the best way to bring about this result is by

Municipality 2012 (9) BCLR 951 (CC), see e.g. J. Dugard, 'Beyond *Blue Moonlight*: The Implications of Judicial Avoidance in Relation to the Provision of Alternative Housing' (2013) 5 *Constitutional Court Review* 264; Ray, 'Evictions, Aspirations and Avoidance', 218–20, describing *Blue Moonlight* as the 'mirror image' of *Saratoga Avenue*'s 'formal procedural' approach.

69 From the Court's perspective, the applicants' challenge based on anticipatory breach in *Saratoga Avenue* did not give the mechanisms that should be primary time to act. Hence the Court's rulings that 'the Court was the inappropriate forum' because for 'logical and practical' reasons the court of first instance should deal with the enforcement of the order (*Ibid.*, paras. 2, 9; generally 7–14), and that the City was now co-operating and should be left to proceed (*Ibid.*, paras. 2, 15–16). Similar institutional concerns may be detected e.g. in *Olivia Road*'s comments that in future not all aspects of agreements after engagement would necessarily need to come before the Court for approval (*Ibid.*, para. 34) and the way that judgment declined to make bolder substantive rulings now that engagement was under way: *Olivia Road*, paras. 32–26; see also Liebenberg, *Adjudicating Socio-economic Rights*, pp. 300–01. Insofar as criticism of the approach in *Saratoga Avenue* is based on the decidedly mixed record of the City's subsequent compliance and its policies on alternative accommodation more generally, it is important to bear in mind that *Saratoga Avenue* is not about deference to the City, but to the joint mechanism of parties, the City and – especially – lower courts. Tentative standard-setting by lower courts has lower risks that the finality of Constitutional Court standards and provides ultimate support for Court activity just as other government activity, or engagement itself (see later) can, and there is a growing body of it, though this record too is mixed: see recently on lower court developments e.g. Wilson, 'Curing the Poor'; Dugard, 'Beyond *Blue Moonlight*'; Bilchitz, 'Avoidance Remains Avoidance'. Whether and when more concrete Court standards would be a positive addition to this situation is (in my view) a good debate, in light of the arguments of this and the previous chapter and the fact that at least some of the problems are to do with the way certain lower court judges apply Court precedents rather than with the precedents themselves, but I take this important future debate no further here.

attracting private property investment. The engagement device produces uncertainty: its results are partly subject to negotiation, and its effects can depend on how long court processes take and how long it takes the municipality to do things such as provide alternative accommodation.[70] The Court has expected private owners to accept ongoing occupation for months, including extensions in light of government delays to provide alternative accommodation, although again it has yet to confront a case where the owner can demonstrate a countervailing urgent need to use her property.[71] The point is not at all that these concerns are or should be decisive. Rather, it is to see that there is no evidence that the Court really redid the inner-city policy calculations with engagement factored in, nor is it clear how it could have done so without a lot of evidence and support. To a socio-economic rights sceptic, this may look like the sort of uneasy judicial confrontation with policy-laden, polycentric matters that shows why socio-economic rights should not be justiciable. To the constitution-building account, this is a Court that cannot have the constitution-building first prize, and must choose between imperfect options. Ideally, urban development planning would not be done this way. That it has been is due to the constitutional inadequacies of the City's approach. If the Court believes the primary constitutional actor is disregarding its constitutional responsibilities, then it can either decide the issues itself and impose its views on the primary constitutional actor, though it might be less institutionally well-suited to make the decision, or it can retreat – or it can find a way to involve other actors in making the decision and, by enlisting this help, avoid resolving newness unilaterally.

This, then, is the first point: engagement represents a more proactive version of the by-now familiar constitution-building move to defer to another mechanism instead of engaging in bold judicial content articulation. The second point of special interest here arises because this use of engagement still relies on constitutionally good things happening as a result of relying other parties. It depends on engagement yielding a

[70] Woolman, *Selfless Constitution*, pp. 328–29; see also Dugard, 'Beyond *Blue Moonlight*', 273, noting a recent example of the tension between the City's prevarication in providing alternative accommodation and the private owner's haste to proceed with the eviction.

[71] See e.g. *Blue Moonlight*, para. 100 (holding that patience can be expected from an owner who knowingly bought an occupied building); *Machele* v. *Mailula*, paras. 30–32 (owner would not suffer irreparable harm if eviction delayed); *Occupiers of Skurweplaas 353 JR* v. *PPC Aggregate Quarries (Pty) Ltd* 2012 (4) BCLR 382 (CC), para. 12 and *Occupiers of Mooiplaats*, para. 18 (both noting that occupiers could stay on land for some months given that the owner was not using it).

constitutionally acceptable compromise or at least enough information and concessions that the Court has a basis on which to move the matter forward itself. These virtuous outcomes will not always come to pass, and in some cases they might be so unlikely that they would not even be worth trying for in the first place. Arguments for trust and deference might be undervalued in scholarship on South Africa but of course they do not always hold.[72] For this reason, engagement in this guise will not always represent a sufficient constitutional response to newness, and its critics may therefore feel entitled to conclude that standards are indeed going to be needed after all. They are not necessarily wrong about this.[73] But we have not yet exhausted engagement's potential to assist in the confrontation with newness.

The argument here can be usefully illustrated with reference to a litigation that has sparked concerns about the engagement device, *Residents of Joe Slovo Community, Western Cape* v. *Thubelisha Homes* ('*Joe Slovo*') – concerns we are now better placed to evaluate. A number of observers of engagement are sympathetic to or at least aware of arguments about what engagement could be, but they worry that in practice it will not turn out that way, and they see *Joe Slovo* as evidence of this.[74] (Even those sympathetic to my analogy to labour law, for example, would worry that engagement might be used to avoid articulating even the degree of substantive framework standards we expect in that context.) In *Joe Slovo*, people were being asked to leave the informal settlement where they lived in order either to move into government housing elsewhere or to be temporarily relocated while service infrastructure and housing were built where they were currently living. When doubts arose about whether enough new houses would be allocated to

[72] As *Olivia Road* recognized: 'Engagement has the potential to contribute towards the resolution of disputes and to increased understanding and sympathetic care if both sides are willing to participate' (*Ibid.*, para. 15); 'the process of engagement will work only if both sides act reasonably and in good faith' (*Ibid.*, para. 20). On this as an inevitable limitation of collaborative approaches, see Fowkes, 'Indian PIL', 458–61; as an limitation of weak-form review, see e.g. D. Landau, 'Aggressive Weak-Form Remedies' (2013) 5 *Constitutional Court Review* 243, esp. 247–48.

[73] See note 69 of this chapter.

[74] See e.g. Liebenberg, 'Engaging the Paradoxes', 19: 'there is a real danger that meaningful engagement as an adjudicatory strategy may descend into an unprincipled, normatively empty process of local dispute settlement'; Ray, 'Evictions, Aspirations and Avoidance', 198: 'I worry [that engagement and techniques like it] will have systematically conservative effects ... because they offer a handy, off-the-shelf, justification for uncritical avoidance'.

the residents, or whether enough houses of the sort affordable to them would be built, portions of the community began to resist the plan, leading to the City's application to evict them. In *Joe Slovo (1)*, the Court had several reservations about the engagement process that had occurred but nevertheless granted the order, subject to further limited engagement on some details of the eviction. This compounds the offense in the eyes of those who see meaningful engagement as a weak device: apparently, engagement does not even have to be meaningful for an eviction to proceed.[75]

In some respects, however, *Joe Slovo (1)* stands to the earlier engagement cases as *Merafong* stands to *Doctors for Life*, and here as there differences in the facts are important in understanding the case. The government actors in *Joe Slovo* had certainly not ignored the occupiers, as those in the seminal cases of *PE Municipality* and *Olivia Road* had done. An important part of the problem with engagement in *Joe Slovo* often seemed to be it had been too unstructured, and that several different officials engaged with the community without co-ordination, creating confusion.[76] This may be bad for other reasons, but to the extent that engagement is about showing respect, unstructured engagement is far less obviously a violation than not deigning to engage at all. This, it should be noted, was not the only concern: Sachs J noted that decision-making by the City on some important issues had been problematically unilateral, for example.[77] But it is here that it matters that engagement, as a device with more than one use, is a more multi-faceted mechanism than the public participation doctrine of *Doctors for Life*. As an exercise in respectful participatory democracy by the government authorities involved, there were certainly flaws with engagement in *Joe Slovo*. It might therefore seem to follow that the process should have been invalidated and redone, just as public participation processes had to be redone following *Doctors for Life* and *Matatiele (2)*. But public participation is just a procedural device; once it is done adequately, the government's preferred outcome may prevail. Engagement is different. The completion of an engagement process by other actors does not alter the fact that a

[75] See e.g. Chenwi, 'New Approach to Remedies', 382–83; McLean, 'Meaningful Engagement', esp. 231, 240–42; Liebenberg, *Adjudicating Socio-economic Rights*, pp. 308–10, 314; Liebenberg, 'Engaging the Paradoxes', 22–25; Ray, 'Engagement's Possibilities', 418–19; Ray, 'Proceduralisation's Triumph', 122–23.

[76] *Joe Slovo (1)*, paras. 25–32, 112 (Yacoob J); 243–46 (Ngcobo J); 301 (O'Regan J); 378–89 (Sachs J)

[77] *Ibid.*, para. 384.

judge needs to decide whether the eviction is just and equitable: a government authority that listens respectfully may not thereafter evict simply because it still thinks that best. Thus in the engagement context meaningful participation, while not merely a means to an end, is also not the only end in play. This is especially important when the eviction is part of a housing upgrade, provided the upgrade itself passes muster.[78] As well as displaying more respectful engagement than the earlier cases, the underlying eviction at issue in *Joe Slovo* also had much more to do with the interests of the community concerned and less to do with clearing people out of places to serve the interests of other groups. The Court's intervention in *Joe Slovo (1)* was thus about policing aspects of the upgrade itself and undertakings about it that had been made during the engagement process, rather than details of the engagement process itself as an exercise in participation and listening. It included one of the most detailed orders the Court has yet issued, specifying precisely what sort of homes the evictees were entitled to, down to the material to be used to build the roofs.[79] Viewed purely from the perspective of participatory democracy, this could be criticized as another high-handed exercise in deciding for the community what was in its interests, continuing the top-down attitude of the City during the original engagement process. But engagement is not purely about participatory democracy, and what *Joe Slovo (1)* reflects is not the erosion of engagement's promise, but merely that it is a device with several uses and the optimal blend of those uses will vary with the facts of particular cases.

Whether the Court truly struck the optimal blend in *Joe Slovo (1)* is a matter for reasonable debate. One can argue that more engagement might have been an all-things-considered better way forward in *Joe Slovo (1)*, not just a more democratically respectful step, and this argument gains strength from what actually happened in the aftermath of *Joe Slovo (1)*. Instead of engaging on the remaining details and then proceeding to the eviction, as *Joe Slovo (1)* had ordered, the community and the City carried on engaging about the relocation more generally. Four times the Court asked the City to report back on compliance with the order, and four times the City duly filed extensive papers reporting on the general engagement, but not on the eviction, which had not been carried out.

[78] See *Ibid.*, esp. paras. 114–16 (Yacoob J), 224–35 (Ngcobo J), 268 (O'Regan J); Currie and De Waal, *Handbook*, p. 586; Ray, 'Evictions, Aspirations and Avoidance', 187; Wilson and Dugard, 'First and Second Waves', p. 49.

[79] *Joe Slovo (1)*, para. 7.

And ultimately, this engagement produced an agreement to conduct an in situ upgrade, in line with international best practice, causing less upheaval to lives and jobs and schools.[80] The community had sought this initially in *Joe Slovo (1)*, and the Court there had noted that it was likely the best option, but the City had argued that an in situ upgrade was not feasible, and the Court declined to second-guess this without evidence. In *Joe Slovo (2)*, while expressing concern about the way its first order had been sidelined, the Court discharged that order, cancelling the eviction and letting what everyone thought was a better option go ahead.[81] I am unsurprisingly sympathetic to the argument that further engagement may have been a better original order, representing as it does a claim that broader deference to other institutions and actors might ultimately have served constitutional ends better than sharper and more substantive judicial intervention. Whether it is right is a matter for speculation: we do not know, for instance, how important the detailed order in *Joe Slovo (1)* was in inducing the government to change its mind on the in situ upgrade. It was also surely important that control of the provincial government funding the project changed during the litigation and the newly installed DA had 'always been critical of the implementation' of the housing project and quickly agreed to revisit it.[82]

My interest here, however, is in the position in which the Court found itself in *Joe Slovo (1)* before this aftermath played out. In that position, stipulating that the upgrade be conducted in situ would have meant taking out of the hands of the primary officials the decision about whether this was the best approach, without very much evidence on the need or wisdom of doing so. We saw the Court's reluctance to engage in such unilateral resolution of newness in the previous chapter. But conversely, a general order to engage again might have looked a rather hopeful gambit. The positions of the community and the City seemed to be familiar to everyone, and there was no particular reason to think the City would change its firm position that an in situ engagement was not feasible. It may have seemed quite likely that a simple order to re-engage would be like the re-engagement order in *Matatiele (2)*, which the community widely saw as an empty charade when they challenged it in

[80] On in situ upgrades, see L. Chenwi, 'Legislative and Judicial Responses to Informal Settlements in South Africa: A Silver Bullet?' (2012) 23 *Stellenbosch Law Review* 540.

[81] *Residents of Joe Slovo Community, Western Cape* v. *Thubelisha Homes (2)* 2011 (5) BCLR 273 (CC).

[82] Wilson and Dugard, 'First and Second Waves', p. 48.

Poverty Alleviation Network, or like the possibility of further engagement in *PE Municipality*, where the Court decided that 'too much water had flowed under the bridge' to attempt court-ordered mediation at a late stage in a protracted dispute.[83] What is crucial for the purposes of the present argument is that it was only because the government stance did, after all, shift that further engagement achieved something after *Joe Slovo (1)*. The Court was still deferring to the government actor on the policy details. Such shifts in government stance are an option to be taken seriously, as cases like *Occupiers* and *Joe Slovo* itself illustrate, but they also do not always happen. If that had been the case after further engagement in *Joe Slovo (1)*, the Court would have been in no better position to second-guess the state policy choice than it was earlier, and it would only have served to delay matters, possibly with the interests of the occupiers less secured in the meanwhile. We thus reach the point noted above in which engagement, despite my arguments, would stand ultimately exposed as the limited and essentially deferent mechanism its critics fear it is.

We can see how in this situation the real game-changer would not be to repeat engagement in its guise as an exercise in getting the parties involved to talk respectfully to each other. That might yield a policy shift, but it also might not, and the Court would have little control over the outcome. And since one would only usually get to this point if the government actors involved had quite consistently stuck to a policy position, expecting a late change might often be something of a shot in the dark (though as South African democracy gets more competitive and populist, and the ANC's enjoyment of slack becomes less secure, it might become costlier to ignore firm community opinion and participatory exercises might achieve more as a result). The real possibility of altering the terms of the constitution-building equation lies instead in the part of engagement that seeks to develop information to assist the Court to make a ruling of its own. And if *that* is the aim, there is no reason to limit the subjects of engagement to the parties involved. The decisive criterion would now be ability to assist the Court with the substantive issue before it, and while this will naturally be true of parties intimately involved in a matter, it will not only be true of them. That engagement is partly about participatory democracy and has its origins partly in that ideal does not alter the fact that, to the extent that the aim of the device is to facilitate the judicial task, it may sometimes

[83] *PE Municipality*, para. 47.

in fact be inconsistent with that aim to confine engagement to the parties involved. We should connect this point to the phenomenon we began to see in cases like *Merafong*, where the optimal resolution of an issue and the novel problems it might raise is not necessarily best pursued within the case as framed by the litigants before the Court. In both instances, there is potentially some tension between the autonomy of the people directly involved and the idea of a court trying to inform itself as best as possible in order to make a judgment about what is constitutional and how what is constitutional is to be brought about, and since both ideas are important that tension will need managing.[84] But this is finer detail of the broader point about the possibilities of engagement, in its various guises, as a judicial toolkit for responding to newness, and having seen how general that challenge is, we can see why this matters far beyond the context of eviction.[85]

Engagement and Its Possibilities: From Eviction to *Prince* to the Future

This argument certainly points beyond engagement's main current usage, but there are already signs within existing practice of the broader potential it holds. The 2011 decision in *Juma Musjid* was an eviction case in relation to a building being used as a school, and so the case was also about the obligations owed to the pupils by the owner and the government department under the right to education. Engagement was ordered, with the Court ruling that the approach to engagement in *PE Municipality*, weighing the right to property and the right to housing, applied 'analogously', since 'normal ownership rights are not counterposed only to constitutional housing rights, but also . . . to other fundamental rights'.[86] Subsequent cases confirm the trend, especially *Welkom High School*, a case that ordered meaningful engagement between school

[84] The parties directly involved would no doubt merit special attention. The special consultative duties owed to 'discrete and identifiable' groups 'directly affected' by a policy, discussed in the public participation cases, may find application here. See *Matatiele (2)*, paras. 68, 79, 100; *Poverty Alleviation Network*, paras. 51–52.

[85] See further comments on judge-led fact-finding in Fowkes, 'Indian PIL', 457–61.

[86] *Governing Body of the Juma Musjid Primary School* v. *Essay NO* 2011 (8) BCLR 761 (CC); the quoted text appears at para. 70. See also Woolman, *Selfless Constitution*, pp. 471–74. *PE Municipality* itself drew inspiration from the role of mediation in other areas of law: see paras. 39–40.

and departmental authorities over a learner pregnancy policy that had nothing to do with eviction.[87]

Blue Moonlight points to another sort of expansion. The City of Johannesburg argued in that case that not it but the province was obliged to fund alternative accommodation, as part of the provisions of the Housing Code created in response to *Grootboom*. The province resisted this suggestion. The Court has not yet had to resolve this point, since it has sufficed to date to find that the City must allocate *some* funds for this purpose, and so the question of how much of the burden must be borne by the province has not had to be decided.[88] But if the standard expected of alternative accommodation rises, or if need does, this question may become a live one, and it will be difficult for the Court to resolve unilaterally. The Constitution offers a ready answer to such a dispute: being one between organs of government, it is governed by the principles of co-operative governance. The Court has ruled that organs of state must try to resolve such disputes themselves before coming to Court, and that it will refuse jurisdiction where such efforts are not made.[89] But if this kind of dispute arises in the context of an ongoing eviction dispute, the Court will be exercising jurisdiction already and may not be able to relinquish it without neglecting the rights of the occupier and the owner: being able to progress on the issue of alternative accommodation will usually be a condition precedent to granting the eviction order. It will be natural, in this context, to require the relevant state organs to engage, resolve the dispute and report back to the Court, drawing on both meaningful engagement and co-operative government. (This implication of the co-operative governance principle has already been important in the education cases just noted).[90] This scenario shows the potential blurring of the line between resolving a concrete situation, which is engagement's current focus, and resolving questions of broader policy

87 *Welkom High School*, esp. paras. 120–28 and the separate concurring judgment of Froneman and Skweyiya JJ, esp. para. 139; I noted the concurrence's broad reading of the ideas of *Doctors for Life* in Chapter 7; see also *MEC for Education in Gauteng Province v. Governing Body of Primary School* 2013 (6) SA 582 (CC), esp. paras. 49, 67–78. The possibility of engagement outside the context of eviction is also readily linked to arguments we have already seen; for example, engagement, so understood, looks quite a lot like what critics were really seeking in *Merafong*.

88 *Blue Moonlight*, paras. 45–50, 57–69.

89 1996 Constitution, s 41; *Premier, Western Cape*.

90 *Rivonia Primary*, paras. 48–49, 77; see also the separate concurrence in *Welkom High School*, paras. 140, 144–47, 161, 164–65.

without judicial unilateralism but within the context of an ongoing exercise of jurisdiction.

In fact, once we look, we will see that steps of this sort already dot the Court's practice, albeit usually in an ad hoc manner, outside the context of cases formally seen as engagement cases. The Court sometimes invites groups not directly involved in a case to participate. These invitations, such as those extended to the Council of Traditional Leaders of South Africa in customary law matters, show the same mix of idea of participation and inclusion, on the one hand, and the perceived potential of the group to contribute to the substance and legitimacy of the Court's decision, on the other, that we see in the engagement cases proper.[91] A case like *Richter* displayed a strongly collaborative element, and while that had a lot to do with the approach of the Electoral Commission, we would presumably appreciate that approach in the same way if it were a product of more exclusively judicial initiative. Suggestions like this will also attract the sympathy of the growing body of work, noted earlier, which draws on dialogue theory or Habermas or experimental constitutionalism more than, say, Dworkin, and would prefer judges to be slower to settle contested questions definitively by bold, principled but unilateral rulings.[92]

In closing this chapter, my particular interest is in applying this thinking to the problematic position in which we left the Court in the controversial equality cases in the first half of it. Having argued that the concern in those cases, unlike more triumphant equality decisions, was the degree of newness they asked the Court to confront unilaterally, what might engagement, as a toolkit for responding to newness, be able to offer?

I take as my illustration the final case to be considered here, *Prince* v. *President, Cape Law Society* ('*Prince*'), another of the Court's regretted refusals of an equality challenge. In *Prince*, a Rastafarian who had completed his law exams wished to register his statutorily required community service, a necessary step to become an attorney. In his application, he revealed that he had two criminal convictions for

[91] Woolman notes this feature of the customary law judgment in *Shilubana* v. *Nwamitwa* 2009 (2) SA 66 (CC); Woolman, *Selfless Constitution*, pp. 456–57.

[92] See sources cited in Chapter 2, n. 38 and Chapter 5 n. 3, and accompanying text. See also discussions of experimental constitutionalism specifically in the socio-economic rights by e.g. Tushnet, *Weak Courts*, p. 249; Chenwi, 'New Approach to Remedies', 383–87; Liebenberg, *Adjudicating Socio-economic Rights*, pp. 434–38.

marijuana possession, and that he intended to keep using marijuana for religious reasons. The law society declined to register his community service on the grounds that his prior illegal behaviour and continued intention to break the law was not fit and proper conduct for an attorney. The Court, ultimately, rejected his challenge to this decision, essentially on the grounds that creating a religious exemption for practicing Rastafarians to the general criminalization of marijuana possession would be too hard to police. *Prince* is less vilified than cases like *Jordan* or *Volks* because it at least recognizes the seriousness of the rights problem at stake, while holding it to be justified. But it nevertheless still did nothing.[93]

For present purposes, what is of particular interest is that when the case first reached the Court, the justices ruled in *Prince (1)* that they lacked the evidence they needed to decide the issue. Instead of dismissing the case, however, the Court called for the parties to supply more evidence in response to specific questions.[94] (It is not uncommon for the Court to call for further argument on a legal issue it feels is important but inadequately traversed on the papers, but it remains very unusual for the Court to call for more evidence on a legal point already squarely raised). In other words, the Court felt unable to decide whether it could order a religious exemption on the basis of the evidence that had been placed before it, so it tried to inform itself. Rather than act as a traditional appeal court and let burdens of proof and pleading rules decide an important question, it tried to alter the terms of the constitution-building equation.

It is also significant, however, that this step did not do all that much to alter that equation. Having received further affidavits, the Court was not much better placed to decide whether an exemption for Rastafarians was feasible and could be policed without undermining the broader objectives behind the general criminalization of marijuana (which was not challenged in the case). There is a sharp difference between the sort of

[93] For criticism and concerns, see e.g. A. Pillay, 'Recent Developments: South Africa' (2003) 1 *International Journal of Constitutional Law* 152; P. Lenta, 'Cultural and Religious Accommodations to School Uniform Regulations' (2008) 1 *Constitutional Court Review* 259, 266–68; A. Smith, 'Equality Constitutional Adjudication in South Africa' (2014) 14 *African Human Rights Law Journal* 609, 617–20.

[94] *Prince* v. *President of the Law Society of the Cape of Good Hope* 2001 (2) SA 388 (CC); see also L. du Plessis, 'Religious Freedom and Equality as Celebration of Difference: A Significant Development in Recent South African Constitutional Case-law' (2009) 12 *Potchefstroom Electronic Law Journal* 10, 19–20.

evidentiary consensus we saw in cases like *Hoffman* and *TAC (2)*, and merely having lots of factual submissions. In *Prince (2)*, the Court split 5–4 on the issue, but it is hard to avoid the impression that neither side was really in much position to decide it.[95] The minority favouring creating an exemption, for example, advance the troubling argument that the state's ban was aimed at protecting citizens from drug-related harm to their health, but that while excessive *smoking* of marijuana causes harm, other Rastafarian practices such as bathing in marijuana or burning it had not been shown to have these harms, and therefore the state's ban was overbroad because it criminalized all these usages alike.[96] This is logically correct, but it is hard to see that it would be possible to police a selective ban on how marijuana may be used, and in any event the applicant had stated that he *did* regularly smoke marijuana, as do many other Rastafarians.[97] The majority was just as uncertain about what might be practicable, but took this as a reason not to impose an order that an exemption be created – thus leaving an admitted problem unremedied, with no apparent prospect that any other institution was going to do anything about it. Neither approach is terribly satisfactory: this is another illustration of the hard choice between deciding on an uncertain basis, or being too uncertain to decide and letting a constitutional problem persist as a result.[98]

How might the Court have done better in *Prince*? For one thing, the suggestion based on s 7(2) made in relation to *Volks* and *Jordan* has appeal in relation to *Prince* too. The judgment in *Prince* in favour of intervention, in one sentence, makes the observation that the legislature had 'never considered' the issue of Rastafarian marijuana use when drawing up the drug control legislation at issue.[99] As in *Jordan*, the statutes concerned were apartheid-era statutes, passed in 1965 and 1992 respectively. Once again, framing the legal question as a challenge to the legislature's breach of its positive s 7(2) duty to promote rights looks promising, as does even the *Mazibuko* prospect of having the government come to Court and make disclosure of its efforts to regulate

95 *Prince (2)*, paras. 4, 31, 107–09.

96 *Ibid.*, paras. 58–59; see also the majority judgment, paras. 116–18, 129–30, 133–42.

97 See also *Ibid.*, paras. 140, 142.

98 It is potentially significant that, in the context of uncertainty, a near-majority of the *Prince (2)* Court were nevertheless willing to issue a definite ruling. This sort of split would be unusual in the socio-economic rights context and may indeed reflect that judges are happier ruling in more traditional contexts like religious exemptions.

99 *Ibid.*, para. 68.

marijuana in light of the special position of Rastafarians. If the Court has to decide whether a violation of religious rights is justified, then the Court has to make a finding on whether an exemption scheme is feasible – which as we have seen it struggled to do even after calling for further evidence. If the challenge is instead directed to the fact that the legislature had apparently never considered the effect on Rastafarians of its criminalization of marijuana possession and use, the violation looks patent coming from the legislature of a pluralist state with rights to religious belief and practice. And because the natural remedy is to refer the matter to the legislature for it to conduct that process, there is no need for the Court to make decisions about feasibility for which it lacked adequate support.

Such a referral, in the age of *Doctors for Life*, would entail public participation in the resulting legislative process, of which consultation with Rastafarian groups would be an essential part. With that element added, we can see the similarities between this result and a general engagement order. The separate judgment of Sachs J in *Prince (2)* records that, in response to a question asked during the hearing, counsel 'indicated that he was not aware of any attempt having been made to contact any Rastafari to see if a reasonable exemption could be worked out with them'. At that time, some years before the engagement remedy he would write about in *PE Municipality*, Sachs J was focused on the interaction of the parties during the court proceedings themselves as 'an important step in the process of accommodation and mutual recognition'.[100] But similar arguments would also suggest the more proactive possibility of ordering the police and other relevant authorities to engage with Rastafarian communities to try and work out an arrangement, both as an exercise in participatory democracy of potentially significant value as a gesture, a learning experience, and a symbol, and as a potential source of help to the Court in moving forward on the matter.[101] Whether one prefers this approach to the legislative referral will naturally depend on arguments from trust and the prior history of the matter: in *Prince (2)*, with no history of prior engagement or even attention, a simple referral to the legislature has appeal, but it is easy to imagine contexts in which an engagement approach within the control of the Court's jurisdiction might seem preferable.

[100] *Ibid.*, para. 162.

[101] For similar comments on *Prince*, see Woolman, *Selfless Constitution*, pp. 427–28; see also his comments, in the context of a different case, on extracting information beyond the parties' papers; *Ibid.*, 442–43.

The limitations of the approach are the same in this context, too. Deferring to action by others, whether via a referral or a judicial engagement exercise, depends on those others producing a constitutionally acceptable result. Just as in *Joe Slovo*, it is easy to imagine scenarios in which a *Prince* referral to the legislature might have yielded only the same ultimate decision that an exemption would be too hard to police, or in which an engagement exercise would not materially shift the positions or information before the Court. In such situations, the Court would again be left with a choice between resolving issues itself in the face of substantial uncertainty (as four judges were willing to do in *Prince (2)*), or decline to act (like the other five), or using further engagement in a still more proactive, inquisitorial way to attempt to resolve some of the factual questions itself, or at least to try and achieve greater certainty about them than the *Prince (2)* Court could from the parties' papers alone. This latter approach, like the basic order of engagement itself, is an act of extended jurisdiction by the Court, and so it runs the same risk we saw in *Nokotyana*: the Court would be embarking on a potentially lengthy exercise of jurisdiction without any guarantee that this would ultimately underwrite a credible order. But *Prince* is more like *Jordan* in that there was much less reason to think the government was taking the underlying issue seriously or that it would act on it, and so non-intervention in *Prince* is less constitutionally appealing than non-intervention in *Nokotyana*. The institutional dynamics, however, are similar whatever the right, because the problem of newness and the judicial response to it are similar across the contexts.

What precise course of action would have been best in *Prince* is a matter of reasonable debate, and again that debate is insolubly dependent on counterfactuals. My comments are less criticisms of the *Prince* judges and litigants – constitution-building is a learning exercise for everyone – than they are directed to the work that remains to be done. *Prince*'s attempt to get the parties to improve the evidentiary position was innovative, but it achieved little and this failure is no doubt an important reason why the approach did not become more common thereafter. Engagement, arising in a different context, marks a renewed effort of this sort, already more advanced than *Prince*'s in its participatory aspects, while still emerging as an evidentiary device. The effort matters because it provides the way out of the stark choice between acting with insufficient support or not acting. On the strength of the arguments of this book, the stance of the ANC government since 1994 has often served to soften this equation, both because the public status it has given to important constitutional ideas has offered support to the Court's position, and because deference in the face of newness is more constitutionally appealing the greater the constitutional quality of the government. But whatever one thinks of such arguments, they have not always held and they will not always hold in the future. The Court will continue to confront newness. The degree to which it does is likely to increase, as invalidating easy apartheid-era unconstitutionalities and vindicating clear products of the nation's rejection of apartheid are increasingly replaced by more contested questions. As more conservative groups start to copy the litigation tactics of their progressive counterparts, sharper contests on the papers before the Court will also become more frequent.[102] These sharper social contests will affect the members and factions of the ANC like everyone else, and the party is less likely to enjoy political slack and to see unpopular constitutional positions enforced by its leadership. If this book is right about the value of the ANC's post-1994 stance to the constitution-building court, than the possible consequences of an erosion of that stance represents the constitution-building approach's greatest unanswered question going forward.

Comparative experience shows how engagement as it currently exists could be only the beginning in this regard, and that there are a range of ways in which the Court can rethink the judicial role and reshape otherwise difficult cases to facilitate their judicial resolution.[103] It also suggests, particularly once other disciplinary work is considered, that this includes the possibility of settling some factual and policy disputes by resort to outside expertise in the manner suggested by the more expansive possible manifestations of the engagement device.[104] Comparative experience also suggest how such steps can become accepted or tolerated

102 Budlender et al., *Public Interest Litigation*, pp. 13–21.

103 India and Colombia are two important but by no means isolated examples here; see Fowkes, 'Indian PIL' and Fowkes, 'Managerial Judge' and further sources there cited. Comparative discussion with other Global South states is, happily, on the rise; see recently e.g. O. Vilhena, U. Baxi and F. Viljoen (eds.), *Transformative Constitutionalism: Comparing the Apex Courts of Brazil, India and South Africa* (Pretoria University Law Press, 2013); D. Bonilla Maldonado (ed.), *Constitutionalism of the Global South: The Activist Tribunals of India, South Africa and Colombia* (Cambridge University Press, 2014).

104 See e.g. the randomized trial approach of the Abdul Latif Jameel Poverty Action Lab (J-PAL), www.povertyactionlab.org; for an accessible introduction to this approach, see A. V. Bannerjee and E. Duflo, *Poor Economics: A Radical Rethinking of the War to Fight Global Poverty* (New York: Public Affairs, 2011).

by political actors, whether because political forces are too divided to oppose them, are grateful for action (and for deniability), or because a government that must remain publicly committed to the rule of law has limited options in clipping a court's wings. Many of these steps could be taken with a high degree of legitimacy, especially if other institutions are acting poorly and if the court is seen as transparent and consultative, and has some credible claim to be seeking the public good. (That said, comparative experience also shows the greater salience that the political calculations analysed by Roux can have in the context of more expansive judicial action, depending on the political context). Much remains to be seen, and to be done: if it is correct that the current model has depended critically for its success on the stance of the ANC, and that the possibility of an erosion of that stance is therefore that model's greatest liability, then alternative institutional strategies to respond to newness will represent the single most important issue for the Court's future work.

As we turn to contemplate that future, however, we should not forget the moral of this book's backward-looking story. All these innovative possibilities represent acceptable interpretations of the Constitution, and they may represent the best available option in particular contexts because they hold out the possibility of constitutional action when it might otherwise seem unlikely or imprudent. But they will still usually represent no more than a constitution-building second prize. The Constitution may underwrite a sweeping judicial mandate, but it has many institutions and allocates responsibilities widely, and does so in large part out of an implicit structural belief that this is the most effective and legitimate pattern of constitutional government. On the strength of the preceding chapters, we can see that South Africa's post-1994 Constitutional Court has not forgotten this. In a context in which other branches of government, whatever their admitted imperfections, have often done a great deal to live up to this constitutional billing, the Court has often had the ability to vindicate a vision of the constitutional mechanism as a whole, not just those parts of it that contemplate bold judicial enforcement of rights. Whether this will remain the case is mostly not up to the Court. The Constitution has made many things into legal issues, and therefore much potentially within judicial control. But it also contemplates much that is new, and unsettled, and uncertain, and therefore much that is not best resolved by courts alone. In this simple fact we see the reason for the heavily institutional work of the constitution-building court.

Conclusion

Constitutionalism, at its best, is a public activity. This book and its case studies have sought to show that this is as true of the celebrated South African example as anywhere. It might therefore be most appropriate to express the conclusions of this book in terms of what I believe they mean for different constitutional actors.

The most important task of an applicant before the constitution-building Court is not to persuade it what a particular provision of the Constitution should be understood to mean, nor even to convince it of the factual existence of a particular constitutional harm – this will be necessary, of course, but not sufficient. It is to show the Court a way in which it can intervene to constitutionally valuable ends. This will be principally an institutional point. It will be harder to demonstrate this the more it is true that action will require the Court to resolve newness unilaterally, and the more the action is the primary responsibility of some other institution which is not itself reneging on that responsibility in some significant way.

This point can seem almost wilfully designed to trip up traditional views of litigation, where proving to the judges what has happened, and persuading them that this is a violation of the law according to the best interpretation of the relevant provisions, is supposed to be the whole of a lawyer's work. But it is not much of an exaggeration to say that the litigant in the constitution-building court who simply argues the facts and the applicable rights will win only by coincidence. Showing that a problem exists does not show the Court that other more constitutionally appropriate actors cannot or will not solve it, and demonstrating to the Court the best interpretation of a piece of law, even if the justices are inclined to agree, does not show that the Court should chose this moment to articulate it. The reason these considerations are important, and that the traditional understanding of lawyers' work does not fit well, is because the Court's task is not just to apply the law – or, perhaps more accurately, because the law it is tasked to apply is expansive and often significantly new, and the task must performed in a context where the mechanisms for constitutional enforcement are often themselves part of what is new and the Court's actions are constantly exposed as potentially presumptuous. As a court of final appeal, interpreting the law is always going to be more important to the Court than settling the facts, but as a constitution-building court confronting newness, the decision of when to act, including when to interpret, is more important still.

For the defendant, in the government or otherwise, the most important task will be to show the Court that it does not need to intervene, and that it can instead show trust. Evidence of good faith and basic competence are the most valuable commodities here. That is not only because the Court is sympathetic to the difficulty of many constitutional tasks and will be pragmatic in its expectations. It is also – less obviously, perhaps, but more importantly – because if another constitutional actor is basically willing and able, then the Court will to an important degree assess that actor's performance against the prospect of its own intervention, in light of its own institutional limitations and the other risks of judicial action. In that scenario, the most important thing is to show the Court that, if it shows trust, it will not look foolish. Signs of bad faith or serious dysfunction will vitiate this default logic. The limitations of judicial intervention will look much less decisive if they are being compared to action by a broken mechanism, or to no action by a defiant one.

The Court has a rather more sophisticated theory of when to intervene than scholarship usually appreciates, but it remains weaker on the question of *how* to intervene. This is a question offering considerable scope for creativity. The fact that traditional understandings of what is expected of litigants do not always fit the demands of constitution-building especially well is an indication that traditional understandings of judicial activity might not always fit it well either. The Court has exercised a range of new powers, but it has sometimes been slow to test the boundaries of novel forms of activity and been ad hoc when it does. Scholars have not been of as much assistance as they might have in this area, because their re-imagining of the Court's institutional role has often been firmly directed to urging it to do more. There is value in exhorting the Court to test its limits, but scholarship informed by the Court's more nuanced theory of when is likely to offer more assistance to the justices, particularly when it comes to showing how the Court might be able to adjust the terms of the constitutional equation somewhat by creative institutional action. We saw some moves in this direction in the last chapter, and partly due to recent personnel changes in recent years, the judges seem to be increasingly willing to reshape cases from the way they litigants have chosen to plead them in order to resolve them in a constitutionally optimal manner. Instead of rejecting a case because it seeks the wrong remedy or is framed in the wrong terms, there appears to be an emerging willingness to reshape it, thus allowing the court to take action on the problem without sacrificing its established craftsmanship and concern for institutional points. This work to reframe the terms of the constitution-building equation is important and needs scholarly support.

Even more important is that the constitution-building account shows us how much constitutional activity happens outside the Constitutional Court, and how much that external activity affects the part that does happen inside it. As an effort to challenge a predominantly Court-centric scholarship, this book has shared some of the sins of its target, but it can at least claim to show why constitutionalism in South Africa should be taken seriously as a broader public activity. Scholarship does exist on the constitutional work done outside the court system – particularly on social movements – but its sum is in any event far below what would be proportional to the amount of constitutional activity that happens there, and important topics are neglected. To take just one example, South Africa has produced one landmark statute after another in the years since 1994, and continues to do so.[1] Individual laws can be criticized, and delays are chronic, but it is nevertheless true that an extraordinary legislative record has been built up. While lawyers naturally look at individual statutes in their fields, the constitutional significance of this work as a body, and of legislatures in the constitutional structure, remains underexamined.

For South Africans, and for South African constitutionalism's many friends abroad, the crucial significance of activity outside the Court should come as encouraging news. Many of the stories told in this book demonstrate how the foundations of great constitutional change are built, and how quite small groups have sometimes done a lot of this construction work, or have been able to trigger it. We are, perhaps, used to a

[1] On the idea of a category of statutes of especial status and entrenchment, but short of truly constitutional status, see Ackerman, *Foundations*, 90–91; B. Ackerman 'Holmes Lectures: The Living Constitution' (2007) 120 *Harvard Law Review* 1737; and for a somewhat different usage also of potential value in the South African context, see W. N. Eskridge, Jnr and J. Ferejohn, 'Super-statutes' (2001–2002) 50 *Duke Law Journal* 1215; Eskridge and Ferejohn, *Republic of Statutes*.

picture in which civil society activity is a clash between settled camps, jostling for small advantages, with decisive change only really possibly if some significant social shift occurs to reset the rules of the game. Sometimes that is accurate, and there are many issues in South Africa with set, powerful groups on all sides, or where this pattern is establishing itself. But since 1994 the country has nevertheless quite often been in a different position. A considerable consensus (albeit an overlapping one) has existed around the need for several kinds of change, some of which has yet to come about. Many implications of the 1996 Constitution remain to be worked out, because the process of getting the new ideas and values into the text is, as we have seen, not the most important factor in realizing their implications in reality. In this situation, the constitution-building work that can be done by small groups of people is not small, especially now that they have precedents for how best to go about this work. While thinking about what it would take to get the constitution-building Court to announce a particular idea to the country as its commitment or to take a certain decision or function out of the hands of other actors is not the only way to plan for social change, its emphasis on how to tackle the uncertainties of newness might make it a good one.

That said, the most important underpinning of the Court's great cases to date has been provided by government action, and a good part of what civil society activity has achieved has been done via government channels, impacting on legislation, or law reform proposals or policy documents. A major theme of this book has been the extent of the ANC's government's contribution in the years since 1994, and the extent to which this goes unconsidered, still less given the constitutional credit it deserves. There are many blots on the ANC's record (and the ink has been falling faster recently), and it is also true that its record in relation to the Court is often better than in many other respects. But if South African constitutionalism itself is so celebrated, and the Constitutional Court would have been at least a nominee for best young court around the world in several years since 1994, the ANC might well have been in the running for best young constitutional government in a good few of those years as well. That there will be resistance to this idea reflects the extent to which suspicion of the government is entrenched, and also the extent to which South Africans tend to make absolute judgments about their government and their politics rather than relative judgments with a calibrating eye on similar contexts elsewhere in the world. It would take much broader comparative study, and more complete examination of the record of the ANC, to test this claim fully, but while it is here offered as a provocation, it is one worth thinking about seriously.

Of course, even if I am right about this happy situation there is no guarantee that it will continue. It already seems a safe bet at this point that South African politics will get more competitive, and that the temptations and rewards of both populism and patronage politics will grow. Among other things, that would reduce political slack, and thus also reduce the incentives and opportunities for government to support policies that are counter-majoritarian in relation to public opinion. Fortune-telling aside, such shifts are not necessarily bad news: they might be good for policies with majoritarian support, such as socio-economic redistribution. They are also not necessarily bad news for the Court. A more fractured, competitive polity is one that may well require the Court to play a larger power-broking role – a classic way for a court to achieve institutional security by being useful to those with power, reinforced by the fact that a fractured power system is less able to pose a threat. Something similar can be true of problems with government inefficiency and incapacity, an issue of huge importance at this point (and one where even small reform gains could produce large benefits). These often manifest as problems at the provincial or local level, problems that the national government is often embarrassed about and keen to fix, and thus problems that may present themselves to the Court as interactions between parts of government, rather than clashes of the Court versus the powerful. (These situations also offer important space for strategically collaborative civil society action.) None of this dispels the possibility that South Africa might move into the more difficult territory for judicial review contemplated in the work of Theunis Roux and others writing on fragile constitutional systems, but this book does not tell us whether or not that will happen. What it does do is show what South African constitutionalism has actually depended on since 1994, so that we can properly appreciate the significance of future developments as shifts in that pattern.

As we look back at the years since 1994, this book sees three things in particular.

The first is a point about the 1996 Constitution. It is aspirational and transformative, but while that it is a way to say that it is a justly celebrated vision, it is also a way to say that it is very open-ended and that its implications are often uncertain. As a result, even as we admire them, we can also see that the words on the page are less decisive than they might be. That is not just because, as with any law, writing down words does not translate automatically into change in the world. It is because compliance with such a text is often a matter of degree to be maximized, rather than a binary matter of obeying or breaking. It because, as we have seen throughout the book, the words on the constitutional page are variously realized in the world, in the acts of those holding democratic power, and in ideas of public status. These are the things that matter most, because they represent the reality in which judges must do their work. These are what fill in what is uncertain in the text, or underwrite that filling in by judges. The constitutionalism matters much more than the Constitution.

This has important and underacknowledged implications for the act of interpretation and the work of the Court. While its critics have been invoking the text and all its promises, battling to defend the idea of transformative rather than preservative constitutionalism, and describing the bolder things the Court could be doing if it would only try, the Court has mostly been confronting a different set of questions. It has had to focus much more often on how and when to protect and promote the promises of the text than on what those promises are – which is why the same is so often true of the points on which the Court itself splits. The line the Court has been working out is often not the one between preservative and transformative constitutionalism, which preoccupies scholarly writing, but the late Chief Justice Langa's line between being transformative and being legislative (which, as is not always remembered, is a line Karl Klare's seminal 1998 paper on transformative constitutionalism aimed to draw too).[2] And because the Court itself is much less court-centric than its critics, it has usually begun its enquiries by asking what other institutions are doing, or might do, and only secondarily about its own powers and how far they can be pushed. This book has attempted to understand the value of the Court's approach by examining factors that are not prominent in the existing scholarship: the challenges of newness and the value of support when judges must confront it; the (related) extraordinary value of trust and the work that creating it takes; and the multi-institutional thinking that follows naturally as soon as the importance of support and trust come into focus.

Finally, the worth or otherwise of this approach depends very heavily on the society in which it is tried. In a different polity, support might be lacking, trust might be naïve, and a court might be forced to go it alone,

[2] Langa, 'Transformative Constitutionalism', 353; Klare 'Transformative Constitutionalism', 150.

or look to other institutions mainly for the purposes of trying not to provoke them. In a different polity, the competing imperatives of constitution-building would be more difficult to align, a constitution-building court would have to make tougher choices between them, and it would be harder and harder to describe its work in terms that could be built into a coherent and satisfyingly legal account. In such a polity, the underlying interpretative approach of this book would often fail, and we would be left either just to describe what had happened, as realists, or to document its legal deficits, as lawyers.

But post-1994 South Africa has mostly not been this polity, or so I have argued in this book. The events of the early 1990s have long been taken as evidence that South Africa was fortunate in her politics. With the passing of that extraordinary time, the inevitable return to politics as normal comes as something of a disappointment. It has sometimes been deceptively easy to mistake the inevitable shift from great to ordinary for the decline from good to bad – easier still because post-1994 South Africa really has experienced shifts to bad politics too. Yet South Africa has often also been fortunate in her post-transition constitutional politics, as we have seen repeatedly. We have seen how each of the most famous members of the Court's canon has been built on the work of others, and been defended by them. We have also seen how a good many of its most criticized decisions represent judgments that court intervention would not be the best way to promote constitutional ends, a judicial luxury that does not exist unless other actors are also sometimes working sincerely for those goals. And we have seen situations where government entities have not been fulfilling their constitutional responsibilities, but where other actors have responded and have helped the Court to compensate for this failure. It is in *this* sort of state that court centrism is often unconvincing, and where taking real constitutional practice seriously is often legally satisfying.

This book has looked backwards, because it has argued that we need to reconsider the ways in which we understand interpretation, South African constitutionalism and the work of the Court. But I will offer one prediction. Despite all the criticism levelled at it, for all the wishing that the ANC were less powerful and multiparty political competition more real, despite all the work that must still be done and all the change we must still aspire to produce, I suspect that we will come to look back with increasing appreciation, and with nostalgia, at the constitutionalism that was possible in the first years of building the South African Constitution.

BIBLIOGRAPHY

South African Constitutions, Statutes and Bills

Basic Conditions of Employment Act 75 of 1997
Constitution Fourteenth Amendment Act of 2008
Constitution Fifteenth Amendment Act of 2008
Constitution of the Republic of South Africa, 1996
Constitution of the Republic of South Africa Act 200 of 1993
Constitution of the Republic of South Africa Act 110 of 1983
Criminal Law (Sexual Offences and Related Matters) Amendment Act 32 of 2007
Criminal Procedure Act 51 of 1977
Domestic Partnerships Bill, 2008, Notice 36 of 2008, *GG* 30663, 14 January 2008
Eastern Cape Liquor Act 10 of 2003
Electoral Act 73 of 1998
Employment Equity Act 55 of 1998
Free State Gambling and Liquor Act 6 of 2010
Gauteng Liquor Act 2 of 2003
Housing Act 107 of 1997
KwaZulu-Natal Elimination and Prevention of Re-emergence of Slums Act 6 of 2007
KwaZulu-Natal Liquor Licensing Act 6 of 2010
Labour Relations Act 66 of 1995
Liquor Act 27 of 1989
Liquor Act 59 of 2003
Local Government: Municipal Structures Act 117 of 1998
Lotteries Act 57 of 1997
Maintenance of Surviving Spouses Act 27 of 1990
Medical Schemes Act 131 of 1998
Mpumalanga Liquor Licensing Act 5 of 2006
National Building Regulations and Building Standards Act 103 of 1997
National Education Policy Act 27 of 1996
National Policy for Health Act 116 of 1990
Northern Cape Liquor Act 2 of 2008

Prevention of Illegal Eviction from and Unlawful Occupation of Land Act 19 of 1998
Promotion of Equality and Prevention of Unfair Discrimination Act 4 of 2000
Riotous Assemblies Act 17 of 1956
Road Traffic Management Corporation Act 20 of 1999
Sexual Offences Act 23 of 1957
South African Civil Aviation Authority Act 40 of 1998
Special Pensions Act 69 of 1996
Western Cape Liquor Act 4 of 2008

Other South African Official Sources

Cabinet of the Republic of South Africa, 'Statement on Cabinet meeting of 17 April 2002', available at www.gcis.gov.za/content/newsroom/media-releases/cabinet-statements/statement-cabinet-meeting-17-april-2002-1

City of Johannesburg, 'Social Package', available at www.joburg.org.za/index.php?option=com_content&task=view&id=3432&Itemid=168

De Klerk, FW, Speech at the Opening of Parliament, 2 February 1990, reproduced in Ebrahim, Hassan, *The Soul of a Nation: Constitution-making in South Africa* (1999)

Department of Health, 'Minister Approaches Constitutional Court on Nevirapine Order' Press Release in the name of Dr Manto Tshabalala-Msimang, 27 March 2002, available at www.doh.gov.za/show.php?id=208

National Strategic Plan on HIV, STIs and TB 2012–2016, www.doh.gov.za/docs/stratdocs/2012/NSPfull.pdf

Department of Human Settlements, National Housing Code (2000)

National Housing Code (2009)

Celebrating 20 years of Human Settlements: Bringing the Freedom Charter to Life (2014)

Government of the Republic of South Africa, Election Regulations, GN R12 *Government Gazette* 25894 (7 January 2004)

Human Sciences Research Council (HSRC), Press Release 'Democracy SA: Update on bar-coded IDs' 12 May 1999, available at www.hsrc.ac.za/Media_Release-96.phtml

Independent Electoral Commission, *Report: National and Provincial Elections 2 June 1999* www.elections.org.za/content/Documents/Election-reports/National-and-Provincial-Elections/1999-National-and-Provincial-ElectionsReport/

'2004 Floor Crossing Results: Summary Reports' available at www.elections.org.za/content/WorkArea/DownloadAsset.aspx?id=1323

'2007 Floor Crossing Results: Summary Reports' available at www.elections.org.za/content/WorkArea/DownloadAsset.aspx?id=1324

KwaZulu Legislative Assembly, Resolution: 'The Constitution of the State of KwaZulu/Natal' (1 December 1992)

Masondo, Amos, 'Statement by the Executive Mayor of Johannesburg, Clr. Amos Masondo, at the media briefing on the City of Johannesburg Expanded Social Package Programme', available at www.joburg.org.za/index.php?option=com_content&task=view&id=4012&Itemid=114

Mbeki, Thabo, State of the Nation Address by the President of South Africa, Thabo Mbeki, 8 February 2002, available at www.sahistory.org.za/archive/2002-president-mbeki-state-nation-address-8-february-2002

National Assembly, Constitutional Review Committee, Minutes, 25 March 1999, available at https://pmg.org.za/committee-meeting/6684/

Constitutional Review Committee, 15 August 2008, record available at https://pmg.org.za/committee-meeting/9505

Internal Question Paper No. 2823, Question 940 for written reply from Mr. AM Shaik Emam (NFP), 21 November 2014, available at https://pmg.org.za/question_reply/497/

Joint Constitutional Review Committee, Minutes, 29 August 2003, available at https://pmg.org.za/committee-meeting/2779/

Joint Constitutional Review Committee, Minutes, 2 February 2004, available at https://pmg.org.za/committee-meeting/3411/

National Assembly debates, *Hansard*, 19 June 1995

National Assembly debates, *Hansard*, 14 November 2006

Private Members' Legislative Proposals and Special Petitions Portfolio Committee, Minutes, 9 September 1998, available at https://pmg.org.za/committee-meeting/6314/

Rules of the National Assembly, available at www.parliament.gov.za/content/NA%20RULES%202014.pdf

Parliament of the Republic of South Africa, *Report of the ad hoc Committee on the Review of Chapter 9 and Associated Institutions* (31 July 2007)

Report of the Committee for Constitutional Affairs on Decision-making and Conflict Resolution Mechanisms and Techniques in Constitutional Systems (PC 1/1990), 20 September 1990

Second Report of the Constitutional Committee of the President's Council on the Adaptation of Constitutional Structures in South Africa (PC 4/1982), not dated

Shilowa, Mbhazima, 'Address by Premier Mbhazima Shilowa at the opening of the Gauteng Provincial Legislature', 18 February 2002; available at www.polity.org.za/polity/govdocs/speeches/2002/sp0218.html

South African Law Commission, *Project 58: Interim Report on Group and Human Rights* (1989)

Project 58: Final Report on Group and Human Rights (1994)

South African Law Reform Commission *Report on Domestic Partnerships* (Project 118) (March 2006)

Books, Articles and Book Chapters

Abel, Richard, *Politics by Other Means: Law in the Struggle Against Apartheid, 1980–1994* (London: Routledge, 1995)

Achmat, Zackie, 'The Treatment Action Campaign, HIV/AIDS and the Government' (2004) 54 *Transformation* 76

'Law, Politics and Social Transformation' (2004) 32 *International Journal of Legal Information* 237

Ackerman, Bruce, *We the People: Foundations* (Harvard University Press, 1991)

The Future of Liberal Revolution (Yale University Press, 1992)

We the People: Transformations (Harvard University Press, 1998)

'The New Separation of Powers' (2000) 113 *Harvard Law Review* 633

'Holmes Lectures: The Living Constitution' (2007) 120 *Harvard Law Review* 1737

We the People: The Civil Rights Revolution (Harvard University Press, 2014)

African National Congress, 'A Bill of Rights for a Democratic South Africa – Working Draft for Consultation' (1991) 3 *African Journal of International and Comparative Law* 608

Albertyn, Cathi, 'Substantive Equality and Transformation in South Africa' (2007) 23 *South African Journal on Human Rights* 253

Albertyn, Cathi and Beth Goldblatt, 'Facing the Challenge of Transformation: Difficulties in the Development of an Indigenous Jurisprudence of Equality' (1998) 14 *South African Journal on Human Rights* 248

Alence, Rod, 'South Africa after Apartheid: The First Decade' (2004) 15 *Journal of Democracy* 78

Amar, Akhil Reed, *America's Constitution: A Biography* (New York: Random House, 2006)

Andenes, Mads Tnnesson and Robert Wintermute (eds.), *The Legal Recognition of Same-Sex Partnerships: A Study of National, European and International Law* (Oxford: Hart, 2001)

Arato, Andrew, *Constitution Making under Occupation: The Politics of Imposed Revolution in Iraq* (Columbia University Press, 2009)

'Post-Sovereign Constitution-Making in Hungary: After Success, Partial Failure, and Now What?' (2010) 26 *South African Journal of Human Rights* 19

Asmal, Kader, David Chidester and Cass Lubisi (eds.), *Legacy of Freedom: The ANC's Human Rights Tradition* (Johannesburg: Jonathan Ball, 2005)

Atkinson, Doreen, 'Taking to the Streets: Has Developmental Local Government Failed in South Africa?' in Sakhela Buhlungu, John Daniel, Roger Southall and Jessica Lutchman (eds.), *State of the Nation: South Africa 2007* (Pretoria: Human Sciences Research Council Press, 2007)

Balkin, Jack M., *Living Originalism* (Harvard University Press, 2011)

Balkin, Jack M., and Sanford Levinson, 'The Canons of Constitutional Law' (1997–1998) 111 *Harvard Law Review* 963 (eds.), *Legal Canons* (New York University Press, 2000)

Ballard, Richard, 'Social Movements in Post-Apartheid South Africa: An Introduction' in Peris Jones and Kristian Stokke (eds.), *Democratizing Development: The Politics of Socio-economic Rights in South Africa* (Leiden: Martinus Nijhoff, 2005)

Bannerjee, Abhijit V., and Esther Duflo, *Poor Economics: A Radical Rethinking of the War to Fight Global Poverty* (New York: Public Affairs, 2011)

Barnard, Jaco, 'Totalitarianism, (Same Sex) Marriage and Democratic Politics in Post-Apartheid South Africa' (2007) 23 *South African Journal on Human Rights* 500

Bauer, Gretchen and Scott D. Taylor, *Politics in Southern Africa: State and Society in Transition* (Boulder: Lynne Rienner, 2005)

Baum, Lawrence, *Judges and their Audiences: A Perspective on Judicial Behavior* (Princeton University Press, 2006)

Berger, Jonathan, 'Litigating for Social Justice in Post-Apartheid South Africa: A Focus on Health and Education' in Varun Gauri and Daniel M. Brinks (eds.), *Courting Social Justice: Judicial Enforcement of Social and Economic Rights in the Developing World* (Cambridge University Press, 2008)

Bhabha, Faisal, 'Disability Equality Rights in South Africa: Concepts, Interpretation and the Transformation Imperative' (2009) 25 *South African Journal on Human Rights* 218

Bickel, Alexander M., *The Supreme Court and the Idea of Progress* (New York: Harper & Row, 1970)

The Least Dangerous Branch: The Supreme Court at the Bar of Politics (2 edn, Yale University Press, 1986)

Bilchitz, David, *Poverty and Fundamental Rights: The Justification and Enforcement of Socio-economic Rights* (Oxford University Press, 2007)

'Is the Constitutional Court Wasting Away the Rights of the Poor? *Nokotyana v Ekurhuleni Metropolitan Municipality*' (2010) 127 *South African Law Journal* 591

'Citizenship and Community: Exploring the Right to Receive Basic Municipal Services in *Joseph*' (2010) 3 *Constitutional Court Review* 45

'Does Sandra Liebenberg's New Book Provide a Viable Approach to Adjudicating Socio-economic Rights?' (2011) 27 *South African Journal on Human Rights* 546

'Does Transformative Constitutionalism Require the Recognition of Animal Rights?' in S. Woolman and D. Bilchitz (eds.), *Is this Seat Taken? Conversations at the Bar, the Bench and the Academy about the South African Constitution* (University of Pretoria Law Press, 2012)

'Avoidance Remains Avoidance: Is It Desirable in Socio-economic Rights Cases?' (2013) 5 *Constitutional Court Review* 296

Bilchitz, David and Melanie Judge, 'For Whom Does the Bell Toll? The Challenges and Possibilities of the Civil Union Act for Family Law in South Africa' (2007) 23 *South African Journal on Human Rights* 466

Bishop, Michael, 'Remedies' in Stuart Woolman and Michael Bishop (eds.), *Constitutional Law of South Africa* (2 edn, Cape Town: Juta & Co., OS 06–08, 2008)

'Vampire or Prince? The Listening Constitution and *Merafong Demarcation & Others v President of the Republic of South Africa*' (2009) 2 *Constitutional Court Review* 313

Bishop, Michael and Ngwako Raboshakga, 'National Legislative Authority' in Stuart Woolman and Michael Bishop (eds.), *Constitutional Law of South Africa* (2 edn, Cape Town: Juta & Co, RS3 05–11, 2011)

Black, Charles L., Jnr., *Structure and Relationship in Constitutional Law* (Lousiana State University Press, 1969)

Impeachment: A Handbook (Yale University Press, 1974)

Bobbitt, Phillip, *Constitutional Fate: Theory of the Constitution* (Oxford University Press, 1982)

Constitutional Interpretation (Oxford and Cambridge [Mass.]: Blackwell, 1991)

Bond, Patrick, *Elite Transition: From Apartheid to Neoliberalism in South Africa* (London: Pluto Press, 2000)

Bonilla Maldonado, Daniel (ed.), *Constitutionalism of the Global South: The Activist Tribunals of India, South Africa and Colombia* (Cambridge University Press, 2014)

Bonthuys, Elsje, 'Women's Sexuality in the South African Constitutional Court' (2006) 14 *Feminist Legal Studies* 391

'Race and Gender in the Civil Union Act' (2007) 23 *South African Journal on Human Rights* 526

Booysen, Susan, 'The Will of the Parties versus the Will of the People? Defections, Elections and Alliances in South Africa' (2006) 12 *Party Politics* 727

'With the Ballot and the Brick . . . the Politics of Service Delivery in South Africa' (2007) 7 *Progress in Development Studies* 21

The African National Congress and the Regeneration of Political Power (Wits University Press, 2014)

Botha, Henk, 'Metaphoric Reasoning and Transformative Constitutionalism' (Part 1) (2002) *Tydskrif vir die Suid-Afrikaanse Reg* 612

'Metaphoric Reasoning and Transformative Constitutionalism' (Part 2) (2003) *Tydskrif vir die Suid-Afrikaanse Reg* 20

'Freedom and Constraint in Constitutional Adjudication' (2004) 20 *South African Journal on Human Rights* 249

'Equality, Plurality and Structural Power' (2009) 25 *South African Journal on Human Rights* 1

Boudin, Chesa and Marlise Richter, 'Adult, Consensual Sex Work in South Africa: The Cautionary Message of Criminal Law and Sexual Morality' (2009) 25 *South African Journal on Human Rights* 179

Bowen, William G. and Derek Bok, *The Shape of the River: Long-term Consequences of Considering Race in College and University Admissions* (Princeton University Press, 1998)

Brand, Danie, 'The Minimum Core Content of the Right to Food in Context: A Response to Rolf Künneman' in D. Brand and S. Russell (eds.), *Exploring the Core Content of Socio-economic Rights: South African and International Perspectives* (Pretoria: Protea Book House, 2002)

'The Proceduralisation of South African Socio-economic Rights Jurisprudence, or "What Are Socio-economic Rights for?"' in Henk Botha, A. J. van der Walt and Johan van der Walt (eds.), *Rights and Democracy in a Transformative Constitution* (Stellenbosch: Sun Press, 2004)

'The Right to Food' in Danie Brand and Christof Heyns (eds.), *Socio-economic Rights in South Africa* (Pretoria University Law Press, 2005)

Brickhill, Jason and Ryan Babuich, 'Political Rights' in Stuart Woolman and Michael Bishop (eds.) *Constitutional Law of South Africa* (2 edn, Cape Town: Juta & Co., OS 03–07, 2007)

Brunner, Georg, 'Structure and Proceedings of the Hungarian Constitutional Judiciary' in László Sólyom and Georg Brunner (eds.), *Constitutional Judiciary in a New Democracy: The Hungarian Constitutional Court* (University of Michigan Press, 2000)

Buckingham, Janet Epp, 'Religious Freedom and Wine Sales on Sunday' (1999) *Stellenbosch Law Review* 117

Budlender, Steven, Gilbert Marcus and Nick Ferreira, *Public Interest Litigation and Social Change in South Africa: Strategies, Tactics and Lessons* (New York: The Atlantic Philanthropies, 2014)

Butler, Anthony, 'The Negative and Positive Impacts of HIV/AIDS' (2006) 23 *Journal of Contemporary African Studies* 3

Calland, Richard, *Anatomy of South Africa: Who Holds the Power?* (Cape Town: Zebra Press, 2006)

The Zuma Years: South Africa's Changing Face of Power (Cape Town: Zebra Press, 2013)

Calland, Richard, and Chris Oxtoby, 'Machiavelli Meets the Constitution: Mbeki and the Law' in Daryl Glaser (ed.), *Mbeki and After: Reflections on the Legacy of Thabo Mbeki* (Wits University Press, 2010)

Calland, Richard and Smita Nakhooda, 'Participatory Democracy Meets the Hard Rock of Energy Policy: South Africa's National Integrated Resource Plan' (2012) 19 *Democratization* 912

Callinicos, Luli, *Oliver Tambo: Beyond the Engeli Mountains* (Claremont: New Africa Books, 2004)

Cameron, Edwin, 'Are Dworkin's "Principles" Really Rules?' (1979) 96 *South African Law Journal* 450

'Legal Chauvinism, Executive-Mindedness and Justice – L C Steyn's Impact on South African Law' (1982) 99 *South African Law Journal* 38

'Sexual Orientation and the Constitution: A Test Case for Human Rights' (1993) 110 *South African Law Journal* 450

'Constitutional Protection of Sexual Orientation and African Conceptions of Humanity' (2001) 118 *South African Law Journal* 642

Witness to AIDS (Cape Town: Tafelberg, 2005)

'Legal and human rights responses to the HIV/AIDS epidemic' (2006) *Stellenbosch Law Review* 47

'Nepal's New Constitution and Fundamental Rights of Minorities – Lessons of the South African Experience', paper delivered at a civil society constitution drafting seminar, Kathmandu, Nepal, 8 January 2007, (2007) 23 *South African Journal on Human Rights* 195

Justice: A Personal Account (Cape Town: Tafelberg, 2014)

Campbell, Catherine, Flora Cornish, Andrew Gibbs and Kerry Scott, 'Heeding the Push from Below: How Do Social Movements Persuade the Rich to Listen to the Poor?' (2010) 15 *Journal of Health Psychology* 962

Chenwi, Lilian, 'A New Approach to Remedies in Socio-economic Rights Adjudication: *Occupiers of 51 Olivia Road and Others v City of Johannesburg and Others*' (2009) 2 *Constitutional Court Review* 371

'Legislative and Judicial Responses to Informal Settlements in South Africa: A Silver Bullet?' (2012) 23 *Stellenbosch Law Review* 540

Chipkin, Ivor, 'Transcending Bureaucracy: State Transformation in the Age of the Manager' (2011) 77 *Transformation* 31

Choudhry, Sujit, '"He Had a Mandate": The South African Constitutional Court and the African National Congress in a Dominant Party Democracy' (2009) 2 *Constitutional Court Review* 1

Christiansen, Eric C., 'Ending the Apartheid of the Closet: Sexual Orientation in the South African Constitutional Process' (1999–2000) 32 *New York University Journal of International Law and Policy* 997

Christianson, Marylyn, 'People with Disabilities Inside (and Outside) the South African Workplace: The Current Status of the Constitutional and Statutory Promises' (2012) *Acta Juridica* 286

Christodoulidis, Emilios A., '"End of History" Jurisprudence: Dworkin in South Africa' (2004) *Acta Juridica* 64

Church, Joan, 'Same-Sex Unions: Different Voices' (2005) 9 *Fundamina* 49

Cock, Jacklyn, 'Rainbow Jurisprudence' (1996) 12 *South African Journal on Human Rights* 1

'Engendering Gay and Lesbian Rights: The Equality Clause in the South African Constitution' (2003) 26 *Women's Studies International Forum* 35

Cockrell, A., 'Rainbow Jurisprudence' (1996) 12 *South African Journal on Human Rights* 1

'The South African Bill of Rights and the Duck/Rabbit' (1997) 60 *Modern Law Review* 513

Coggin, Thomas and Marius Pieterse, 'Rights and the City: An Exploration of the Interaction between Socio-economic Rights and the City' (2012) 23 *Urban Forum* 257

Collings, Justin, *Karlsruhe Republic: A History of the German Constitutional Court* (Oxford University Press, 2015)

Commonwealth Observer Group, *The National and Provincial Election in South Africa 2 June 1999* (Commonwealth Secretariat, 1999)

Cooke, Anita, 'Choice, Heterosexual Life Partnerships, Death and Poverty' (2005) 122 *South African Law Journal* 542

Cornell, Drucilla and Nick Friedman, 'The Significance of Dworkin's Non-positivist Jurisprudence for Law in the Post-colony' (2010) 4 *Malawi Law Journal* 1

Croucher, Sheila, 'South Africa's Democratization and the Politics of Gay Liberation' (2002) 28 *Journal of Southern African Studies* 315

'South Africa: Opportunities Seized in the Post-Apartheid Era' in Manon Tremblay, David Paternotte and Carol Johnson (eds.), *The Gay and Lesbian Movement and the State: Comparative Insights into a Transformed Relationship* (Surrey: Ashgate, 2011)

Currie, Iain, 'Judicious Avoidance' (1999) 15 *South African Journal on Human Rights* 138

Currie, Iain and Johan de Waal, *The Bill of Rights Handbook* (6 edn, Cape Town: Juta & Co., 2013)

Damaška, Mirjan R., *The Faces of Justice and State Authority: A Comparative Approach to the Legal Process* (Yale University Press, 1986)

Daniels, Reynaud N. and Jason Brickhill, 'The Counter-Majoritarian Difficulty and the South African Constitutional Court' (2006–2007) 25 *Pennsylvania State International Law Review* 371

Davis, Dennis, *Democracy and Deliberation: Transformation and the South African Legal Order* (Cape Town: Juta & Co., 1999)

'Dworkin: A Viable Theory of Adjudication for the South African Constitutional Community?' (2004) *Acta Juridica* 96

'Adjudicating the Socio-economic Rights in the South African Constitution: Towards "Deference Lite"?' (2006) 22 *South African Journal on Human Rights* 301

'Transformation and the Democratic Case for Judicial Review: The South African Experience' 5 *Loyola University Chicaga International Law Review* 45 (2007–2008)

'Socioeconomic Rights: Do They Deliver the Goods?' (2008) 6 *International Journal of Constitutional Law* 687

'Transformation: The Constitutional Promise and the Reality' (2010) 26 *South African Journal on Human Rights* 85

Davis, Dennis M. and Karl Klare, 'Transformative Constitutionalism and the Common and Customary Law' (2010) 26 *South African Journal on Human Rights* 403

De Klerk, F. W., *The Last Trek: A New Beginning: The Autobiography* (Johannesburg: Jonathan Ball, 1999)

De Villiers, Fleur (ed.), *Bridge or Barricade? The Constitution – A first appraisal* (Johannesburg: Jonathan Ball, 1983)

De Vos, Pierre, 'The "Inevitability" of Same Sex Marriage in South Africa's Post-Apartheid State' (2007) 23 *South African Journal on Human Rights* 432

De Vos, Pierre and Jaco Barnard, 'Same-Sex Marriage, Civil Unions and Domestic Partnerships in South Africa: Critical Reflections on an Ongoing Saga' (2007) 124 *South African Law Journal* 795

Devenish, George, 'Political Musical Chairs: The Saga of Floor-crossing and the Constitution' (2004) 15 *Stellenbosch Law Review* 52

Dickinson, Gerald S., '*Blue Moonlight* Rising: Evictions, Alternative Accommodation and a Comparative Perspective on Affordable Housing Solutions in Johannesburg' (2011) 27 *South African Journal on Human Rights* 466

Dixon, Rosalind, 'Creating Dialogue about Socioeconomic Rights: Strong-Form versus Weak-Form Judicial Review Revisited' (2007) 5 *International Journal of Constitutional Law* 391

Dixon, Rosalind and Tom Ginsburg, 'Deciding Not to Decide: Deferral in Constitutional Design' (2011) 9 *International Journal of Constitutional Law* 636

'The South African Constitutional Court and Socio-economic Rights as "Insurance Swaps"' (2011) 4 *Constitutional Court Review* 1

Dodek, Adam M., 'A Tale to Two Maps: The Limits of Universalism in Comparative Judicial Review' (2009) 47 *Osgoode Hall Law Journal* 287

Du Bois, Francois, 'Preface: The Practice of Integrity' (2004) *Acta Juridica* i

Du Plessis, Lourens, 'Interpretation' in Stuart Woolman and Michael Bishop (eds.), *Constitutional Law of South Africa* (2nd edn., Cape Town: Juta & Co., OS 06–08, 2008)

'Religious Freedom and Equality as Celebration of Difference: A Significant Development in Recent South African Constitutional Case-Law' (2009) 12 *Potchefstroom Electronic Law Journal* 10

Du Plessis, Max, 'Between Apology and Utopia – The Constitutional Court and Public Opinion' (2002) 18 *South African Journal on Human Rights* 1

Dubow, Saul, *Apartheid, 1948–1994* (Oxford University Press, 2014)

Dugard, Jackie, 'Court of First Instance? Towards a Pro-Poor Jurisdiction for the South African Constitutional Court' (2006) 22 *South African Journal on Human Rights* 261

'Judging the Judges: Towards an Appropriate Role for the Judiciary in South Africa's Transformation' (2007) 20 *Leiden Journal of International Law* 965

'Courts and the Poor in South Africa: A Critique of Systemic Judicial Failures to Advance Transformative Justice' (2008) 24 *South African Journal on Human Rights* 214

'Civic Action and Legal Mobilisation: The Phiri Water Meters Case' in Jeff Handmaker and Remko Berkhout (eds.), *Mobilising Social Justice in South Africa: Perspectives from Researchers and Practitioners* (The Hague: ISS and Hivos, 2010)

'Urban Basic Services: Rights, Reality, and Resistance' in Malcolm Langford, Ben Cousins, Jackie Dugard and Tshepo Madlingozi (eds.), *Socio-economic Rights in South Africa: Symbols or Substance?* (Cambridge University Press, 2014)

'Beyond *Blue Moonlight*: The Implications of Judicial Avoidance in Relation to the Provision of Alternative Housing' (2013) 5 *Constitutional Court Review* 264

Dugard, Jackie and Malcolm Langford, 'Art or Science? Synthesizing Lessons from Public Interest Litigation and the Dangers of Legal Determinism' (2011) 27 *South African Journal on Human Rights* 39

Dugard, Jackie and Theunis Roux, 'The Record of the South African Constitutional Court in Providing an Institutional Voice to the Poor' in Roberto Gargarella, Pilar Domingo and Theunis Roux (eds.), *Courts and Social Transformation in New Democracies: An Institutional Voice for the Poor?* (Hampshire: Ashgate, 2006)

Dugard, John, 'The Judicial Process, Positivism and Civil Liberty' (1971) 88 *South African Law Journal* 181

Human Rights and the South African Legal Order (Princeton University Press, 1978)

Dworkin, Ronald, *Law's Empire* (Harvard University Press, 1986)

'The Order of the Coif Lecture: In Praise of Theory' (1997) 29 *Arizona State Law Journal* 353

Sovereign Virtue: The theory and practice of equality (Harvard University Press, 2002)

'Keynote Address: The Practice of Integrity' (2004) *Acta Juridica* 1

'Keynote Address: Rawls and the Law' (2004) 72 *Fordham Law Review* 1387

Justice for Hedgehogs (Harvard University Press, 2011)

Dyzenhaus, David, *Judging the Judges, Judging Ourselves* (Oxford: Hart, 1996)

'Law as Justification: Etienne Mureinik's Conception of Legal Culture' (1998) 14 *South African Journal on Human Rights* 11

Ebrahim, Hassan, *The Soul of a Nation: Constitution-Making in South Africa* (Oxford University Press, 1999)

Electoral Institute of South Africa, *South Africa's Second Democratic Election 1999: An Annotated Bibliography* (Electoral Institute of South Africa, 2001)

Ely, John Hart, *Democracy and Distrust: A Theory of Judicial Review* (Harvard University Press, 1980)

Endresen, Kristin and Astrid von Kotze, 'Living while Being Alive: Education and Learning in the Treatment Action Campaign' (2005) 24 *International Journal of Lifelong Education* 431

Epp, Charles R., *The Rights Revolution: Lawyers, Activists, and Supreme Courts in Comparative Perspective* (University of Chicago Press, 1998)

Making Rights Real: Activists, Bureaucrats, and the Creation of the Legalistic State (University of Chicago Press, 2010)

Eskridge, William N., Jnr., 'Backlash Politics: How Constitutional Litigation Has Advanced Marriage Equality in the United States' (2013) 93 *Boston University Law Review* 275

Eskridge, William N., Jnr. and John Ferejohn, 'Super-Statutes' (2000–2001) 50 *Duke Law Journal* 1215

Republic of Statutes: The New American Constitution (Yale University Press, 2010)

Farlam, Paul, 'The Ambit of the Right to Freedom of Religion: A comment on *S v Solberg*' (1998) 14 *South African Journal on Human Rights* 298

Fick, Nicolé, 'Well Intentioned but Misguided? Criminalizing Sex Workers' Clients' (2007) 22 *SA Crime Quarterly* 33

Fine, Derrick and Julia Nicol, 'The Lavender Lobby: Working for Lesbian and Gay Rights within the Liberation Movement' in Edwin Cameron and Mark Gevisser (eds.) *Defiant Desire: Gay and Lesbian Lives in South Africa* (New York: Routledge, 1995)

Finkel, Jodi S., *Judicial Reform as Political Insurance: Argentina, Peru, and Mexico in the 1990s* (University of Notre Dame Press, 2008)

Fombad, Charles M., 'Challenges to Constitutionalism and Constitutional Rights in African and the Enabling Role of Political Parties: Lessons and Perpsectives from Southern Africa' (2007) 55 *American Journal of Comparative Law* 1

Fowkes, James, 'How to Open the Doors of the Court – Lessons on Access to Justice from Indian PIL' (2011) 27 *South African Journal on Human Rights* 434

'Civil Procedure in Public Interest Litigation: Tradition, Collaboration and the Managerial Judge' (2012) 1 *Cambridge Journal of International and Comparative Law* 235

'Constitutional Civil Procedure and the Limits of Party Autonomy in Private Cases: *Maphango v Aengus Lifestyle Properties (Pty) Ltd* (2013) 5 *Constitutional Court Review* 308

'Founding Provisions' in Stu Woolman and Michael Bishop (eds.), *Constitutional Law of South Africa* (2 edn, Cape Town: Juta & Co., RS6, 04–14, 2014)

'Right After All: Reconsidering *New National Party* in the South African Canon' (2015) 31 *South African Journal on Human Rights* 151

'The People, the Court, and Langa Constitutionalism' (2015) *Acta Juridica* 75

'Apartheid Judging and Dugard's Question: Re-examining the Legend' (forthcoming)

'More Power than Pact: The Over-emphasis on the Negotiated Origins of South Africa's Constitution' (forthcoming)

'Two Concepts of Transformative Constitutionalism' (forthcoming)

'Normal Rights, Just New: Understanding the Judicial Enforcement of Socio-economic rights' (forthcoming)

Fowkes, James and Michaela Hailbronner, 'Courts as the Nation's Conscience: Empirically Testing the Intutions Behind Ethicalization' in Silja Vöneky, Britta Beylage-Haarman, Anja Höfelmeier and Anna-Katharina Hübler (eds.), *Ethics and Law: The Ethicalization of Law / Ethik und Recht: Ethisierung des Rechts* (Heidelberg: Springer, 2013)

Friedman, Steven, and Shauna Mottiar, 'A Rewarding Engagement? The Treatment Action Campaign and the Politics of HIV/AIDS' (2005) 33 *Politics & Society* 511

Fritz, Nicole, 'Crossing Jordan: Constitutional Space for (un)Civil Sex?' (2004) 20 *South African Journal on Human Rights* 230

Fukuyama, Francis, *Trust: The Social Virtues and the Creation of Prosperity* (New York: The Free Press, 1995)

Geffen, Nathan, *Debunking Delusions: The Inside Story of the Treatment Action Campaign* (Johannesburg: Jacana, 2010)

Gevisser, Mark, *The Dream Deferred: Thabo Mbeki* (Johannesburg: Jonathan Ball Publishers, 2007)

Gilliomee, Hermann, *The Afrikaners: Biography of a People* (2 edn, UK: Hurst, 2009)

The Last Afrikaner Leaders: A Supreme Test of Power (Cape Town, Tafelberg: 2012)

Ginsburg, Tom, *Judicial Review in New Democracies: Constitutional Courts in Asian Cases* (Cambridge University Press, 2003)

'The Politics of Courts in Democratization' in James L. Heckman, Robert L. Nelson and Lee Cabatingan (eds.), *Global Perspectives on the Rule of Law* (Routledge, 2010)

Ginsburg, Tom and Tamir Moustafa (eds.), *Rule by Law: The Politics of Courts in Authoritarian Regimes* (Cambridge University Press, 2008)

Glendon, Mary Ann, *A Nation Under Lawyers: How the Crisis in the Legal Profession is Transforming American Society* (Harvard University Press, 1996)

Goldblatt, Beth, 'Regulating Domestic Partnerships: A Necessary Step in the Development of South African Family Law' (2003) 118 *South African Law Journal* 610

Gouws, Amanda and Paul Mitchell, 'South Africa: One Party Dominance Despite Perfect Proportionality' in Michael Gallagher and Paul Mitchell (eds.), *The Politics of Electoral Systems* (Oxford University Press, 2005)

Gouws, Amanda and Lourens M. du Plessis, 'The Relationship between Political Tolerance and Religion: The Case of South Africa' (2000) 14 *Emory International LR* 657

Graber, Mark A., 'Review: Constitutional Politics and Constitutional Theory: A Misunderstood and Neglected Relationship' (2002) *Law and Social Enquiry* 309

Graham, Paul, 'Opening the Door to Crossing the Floor' (2003) 11 *Democracy in Action* 6

Green, Pippa, *Choice, Not Fate: The Life and Times of Trevor Manuel* (Johannesburg: Penguin, 2008)

Guelke, Adrian, *South Africa in Transition: The Misunderstood Miracle* (London: Tauris, 1999)

Gumede, William, *Thabo Mbeki and the Battle for the Soul of the ANC* (Updated ed.), Cape Town: Zebra, 2007)

Gumedze, Sabelo, 'HIV/AIDS and Human Rights: The Role of the African Commission on Human and People's Rights' (2004) 4 *African Human Rights Law Journal* 181

Gunther, Gerald, 'The Subtle Vices of the 'Passive Virtues' – A Comment on Principle and Expediency in Judicial Review' (1964) 64 *Columbia Law Review* 1

Hailbronner, Michaela, *Tradition and Transformation: The Rise of German Constitutionalism* (Oxford University Press, 2015)

Handley, Antoinette, *Business and the State in Africa: Economic Policy-Making in the Neo-Liberal Era* (Cambridge University Press, 2008)

Harber, Anton, *Diepsloot* (Johannesburg and Cape Town: Jonathan Ball, 2011)

Harris, Peter, *Birth: The Conspiracy to Stop the'94 Election* (Cape Town: Umuzi, 2010)

Haysom, Fink, 'Constitutionalism, Majoritarian Democracy and Socio-economic Rights' (1992) 8 *South African Journal on Human Rights* 451

Hessebon, Gedion T., 'Some Major Themes in the Study of Constitutionalism and Democracy in Africa' (2013) 7 *Vienna Journal on International Constitutional Law* 28

Heywood, Mark, 'Preventing Mother-to-Child HIV Transmission in South Africa: Background, Strategies and Outcomes of the Treatment Action Campaign Case against the Minister of Health' (2003) 19 *South African Journal on Human Rights* 278

'Shaping, Making and Breaking the Law in the Campaign for a National HIV/AIDS Treatment Plan' in Peris Jones and Kristian Stokke (eds.), *Democratizing Development: The Politics of Socio-economic Rights in South Africa* (Leiden: Martinus Nijhoff, 2005).

'South Africa's Treatment Action Campaign: Combining Law and Social Mobilization to Realize the Right to Health' (2009) 1 *Journal of Human Rights Practice* 14

'Civil Society and Uncivil Government: The Treatment Action Campaign versus Thabo Mbeki, 1998–2008' in Daryl Glaser (ed.), *Mbeki and After: Reflections on the legacy of Thabo Mbeki* (Wits University Press, 2010)

Hirsch, Alan, *Season of Hope: Economic Reform under Mandela and Mbeki* (University of KwaZulu Natal Press, 2005)

Hirschl, Ran, 'Reply: Constitutionalism, Judicial Review, and Progressive Change: A Rejoinder to McCain and Fleming' (2005) 84 *Texas Law Review* 471

Towards Juristocracy: The Origins and Consequences of the New Constitutionalism (Harvard University Press, 2007)

'On the Blurred Methodological Matrix of Comparative Constitutional Law' in Sujit Choudhry (ed.), *The Migration of Constitutional Ideas* (Cambridge University Press, 2007).

Hirschman, Albert O., *Exit, Voice, and Loyalty: Responses to Decline in Firms, Organizations, and States* (Harvard University Press, 1970)

Hoeane, Thabisi, 'Floor-crossing in South Africa: Entrenching or Undermining Democracy? (2008) 27 *Politeia* 70

Hoexter, Cora, *Administrative Law in South Africa* (2 edn, Cape Town: Juta & Co., 2012

Hopkins, Kevin, 'Shattering the Divide – When Judges Go Too Far' (March 2002) *De Rebus* 23

'Democracy in a Post-TAC Society' (November 2002) *De Rebus* 14

Human Sciences Research Council, *Opinion 1999: Voter Participation in the 1999 Elections* (Pretoria: Human Sciences Research Council Press, 1999)

Humphries, Richard, 'Assessing the 1999 Election Machinery: Views of Political Parties, and Other Stakeholders' in Yvonne Muthien (ed.), *Democracy South Africa: Evaluating the 1999 Election* (Pretoria: Human Sciences Research Council Press, 1999)

Isacharoff, Samuel, 'Constitutional Courts and Democratic Hedging' (2011) 99 *Georgetown Law Journal* 961

'The Democratic Risk to Social Transitions' (2013) 5 *Constitutional Court Review* 1

Jagwanth, Saras, 'Expanding Equality' (2005) *Acta Juridica* 131

Jolobe, Zwelethu, '"Things Fall Apart, Can the Centre Hold?" The State of Coalition Politics in the Cape Metropolitan Council' in Sakhela Buhlungu, John Daniel, Roger Southall & Jessica Lutchman (eds.), *State of the Nation: South Africa 2007* (Pretoria: Human Sciences Research Council, 2007)

Jung, Courtney, Ellen Lust-Okar and Ian Shapiro, 'Prospects for Democratic Settlements: South Africa as a Model for the Middle East and Northern Ireland?' (2005) 33 *Politics & Society* 277

Jung, Courtney and Ian Shapiro, 'South Africa's Negotiated Transition: Democracy, Opposition, and the New Constitutional Order' (1995) 23 *Politics & Society* 269

'South African Democracy Revisited: A Reply to Koelble and Reynolds' (1996) 24 *Politics & Society* 237

Kahn, Paul W., 'Comparative Constitutionalism in a New Key' (2002–2003) 101 *Michigan Law Review* 2677

Kende, Mark S., 'The South African Constitutional Court's Construction of Socio-economic Rights: A Response to Critics' (2003–2004) 19 *Connecticut Journal of International law* 617

Constitutional Rights in Two Worlds: South Africa and the United States (Cambridge University Press, 2009)

Khosa, Meshack, 'Voting in Action: Focus Group and Workshop Findings' in Yvonne Muthien (ed.), *Democracy South Africa: Evaluating the 1999 Election* (Pretoria: Human Sciences Research Council Press, 1999)

Klaaren, Jonathan, 'Case Reports: Executive Council, Western Cape Legislature, and Others v President of the Republic of South Africa and Others CCT/27/95, 1995 (4) SA 877 (CC); 1995 (10) BCLR 1289 (CC)' (1996) 12 *South African Journal on Human Rights* 158

'Structures of Government in the 1996 South African Constitution: Putting Democracy Back into Human Rights' (1997) 13 *South African Journal on Human Rights* 3

Klare, Karl E., 'Legal Culture and Transformative Constitutionalism' (1998) 14 *South African Journal on Human Rights* 146

'Legal Subsidiarity and Constitutional Rights: A Reply to AJ van der Walt' (2008) 1 *Constitutional Court Review* 90

Klarman, Michael J., *From Jim Crow to Civil Rights: The Supreme Court and the Struggle for Racial Equality* (Oxford University Press, 2004)

Kleinbooi, Hein, 'Identity Crossfire: On Being a Black Gay Student Activist' in Edwin Cameron & Mark Gevisser (eds.), *Defiant Desire: Gay and Lesbian Lives in South Africa* (New York: Routledge, 1995)

Klug, Heinz, 'Constitutional Law' (1992) *Annual Survey* 693

'Constitutional Law' (1993) *Annual Survey* 1

'Striking Down Death' (1996) 12 *South African Journal on Human Rights* 61

Constituting Democracy: Law, Globalism and South Africa's Political Reconstruction (Cambridge University Press, 2000)

'Participation in the Design' in Penelope Andrews and Stephen Ellmann (eds.) *Post-Apartheid Constitutions: Perspectives on South Africa's Basic Law* (Ohio University Press, 2001)

'Five Years On: How Relevant Is the Constitution to the New South Africa?' (2001–2002) 26 *Vermont Law Review* 803

The Constitution of South Africa: A Contextual Analysis (Oxford: Hart, 2010)

Koelble, Thomas and Andrew Reynolds, 'Power-Sharing Democracy in the New South Africa' (1996) 24 *Politics & Society* 221

Krüger, Rósaan, 'Sex Work from a Feminist Perspective: A Visit to the *Jordan* Case' (2004) 20 *South African Journal on Human Rights* 138

Kruuse, Helen, '"Here's to You, Mrs Robinson": Peculiarities and Paragraph 29 in Determining the Treatment of Domestic Partnerships' (2009) 25 *South African Journal on Human Rights* 380

Landau, David, 'Aggressive Weak-Form Remedies' (2013) 5 *Constitutional Court Review* 243

Langa, Pius, 'Transformative Constitutionalism' (2006) 17 *Stellenbosch Law Review* 351

Langford, Malcolm, Richard Stacey and Danwood Chirwa, 'Water' in Stuart Woolman and Michael Bishop (eds.), *Constitutional Law of South Africa* (2 edn, Cape Town: Juta & Co., RS3 05–11, 2011)

Lave, Tamara Rice, 'A Nation at Prayer, a Nation in Hate: Apartheid in South Africa' (1994) 30 *Stanford Journal of International Law* 483

Le Roux, Wessel, 'Bridges, Clearings and Labyrinths: The Architectural Framing of Post-Apartheid Constitutionalism' (2004) 19 *SA Public Law/SA Publiekreg* 629

Lehmann, Karin, 'In Defense of the Constitutional Court: Litigating socio-economic rights and the myth of the minimum core' (2006–2007) 22 *American University International Law Review* 163

Lenta, Patrick, 'Judicial Restraint and Overreach' (2004) 20 *South African Journal on Human Rights* 544

'Looking Sideways: Constitutional Interpretation, Ethics and Theory' (2004) 15 *Stellenbosch Law Review* 3

'Cultural and Religious Accommodations to School Uniform Regulations' (2008) 1 *Constitutional Court Review* 259

Leon, Tony, 'Etienne Mureinik's Role in Securing and Constitutionalising the Independence of the Universities and Judicial Selection' (1998) 12 *South African Journal on Human Rights* 190

Leonard, Alvereen, 'To Test or Not to Test Employees for HIV' (2003) *Juta's Business Law* 140

Levine, Michael E. and Jennifer L. Forrence, 'Regulatory Capture, Public Interest and the Public Agenda: Towards a Synthesis' (1990) 6 *Journal of Law, Economics and Organization* 167

Liebenberg, Sandra, 'The Interpretation of Socio-economic Rights' in Stuart Woolman and Michael Bishop (eds.), *Constitutional Law of South Africa* (2 edn, Cape Town: Juta & Co., OS 12–03, 2003)

Adjudicating Socio-economic Rights under a Transformative Constitution (Cape Town: Juta & Co., 2010)

'Engaging the Paradoxes of the Universal and Particular in Human Rights Adjudication: The Possibilities and Pitfalls of "Meaningful Engagement"' (2012) 12 *African Human Rights Law Journal* 1

Lind, Craig, 'Domestic Partnerships and Marital Status Discrimination' (2005) *Acta Juridica* 108

Llewellyn, Karl N., *The Common Law Tradition: Deciding Appeals* (Boston: Little, Brown & Co., 1960)

Jurisprudence: Realism in Theory and Practice (Chicago University Press, 1962)

The Case Law System in America (Paul Gewirtz, ed.; Michael Ansaldi, tr.) (Chicago University Press, 1989)

Lodge, Tom, 'The South African General Election, April 1994: Results, Analysis and Implications' (1995) 94 *African Affairs* 471

Lodge, Tom, Denis Kadima and David Pottie, 'South Africa' in Tom Lodge, Denis Kadima and David Pottie (eds.), *Compendium of Elections in Southern Africa* (Electoral Institute of South Africa, 2002)

Luwaya, Nolundi, 'Report on the Provincial Traditional Courts Bill Hearings: Exploring Rural People's Democratic Participation and Freedom of Expression' (2012) 2 *Issues in Law and Society* 1

Macmillan, Hugh, *The Lusaka Years: The ANC in Exile, 1963–1994* (Auckland Park: Jacana Media, 2013)

Maguire, Sebastian, 'The Human Rights of Sexual Minorities in Africa' (2004–2005) 35 *California Western International Law Journal* 1

Mandel, Michael, 'A Brief History of the New Constitutionalism, or "How We Changed Everything so that Everything Would Remain the Same"' (1998) 32 *Israel Law Review* 250

Maphai, Vincent T., 'A Season for Power-Sharing' (1996) 7 *Journal of Democracy* 67

Mashaw, Jerry L., and David. L. Harfst, *The Struggle for Auto Safety* (Harvard University Press, 1990)

Massoud, Mark F., 'The Evolution of Gay Rights in South Africa' (2003) 15 *Peace Review* 301

Mattes, Robert B., 'South Africa: Democracy Without the People?' (2002) 13 *Journal of Democracy* 22

Mbazira, Christopher, 'Service Delivery Protests, Struggle for Rights and the Failure of Local Democracy in South Africa and Uganda: Parallels and Divergences' (2013) 29 *South African Journal on Human Rights* 251

Mcconnachie, Cameron and Chris Mcconnachie, 'Concretising the Right to a Basic Education' (2012) 129 *South African Law Journal* 554

McCraw, Thomas K., *Prophets of Regulation: Charles Francis Adams, Louis D. Brandeis, James M. Landis and Alfred E. Kahn* (Harvard University Press, 1984)

McKinley, Dale T., *The ANC and the Liberation Struggle: A Critical Political Biography* (London: Pluto Press, 1997)

McLaughlin, Eric, 'Electoral Regimes and Party-switching: Floor-crossing in South Africa's Local Legislatures' (2012) 18 *Party Politics* 563

McLean, Kirsty, 'Housing' in Stuart Woolman and Michael Bishop (eds.), *Constitutional Law of South Africa* (2 edn, Cape Town: Juta & Co., OS 07–06, 2006)

Constitutional Deference, Courts and Socio-economic Rights in South Africa (Pretoria University Law Press, 2009)

'Meaningful Engagement: One Step Forward or Two Back? Some Thoughts on *Joe Slovo*' (2010) 3 *Constitutional Court Review* 223

Metz, Thaddeus, 'Animal Rights and the Interpretation of the South African Constitution' in Stu Woolman and David Bilchitz (eds.), *Is this Seat Taken? Conversations at the Bar, the Bench and the Academy about the South African Constitution* (University of Pretoria Law Press, 2012)

Meyersfeld, Bonita, *Domestic Violence and International Law* (Oxford and Portland, Oregon: Hart Publishing, 2010)

'If You Can See, Look: Domestic Partnerships and the Law' (2010) 3 *Constitutional Court Review* 271

Meyerson, Denise, 'Does the Constitutional Court of South Africa Take Rights Seriously? The Case of *S v Jordan*' (2004) *Acta Juridica* 138

'Who's In and Who's Out? Inclusion and Exclusion in the Family Law Jurisprudence of the Constitutional Court of South Africa' (2010) 3 *Constitutional Court Review* 301

Michelman, Frank, 'The Constitution, Social Rights and Reason: A Tribute to Etienne Mureinik' 14 *South Africa Journal on Human Rights* (1998) 499

Michie, Jonathan and Vishnu Padayachee (eds.), *The Political Economy of South Africa's Transition: Policy Perspectives in the Late 1990s* (London: Dryden Press/Harcourt, 1997)

Milgrom, Paul and John Roberts, *Economics, Organization and Management* (Englewood Cliffs, NJ: Prentice Hall, 1992)

Misra-Dexter, Neeta and Judith February (eds.), *Testing Democracy: Which Way Is South Africa Going?* (Cape Town: IDASA, 2010)

Moellendorf, Daryl, 'Reasoning about Resources: *Soobramoney* and the Future of Socio-economic Rights Claims' (1998) 14 *South Africa Journal on Human Rights* 327

Mompati, Ruth, 'Foreword' in Neville Hoad, Karen Martin and Graeme Reid (eds.), *Sex and Politics in South Africa* (Cape Town: Juta & Co., 2005)

Moseneke, Dikgang, 'Striking a Balance between the Will of the People and the Supremacy of the Constitution' (2012) 129 *South African Law Journal* 9

Munro, Brenna M., *South Africa and the Dream of Love to Come: Queer Sexuality and the Struggle for Freedom* (University of Minnesota Press, 2012)

Muntingh, Lukas, 'The State of Civil Society Participation in Parliament' (2012) 16 *Law, Democracy and Development* 29

Mureinik, Etienne, 'Fundamental Rights and Delegated Legislation' (1985) 1 *South African Journal on Human Rights* 111

'Administrative Law in South Africa' (1986) 103 *South African Law Journal* 615

'Security and Integrity' (1987) *Acta Juridica* 197

'Dworkin and Apartheid' in Hugh Corder (ed.), *Essays on Law and Social Practice in South Africa* (Cape Town: Juta & Co., 1988)

'Beyond a Charter of Luxuries: Economic rights in the Constitution' (1992) 8 *South African Journal on Human Rights* 464

'Emerging from Emergency: Human Rights in South Africa' (1994) 92 *Michigan Law Review* 1977

'A Bridge to Where? Introducing the Interim Bill of Rights' (1994) 10 *South African Journal on Human Rights* 31

Murcott, Melanie, 'The Role of Administrative Law in Enforcing Socio-economic Rights: Revisiting *Joseph*' (2013) 29 *South African Journal on Human Rights* 481

Muriaas, Ragnhild Louise, 'The ANC and Power Concentration in South Africa: Does Local Democracy Allow for Power-sharing?' (2011) 18 *Democratization* 1067

Muthien, Yvonne (ed.), *Democracy South Africa: Evaluating the 1999 Election* (Pretoria: Human Sciences Research Council Press, 1999)

Nattrass, Nicoli, *Mortal Combat: AIDS Denialism and the Fight for Antiretrovirals in South Africa* (University of KwaZulu-Natal Press, 2007)

Newstrom, Linda, 'The Horizon of Rights: Lessons from South Africa for the Post-Goodridge Analysis of Same-Sex Marriage' (2007) 40 *Cornell International Law Journal* 781

Nyati, Linda, 'Public Participation: What Has the Constitutional Court Given the Public?' (2008) 12 *Law, Democracy and Development* 102

O'Donovan, Michael, 'Election Day Exit Poll' in Yvonne Muthien (ed.), *Democracy South Africa: Evaluating the 1999 Election* (Pretoria: Human Sciences Research Council, 1999)

O'Regan, Catherine, 'No More Forced Removals? An Historical Analysis of the Prevention of Illegal Squatting Act' (1989) 5 *South African Journal on Human Rights* 361

'Helen Suzman Memorial Lecture: A Forum for Reason: Reflections on the role and work of the Constitutional Court' (2012) 28 *South African Journal on Human Rights* 116

Olivier, Johan, 'The Independent Electoral Commission (IEC): The Quest for Free and Fair Elections' in Yvonne Muthien (ed.), *Democracy South Africa: Evaluating the 1999 Election* (Pretoria: Human Sciences Research Council Press, 1999)

Palmberg, Mai, 'Emerging Visibility of Gays and Lesbians in Southern Africa: Contrasting Contexts' in Barry D. Adam, Jan Willem Duyvendak and André Krouwel (eds.), *The Global Emergence of Gay and Lesbian Politics* (Philadelphia: Temple University Press, 1999)

Pieterse, Marius, 'Coming to Terms with the Judicial Enforcement of Socio-economic Rights' (2004) 15 *South African Journal on Human Rights* 383

'What Do We Mean When We Talk about Transformative Constitutionalism' (2005) 20 *SA Public Law/SA Publiekreg* 155

'Health Care Rights, Resources and Rationing' (2007) 124 *South African Law Journal* 514

'Indirect Horizontal Application of the Right to Have Access to Health Services' (2007) 23 *South African Journal on Human Rights* 157

'Procedural Relief, Constitutional Citizenship and Socio-economic Rights as Legitimate Expectations' (2012) 28 *South African Journal on Human Rights* 359

'Development, the Right to the City, and the Legal and Constitutional Responsibilities of Local Government in South Africa' (2014) 131 *South African Law Journal* 149

Pillay, Anashri, 'Recent Developments: South Africa' (2003) 1 *International Journal of Constitutional Law* 152

Pillay, Kameshni, 'Implementing *Grootboom*: Supervision Needed' (July 2002) 3 *Economic and Social Rights Review* 16

Post, Robert, 'Foreword: Fashioning the Legal Constitution: Culture, Courts and the Law' (2003) 117 *Harvard Law Review* 4

Pretorius, Loot, 'A Response to Professors Michelman and Van der Walt' (1998) *Acta Juridica* 282

Price, Alistair, 'The Content and Justification of Rationality Review 25 *SA Public Law/SA Publiekreg* 345 (2010)

Psygkas, Athanasios, 'Revitalizing the "Liberty of Ancients" through Citizen Participation in the Legislative Process' (2010) 5 *Annuaire International des Droit de l'Homme* 720

Quinot, Geo and Sandra Liebenberg, 'Narrowing the Band: Reasonableness Review in Administrative Justice and Socio-economic Rights Jurisprudence in South Africa' (2011) 22 *Stellenbosch Law Review* 639

Rautenbach, I. M., 'Die konstitusionele hof se riglyne vir die toepassing van die reg op gelykheid II [The Constitutional Court's guidelines for the limitation of the right to equality II]' *Tydskrif vir die Suid-Afrikaanse Reg* 329 (2001)

'Means-End Rationality in Constitutional Court Judgments' (2010) *Tydskrif vir die Suid-Afrikaanse Reg* 768

Ray, Brian, '*Occupiers of 51 Olivia Road v City of Johannesburg*: Enforcing the Right to Adequate Housing through Engagement' (2008) 8 *Human Rights Law Review* 703

'Engagement's Possibilities and Limits as a Socioeconomic Rights Remedy' (2010) 9 *Washington University Global Studies Law Review* 399

'Proceduralisation's Triumph and Engagement's Promise in Socio-economic Rights Litigation' (2011) 27 *South African Journal on Human Rights* 107

'Evictions, Aspirations and Avoidance' (2013) 5 *Constitutional Court Review* 172

Raz, Joseph, *Between Authority and Interpretation: On the Theory of Law and Practical Reason* (Oxford University Press, 2009)

Roach, Kent, 'Sharpening the Dialogue Debate: The Next Decade of Scholarship' (2007) 45 *Osgoode Hall Law Journal* 169

Roach, Kent and Geoff Budlender, 'Mandatory Relief and Supervisory Jurisdiction: When It Is Appropriate, Just and Equitable?' (2005) 122 *South African Law Journal* 325

Robins, Steven L., *From Revolution to Rights in South Africa: Social Movements, NGOs & Popular Politics After Apartheid* (University of KwaZulu-Natal Press, 2008)

Roederer, Christopher J., 'Judicious Engagement: Theory, Attitude and Community' (1999) 15 *South African Law Journal* 486

Roithmayr, Daria, 'Lessons from *Mazibuko*: Persistent Inequality and the Commons' (2010) 3 *Constitutional Court Review* 317

Rose-Ackerman, Susan, Stefanie Egidy and James Fowkes, *Due Process of Lawmaking: the United States, South Africa, Germany and the European Union* (Cambridge University Press, 2015)

Rosenberg, Gerald N., *The Hollow Hope: Can Courts Bring about Social Change?* (2 edn, University of Chicago Press, 2008)

Roux, Theunis, 'Legitimating Transformation: Political Resource Allocation in the South African Constitutional Court' (2003) 10 *Democratization* 92

'Continuity and Change in a Transforming Legal Order: The Impact of Section 26(3) of the Constitution on South African Law' (2004) 121 *South African Law Journal* 466

'Democracy' in Stuart Woolman and Michael Bishop (eds.), *Constitutional Law of South Africa* (2 edn, Cape Town: Juta & Co., OS 07–06, 2006)

'Principle and Pragmatism on the Constitutional Court of South Africa' (2009) 7 *International Journal of Constitutional Law* 106

'Transformative Constitutionalism and the Best Interpretation of the South African Constitution: Distinction Without a Difference?' (2009) 20 *Stellenbosch Law Review* 258

The Politics of Principle: The First South African Constitutional Court 1995–2005 (Cambridge University Press, 2013)

'The South African Constitutional Court's Democratic Rights Jurisprudence' (2013) 5 *Constitutional Court Review* 33

Rubenfeld, Jed, 'Reading the Constitution as Spoken' (1995) 104 *Yale Law Journal* 1119

Freedom and Time: A Theory of Constitutional Self-Government (Yale University Press, 2001)

Revolution by Judiciary: The Structure of American Constitutional Law (Harvard University Press, 2005)

Rule, Stephen, 'Eyes on the Ground: Fieldworker Observations' in Yvonne Muthien (ed.), *Democracy South Africa: Evaluating the 1999 Election* (Pretoria: Human Sciences Research Council, 1999)

Sachs, Albie, *Protecting Human Rights in a New South Africa* (Oxford University Press, 1990)

'Book Review: Cass R. Sunstein, One Case at a Time: Minimalism on the Supreme Court and Ian Loveland, Racial Discrimination and the Right to Vote in South Africa 1855–1960' (2001) 51 *University of Toronto Law Journal* 87

The Strange Alchemy of Life and Law (Oxford University Press, 2011)

Sarkin, Jeremy, 'The Political Role of the South African Constitutional Court' (1997) 114 *South African Law Journal* 134

Schlemmer, Lawrence, 'Bridges that Have to Be Built' in Fleur de Villiers (ed.), *Bridge or Barricade? The Constitution – A First Appraisal* (Johannesburg: Jonathan Ball, 1983)

Seafield, Lucrecia, 'South Africa: The Interdependence of All Human Rights' in Adbullai Ahmed An-Na'im (ed.), *Human Rights under African Constitutions: Realizing the Promise for Ourselves* (University of Pennsylvania Press, 2003)

Seekings, Jeremy and Nicoli Nattrass, *Class, Race and Inequality in South Africa* (Yale University Press, 2005)

Shapiro, Martin, *Courts: A Comparative and Political Analysis* (University of Chicago Press, 1981)

Sibanda, Sanele, 'Not Purpose-Made! Transformative Constitutionalism, Post-Independence Constitutionalism and the Struggle to Eradicate Poverty' (2011) 22 *Stellenbosch Law Review* 482

Simeon, Richard and Christina Murray, 'Reforming Multi-level Government in South Africa' (2009) 43 *Canadian Journal of African Studies* 536

Sinclair, June, 'Poverty: Giving Meaning to the Right to Social Assistance' (2012) *Stellenbosch Law Review* 191

Sisk, Timothy D., *Democratization in South Africa: The Elusive Social Contract* (Princeton University Press, 1995)

Smit, Marius, '"Collateral Irony" and "Insular Construction" – Justifying Single-Medium Schools, Equal Access and Quality Education' (2011) 27 *South African Journal on Human Rights* 398

Smit, Nicola and Steve Cornelius, 'South African Perspectives on HIV/AIDS in the Workplace' (2005) 36 *Cambrian Law Review* 73

Smith, Anne, 'Equality Constitutional Adjudication in South Africa' (2014) 14 *African Human Rights Law Journal* 609

Smith, Bradley S., '*Parker*, Life Partnerships and the Independent Trustee' (2013) 130 *South African Law Journal* 527

Sólyom, László, 'The Role of Constitutional Courts in the Transition to Democracy, with Special Reference to Hungary' in Saïd Arjomand (ed.), *Constitutionalism and Political Reconstruction* (Leiden: Brill, 2007)

Southall, Roger, 'The State of Party Politics: Struggles within the Tripartite Alliance and the Decline of Opposition' in John Daniel, Adam Habib and Roger Southall (eds.), *State of the Nation: South Africa 2003–2004* (Pretoria: Human Sciences Research Council, 2003)

Spitz, Richard with Michael Chaskalson, *The Politics of Transition: A Hidden History of South Africa's Negotiated Settlement* (Witwatersrand University Press, 2000)

Stein, Anthony, 'Constitutional Jurisprudence' (1997) *Annual Survey* 45

Steinberg, Jonny, *Three Letter Plague: A Young Man's Journey through a Great Epidemic* (Johannesburg: Jonathan Ball Publishers, 2008)

AIDS and AIDS Treatment in a Rural South African Setting (Pretoria: Institute for Security Studies, 2008)

Steytler, Nico, and Jaap de Visser, 'Local Government' in Stuart Woolman and Michael Bishop (eds.), *Constitutional Law of South Africa* (2 edn, Cape Town: Juta & Co., OS 06–08, 2008)

Stone Sweet, Alec, *Governing With Judges: Constitutional Politics in Europe* (Oxford University Press, 2000)

'Constitutional Courts and Parliamentary Democracy' (2002) 25 *West European Politics* 77

Strauss, Piet, 'Church Polity in a Changing South Africa: A Study of Two Reformed Churches' (2013) 39 *Studia Historiae Ecclesiasticae* 129

Sundquist, James L., *Dynamics of the Party System: Alignment and Realignment of Political Parties in the United States* (Washington, DC: Brookings Institution, Rev. Ed., 1983)

Sunstein, Cass R., *Legal Reasoning and Political Conflict* (Oxford University Press, 1996)

'The Order of the Coif Lecture: Response: From Theory to Practice' (1997) 29 *Arizona Law Journal* 389

One Case at a Time: Judicial Minimalism on the Supreme Court (Harvard University Press, 1999)

Designing Democracy: What Constitutions Do (Oxford University Press, 2001)

'Problems with Minimalism' (2005–2006) 58 *Stanford Law Review* 1889

Tatchell, Peter, 'The Moment the ANC Embraced Gay Rights' in Neville Hoad, Karen Martin and Graeme Reid (eds.), *Sex and Politics in South Africa* (Cape Town: Juta & Co., 2010)

Taylor, Scott D., *Business and the State in Southern Africa: The Politics of Economic Reform* (Boulder: Lynne Rienner, 2007)

Thipe, Thuto, 'Voices in the Legislative Process: A Report on the Public Submissions on the Traditional Courts Bill (2008 and 2012)' (2012) 1 *Issues in Law and Society* 1

Thipe, Thuto, Monica De Souza and Nolundi Luwaya, '"The Advert Was Put Up Yesterday": Public Participation in the Traditional Courts Bill Legislative Process' (2015–16) 60 *New York Law School Law Review* 519

Tirole, Jean, 'Incomplete Contracts: Where Do We Stand?' (1999) 67 *Econometrica* 741

Trochev, Alexei, *Judging Russia: Constitutional Court in Russian Politics, 1990–2006* (Cambridge University Press, 2008)

Tushnet, Mark, 'The Possibilities of Comparative Constitutional Law' (1998–1999) 108 *Yale Law Journal* 1225

Weak Courts, Strong Rights: Judicial Reivew and Social Welfare Rights in Comparative Constitutional Law (Princeton University Press, 2008)

Twining, William, *Karl Llewellyn and the Realist Movement* (London: Weidenfeld & Nicolson, 1973)

Van der Merwe, Johan, 'The Dutch Reformed Church from *Human Relations and the South African Scene in the Light of Scripture* to *Church and Society:* The Struggle Goes On' (2013) 39 *Studiae Historiae Ecclesiasticae* 137

Van der Walt, A. J., 'Dancing with Codes – Protecting, Developing and Deconstructing Property Rights in a Constitutional State' (2001) 118 *South African Law Journal* 258

Constitutional Property Law (3 edn, Cape Town: Juta & Co., 2011)

Van der Walt, Johan, Law and Sacrifice: Towards a Post-Apartheid Theory of Law (New York: Routledge, 2005)

'Normative Pluralism and Anarchy: Reflections on the 2007 Term' (2008) 1 *Constitutional Court Review* 77

Van Niekerk, Barend, '... Hanged by the Neck until You Are Dead: Some Thoughts on the Application of the Death Penalty in South Africa' (1969) 86 *South African Law Journal* 457

Venter, Roxanne, 'Motions of No Confidence: Parliament's Executive Check and Checkmate' (2014) *Tydskrif vir die Suid-Afrikaanse Reg* 407

Vilhena, Oscar, Upendra Baxi and Frans Viljoen (eds.), *Transformative Constitutionalism: Comparing the Apex Courts of Brazil, India and South Africa* (Pretoria University Law Press, 2013)

Waldron, Jeremy, 'The Core of the Case Against Judicial Review' (2006) 115 *Yale Law Journal* 1346

Wall, Alan, 'South Africa' in Astrid Evrensel (ed.), *Voter Registration in Africa: A Comparative Analysis* (Electoral Institute for the Sustainability of Democracy in Africa, 2010)

Welsh, David, *The Rise and Fall of Apartheid* (University of Virginia Press, 2010)

Wesson, Murray, 'Reasonableness in Retreat? The Judgment of the South African Constitutional Court in *Mazibuko v City of Johannesburg*' (2011) 11 *Human Rights Law Review* 390

Wildenboer, Liezl, 'Marrying Domestic Partnerships and the Constitution: A discussion of Volks v Robinson 2005 5 BCLR 446 (CC)' (2005) *SA Publiekreg/SA Public Law* 459

Williams, Kerry, 'I Do or We Won't: Legalising Same-Sex Marriage in South Africa' (2004) 20 *South African Journal on Human Rights* 32

Williams, Lucy A., 'The Role of Courts in the Quantitative-Implementation of Social and Economic Rights: A Comparative Study (2010) 3 *Constitutional Court Review* 141

Wilson, James Q., *Bureaucracy: What Government Agencies Do and Why They Do It* (New York: Basic Books, 1989)

Wilson, Stuart, 'Breaking the Tie: Evictions from Private Land, Homelessness and a New Normality' (2009) 126 *South African Law Journal* 270

'Litigating Housing Rights in Johannesburg's Inner City: 2004–2008' (2011) 27 *South African Journal on Human Rights* 127

'Curing the Poor: State Housing Policy in Johannesburg after *Blue Moonlight*' (2013) 5 *Constitutional Court Review* 279

Wilson, Stuart and Jackie Dugard, 'Taking Poverty Seriously: The South African Constitutional Court and Socio-economic Rights' (2011) *Stellenbosch Law Review* 644.

'Constitutional Jurisprudence: The First and Second Waves' in Malcolm Langford, Ben Cousins, Jackie Dugard and Tshepo Madlingozi (eds.), *Socio-economic Rights in South Africa: Symbols or Substance?* (Cambridge University Press, 2014)

Wiredu, Kwasi, 'Democracy by Consensus: Some Conceptual Considerations' (2001) 30 *Philosophical Papers* 227

Woolman, Stu, 'The Amazing Vanishing Bill of Rights' (2007) 124 *South African Law Journal* 762

The Selfless Constitution: Experimentalism and Flourishing as Foundations of South Africa's Basic Law (Cape Town: Juta & Co., 2013)

Woolman, Stu, and Brahm Fleisch, *The Constitution in the Classroom: Law and Education in South Africa 1994–2008* (Pretoria University Law Press, 2009)

'The Problem of the "Other" Language' (2013) 5 *Constitutional Court Review* 135.

Woolman, Stu, and Danie Brand, 'Limitations' in Stuart Woolman and Michael Bishop (eds.), *Constitutional Law of South Africa* (2 edn, Cape Town: Juta & Co., OS 07–06, 2006)

Wouters, Edwin, H. C. J. van Rensburg and H. Meulemans, 'The National Strategic Plan of South Africa: What Are the Prospects of Success after the Repeated Failures of Previous AIDS Policy?' (2010) 25 *Health Policy and Planning* 171

Young, Katharine G., 'The Avoidance of Substance in Constitutional Rights' (2013) 5 *Constitutional Court Review* 232

Zlotnick, Myron, 'The Death Penalty and Public Opinion' (1996) 12 *South African Journal on Human Rights* 70

Other sources

Achmat, Zackie, 'We Mourn Simon Tseko Nkoli' *Equality*, No. 4, 4 June 1999, reproduced in Neville Hoad, Karen Martin and Graeme Reid (eds) *Sex and Politics in South Africa* (Cape Town: Juta & Co., 2005)

African National Congress, 'United Nations Must Take Action to Destroy Apartheid' Statement at the meeting of the Special Political Committee of the General Assembly, New York, 29 October 1963, available at www.anc.org.za/show.php?id=4202

'Comments and Observations on Proposals for a United Nations Security Council Resolution on Apartheid', New York, 1 November 1963, available at www.anc.org.za/show.php?id=4265

'Constitutional Guidelines for a Democratic South Africa' (1989), available at www.anc.org.za/show.php?id=294

'A Bill of Rights for a New South Africa – Preliminary Revised Text, February 1993', available at www.anc.org.za/show.php?id=231

Anti-Apartheid Movement, Resolution by the Conference for a Democratic Future on Negotiations and the Constituent Assembly, 8 December 1989, reproduced in Hassan Ebrahim, *The Soul of a Nation: Constitution-Making in South Africa* (Oxford University Press, 1999)

Cilliers, Johann, 'Preaching between Assimilation and Separation: Perspectives on Church and State in South African Society', paper delivered at the Homilectics Seminar for Danish Pastors, Copenhagen, 19–20 June 2008, available at http://academic.sun.ac.za/theology/Profiles/Profile_documents/Johan_Cilliers_PREACHING_BETWEEN_ASSIMILATION_AND_SEPERATION.pdf

Daley, Suzanne, 'Head of South Africa's Election Commission Resigns Suddenly', *New York Times*, 27 January 1999.

Davis, Ken, 'Hamba Kahle (Farewell) Simon Nkoli', *Green Left Weekly*, January 20, 1999, www.greenleft.org.au/1999/345/19684

Equal Education, School Infrastructure Campaign, materials available at www.equaleducation.org.za/campaigns/minimum-norms-and-standards

Fowkes, David, 'The Democratic Escape from the Populist Cycle – A Comparative Case Study of Five Highly Unequal Democracies', unpublished PhD Dissertation, School of Advanced International Studies, Johns Hopkins University, 2011

Inter-Parliamentary Union, *Parliamentary Involvement in International Affairs* (Report to Second World Conference of Speakers of Parliaments, September 2005) available at www.ipu.org/splz-e/sp-conf05/involvement-rpt.pdf

Khosa, Meshack and Yvonne G. Muthien, 'Election Management in South Africa: An Evaluation of the 1999 Election' in International IDEA Conference–Towards Sustainable Democratic Institutions in Southern Africa, http://archive.idea.int/ideas_work/22_s_africa/elections_3_south_africa.htm

Keller, Bill, 'How to Lose a Country Gracefully' *New York Times Magazine*, March 6, 2011

Lekota, Patrick Mosiuoa 'Terror', 'Address at Simon Nkoli's Memorial Service, St Mary's Cathedral, Johannesburg, December 1998', reproduced in Neville Hoad, Karen Martin and Graeme Reid (eds) *Sex and Politics in South Africa* (Cape Town: Juta & Co., 2005)

Masemola N. P. K., 'Floor-crossing and Its Political Consequences in South Africa' (Electoral Institute of South Africa Occasional Paper No. 44, June 2007)

Mbeki, Thabo, Telex from Thabo Mbeki to Peter Tatchell, dated 24 November 1987, reproduced in Neville Hoad, Karen Martin and Graeme Reid (eds.) *Sex and Politics in South Africa* (Cape Town: Juta & Co., 2005)

National Union of South African Students, 'NUSAS Talks to the ANC: Reportback on Meeting between the National Union of South African Students and the African National Congress Held from Sunday, 31 March to Tuesday, 2 April in Harare, Zimbabwe' (1986), available at www.disa.ukzn.ac.za/index.php?option=com_displaydc&recordID=pam19860400.026.022.000

Organization of African Unity, Declaration of the Organization of African Unity (OAU) ad hoc Committee on Southern Africa on the question of South Africa, Harare, Zimbabwe, 21 August 1989

Sachs, Albie, 'The Third Ernie Wentzel Memorial Lecture "Watch out – There's a Constitution about": Preparing Ourselves for the Era of Constitutionalism' 8 May 1991 (Centre for Applied Legal Studies (CALS) Pamphlet, 1991)

Socio-economic Rights Institute of South Africa, *A Resource Guide to Housing in South Africa 1994–2010: Legislation, Policy, Programmes and Practice* (2011), www.urbanlandmark.org.za/downloads/SERI_Housing_Resource_Guide_Feb11.pdf

Thatchell, Peter, 'ANC Dashes Hopes for Gay Rights in SA', *Capital Gay*, 18 September 1987, reproduced in Neville Hoad, Karen Martin & Graeme Reid (eds.) *Sex and Politics in South Africa* (Cape Town: Juta & Co., 2010).

Treatment Action Campaign, *Fighting for Our Lives: The History of the Treatment Action Campaign 1998–2010* (2010), available at www.tac.org.za/files/10year book/index.html

Tutu, Desmond, Submission to Theme Committee Four, Constitutional Assembly from Desmond Tutu, Anglican Archbishop of Cape Town, 2 June 1995, reproduced in Neville Hoad, Karen Martin & Graeme Reid (eds.) *Sex and Politics in South Africa* (Cape Town: Juta & Co., 2005)

Zapiro, Cartoon, *Mail & Guardian*, August 6, 2010

[unattributed], 'How Many People Will Be Able to Vote?' (1999) 13(1) *Focus*

INDEX

For EU product safety concerns, contact us at Calle de José Abascal, 56–1°, 28003 Madrid, Spain or eugpsr@cambridge.org.

www.ingramcontent.com/pod-product-compliance
Lightning Source LLC
LaVergne TN
LVHW011530200926
848484LV00001B/221

* 9 7 8 1 1 0 7 1 2 4 0 9 7 *